I0121168

Old World Roots of the Cherokee

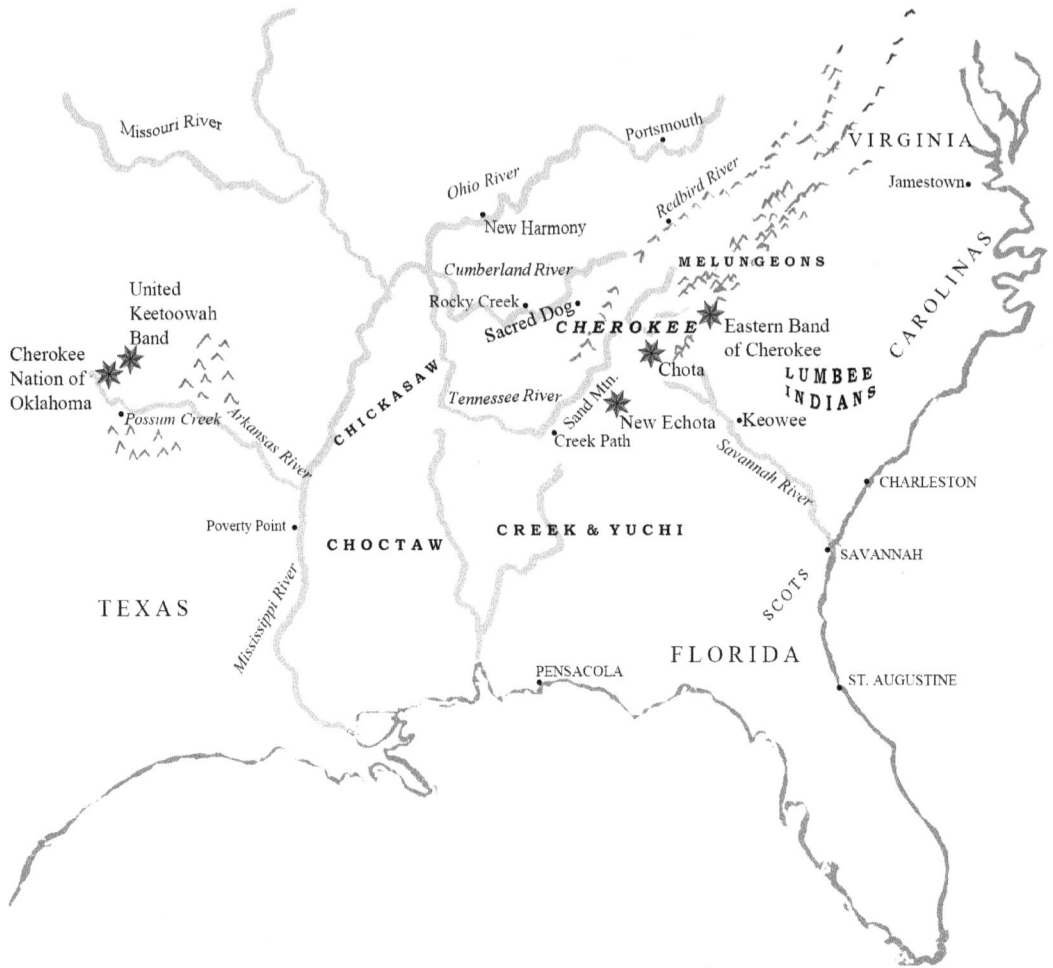

The Cherokee Anomaly (copyright Donald N. Yates, 2011).

# Old World Roots of the Cherokee

*How DNA, Ancient Alphabets and
Religion Explain the Origins
of America's Largest Indian Nation*

Donald N. Yates

*Foreword by* Richard Mack Bettis

McFarland & Company, Inc., Publishers
*Jefferson, North Carolina, and London*

Library of Congress Cataloguing-in-Publication Data

Yates, Donald N., 1950–
Old world roots of the Cherokee : how DNA, ancient alphabets
and religion explain the origins of America's largest Indian nation
/ Donald N. Yates ; foreword by Richard Mack Bettis.
p.    cm.
Includes bibliographical references and index.

ISBN 978-0-7864-6956-7
softcover : acid free paper ∞

1. Cherokee Indians— Origin.    2. Cherokee Indians— Migrations.
3. Cherokee language — Alphabet.    4. Cherokee language — Etymology.
5. Indians of North America — Transatlantic influences.
6. Human population genetics— Mediterranean Region.    I. Title.
E99.C5Y39 2012        975.004'97557 — dc23        2012019546

British Library cataloguing data are available

© 2012 Donald N. Yates. All rights reserved

No part of this book may be reproduced or transmitted in any form
or by any means, electronic or mechanical, including photocopying
or recording, or by any information storage and retrieval system,
without permission in writing from the publisher.

On the cover: *clockwise from top* wampum image © 2012 clipart.com
with inset of *Tanawa* from New Guinea cave (illustration by
Christopher C. Vigil); DNA helix © 2012 Shutterstock;
map of places mentioned in the book created by author;
*background* detail from *The Constitution and Laws
of the Cherokee Nation*, published in Cherokee, 1875

Manufactured in the United States of America

McFarland & Company, Inc., Publishers
Box 611, Jefferson, North Carolina 28640
www.mcfarlandpub.com

To Cherokee descendants everywhere

# Contents

# Introductory Note

Donald Yates burst onto the scene clarifying Melungeons and went on to explain many more peoples via pioneering researches in DNA. A classically grounded scientist who is conversant with Hebrew, he detected Cherokee as Greek in what can only be called an epochal shift of thinking, posing the historical challenge of getting Alexandrine and Mediterranean *koine* to Tennessee ahead of Hernando De Soto.

Oklahomans have long recognized the passion for excelling of gifted Cherokee. As an Oklahoman I fully acknowledge that tradition and as a North Carolinian have been dismayed that this state does not equally celebrate it, as inevitably it will. Yates' momentous book surely will have numerous noteworthy successors.

Cyclone Covey
Professor of History Emeritus
Wake Forest University
Winston-Salem, North Carolina

# Acknowledgments

The road to this book's appearance has been a long one. It is a pleasure for me to acknowledge the help of the following individuals for their roles small and large along the way: Bett Yates Adams, DeWayne Adamson, Steve Adkins, Judith Alef, William L. Anderson, Charles E. Austin, Bobbi Bacha, Joseph F. Bailey, Sandra Ballard, Dennis Banks, Michelle Baugh, Sharon Crisp Bedzyk, Rabbi Arnold Mark Belzer, Mabel Bentley, Richard Mack Bettis, the late Wallace Black Elk, Judy Douglas Bloom, Brent S. Vaughn Blount, Francesca Bortolaso, Lisa Bowes, Doris Cooper Bowman, the late John Bozowski, Edith Breshears, Donal Buchanan, Leah Laura Bulgariev, James H. Burchell, Linda Burckhalter, John (Dick) Caldwell, Virginia Caldwell, Helen Campbell, Francesca Cappellini, George Carter, Manfred Clauss, Ernest Cline, Doloris C. Cogan, William Collins, Grady Cooper, Jamie Cooper, Troy Cooper, Windham Cooper, Andre Copeland, Cyclone Covey, Brent Yanusdi Cox, Lauren T. Crews, Dr. Bruce Linton Dean, Gail Lynn Dean, the late Vine Deloria, Jr., Tom Diaz, Susan Drinan, Edmund F. Durfee, Werner Eck, Pamela G. Edwards, Bill Emmett, Momfeather Erickson, Debbie Erskine, the late Gloria Farley, Tommy Doyle Fields, Joseph Flynn, Flick Ford, Beatrice L. Frost, Ida Jane Gallagher, Mary M. Garrabrant-Brower, Michael E. Gilbert, Kelly Strater Gilroy, Mary Goodman, Cheryl Lynn Green, Alan Greth, Reagan L. Grimsely, the late Floyd Milton Grimwood, Billie Groening, R. L. Guffin, James L. Guthrie, Edmund Haag, Peter Haarer, Linda Haberlin, Ann Reagan Haines, Jess Hair, Linda Barnett Hall, Klaus Hallof, Zena Halpern, Florine Hamm, Nancy E. Hammes, Morton A. Harris, LaSonya Hayes, Marjorie Hecht, Kimberly McFadden Hill, Jacqueline Hines, Elizabeth Caldwell Hirschman, Denise Holmes-Kennedy, Raymond Hurst, John R. Ihlefeld, Paul Iverson, Ola Faye James, Stephen C. Jett, Roger L. Jewell, Carl Johannessen, the late Dorothy Randell Johnson, Nini Johnston, J. Jones, Pat Goin Jones, Rolling Thunder Justice, Pam Kahler, N. Brent Kennedy, Richard Kennedy, Miranda King, Willora Glee Krapf, Margaret E. Kross, Brenda LaForce, Everett LaForce, Page Lambert, Jessica Kiely Law, Eleanor M. Leonard, Rabbi Shmuel Lerer, David E. Lewis, Elisha Linder, Strawberry Luck, Bonnie J. Lyda, Juan B. Madrid, MeriDee Orvis Mahan, Thomas Mahar, Ronald Martin, Karen Mattern, Michelle Maxwell, Wayne May, Robert English McBeath, Peter McCormick, J. Huston McCulloch, Dorman McDonald, Barry McLerran, Russell Means, Matthew Mebust, Brian Mickelsen, Sebenia Ann Milbacher, Nicholas J. Millington, Thomas O. Mills, Karen Sue Mitchell, Debra Modrall, Holli S. Molnar, the late Jerry W. Moore, Michael M. Moore, Nola W. Moyers, Nelson Morgan, Nancy Sparks Morrison, Lars Mouritsen, David Mowa, Charley Myers, Maxine Nethercutt, Susan Newton, the late David Nitchman, Daisy Njoku, Stedman B. Noble, Esther P. Noffsinger, Barbara Roasting Ear Oliver, Rick Osmon, Teresa A. Panther-Yates (with special gratitude for all her assistance in making this long effort a success), Marshall Payn, Warren D. Pearson, Ella Mae Perkinson, Felicia Pickering, Dan E. Pomeroy, Gerald Potterf, Deborah Pritchett, Patrick Pynes, Alice E. Richards, the late James Riddle,

Jimi Riddle, JonLyn L. Roberts, Nadine Rosenbush, Molly Running Wolf, Paul Russell, the late Sonyaquay Russell, Larry Rutledge, Kathy Ryder, Rick Sanders, Michael Satlow, Betty Sue Price Satterfield, Arcelle Sawyer, Steve Shaffer, Billy Shaw, Rose C. Shockerly, Carole C. Sides, Billy Sinor, Amy Yates Smith, Bruce Smith, David Ray Smith, Robert D. Starling, Billy Starnes, Julia Starnes, Keely Starnes, Phyllis E. Starnes, George Starr-Bresette, Neil Steede, Marc K. Stengel, Richard Stewart, Kenneth B. Tankersley, Malee Thomas, Bart Torbert, the late Lupe Trejo, Jr., Elizabeth Trupin-Pulli, Gunnar Thompson, D. J. Thornton, Elizabeth Pearl Thurman, Bertram Tsavadawa, Kaye M. Viars, Edward Viera, Christopher C. Vigil, Orlando Vigil, Jay Stuart Wakefield, Skip Whitson, Joe White, Willie Marie Williams, Cecil Wooten, George Wickliffe, Brian E. Wilkes, Marie Wilkins, Gayl A. Wilson, Paul Minus Williams, Wayne Winkler, Celia Wyckoff, Dana Yarbrough, the late Bessie C. Yates, the late Cooper Leland Yates, Dustin Blake Yates, Lawden H. Yates, Paul G. Yates, William E. Yates, Madolyn York and Ju Sun Yi.

# Foreword

## by RICHARD MACK BETTIS

This book is relevant and would have been so even two hundred or five hundred years ago. Histories of America conventionally start in 1492 with Columbus and other European explorers. They all are supposed to discover savages of the lowest order. Thankfully, Donald Yates is not burdened by such stereotypes. As an expert in genetics who knows history, he answers only to those seeking truth. His interdisciplinary approach is relatively new, but its use is exploding.

As a historical investigator who uses the science of DNA as the perfect tool, Yates does not buy into the idea that everything discovered must have the stamp of Western Europe on it to be civilized and worthwhile. His many questions come from an extensive education in the humanities, but his final answers derive from science. He rightfully probes some of our ironclad assumptions about early America — its artifacts, architecture, skills, sciences of astronomy and mathematics and other knowledge surpassing that of the later explorers. He finds languages and customs from places around the world.

The book becomes more relevant when Yates merges DNA with history on the subject of Greeks, Jews, Egyptians and American Indians. His results constitute a rediscovery of an important part of America. Enrolling descendants of the earliest and best-known Cherokee families, he began the DNA project in 2003 and confirmed that Cherokee blood was mixed with the Blood of Israel and other ancient East Mediterranean peoples.

Readers of the work will encounter Hebrews in America, but in a scholarly and objective manner. The world history of the Cherokee has been rewritten, and the histories of other Native peoples have been placed on a different footing. In the context of what it means to be Cherokee, the word "world" is not overstated. Updated histories of other peoples will follow, with the same laboratory accuracy. Just like this work, such histories will approach the past differently and examine the present with new eyes. Past and present converge in the science of history as well as history of science. The tried and proven method of empirical research is still essential to answer the what, when, where and how of history, but for the who, science now provides an answer. And that is exciting. Our thinking must be radically readjusted. We just don't know how much, yet. The hint and suggestion of wider import is found in these test groups of "anomalous" Southeastern Indians and Jews.

Molecular biology is today's most accurate means of identifying any given individual in relation to all other human beings in the world. Physical science can now group people of the same and similar genetic backgrounds into any number of classifications, wherever found and tested, regardless of previously conceived ideas about their heredity. Rapid improvements are being made as larger world DNA databases are being assembled, as the science becomes better understood and refined.

Since blending history and science in this way alters many long-accepted beliefs, the concept for some will be unpalatable, acceptable only through gradual understanding. But it won't go away. It is important to recognize that this methodology only defines one's physical makeup — not beliefs, culture, religion or a geopolitical home address. No one can know all his or her variegated ancestry, but those who want to will now be able to learn more as studies and data grow.

For some historians, genealogists, Cherokee people and Jews, this information will be especially compelling. It will spark insight to long-standing questions about their ancestors. For anthropologists, a more accurate understanding of human geographic dispersion and identification will be the result — or can be. Truth is where you find it.

Earlier histories have been written primarily on the basis of cultural observation, perhaps also pieced together from archaeological digs and oral and written records. All these important data need not wait for the slow-moving test of time but can now be submitted to the more summary judgment of science. Yates has taken this long step back in time, and it leaves a lasting footprint.

I myself have Cherokee blood and have searched for over fifty years to learn of the component ethnic types of the Cherokee people. New leads always presented new questions. The tasks of tracking the truth became increasingly circuitous. Research in the past could provide only partial answers. In trying to identify who the Cherokee really were I confronted the following mysteries, plus many others. The Hebrews and Middle East seemed believably evident, by admission and observation. The sea-peoples and transoceanic trade were also apparent, through palpable evidence and Cherokee oral history. The tongue-twisting syllables *tli, tlo, tla,* etc., of Southern Mexico and Central America (Maya, Toltec, Aztec) were obvious, as were rituals of the Old Testament, i.e., sacrificial fire and offerings, which are still here to see. It is recorded that some early Cherokee spoke Hebrew and others, Welsh. The existence of a Hebrew inscription on the Bat Creek Stone from a mound in the Cherokee homeland of Tennessee cannot be denied, and I have examined it. Numerous other pieces of evidence are offered by Yates to validate multiple origins and diverse currents of influence.

As Dr. Cyrus Gordon, late professor of Mediterranean studies at Brandeis University, put it in a talk given in Tulsa some thirty-five-plus years ago regarding some of these observations, there is "more sameness than similarity." This observation suggested there might one day come a redeeming scientific finality. I waited, frequently impatiently. Now Dr. Yates has invoked DNA to reveal to us places, peoples, and times where genetic markers of today's Cherokee are and have been found. For students of the Cherokee, valid and trustworthy answers are here. Not all yet, but a significant start. And his data have many other applications.

Such new and growing libraries of DNA will begin to unravel the most debated questions about American history. Who was here before Columbus? From what lands did they migrate to this hemisphere? How? By whom were they met upon arrival? What is the time depth?

Besides these questions, an even greater issue is raised and fairly screams out to us: At what point do we have, or how can we now define, what is "American"? According to what authority and in relation to what time? That definition remains one of those moving targets! This book is not telling us what to believe, but it does give us important new information so we can decide for ourselves.

Because of the problematic definitions of what makes a Cherokee, and who or what is an American, it is ironic that diffusionists (those who hold identical cultural traits have a common origin somewhere) owe anti-diffusionists and isolationists (those who believe the opposite, in independent origins) a heavy debt, for working so long and hard to point up information demanding critical review. It is satisfying to consider that this work is part of a new discipline to provide that critical review. Their sometimes dogmatic position has become more and more vulnerable. Such icons as the Bering land bridge are beginning to tumble.

Yates comes with well-researched and personal knowledge from his study of the Cherokee — the Ani-Yun-wiya or, Principal People. He introduces us to them in a book that could only be written in the information age, where there are an abundance of connections available through the Internet. A common legal phrase seems on point here: *res ipsa loquitur* — The thing speaks for itself.

Indeed, the ancient peoples thesis is not at all a novel historical concept. Yates points up what students of the Cherokees have long known. Three of the best-informed early authors of Cherokee history, independently, described a poignant sameness in Old Testament Hebrew traditions and ceremonies practiced by the Cherokee. Those historians are James Adair, Elias Boudinot and Dr. Emmet Starr. However, their characterizations of the Cherokee as remnants of Israel have never been taken seriously by mainstream historians. With Dr. Yates's research, these three sources have been vindicated. They enjoy, by now, some degree of emeritus status. The same can be said for Constantine Rafinesque, the discoverer of the Wallam Olum.

Exceptions to the common dismissal of Jewish connections are and always have been the traditional Keetoowahs. These last holdouts are descendants of people from the ancient mother town of Kituwha, a city of refuge in the mold of ancient Judea in present-day North Carolina. They still gather in Northeast Oklahoma to relate their Old Testament beliefs, in solemn ceremonies. Yates discusses this and offers a photograph of the sacred peace belts which those traditionalists have used to teach their history. The belts, reportedly, are gifts of great value reflecting long alliances with the Iroquois Confederacy. As such, they date into antiquity, or pre-history. The seven belts are highly revered and protected, as they should be.

It is important for readers of this book to realize that they are being guided, ever so surely and carefully, through the Cherokees' own insider history of themselves. Into this history is infused genetic information. We meet in this work the rare author who is both historian and scientist. He adds to these strengths family history, for Yates is also a genealogist. We come to realize how biochemical fingerprints make each of us different from others and at the same time related, how such a database of information contains the lives of our parents, and all our ancestors having the same genetic markers, back through time to the first mutation distinguishing a certain line.

I am aware that DNA evidence is scientifically accurate to approximately one in a trillion. As an attorney, I know that prior to DNA as a legal tool, you could take one, or one hundred pieces of circumstantial evidence to court, and none of it could ever amount to more than just circumstantial evidence. Today, however, one valid piece of DNA evidence trumps it all.

A survey of the amalgam of people we call Cherokee reveals multiple migrations and diverse places of origin. It is fact that the Cherokees' own origin stories include the East, the North, the South and the West. We Cherokee claim to come from the Mediterranean, Middle East, all of Europe, Africa, the Tarim Basin, the Indus Valley, Asia, a sunken island (Atlantis?) and South and Central America. We were always here where the Creator put us.

The spread of pins trailing across the world map seems to verify that we are an honest people — the Cherokees do derive from very diverse geographical and genetic sources.

The surprising nature of this information has caused the scholar (and fellow Oklahoman, friend and mentor) Dr. Cyclone Covey, professor emeritus at Wake Forest University, to refer to such a mix of peoples as "the Cherokee enigma." The seemingly contradictory strains seem to beg many questions, and this book responds to some key elements. Interestingly, its chapters reiterate the Cherokees' own identification with ancient peoples and their role as survivors and teachers for the dispersed remnants. Setting aside Rome and the civilizations of Greece, Egypt and Judea from which they derive, the Cherokee are, in fact, the oldest civilization outside China and India in continuous existence today. They have subsisted for over 2,200 years since their founding, as described in this account. History will want to turn new eyes on them for their longevity as a people, if nothing else.

We learn that the Cherokee are part of the blood of an ancient dispersion, and they come from more than one group. After all, the earliest published history on the Cherokee, by Adair (1775), as well as many early Europeans, accepted Cherokees as descendants of the Lost Ten Tribes of Israel. In any case, a valid historical and religious question seems apropos: Was the Diaspora, or dispersion of Israel, really a punishment, or actually a greater plan for survival? Either way, preservation of the bloodline was the result. DNA has proved it by tracking some of the wanderers.

After a lifetime of living among other Cherokee and researching my heritage, I have come to know them as good people and good citizens. I would go further and postulate that the original nucleus of men and women who became Cherokee banded together with like people in an effective alliance. It was made up of groups from earlier diffusions. Taking with them the best of all worlds wherever they went, and leaving behind a distinct memory of their presence and influence, the Cherokee emerged in a centralized confederacy that dominated the wide area where the Spanish and various Europeans first encountered and misnamed them — in our Central and Southeastern Woodlands.

The author goes into some detail regarding neighboring groups such as the Creek and Choctaw, Shawnee and Yuchi. He shares DNA test results documenting a great hybrid vigor from the distant, as well as a not-so-distant, past. It is ironic that in 2004, I prepared a paper in response to the specific question raised by Covey — who are the Cherokee? I believe that much of the content of this paper is now finally validated, and vindicated. Again: DNA trumps circumstantial evidence.

During their centuries of organized strength the Cherokee maintained Native confederacies to both the north and south, which the colonists recognized and were forced to respect. After about 1700, however, they were on a rapid downward slide. So many Europeans pushed for land that the strongest union of even the Five Civilized Tribes and their allies was ineffectual. All had to strain to merely survive. And they did survive, but only by forced removal. One more ironic sameness: Like the Hebrews, the Cherokee had their Exodus. Because of it, their blood survives today. History repeats itself? Seems so!

The American colonial period brought a welter of European immigrants to these shores. Here again DNA has something to say. Yates presents straightforward examples of Jewish lines found in several prominent early immigrant–Indian families. Descendants of several of those lines — the Cherokee families Tassel, Dragging Canoe, Ward, Grant, Dougherty, Rogers, Cooper and Gist, as well as some Choctaw surnames — were and are family friends of this writer, so their history is now richer for me personally.

Because of the book's information, or rather, evidence, we must revise many notions about Cherokee history. More specifically, our national historical thinking must recognize that many of the immigrants who described themselves as Scot, Irish, Spanish, French, English or other nationalities actually were only declaring the nations from which they had sailed. After settling, after intermarriage, remaining as crypto–Jews, or openly returning to an identity of choice, they, and all others, became just as American as any other immigrants. Surely they helped introduce the theme of tolerance in our early history. Avoiding unfair bias has allowed many good, but unknown, people to be accepted as valued and respected neighbors.

Incidentally, the earliest previous evidence known to me to provide conclusive proof of pre–Columbian sea travel to the Americas were tests by German scientists published in the 1970s. From bone samples, soft tissue and hair of Ramses II and at least eight other mummies they isolated cocaine and tobacco— plants native only to the Americas. This was reported in a *Nova* documentary.

Another plant coming from Egypt to Peru is cotton, genetically the same in both nations. These examples stand as proof of sea travel to and from the Americas. More recently, a mutated gene occurring in Southeast Asia some 6000 years ago has been identified in South and Central America. It came via the South Pacific, since it is not found in any peoples of Alaska, the Northwestern U.S., Canada, or in any populations associated with the so-called Bering Land Bridge. Heyerdahl has shown us how these trips could be made, with the simplest of crude ships, though he was wrong about the direction of the voyages, which genetics has shown went from west to east rather than the other way around. These discoveries were reported in studies sponsored by Brigham Young University and the University of Pennsylvania in the 1990s. John L. Sorenson and Carl L. Johannessen's definitive *World Trade and Biological Exchanges* catalogs 100 species of cultivated plants (among which are the sweet potato and corn), 19 species of micro-predators and seven other species of fauna, including hairless dogs, turkeys and the common chicken, that were shared between the Old and New World long before Columbus. Yates tracks Cherokee genes from New Guinea and Polynesia through South and Central America and Mexico, confirming such early connections.

Ideas suggested in this book are consistent with Old Testament and the histories written by Josephus. Ancient Hebrews ultimately went to many places at different times. But where? And are they really lost? Is it not possible that those thought to be lost might be found and accounted for in a completely scientific way, such as a simple swab of the cheek? The reader may be literally holding the answer.

Consider that Egypt was the magnetic center of wealth, culture and military dominance in that part of the world. It had drawn people both by land and sea, from every known country, for trade and commerce. The Hebrews left Egypt with knowledge of stone building (even about pyramids and palaces), of sea travel, trading and of languages of all who came there. With such valuable knowledge, they could blend, co-exist, serve as translators, scribes and valuable leaders for people they already knew, as well as those they might encounter later. In Yates's Rafinesque chapter, he describes the Cherokees' innate talents as ombudsmen, arbitrators, negotiators and assimilators. Some more sameness? For sure!

It is also fact that the Famous Sea Dogs, as Homer describes the Phoenicians, were from the city-states of Sidon, Lebanon, Canaan and Tyre, along with some Carthaginians. They were all among the mercantile and mercenary allies of Egypt. Phoenicians established the first international trade cartels (*Nova*, April 2006). What priceless experience and abilities the Hebrews took with them! That *Nova* documentary revealed that Lebanese and

Canaanites carried and still carry Phoenician genes, as did apparently Charlemagne and Thomas Jefferson (both of whom are believed to belong to the lineage known as T).

Bernard Malamud once remarked: Every man is a Jew though he may not know it. Could this be literally as well as figuratively true? Let's just refer to some of the most fundamental annals of mankind. In Genesis 1:28, Yehowah of the Cherokee, the Biblical Jehovah, creates Adam and Eve and gives them certain instructions. This story is essentially identical in the Torah, Quran, and Flavius Josephus. Southeastern Indians also acknowledged the Hebrew God, and even today their drum songs often contain the repeated syllables of Ye-Ho-Wah. While Adam and Eve and their descendants did not do everything as admonished, they and theirs did follow what is perhaps the most gratifying of human tasks: Go forth and multiply. History has argued, and now science proves, that they are among us.

As suggested above, Dr. Yates is sticking pins in maps, points representing times and locations in the world where genetic markers have been found matching Cherokees, Hebrews, or Jews. We learn where so-called points A and B and other significant places and genes converge, time and again. The Americas are loaded with stories of white men, even bearded white men, who came to this hemisphere in ships. Petroglyphs of such people are plentiful. One witness to such lore is the Popul Vuh of the Maya. Recently, Kennewick Man in the Pacific Northwest validates the supposition in a concrete way.

So we follow through the colonial period when the Cherokee people, at their zenith, are suddenly threatened with cataclysmic change, first by a few immigrants, then soon by militant hoards. It is a historical truism: Whatever invaders consider valuable, if superior in number and might, they take. The Cherokee had land; and then word of gold got out. The Cherokee were no longer safe at home. In fact, they no longer had a home.

Military conquest, germ warfare and every device available were used to force treaties requiring the Cherokee and others to go. However, the greatest loss of Cherokee blood was, as Yates describes, by the most natural way, assimilation. To the Cherokee in 2012, the mortal enemy, seen every day in plain sight, is still blood dilution. With it goes loss of language and segment after segment of the culture. Today, there is no Will Usti to help slow or reverse the process.

Among Western or Oklahoma Cherokee, there began early on, and continues to exist, a division between the low-blood quantum and higher blood-quantum groups. The split is a continuation of the historical blood feud between strong traditionalists and assimilationists; it really goes back to the Treaty Party controversy during Removal. The *Ani-gi-du-wha-gi* or self-help groups (not too different from the Jewish term "kibbutz") still function today, especially among the more traditional small communities or stomp dance grounds inside the Cherokee world. But the people must of necessity co-exist with the outside world. They all shop at Walmart and Target, and most work or go to schools or church together. Through the dimming veil of differences, pride still exists within an inner circle, and from time to time, a resurgence of teaching the language and history starts up with renewed interest.

Traditional ceremonies of the Keetoowah Society are held, but they are infrequent. The Seven Clans Society still has meetings, but they are also fewer. Most "fires" or towns no longer exist. Since its 1946 reformation by Act of Congress and subsequent award of federal recognition, the United Keetoowah Band of Cherokee Indians in Oklahoma is today stronger and larger than ever. It took advantage of every legal right to preserve its sovereign status under State and Federal Reorganization Acts. It now has a one-quarter blood-quantum membership rule. The largest and most widely known group is the Cherokee

Nation of Oklahoma, with very large numbers of very low blood-quantum members. They have successful hospitals, clinics, home building programs, and several casinos and tribal businesses. In the eyes of the majority culture, numbers still matter when it comes to government programs, as Yates reminds us in remembering Dr. Angie Debo, prophetess and historian of Oklahoma Indian Tribes.

Cherokees have been and still are intelligent and resilient. Throughout the present book we see many reasons why: their hybrid vigor, diverse history, the flexibility to recognize and accept better ways to do things and a resolute determination to not quit. These reasons will ensure that many of the Cherokee names we come across today will still be in future census records and in prominent roles in their communities. After this book becomes available, it is predicted that more Cherokee will learn of Jewish and related — Arabic, Berber and North African — roots.

The exceptionally welcome opportunity to learn the truth of things believed but unproven, to add new, valuable knowledge to earlier research, is a special pleasure for me. To read such a book of the science of history brings understanding, insights and thoughts of lasting value. I have felt a responsibility to communicate thoughts equal in some small part to the important knowledge shared with us in this benchmark work. I hope I have done so. This book is timely and long awaited by many. History today, as you now are reading it, no longer has to be educated guess, observation or long-accepted-but-often-wrong ideas. Newer, better science is finally here and is being added to and improved.

For Hebrews and Jews, past and present, who have contributed to our Cherokee way of life, *wa-do*, or thank you. Sequoyah's syllabary, of whatever origin, still endures on our talking leaves. Likewise, my heart goes out to the Jewish people that something from individual or from all Cherokees has been beneficial, in some way, to them. Gratitude to the Jewish people is personalized for me, inasmuch as my wife has genes from an early Jewish merchant, as well as from the Cherokee. Today, our children and grandchildren share that blood, plus the Cherokee and other blood on my side.

*Richard Mack Bettis earned a J.D. degree from Oklahoma City University Law School and has lived in Tulsa on the borderline of the former Cherokee Nation of Oklahoma since 1955. A prominent voice in Indian cultural and legal affairs, he has known many of the leaders of Cherokee government, including chiefs W. W. Keeler, Ross Swimmer and Wilma Mankiller.*

# Introduction

According to the title of a popular book, there are 500 Indian nations. The U.S. Bureau of Indian Affairs today lists over 800 Indian "groups." Not one of them has a satisfactory history, by which I mean a competent, written account of their past. Rather than tackle the particular details of a single tribe, their unique language or a distinct period in a tribe's history, writers have preferred to author general histories or omnibus compilations ... with titles like *500 Nations*. For a variety of reasons, none of these treatments can be said to be authoritative or complete. The encyclopedic approach suffers because of a dearth of individual studies, and the "first-cut" journal articles that might be expected to contribute to a gradually accumulating body of knowledge about American Indians are stillborn for lack of a settled framework in the field as a whole.

Of the "500," it is the Cherokee who are most harmed by the confused state of affairs. They comprise the largest nation. If we cannot understand who the Cherokee are we are not very advanced in our knowledge of American Indians.

One might think that the problem could be solved by having more Native authors writing history. But that only compounds the confusion, because Native authors are often fighting old wars. At any rate, they founder like all the others. Either they are engulfed by the chimerical Scylla of case studies or wrecked on the massive, unformed Charybdis of the discipline itself.

The latest history of the Cherokee by Robert Conley was commissioned by a principal chief of the Cherokee Nation of Oklahoma. It is a general treatment of a particular subject, combining the failings inherent in both approaches. As in so many other tribal monographs, politics and equivocation seem to have hijacked objectivity. The Cherokee Nation of Oklahoma is not coterminous with the Cherokee people. There are more Cherokees that do not belong to the Cherokee Nation of Oklahoma than who belong to it as citizens with roll numbers and quantum blood certificates. Its history is neither comprehensive nor even representative of Cherokee history, for it begins only in 1838, the year of the final, legal defeat of the Cherokee by the U.S. government and their removal on the Trail of Tears to Indian Territory. Like his patron, Conley has axes to grind. He glosses over the pre–1838 past and ignores many events that take place in the Cherokee homeland in the East. On the issue of origins, he simply lists the various theories without taking a considered position.

Cherokee historiography falls into the same periods as federal Indian policy, whose precedents are all traceable in British Indian trade relations. Except for James Adair's *History of the American Indians*, published in London in 1775, no study of the subject of American Indians was attempted in monograph form during the Colonial period. To be sure, several classic treatments existed in Spanish. One was Gregorio de Garcia's *Origen de los Indios del Nuevo Mundo e Indias Occidentales* (Valencia, 1607), a work that summarized all the learned hypotheses advanced to that time. (It concluded that American Indians were human beings.)

Another was Bartolomé de las Casas' *Historia de las Indias,* so radical in its pleas for Indian rights that it was not published in its entirety until the nineteenth century.

In the Peace of Paris that concluded the American Revolution in 1783, Americans (as Native Americans were then called) were ignored. The very mention of Indians was tabled by both British and Americans (as the Colonials were now called). The sovereignty of Indian tribes, validity of Indian treaties and status of Indians as individuals were subjects simply not addressed, although some tribes (like the Iroquois) had fought on the side of the rebels and others (like the Cherokee) on the side of the British. Theoretically, reparations and damages might have been discussed. No peace treaty, at any rate, was signed with any Indians. The whole topic was sublimely avoided.

The new nation's Indian policies began to take shape after the election of the first president, George Washington, in 1792. The person of the president emerged as the Great White Father, taking the place of King George, awarding medals of a new George to what became "medal chiefs." The U.S. Senate took on the role of guarantor of Indian rights and treaties. During the interregnum, a good deal of encroachment had taken place on Indian lands. The states of Kentucky and Tennessee were carved out of Cherokee territory after two illegal states were attempted, Watauga Country and the State of Franklin. The Great White Father was given a list of 500 names of white men settled illegally in the Cherokee Nation. He was given the list by white men lobbying the government to allow them to stay. It is an indication of how admixed the nation already was. Some of these events are reviewed in Chapter 11: Phoenix Rising.

There was every reason to place the Indians under the care of the Senate, for this chamber of government also had the authority to declare war and make peace. From 1790 until the 1860s, Indian affairs were regulated by the War Department. Studies of Indians took on the character of language manuals, musters of soldiers, warrior counts, auditor's records and fatality lists. Indian eloquence was spent on polemic speech after polemic speech (think of Red Jacket or Tecumseh). Henry R. Schoolcraft, an Indian agent, published his massive work, *Historical and Statistical Information Respecting ... the Indian Tribes of the United States* in six volumes from 1851 to 1857. Portraits of chiefs were commissioned and displayed, somewhat like a baseball card collection, at the Indian Gallery of the Department of War in Washington. Constantine Rafinesque flourished during this period as a lone well-informed, European–trained and unprejudiced scholar in matters of Indian prehistory and the archeology of ancient Native America (Chapters 4 and 5 in this book).

The last treaty with an Indian Nation was signed in 1867, after which treaty making was suspended. Two Indian wars ended without any treaty — the Second Seminole War (1835–1842) and the Sioux Wars (beginning 1854 and continuing with the Indian victory at the Battle of Little Big Horn in 1876 and U.S. army Massacre at Wounded Knee in 1890). The Seminole War was the most expensive Indian war fought by the United States. It cost the government $1 million for every Seminole killed and lasted longer than any other engagement. The last Indian wars were fought with the Apaches and Utes and ended without any pretense of treaty making. Most information about American Indians appeared in the popular press, with the result that the "newspaper Indian" came into being. He was succeeded by the "Hollywood Indian."

By the 1880s all Indians within the bounds of the United States were thought to be situated on reservations. These desolate tracts of land unwanted by the government all lay west of the Mississippi with the exception of a handful of tiny acreages like those of the Mohawks of New York and Cherokee Indians of North Carolina, both of which were given to the Indians by local white people. The next chapter in Indian policy is usually known as the Dawes Act years or period of severalty. Congress passed the Dawes Severalty Act in 1887. Among the measures in this law was one to terminate Indian communal ownership of the land on their reservations "as rapidly as possible." Indian governments were also ended. This era witnessed the rise of an imperial school of American Indian anthropology based in the Bureau of American Ethnology at the Smithsonian Institution. The bureau's founding director, John Wesley Powell, sought "to organize anthropologic research in America." At this time, there appeared James Mooney's *Sacred Formulas of the Cherokees* and *Myths of the Cherokee* (as the 7th and 19th annual reports of the bureau). He also wrote *Historical Sketch of the Cherokee*, reissued in 1975 after the Cherokee Nation of Oklahoma regained its standing and began to function as a government again. The author of our foreword, Richard Mack Bettis, wrote the introduction to that book.

The government of the Cherokee Nation of Oklahoma (the only officially recognized Cherokee Indian group at that time) was discontinued in 1903. The rolls were closed. There were to be no new Indians after this, maybe a few stragglers. But to be enrolled in a federally-recognized Indian tribe henceforth meant that one had to provide the Bureau of Indian Affairs (successor to the War Department) with a paper trail of birth and death certificates leading back to someone explicitly named on the final rolls. In the case of the Cherokee Nation of Oklahoma, this meant the Dawes Roll of 1898. For the belatedly-recognized Eastern Band of Cherokee Indians in North Carolina, it meant the Baker Roll of 1924. Most Cherokee genealogy research today focuses on these two rolls.

In 1924, U.S. citizenship was extended to all American Indians. For the first time since European contact 400 years ago, more American Indians were being born than were dying. Their population was slowly increasing. In 1922, the first advocacy group, the Association on American Indian Affairs, was founded in New York. For the Cherokee, these years are memorable for the publication in 1921 of Emmet Starr's *History of the Cherokee Indians and Their Legends and Folklore*, still today the master compendium of Cherokee family history and clans.

Republican presidents ended a decade of supremacy in 1932. The New Deal under Democrat Franklin D. Roosevelt began. The Indian New Deal could be summed up in the single figure of John Collier, commissioner of Indian Affairs 1932–1945. He was the first high-ranking government official to conduct what we would call today a "needs assessment" of what was called then "the Indian problem." The result was a rejuvenation of Indian self-sufficiency and a thorough reorganization of the reservation system. As Vine Deloria once remarked, the whole effort of Indians at that time was to learn administrative law. The rising stars on a reservation, if they escaped boarding school, read Felix Cohen's bulging *Handbook of Federal Indian Law* with a flashlight in their tipis. Concurrently, many anthropologists of the John Wesley Powell and Franz Boas schools were collecting the traditions of various tribes and putting them on the shelves of libraries for the first time. Unfortunately for Cherokee studies, there was not much attention from anthropologists or administrators during these years, partly because the Cherokee were too assimilated and ubiquitous to be regarded with much curiosity. Their secrets continued to slumber.

The period known as Termination and Relocation began in 1945 and lasted into the 1970s. Some tribes, like the Menominee, were abolished altogether. Under Dillon Meyer, treaty rights, payments and federal benefits to tribes were to be stopped. Reservation youths were to be relocated to urban centers where they could be schooled and find employment. It was a disastrous time for American Indians, including the Cherokee, for whom the watchword of the day was assimilation. Little interest was shown in Indian history until the efforts of the National Congress of American Indians (founded 1944) began to galvanize Indians to political activism. A pan–Indian consciousness and self-determination movement came into being during the late 1960s and early 1970s.

The period known as Self-Determination began with the American Indian occupation of Alcatraz Island (1969–1971), American Indian Movement seizure of Bureau of Indian Affairs (BIA) headquarters in Washington, D.C., in 1972 and Wounded Knee Incident of 1973. It witnessed the achievement of civil rights by American Indians and a prolific output of literature, scholarship, journalism and political writings. The *Journal of Cherokee Studies* and *American Indian Quarterly* were established. Dominant figures in American Indian letters were Vine Deloria, Jr., author of *Custer Died for Your Sins* and *God Is Red*, Angie Debo (*And Still the Waters Run*, 1973) and Dee Brown (*Bury My Heart at Wounded Knee*). Although these books set the tone for many subsequent historical works, they were far from objective and unbiased. They raised few historical problems that had to be worked out. They did not break any new ground. The state of the science of Indian linguistics and study of Indian languages and literature was very backward indeed.

The present period of American Indian studies may be called the Academic. In Cherokee studies, Mooney and Royce are reprinted. It has been marked by professionalism — professional teachers, professional artists, professional professors, professional journalists, professional gaming experts, professional musicians, professional administrators, on and on. It is not impossible that there exists something by now called a professional Indian.

General studies, it seems, continued along their own way with a proliferation of coffee-table books. My favorite is the series by artist Thomas Mails (e.g., *The Mystic Warriors of the Plains*). The turn of the twenty-first century is a ripe moment for harvesting innovative tribally-specific works and listening to original new voices. Robert Warrior has gone so far as to write an American Indian intellectual manifesto (*Tribal Secrets*).

A wave of political correctness and ethnic bias, however, has swept over editors and academic institutions. American Indian studies by American Indians and American Indian studies by Americans are two different animals. Under the circumstances, little collaboration is possible. A true cross-pollinating or interdisciplinary effect is rare given the antipathy between the two camps, which emphasize professions and specialties. Characteristic of the times are scholarly compendiums like the *Handbook of American Indians* and *American Indian Religious Traditions: An Encyclopedia*. Programs in universities are liable to be called Indigenous and Southwest Studies. They can be housed in English, sociology, anthropology, archeology, history or American studies departments. Europeans keep a respectful distance.

For my part, I see no reason why an American Indian cannot go to Hollywood and get a part that is not one playing an American Indian. Russell Means is in the same position today as Hattie McDonald was seventy years ago when she played Mammy in *Gone with the Wind*. I think an American Indian choosing, say, Victorian literature for their doctoral dissertation would not only be a boon to Victorian literary criticism but also a beneficial role model for other American Indians. I see no reason to shoo the anthropologists and "other friends" off the reservation. As a mixed blood, I have sometimes felt compelled to shoot arrows and race over to the other side to get hit. Telling me I can't have an Indian card and become a ward of the government is like forbidding me from joining the French Foreign Legion.

So where does this sketch of Indian studies leave us? Nature does not like a vacuum. The scientists and historians who study nature do not like one either. Rather than say those three little words "I don't know," they have filled the gaps in our knowledge with assumptions and generalizations. I will examine some of those in the case of American Indian genetics in Chapter 3.

If mainstream scholars keep patching up the field of American Indian studies with the same stubborn glue-all, the "diffusionists" err in the opposite direction. They pump American Indian studies too full of airy, ecumenical notions. That Roman brick masons may have been responsible for the Roman brick mason marks catalogued on thousands of bricks at the ancient Mexican site of Comalcalco is already difficult for many Smithsonian–schooled archeologists to accept. But to entertain the thought that Chinese, Indonesians, Indians, Egyptians, Carthaginians, Romans, Greeks, Jews and West Africans may have blended and interacted in the creation of Classic Maya is too much. It is beyond the academic pale and will usually evoke nothing but silence and silencing.

Mainstream anthropologists dismiss all evidence for contact (not to say influence) between Old and New World peoples before Columbus. Diffusionism is classed with conspiracy theories, racist agendas and amateur science. Anyone who listens to it or is lured by it is to be pitied — or perhaps protected by the equivalent of a consumer rights bureau.

One might wonder why all the passion. I have belonged at different times to both camps. I have witnessed academic scholars demolish the arguments of what they regard as the lunatic fringe with a glee out of all proportion both to the effort and the accomplishment. I have also mingled with the enemy at conferences like those of the Epigraphic Society. Here I could detect only a feeling of weary resignation. It is not so much a case of "ignorant armies clashing by night" as of two involuntary duelers meeting at dawn. Do we really have to do this? In the spirit of humility, one should always bear in mind that it is just as difficult to disprove something as to prove it.

We can see some of these dynamics in the case of the Melungeons, a multi-ethnic group (some say) with a distinct culture and religious practices (some say) that long went undetected, although they had been dwelling (some say) in the Cherokee Indians' former territory in the southeastern United States for between 300 and 500 years, perhaps longer. Typically, they are described as having dark skin, black or dark-brown straight hair, brown or blue eyes and European features. A book written in 1994 by a self-identifying Melungeon, Brent Kennedy, renewed interest in them and stimulated a burst of memoirs and informal research. The Melungeon Heritage Association was founded in Wise, Virginia, in 1997. Helen Campbell created a Web site with monthly publications at Melungeons.com in 2002. Studies that included DNA analyses by Elizabeth Hirschman of Rutgers University and me as co-investigators supported what Kennedy had earlier proposed: The Melungeons were a Sephardic Jewish and Moorish community that began perhaps as early as 1540 with the De Soto expedition. Over the centuries, incoming Sephardic Jews and Spanish Muslims augmented their numbers after fleeing the Spanish Inquisition and finding refuge in such way stations as the Low Countries, Germany, France, Italy, Greece, Switzerland, the Ottoman Empire, Egypt, Scotland, Ireland and England.

Many people deny the existence of Melungeons altogether. They argue that what others call the Melungeons are simply the pioneer descendants of English land grantees from the Northern Neck of Virginia who settled in the East Tennessee area, or that they are Scots-Irish or German or otherwise indistinguishable from the general population. On the Internet there is endless, almost ontological quibbling about what makes one a Melungeon. Is the term to be restricted to Collins and Goins descendants on Newmans Ridge in Hancock County, Tennessee, or can it be extended to those across the Virginia border and to other ethnically mixed groups such as the Redbones of Louisiana, Carmel Indians of Ohio and Lumbee Indians of North Carolina? What most participants in the controversy overlook is the question I began and ended with: What is the connection between Melungeons and Cherokees? Why was I both? Could it be that the Judaic/Islamic roots of the Melungeons were older than had been postulated even by the most daring believers in such a thesis?

Certainly the trail is obvious as far back as the seventeenth century. Melungeons are sometimes referred to as Black Dutch, a usage common especially among mixed blood Cherokee people. This term originally referred to Hollanders of dark appearance during the Spanish occupation of the Netherlands in the 1600s. After Dutch independence, colonial Virginia and Carolina records called the same people Portuguese. A connection between the two lay in judaizing (returning to Judaism after forced or feigned conversion to Christianity) Sephardic merchants, or Marranos (Spanish-Portuguese bankers and merchants), who settled in the Dutch Republic following its separation from Spain. These called themselves, ambiguously, *gente del linaje,* or *homens da nação,* and in English, "Hebrews of the Portuguese Nation." Following the introduction of the Spanish Inquisition in the 1490s, and especially as it was stepped up by Catholic authorities after 1580, they streamed into Britain, especially Scotland, and thence to America.

One theory about the meaning of the word Melungeon is that it is an Arabic word meaning "cursed souls." This is an apt description for a people who seemed to be dogged by persecution. Another explanation of the epithet lays in the use of melongena, an archaic word for eggplant, a term applied in Inquisitorial Spain, Portugal and Italy to crypto–Jews, who favored eggplant stew over pork. Comparable racial terms are *melanzana* in Italian, *mulenyam* in Sicilian and *molonjohn* in English. It may be nothing more than a nonce word coined on the basis of French mélange, as some maintain, but the eggplant allusions permeate the hidden meaning in Cervantes' Don Quixote with its crypto–Jewish, crypto–Muslim narrator Cide Hamete Benengeli, Mr. Eggplant. The surname Benenhaley persists among South Carolina's mixed-blood Turks, whose DNA matches show Portuguese, Moroccan, Brazilian, Berber, Egyptian and Arab, as well as Native American and Sub-Saharan African origins. As late as the 1950s, health officials in several Southern states, notably Walter Plecker in Virginia, maintained lists of Melungeon surnames that belonged, they said, to degenerate "mongrel breeds," the products of miscegenation. Almost every one of the surnames mentioned in this book appears on these lists. My mother did not have a birth certificate. It was destroyed, presumably because of what it said or implied about her "race."

In my reading of the archeological record, the story of Jews and related peoples among the Indians goes back many centuries before any Sephardic Jew set foot on these shores. Perhaps the most astonishing piece of evidence for ancient contact between the Old and New World is the Bat Creek Stone (see Chapter 9), an inscription from an Indian tomb in Tennessee that has been interpreted as a Hebrew record of the Simon Bar Kochba revolt of 135–6 C.E. It is fashionable to scoff at artifacts brought to light by amateurs or members of the public, but the Bat Creek Stone was excavated under the direction of the Smithsonian Institution's Cyrus Thomas. Strict archeological protocol was observed. This was the heartland of the Cherokee, near Knoxville, Tennessee. Again, we find the congruence and contemporaneity of Jews and Cherokees.

Small and scattered as these artifacts are, they seem to present a case that can no longer be dismissed. Although overlooked in the usual historical accounts of America, Mediterranean peoples evidently made their way to North America far earlier than previously thought.

Another enigma that spurred me on in my research was the unusual genetics of my mother's family. DNA studies of the Cherokee and Melungeons show a very different story from that routinely taught in schools and universities (see Chapter 3: DNA). The project I started nearly ten years ago titled Southeastern U.S. Indian DNA ended up adding Mediterranean gene types U, J, H and T, among others, to the established set of common mitochondrial (maternal) lineages of ancient Cherokee Indians (A, B, C, D and X). Phase II and III investigations confirmed these anomalous lineages. Population geneticists have previously classified Native American DNA into five Asiatic gene types (although haplogroup X is now conceded by most to be Eurasian and trans–Atlantic in origin, with its worldwide center of diffusion in Lebanon and northern Israel). Whether the presence of these genes is the effect of a dwindling genetic inheritance from an ancient population that joined with Asiatic Indians, one that ran very thin, or of a later minor influx and blending, these genes can in no way be the result of post–1492 admixture. The best explanation is that Romans, Greeks, Jews, Phoenicians and other ancient peoples intermingled with Asiatic Indians in America during the period we call Classical Antiquity. I argue that their contributions to Indian societies, particularly the Cherokee, did not disappear but were recognized by later Jewish immigrants arriving on American shores (see Chapters 10 to 12).

A critical piece of the puzzle was the discovery by Gloria Farley of an ancient rock inscription in Oklahoma, the Possum Creek Stone (see Chapter 10: Sequoyan Syllabary). The writing, she postulated, suggests a Mediterranean origin for the Cherokee syllabary conventionally attributed to Sequoyah. Once we accept such Old World peoples among the Cherokee, it seems reasonable to suppose that Mediterranean civilizations contributed cultural characteristics and religious beliefs, as well as genes and physical traits. Some of the customs I single out to investigate are the Cherokees' bathing practices, athletics, military organization, rich folklore concerning fairies and reference to themselves as a "nation" (Chapter 8: She Who Walks with the Little People and Chapter 9: Yom Kippur with the Cherokee).

The final chapter of the book brings us down almost to the present with a genealogical study of Melungeon families on Sand Mountain in Alabama. Here I return full circle to my unique family history, for my mother, Bessie Cooper, was born on Sand Mountain and was descended from Cherokee chiefs. With the defeat of the Echota Cherokee by the Tennesseans, the population center of the Melungeons shifted down the Appalachian chain to Waldens Ridge and Sand Mountain, following in the same direction of the relocation of Cherokee towns to Sequatchie Country and northern Georgia and Alabama. Already the Cherokee "Nation," as it was to be known, consisted of fifty percent mixed bloods and intermarried whites. Prominent among these settlements was Creek Path, the seat of Chief Black Fox. Among the Melungeon families studied are those allied with this new Chickamauga hierarchy, including surnames Cooper, Brown, Justice and Lowrey. (So there can be no mistake in the genealogical documentation, we have taken pains to cite land deeds and other local records in what many might consider exiguous detail.) We follow their fate through the 1860s and '70s, when the growth of Nativist and white supremacist movements like the Ku Klux Klan forced them to become more secretive, to withdraw from mainstream society, or to move away. By the third generation, knowledge of their true origins was rare. Family by family, their rich heritage was lost as they were forced to fight a double prejudice, anti–Indian and anti–Semitic.

Pushing the story of my ancestors further and further back, I was forced to develop a tentative chronology of Indian nations (see Chapter 5: America's Middle Ages). The basis for this was the work of Constantine Rafinesque, together with the Wallam Olum and other Indian traditions used by him. Before using these witnesses, however, I had to establish Rafinesque's veracity and trustworthiness and attempt to restore his reputation as an antiquarian scholar (Chapter 4: Ancient History of the Indians).

A similar transformation had to occur in the case of James Adair, the spinner of a theory of the Jewish origins of American Indians (Chapter 6: James Adair and the Lost Tribes of Israel). Adair was wrong for the right reasons. That he was mistaken in his conclusions should not prevent us from examining his evidence and the grounds for his thinking. He was uniquely situated to observe Chickasaw, Choctaw, Creek and Cherokee society. He has rightly been called — even by non-diffusionists like Charles Hudson — the founder of American Indian anthropology. Adair was the first to note that the name of one American Indian tribe (Conoy) was the same as the name of the ancient Phoenicians (Chnai).

I have been not only surprised but also a little sorry to have arrived at the conclusions I was forced to draw from this personal odyssey. I wish it had been otherwise. I wish that my Cherokee ancestors had turned out to be the numinous, proud figures I knew from tales and textbooks, that their original homeland had ever been the Great Smoky Mountains where my family vacationed and that they were by nature a people who turned their backs on the allurements of technology, physical comfort and material gain to embrace a spiritual life. The reality is that they were more like ancient Greeks, Egyptians and Jews, the acknowledged founders of modern Western civilization. This is not to rob them of any mystery. It should make us both closer and more akin to each other, and it should invite an explosion of new studies. I hope it is the beginning of a more nuanced understanding of our common mysteries, our common diversity and the factors that have made the Cherokees one of the most enduring of all peoples. The ancient Greeks, Phoenicians, Israelites and Egyptians are gone. The Cherokees remain.

# Chapter 1

## *Secret of the Keetoowah Priests*

*What we know is not much*
*What we do not know is immense* — Pierre-Simon Laplace

Cherokee traditions are incomplete and contradictory about their origins. Official treatments — including Robert Conley's tribal history commissioned by Wilma Mankiller when she was chief of the Cherokee Nation of Oklahoma and the U.S.–government-sponsored *American Indian Handbook* from as late as the year 2004 — make little attempt to analyze or reconcile the various accounts preserved by explorers, anthropologists, missionaries and the Cherokee themselves.[1] Some legends say the Cherokee came from the west, others from the northeast, still others out of Mexico to the south. No one can agree if they came with other American Indians across the Bering Strait or originated from some other direction. Estimates of their first emergence as a people vary from tens of thousands of years ago to less than 1,000. One of the oldest recorded versions was a migration story told to the Carolina merchant and Scotsman Alexander Long in 1717. It goes as follows:

> For our coming here, we know nothing but what was had from our ancestors and has brought it down from generation to generation [*sic*]. The story is thus. [We] belonged to another land far distant from here, and the people increased and multiplied so fast that the land could not hold them, so that they were forced to separate and travel to look out for another country. They traveled so far that they came to another country that was so cold.... Yet going still on, they came to mountains of snow and ice. The priests held a council to pass these mountains, and that they believed there was warmer weather on the other side of those mountains because it lay near the sun setting. [It] was believed by the whole assembly we were the first to make [snowshoes] to put on our old and young. [We] passed over these mountains till we lost sight of the same and went through darkness for a good space, and then [saw] the sun again, and going on we came to a country that could be inhabited.[2]

With its confusing directions and lack of context and chronology as well as vagueness about distances, not to mention its silence on sources, Long's account is not very useful for understanding who the Cherokee are or where they came from.

Don't the Cherokee have a creation story or national narrative like the Hopi in Arizona, Algonquian tribes or other American Indians? Don't they have a uniform mythology similar to the Romans, Greeks and British with their traditional epic foundation stories or, for that matter, Americans with their tales of the Pilgrims and Lexington and Concord and Declaration of Independence? As it turns out, the answer to this question, due to recent discoveries is, yes, they do.

It may be that the secret of the Cherokees has been placed right in front of us all the time. For it is widely known that the Cherokees had writing with the so-called Sequoyan syllabary, that they were literate from an early period of their existence. What is not well appreciated is that they had schools, learned societies, oral traditions memorized and transmitted from generation to generation, and even universities. At a time when most of the rest of the country lacked public schools and universal schooling requirements for children, the Cherokee built colonnaded brick campuses for males and females in the scrub hills of Indian Territory. In 1907, an ordinary product of the female seminary, Narcissa Owen, wrote her memoirs. It was a literary sketch of the tribe's removal west, her life as an artist, storyteller and music teacher, her marriage to a businessman and the upbringing of their son, the first Native American senator in U.S. history.[3] Since the 1820s, the Cherokee have maintained bilingual newspapers published in their own language and unique syllabary.

In 1880, the Cherokees of Oklahoma received their first full-fledged institution of higher education when the American Baptist Home Mission Society started Indian University in Tahlequah. Renamed Bacone University, it eventually developed a press. One of the press's first publications was a slender little octavo-sized book titled *A Cherokee Vision of Eloh*.'[4] Based on a report in the newspaper *Indian Chieftain* by Cornsilk (Cherokee name of William Eubanks)[5] rendering the deposition of Sakiyah Sanders, a member of the secret priestly society of the Keetoowahs in the 1890s, this *Cherokee History of the World* (as the original title may be literally translated) tells of a unique "heritage of history, spirituality and prophecy ... in a matter sensitive to native

Fig. 1.1. Sam Smith, son of RedBird Smith, first chief of the Keetoowah Society, ca. 1900, RedBird Smith Ceremonial Ground near Blackgum, Oklahoma. He holds what is believed to be a large peace calumet given by the British to the Six Nations Confederacy in 1756 and later presented to the Cherokee. There are wampum belts displayed in the background, emblems of other treaties, as well as one hanging about his neck. Courtesy Richard Mack Bettis.

understanding" (11). The document narrates in Cherokee and English on facing pages the story of the travels of twelve original clans to North America across a large western body of water that can only be the Pacific Ocean. They migrate to escape overcrowding and frequent floods in the old country. Before leaving, the Cherokees, whom the document names Eshelokee, build a "store reaching to heaven," but this is destroyed "by the gods" (17).

For Indians, oral tradition is sacrosanct. It occupies the same sort of primacy and immediacy as the written word in Western civilization. The term "vision" is proper in the Vision of the Elohi. Pronouncements of a seer can concern past deeds, the people's present spiritual condition or religious state, or future developments and things to come. Visions can act as history, commentary and deliberation on current events, or prophecy. In the native worldview, present, past and future are fused together into one.[6]

According to the Keetoowah text, "Other red tribes or clans to the Cherokee tribe began to come also from the old country," and "in the course of time the old pathway which had been traveled by the clans was cut [broken] by the submergence of a portion of the land into the deep sea. This path can be traced to this day by the broken boulders. This was of no surprise to the clans as they were used to the workings of the floods" (17).

For many years after establishing their new homes, the settlers searched for the missing five clans. Unable to find them, they "gave it up and established a new system of seven sacred clans to the tribe. From that day to this[,] they have been searching for the five lost clans of the Cherokee" (17). At some point in the Eshelokees' wanderings, it is not clear when, or where, "a black race of terrible invaders came in boats over the sea" (19). The first wave is repulsed by the Cherokee warriors, as are "thousands upon thousands" of them, until the Cherokees discover the poison of a dragon, the dread Uktena, to kill them and prevent any further irruptions. After that, they live "for ages" in peace, and "knowledge of the war with the dark invader became in the course of time only a story" (23).

Brian Wilkes, an expert on the Cherokee language and traditions, says there were four invasions of the old land, called Elohi Mona in song.[7] On the fourth invasion, the Cherokees used the monstrous Uktena's venom but in so doing contaminated the land and rendered it unfit for habitation. The poison destroyed the invaders, but the land was so devastated it soon afterward "sank into the ocean." Such a chain of events could well pass today for a fable of environmental disaster.

The rest of the text describes the coming of Europeans, whom the Cherokee welcome at first but soon discover to be a "race of deceit and cunning" (29). Christianity is called "the writing of a strange teaching that the white invader claimed to have spoken from heaven[,] the truth or untruth of which the red tribe had to find out for themselves" (27).[8] Notably, there are multiple waves of white people landing in North America in this version of history, suggesting a much deeper time frame than 1492, the date most of us are fixated on for entry of Europeans into the Americas. Twelve divisions of the Eshelokee are presented. Are they a memory perhaps of the tribes of Israel? In the Biblical account, Judah occupies the south, Benjamin the area around Jerusalem, Ephraim the north and so forth. Whether that explanation is applicable or not, it is likely that the Cherokee clans came from different homelands in the "old country." The clans represent biogeographical or genetic moieties in a political confederation.

Few can fail to miss the obsession with seven as a magical number in the *Cherokee History of the World*. It may be significant that both the Hebrews and other ancient Mediterranean peoples and Cherokee counted seven days in a week. The Cherokee appear to be unusual, if not unique, among Indian tribes for having done so.[9] According to tradition, their seven clans reflect occupational castes of warriors, foragers, hunters, builders, healers, priests and messenger/diplomats. As for the floods in the Keetoowah origin story, these details agree with the ancestral homeland of the Cherokees described in their ritual recitation at the green-corn dance, where keepers of sacred stories performed enormous feats of memory annually with the help of wampum belts for the benefit of the young people. This origin-place of the Cherokees contained great snakes and water monsters, "for which reason it was supposed to have been near the seacoast" according to anthropologists.[10] Another Cherokee tradition tells of a single devastating flood, triggered by earthquakes.

The Keetoowah text mentions a "store reaching to heaven," destroyed in the old home-land. The Tower of Babel myth, as has been revealed by recent ethnographic research, goes far beyond Mesopotamia and the Fertile Crescent. It has roots in the Far East. Oxford genetics professor Stephen Oppenheimer derives tales of a primordial tower built in defiance of heaven from a civilization situated east of India and even Burma, evidently an Austronesian one.[11] In the Keetoowah account we are told of invasions by a fierce race of black men. This detail seems puzzling at first since, according to Cornsilk (or Sanders), the Cherokees' lost ancestral home lies beyond the western shores of the Pacific Ocean. Although called dark, and black, the invaders do not seem to be Africans. They are said to come from the west. They arrive by sea.

In this Cherokee religious narrative, we read that "the ancient worship of the wise ones of heaven" was brought over from the old country "beyond memory" and "reorganized in the new country [America] as the ancient religion" (23). Once the last wave of invaders, the white men, gain a foothold and begin dispossessing them of their land, the Cherokee are ultimately "driven to the seashore [of the West Coast], where they will cross the waters ... landing in the old country from when[ce] they came." There, they "will find the five lost clans, became [*sic*] reunited into twelve clans, into one people again, will become a great nation known as the Eshelokee of the half-sphere temple of light" (29).

A word that leaps from the page in this strange account is *cahtiyis*, the "half-sphere temple of light," glossed as "possibly a reference to town house" (23, 35). It is left in its original language, whatever that might be. Obviously it was an enigma to the Cherokee editors. *Cahtiyis* provides an important and authentic clue to the origins of these seaborne migrants with their institutions of multiple gods, temples, flags and council houses. True, modern Cherokee does have the words *gatiyi* and *digatiyo*, used for stomp dance grounds and structures, but these do not seem to be composed of Cherokee elements. If *cahtiyis* is a foreign word, as it appears to be, what language does it come from? Suggestively, almost letter for letter, it is Doric Greek, formed from the root *kata-* "sit," plus the noun suffix *-is*. The literal meaning is "a sitting down," which fits well in the context of the Keetoowah text. It is the standard Greek name for an assembly hall.[12] These public buildings were often constructed in a circular shape to emphasize egalitarian principles. The assembled citizenry, arranged by tribe and clan, sometimes reclined on bench-like couches or rafters, as do many American Indians even today.

The word applies well to a rotund style of architecture whose social function as a dome-shaped place of worship evokes the Southwestern American Indian kiva (Fig. 1.2) as well as the Cherokee council house familiar to us from eighteenth-century travelers' accounts. Although no such structure survives today, the heptagon (as it is sometimes called) seems to have been a round tripartite structure with the symbolism of the seven clans expressed in its seating arrangements. There is a drawing based on excavations of such a "town house" built in the 1740s or 1750s in Chota, the Cherokee capital, in the official *Handbook of the American Indian*. Here is the description:

> About 18.3 m [60 feet] in diameter, it had 8 major roof supports, a central hearth, tiers of benches around the walls, and a south-facing, enclosed entrance. The low wattle-and-daub walls supported wood rafters and steep bark roof covered with soil.... European visitors in 1758 and 1761–1762 estimated it could seat 400–500 individuals.[13]

Note that, strictly speaking, the historical Cherokee assembly hall is not really a domed "half-sphere temple." It is neither hemispherical nor a place of worship. One can only consider it a half-sphere in a figurative sense. The light mentioned in the text must be that of

Fig. 1.2. Reconstructed kiva, Aztec Ruins, New Mexico. Author's photograph.

the fire in the center of the floor, symbolic of some other greater light. All things considered, we may speculate that the Cherokee capitol mirrors a rotunda-like model from the old country, where building materials like stone might have been available. Are we dealing with a situation where worship of the light of heaven and gods above has somehow been transferred or accommodated to new conditions?

The use of columns is especially striking, as is the forthright use of the word "temple." The Doric Greek architecture of the *tholos* seems pertinent here. In its classic shape, the *tholos* consisted of a circular drum of columns covered by a parasol-shaped roof supported by internal wooden posts.[14] The form also appears in tombs and is notable in the monumental national architecture of Washington, D.C.

Also relevant may be the institution of the Dorian Greek annual assembly called Apellai, after Apollo, god of light. At this festival all citizens of the state come together under one roof to celebrate the arts and enlightenment of their patron god Apollo. They ceremoniously renew the sacred fire representing him in his aspect of the Sun. The best-known of the Apellai festivals took place each year in the North African Dorian city of Cyrene, where pilgrims from all over the ancient world converged to honor Apollo. He was equated with the Egyptian god Ammon, whose temple stood in the Oasis of Siwa in the Libyan interior. Famously, Alexander the Great made a pilgrimage to the oracle there following his conquest of Egypt in 331 B.C.E. Ammon's speaking head, manipulated by the Siwa priests, greeted him as Son of God, or Pharaoh.

An important part of the ceremonies conducted in both the Cherokee council house and temples of Apollo was to introduce young men who had come of age in the intervening year into the community to take their rightful position in their clan, phratry (fraternity), military unit, priesthood or other social division. The same function was, and is, fulfilled each year in the Southwestern Indian kiva. The dimensions of the largest of these are comparable to the Cherokee heptagon and Greek *tholos*. Note that the Cherokees' whitewashed townhouse posts echo the marble columns in a Greek temple.

Although called a heptagon, the Cherokee national assembly hall was seven-sided only in a figurative sense. In actuality it was octagonal. Inside, along the eighth wall in front sat the "peace" or White Chief and "war" or Red Chief flanked by assistants and counselors with a screen separating the public or profane space from the sacred area or inner sanctum behind them. The medicine bundle, or "ark of the nation," was kept here in the same way as the Ark of the Covenant was concealed in the Holy of Holies in the Temple in Jerusalem, or as the religious paraphernalia of gods and goddesses were hidden from common view in the cella of a Greek temple. In the Cherokee "temple," there was a flag outside the narrow entrance portico and painted standards with calendrical symbols of the sun and moon attached to the posts inside.[15]

Along with *cahtiyis*, the "half-sphere temple of light," the word Eloh' may also have Greek roots. Cognate with the Doric *alaan* ("be driven"), *Eloi* can be taken to signify "wanderers."[16] Homer, whose works were learned by rote by schoolchildren and who was often quoted in the ancient world, uses the related word *ala* of Odysseus' wandering or roaming without home or hope of rest. This interpretation fits with the name of the ancestral land in Cherokee legends, Elohi Mona, for Mona can also be read as strict Doric Greek: *mona*, "abiding place, a place to stay in." Hence the name preserved in Cherokee song seems to mean Place Where the Wanderers Tarried. Their immediate provenance, the Old Country of the Keetoowah, is apparently not the same as a more distant homeland. It is a way-station or entrepôt.

Could the other untranslated word in the treatise, Eshelokee, also be Greek? The author recalls a remark by Paul Russell, the Potawatomi-Shawnee-Cherokee elder who was one of his teachers: "Nobody really knows where the name Tsalagi [pronounced Cha-la-kee] comes from. It's odd that the Tsalagi Warrior Society always pronounces it Shalokee, with an *s* and *h*."[17] Members of the Warrior Society, which still flourishes in parts of Tennessee and North Carolina, distinguish themselves in this way from the overarching tribe, the Tsalagi, with its *ts* sound.

Eshelokee, which specifically refers to the warrior caste and is, after all, the foundation of *Vision of the Elohi*, appears to be the same word as Greek *etheloikeoi*, "willing settlers, colonizers."[18] The *th* sound of the Greek is replaced by an *sh* sound. Cherokee, like many Native American languages, has no exact equivalent. This is evidently a proper name for those who joined the travels across the face of the earth or Elohi — the crew members, conscripts and other members of an expedition. Such a derivation may explain why the customary name for the Cherokee — Tsalagi — notoriously resists all efforts to etymologize it. In the form *choloki*, according to anthropologists, it designates "people of foreign speech."[19] This is the most common explanation, resting on a lingua franca of the Southeastern Indians called Choctaw trade jargon. But that interpretation begs a question. There are other etymologies, although none is capable of being analyzed into elements of the Cherokee language.

According to the author of a recent grammatical study of Oklahoma Cherokee, Brad Montgomery-Anderson, "There are several beliefs about the origin of the name *jalagi*, but it appears that the word itself is not a native Cherokee word."[20] The names used for Cherokee people by their neighbors and surrounding Indian nations vary widely. The Seneca and other northern tribes call them "cave people" (*Oyatakea*), others, "record keepers," still others, including themselves, "dog people."

## Fig. 1.3. Greek Words in Cherokee

*Sources:* Liddell and Scott's *Greek English Lexicon (1996);* Durbin Feeling's *Cherokee English Dictionary (1975);* Robinson *(1996);* Mooney; Meredith and Milan.

| Greek | Meaning | Cherokee | Meaning |
|---|---|---|---|
| alomenoi | wanderers (in a hopeless sense) | eloh'; elohi | migrants, wanderers; earth |
| dakos | noxious, devouring beast, whale | dakwa | mythic great fish |
| dasis | hairy, shaggy like a beast (walrus?) | dachi | hairy water monster |
| etheloikeoi* | volunteer settlers | eshelokee | Cherokee |
| gennadas | noble | kanat(i) | doctor, hunter |
| huios Dios | Son of Zeus (title of Herakles) | Su-too Jee | mythic strong man |
| illo, illas* | wrap, twist; rope | gilohi | twisted (cf. Hawaiian *hilo*) |
| kakotechneo | base arts,, perjury, fraud | kaktunta | taboo regulation |
| kanon | straight-edge used by athletes | canuga | scraper used by ballplayers |
| karanos | a chief | Koranu† | war chief title |
| kateis* | assembly | cahtiyis | assembly house |
| kerux | herald | skarirosken† | speaker, herald |
| mona* | stopping place, way-station | mona | land where the Elohi tarried |
| neika* | contest | anetcha | ballplay |
| ooktenna | one not killed | Uktena | name of a dragon or serpent |
| oulountata | declared healthy | oolungtsata | divining crystal for health |
| styx | abominable | Stichi | name of dangerous serpent |
| tanawa* | astronomical instrument | Tlanua | Great Hawk |
| (hoi en) telei | those in authority | tilihi | brave, warrior |
| theatas* | spectator in a play | tetchata | Playful Cherokee fairy |
| theatron | theater, assembly | tetchanun | ceremonial enclosure |
| typho | raise a smoke, make sacrifice | Tathtowe | ceremonial title; firecracker bringer (Santa Claus) |

*Denotes Doric Greek form.*
†*Denotes Lower Cherokee dialect.*

Cherokee elders say many of these are attempts by unrelated tribes to find a similar sounding word to Tsalagi (pronounced approximately Tchalakee or Cholokee) in their own respective language. The proof of this seems to be that no one can offer a convincing etymology for "Cherokee" in the Tsalagi language itself. Other interpretations include *tsad'halagi,* "people who took a different path," and *atsilahagi,* "fire carriers." Several Mississippi Valley nations still refer to the Cherokee as the Shanogi, or Shannakiak. Linguistically, each of these is problematic. In brief, there is no agreement among American Indian scholars or the Cherokee themselves on the true origin of the name Tsalagi. Many of the proffered word-origins appear to be nothing but rationalizations.

The Cherokee language is spoken today as their primary language by fewer than a hundred human beings on the planet, most of these rural Oklahomans well advanced in years. To be sure, it is being preserved in libraries and language programs as a second language, notably by the Cherokee Nation of Oklahoma, Oklahoma State University and others. In a few years, though, the last link to fluent native speakers will be broken. Cherokee will join other dead languages like Latin, Aramaic and Ancient Egyptian. That may not matter when it comes to studying the language and reaping its store of knowledge, for from a linguistic point of view, Cherokee is something of a historical riddle as it is. The remaining speakers speak versions and dialects that only complicate the issue. Once it is locked away in books and recordings it may actually stimulate us to study it.

Unfortunately, the first descriptions were made by American traders, agents and missionaries, and none of their reports survives. Lost are a grammar and dictionary by Samuel Worcester, the missionary whose activities in the tribe led to the seminal Supreme Court case *Worcester vs. Georgia* in 1832 and who first wrote down the syllabary. At a time when the well educated in America still learned Greek and Latin in school, field ethnographer John McIntosh reported that Huron, another Iroquoian language, shared grammatical peculiarities with Greek. "As to the number and tenses, they have the same differences, as the Greek and some languages spoken in the north east of Asia.... The action is expressed differently in respect to anything that has life, and an inanimate thing; thus, *to see a man*, and *to see a stone*, are two different verbs; and to make use of a thing that belongs to him who uses it, or to him to whom we speak, are also two different verbs."[21] Cherokee makes many of the same syntactical distinctions. Most people if asked today would probably take the position, as do most linguists, that Cherokee is "the sole representative of the Southern branch of the Iroquoian family of languages."[22]

If, however, as the linguists believe, Cherokee split off from a proto–Iroquoian language at a distant remove in time equal about to the divide that separates the descendants of Swiss or Bavarian Low German and standard High German, or Czech and Polish, or French and Provençal, disturbing questions arise about the relationship of Cherokee and other Iroquoian languages. Why are the two languages not mutually intelligible? A Cherokee speaker has the same odds of being understood by a Haudenosaunee or Mohawk speaker as a Russian by a Vietnamese or Anglo-Saxon warlord by a BBC newscaster. Why does Mohawk have two or three times as many words as Cherokee? Why does Cherokee have a radically different syntax and grammar from Mohawk? Compared to Mohawk, Cherokee is so stripped bare and simple it comes across as pidgin English. Could that simplicity be illusory? Are we misled by the fact that it is spoken so poorly now as a second language? Why is two-thirds of its vocabulary non-cognate, not sharing the same roots as Mohawk? The lack of overlap extends to basic words like the names of numbers.[23] In Mohawk, seven is *tsjada.* In Cherokee it is *gahlgwogi.*

Could the original Cherokee, the Eshelokee, have spoken a non–Indian language, and might it have been a form of Greek? According to our informant Brian Wilkes, before they relocated to the Smoky Mountains, the Cherokees lived for generations in the Ohio Valley. Here they quarreled with Iroquoian people, who had been their allies and fellow travelers in recent migrations. To resolve that conflict, it was decided it would be easier for the Cherokees to learn the local tongue Mohawk than for the Iroquois to switch to the difficult language the Cherokees spoke. Since that time, the Cherokees have spoken a form of Iroquoian. Wilkes goes on to say, "When the conflicts arose again, the Cherokees and their close relations the Tuscaroras went south, the Cherokees settling in the mountains and the Tuscaroras settling closer to the coast. After clashing with the English, the Tuscarora returned north in 1718, becoming the sixth nation of the Haudenosaunee [Iroquois Confederacy]. The Cherokees were also invited to return, but history sent them in a different direction."[24]

Some say the old language was similar to Hopi, Wilkes adds, and that the Cherokees who went east after forking off from the main group in Arkansas are the Bahana or Elder White Brother of Hopi prophecy. Others say the discarded language is Mayan, and the Cherokee are the *Chan,* the Snake People (boat builders) who went north, according to Maya elders. "Boat people" refers to their origins as seafarers because Chan means both "snake" and "canoe, boat." We have seen some tribes in the lower Mississippi River valley call the Cherokee by the name Shanogi. "Feathered serpents" are ships with sails. Further, according to several accounts, the Cherokee acquired this name among the Incas of South America, with whom they also first learned to smoke tobacco. Down to the present time, the Cherokee are regarded by other Southeastern tribes as having a franchise on tobacco. Only they are entitled to carve the image of a snake on their pipes; only they know how to "remake" or sanctify tobacco.

This persuasive if untidy account is supported by the linguistic relationship of the Cherokee, Tuscarora and Iroquois, by the immediate provenance of the Cherokee from the Ohio Valley, by the traditional enmity between the Iroquois and Cherokee, and by certain connections between the Hopi, Cherokee, Maya and Incas.

At any rate, it is clear that a substantial number of Cherokee words are of foreign extraction. Similarly, several of the details of the Eshelokee origin-story evoke similar ones in the mythology of people on the other side of the world. Take the Uktena, for example, the dragon whose venom allows the Cherokee to repulse the foreign black invaders before its poison pollutes the land. This word makes perfect sense in the Greek language. It cannot be analyzed into Cherokee elements—a failing which suggests foreign roots. It probably derives, unless I am mistaken, from *ou* "not" and *ktennais* "slain." In technical terms, it is the aorist participial form of Greek *kteino* "kill, slay."[25] The literal meaning is unslayable one. What better epithet for a serpent than Unslayable? The usage is Homeric and was followed by all early authors writing in the Greek language.

The name of another dangerous serpent, Ustutli (pronounced Stichi), also appears to be Greek, perfectly Homeric. It seems to be a rendering of the word Styx, a curse word used for that which is hated, an abomination: "the most powerful warranty for oaths."[26] Further, two more Cherokee names for fabulous beasts appear to come from Greek: *dakwa*, a mythic great fish, from *dakos* "noxious, devouring beast," used by classical writers to describe a whale (but in our context probably to be understood as referring to a shark), and *datsi*, a water monster, from *dasys* "shaggy, bristly like a beast," perhaps the walrus.[27] A tentative list of words of apparent Greek origin found in the Cherokee language is given in figure 1.3. If these correspondences are true, they work better in the Doric dialect of Greek than in the more common Attic.

Evidence for Doric Greek words in Cherokee is compelling and cogent. Nearly all those adduced are proper nouns, titles, religious terms and the like—just the sort of words one might expect to survive when people adopt a new language but retain some of the old tongue and culture. An analogy would be Hebrew words scattered through Yiddish or Latinate vocabulary found in English law and government. But what bizarre link could connect Bronze Age Dorian Greeks with an American Indian tribe?

The perfect tool for answering such a question is a classical education from the time of Matthew Arnold ... or the monumental *Pauly-Wissowa*. This hundred-headed hydra served as a bible to generations of classicists. Written in crabbed German from the Age of Goethe, with arcane abbreviations, the set takes up an entire bay in the stacks of any library fortunate enough to possess a copy. There are few west of the Mississippi in the United States. It used to be a rite of passage for any student in classical philology. Today it is still living out an existence of sort—think shades of heroes in the underworld—in the form of *Der Kleiny Pauly*, a mere five volumes averaging 1500 pages each.

All clues to the Cherokee mystery lead to Cyrene. After long study, I am persuaded that the Wanderers described in the Vision of Elohi most likely originated in this important Doric-speaking colony of Sparta, modern Shahat in Libya. Spartans were transplanted there en masse following their defeat in the Peloponnesian War of 431–405 B.C.E. Cyrene had been founded by Dorian Greeks from the island of Thera, modern-day Santorini, near Crete, and owed its first cultural influences to the Minoans, who ruled Thera until the devastating volcanic eruption of 1650–1500 B.C.E. Cyrene and the surrounding area flourished for nearly a thousand years, first as a kingdom, briefly as a republic, then as a city-state or polis within the domain of Carthage. Under the Ptolemies it was an allied client state of Egypt; its port of Apollonia was second only to Alexandria, the Ptolemaic capital. Finally, it became the Roman province of Cyrenaica. The Romans reunited it with Crete, bringing its history full circle. Importantly, Cyrene was the chief cult city of Apollo. Apollo's temple there was the most famous shrine of the sun-god in the ancient world.

Dorian Sparta was the traditional rival to Ionian Athens, ultimate winner in a bitter power play between the two city-states, and it is not surprising that little attention has been given to it in the history books. Sparta and its colonies got poor press in the writings of Thucydides and Aristotle, where they are portrayed as crass militaristic slave-states. Hence our word "Spartan," meaning overly disciplined, and the term "laconic," applied to anything terse and unadorned. Sparta dominated the region of Laconia in the Peloponnese. Just as Carthage was destroyed by the conquering Romans at the end of the Third Punic War in 147 B.C.E., and quietly subjected to an official *obliteratio memoriae*, so also did Sparta and Cyrene suffer at the hands of later historians. After choruses of "Carthage must be destroyed" in the Roman senate, its conquering armies sowed salt in the soil of the Punic capital. Sparta was likewise relegated to a role of non-importance by other Greeks, who belonged to the Ionian stock, not Dorian.

But Cyrene was the Dorian Greeks' pride and glory. The North African colony to which the Peloponnese Spartans fled after their defeat by Athens became known as a place of refined luxury and high culture. Its constitutional government was the admiration of all. The Dorian Greeks of Libya held a monopoly on the silphium trade, a now-extinct hallucinogenic pharmaceutical used as a cure-all. They vied with the Phoenicians as merchants to the world. They developed a distinctive school of philosophy, the Cyrenaics, who believed sensory pleasure to be the supreme good, and a tradition of learning and literature that included some of the most famous names of antiquity. One was Callimachus, an important poet and head of the Library of Alexandria. Another was Eratosthenes, the first geographer to measure and chart the world in the round, also head of the same library. Eratosthenes' estimate of the earth's circumference was astonishingly accurate and not improved upon until 2,000 years later.[28] With a population of 135,000 people, Cyrenaica was home to one of the largest and most prosperous Jewish communities outside ancient Israel. It was surpassed only by Alexandria, the Egyptian capital and greatest merchant port of its day. At this time Jews were thoroughly Hellenized. They not only spoke Greek as their first language, even at the High Temple in Jerusalem, but had adopted customs such as play-going and public baths.[29] Judaism had absorbed many elements of pagan Greek and Egyptian religion.

Classical scholar Shimon Appelbaum, an authority on ancient Cyrene, estimates 5,000 Jews lived in the capital city.[30] The Roman Jewish historian Josephus says they enjoyed equal rights before the law with other inhabitants. The country adopted a progressive form of government as early as the fifth century B.C.E. and developed a fully democratic constitution modeled on that of Athens about 375 B.C.E. This protected the rights of all citizens and *perioikoi* (native Libyans living in the vicinity), creating a celebrated harmony of civic life, according to Appelbaum. One-quarter of the population were metics, workers and tradesmen of various nationalities; half of the population were Berbers. Into this polyglot and multi-ethnic mix of peoples, Jewish merchants entered and interacted extremely well.

Josephus calls the first Jews in Cyrenaica *katoikoi*, military settlers with land grants, a word not dissimilar to *etheloikeoi*, or Eshelokee.[31] By the middle of the third century, Jews were already living in concentrated villages and were organized into strong communities. Perhaps more than any other Jewish colony, Cyrenaican Jewry not only had a pronounced commercial and political character but also enjoyed a vast land base. In the interior, landowners managed an economy that made Cyrene a byword for wealth, luxury and productivity. In addition to being the granary of the Mediterranean world, it was also the terminus for trading routes that led across the Sahara to African gold, ivory and slaves.

Ptolemy III is credited with the initial large settlement of Jews in Libya in the third century B.C.E., but there were traces already of Jewish settlement on the coast of the Gulf of Syrta (now Sydra) to the west, where local legend places the first synagogue in Solomonic times (about 1000 B.C.E.). His predecessor Ptolemy II freed 120,000 Jewish prisoners in the Syrian wars, a not inconsiderable number, and settled most in Egypt, placing 30,000 of them in his fortresses on the Libyan and Sudanese frontier. The Egyptian term *marranu*, "military lord," is likely the origin of the word Marrano in its sense of "Jewish prince in exile."

Shimon Appelbaum manages to put a face on Cyrenaic Jews. On the Cyrenean plateau in the hinterland west of the city of Cyrene was the ancient village of Messa, which the local Libyan inhabitants today call Place of the Jews. "The representation of a menorah, cut deeply in the ancient rock-cut road a short distance south of the site, is proof that the name reflects historical reality," he writes. Not only in Cyrene and its port of Apollonia (considered one city in antiquity) but in Berenice in the western part of the country, today Bengazi, Jews were numerous and prominent. "Jewish inscriptions found at Bengazi inform of a comfortable and even wealthy stratum which constituted the leadership of the community." They maintained several synagogues and even an amphitheater and were thoroughly Hellenized, with names like Julius son of Jesus and Agathocles son of Elazaros. There are scattered archeological records of Jewish farmers, merchants, soldiers, civil servants, stonemasons, potters, a painter, mint-workers, weavers and sailors.

For our purposes, the most fascinating aspect of ancient Cyrene that Appelbaum brings into relief is the unusual structure that served as a synagogue. It is apparently modeled after the amphitheater in the port of Apollonia, where the city-state's rites in honor of the sun-god Apollo/Ammon were carried out along with other solemn civic functions. The floor and pillars of the Jews' place of worship were plastered white, just as in a ritual performed anew each year in the Cherokee national heptagon. The walls were colorfully painted—again like the Cherokee assembly hall and Pueblo Indian kiva. The architecture with its drum-like roof and seating arrangement about a hypostyle bear a striking resemblance to the Cherokee layout.

But if the original language of the Keetoowah priests was Doric Greek as spoken in ancient Cyrene, what could be the historical link between Greeks, Jews, Libyans and Egyptians of that fabled cosmopolitan city-state and today's Cherokee of the Ozarks and Appalachians? How did they get from there to here? In the next chapter we suggest a motive and a way.

# Chapter 2

## *Around the World*

*Condemnation without investigation is the height of ignorance.*— Albert Einstein

When I was invited to give an address at the annual conference of the Institute for the Study of American Cultures (ISAC) several years ago, I had no idea what to expect. I found a small crowd of specialists from a variety of disciplines running the gamut from archeology to zoology. Elephants in America! Jews in aboriginal New Mexico! Coxca in Mexico the hiding place of ancient Maya secrets! How Egyptians measured the equinox! Borneo the cradle of agriculture and navigation! Puebla site near Mexico City 400,000 years old! The atmosphere was invigorating. My topic of crypto–Jews and crypto–Muslims among the Cherokee seemed, by comparison, tame.

If there is such a thing as the leading edge in academic studies, ISAC and its diffusionists occupy the *bleeding edge*. A diffusionist is one who believes in cross influences. The opposite is a non-diffusionist, a scholar who regards Indians of North and South America, for instance, as having been essentially on their own until 1492. Although anthropological orthodoxy labels the work of diffusionists crackpot science — "Why do such lunatic ravings persist?" asks popular archeologist Brian Fagan in his book on human prehistory *The Great Journey: The Peopling of Ancient America*— diffusionist doctrine has been inching its way into the mainstream with such books as Gavin Menzies' *1421: The Year China Discovered America* and TV shows like those on the Discovery Channel.[1]

A case in point is a Greek admiral named Maui who, it is claimed, left inscriptions as far distant as New Guinea and Chile. According to Harvard biology professor Barry Fell, Maui was a third-century B.C.E. North African navigator in command of a large Libyan-Egyptian fleet. An extensive body of folklore survives throughout Polynesia concerning his exploits as a trickster and culture-bearer who "fished islands from the deep," somewhat like "many-wiled" Odysseus.[2] It has frequently been noted that Polynesians—one of the oceanic peoples expanding into and around the Pacific from Island Southeast Asia —combine the characteristics of many different ethnic groups, including Malaysians, Melanesians, Austronesians, Mongoloids, Japanese, Cambodians, Hindus and even Mediterranean types.[3] The Mesopotamian sun god Ra is the same as the Polynesian god Ra, and the plumed head-dress of Hawaiian royalty (which echoes that of Tibetan Buddhist monks) is said to reproduce that of a Greek hoplite (fig. 2.1).[4]

A New Zealander, Fell was keenly interested in elucidating the origins of the Maori, the ancient first settlers of his native land. He came upon cave drawings at Sosorra in western New Guinea, which he connected with an inscription in a cave near Santiago, Chile. After spending eight years "ransacking" Harvard's Widener Library, he was able to decipher the latter as an example of "standard Libyan ... a dialect of Egyptian spoken by the brown-skinned fisher folk whom the Greeks called Mauri" (that is Moors, hence Maori).

There were hundreds of similar inscriptions scattered throughout the Pacific. Comparing the Santiago inscription and Sosorra drawings, which included paintings, astronomical and navigational diagrams and calculations in Greek and Egyptian, Fell reconstructed the events of an amazing feat of navigation in the ancient world. A Libyan fleet was dispatched between 235 and 225 B.C.E. under the auspices of Eratosthenes, director of the Library at Alexandria. Sponsored by the Egyptian pharaoh, its mission was to circumnavigate the world. It established what we now know as the international dateline (fig. 2.2). The admiral in charge was Maui, and the captain of one ship (the total number is variously given as six, ten and 12) was Rata.

Berkeley geographer George Carter translates the Santiago inscription as follows:

> Southern limit of the coast reached by Maui. This region is the southern limit of the mountainous land the commander claims, by written proclamation, in this land exulting. To this southern limit he steered the flotilla of his ships. This land the navigator claims for the King of Egypt, for his Queen, and for their noble son, running a course of 4,000 miles, steep, mighty, mountainous, on high uplifted. August, day 5, regal year 16.[5]

The king, or pharaoh, referred to in this inscription is believed to be Ptolemy Euergetes III, called the Benefactor, whose wife was the Cyrenaic empress Berenice. He ruled until 221 B.C.E. Ptolemy III not only subjugated Libya (Cyrene) but his power is known to have extended as far eastward as India, where King Asoka was his ally. These facts date the landfall made by Maui's ships in South America to 230 as Ptolemy III began his reign in 246. Fell concludes that Rata, Maui and the three hundred or so other members of this expedition were the founding fathers of Polynesia.

If the Libyan presence in the Pacific during the third century B.C.E. consisted of an entire fleet, one separated from its homeland for several years, women were most likely aboard. The expedition was probably a colonizing effort. Perhaps like a Phoenician expedition under Pharoah Necho in the seventh century B.C.E., members spent some time between voyages on dry land raising crops for food.

Greek colonies, of course, were not unusual, even outside the Mediterranean. The ancient geographer Agatharchides[6] employed by the Library at Alexandria wrote a treatise on the Indian Ocean in which he mentions a Greek colony on the unidentified island of Socotra. The name is usually glossed as a Greek form of Sanskrit *Dvipa Sukhatara,* meaning "the Happy, or Blessed Isles." Most commentators place this colony somewhere close to the mouth of the Red Sea, but a simpler solution is that this is a reference to Sukatra (Java in Indonesia), whose name means "beloved, blessed, blissful." Java, of course, has been the ultimate destination for spice merchants since the beginning of history. The Egyptians mined gold in Sumatra, especially during the Ptolemaic period when Egypt was ruled by the Greeks. Spice like nutmeg, which grew only on those islands, comprised essential ingredients in the mummification process of Egyptian kings. Taprobana was the island on the edge of the known world, first reported by the Greek geographer Megasthenes around 290 BCE. It appeared on maps produced under Eratosthenes' direction[7] and is believed by some to be Sumatra, the largest, westernmost of the Sunda islands.

The idea of a Ptolemaic colony in the Far East is borne out by the presence of Mediterranean mitochondrial DNA in Southeast Asia, Indonesia, New Guinea and Polynesia. Mitochondrial DNA is passed from a mother to her children unchanged over millennia, so it is a good tool for determining the founding mothers of populations. One study of New Guinea lineages finds a sizable degree of haplogroup (maternal lineage) H, a specifically European type. Its incidence does not seem likely to be due to modern admixture, as often claimed

*Top left:* Fig. 2.1a. Greek hoplite on a clay plaque from the Athenian Acropolis, ca. 500 B.C.E. *Top right:* Fig. 2.1c. Mississippian era warrior from Moundville, Alabama. *Bottom left:* Fig 2.1b. Cherokee chief in battle array from Tennessee, ca. 1200 c.e. *Bottom right:* Fig. 2.1d. Hawaiian warrior in traditional regalia. Illustrations by Christopher C. Vigil.

of such an anomaly, for such a conclusion would entail a nineteenth or twentieth-century European woman (say, an adventurous Victorian schoolteacher) marrying a native man. There was a paucity of European women in Papua New Guinea then and now. The same study lists moderately high frequencies of the following European and Middle Eastern haplogroups: H (4), T (perhaps Egyptian, 3), I (7), J (2), G (15), K (2), and U (extremely common in North Africa, 19).[8] These are not numbers to be dismissed lightly. Possibly, they are the genetic trail of Greek, Jewish, Libyan and Egyptian women in an ancient New Guinea settlement.

    Among the drawings in the New Guinea cave studied by Fell was a figure he identified as an "ancient Libyan instrument called the Tanawa, or 'Reckoner,' a mechanical calculator of the third century B.C. intended to aid the study of planetary motions by converting posi-

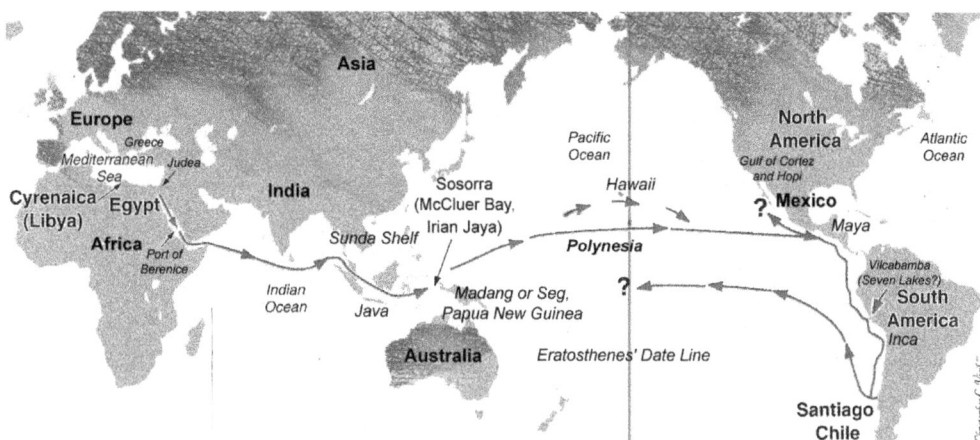

Fig. 2.2. Probable route of the Egyptian fleet in the third century B.C.E. Illustration by Christopher C. Vigil.

tion angles from polar to ecliptic coordinates." Two subsequent experiments built models of the *tanawa* (from Greek ταυάν, 'outstretched, long') and proved it was used to determine longitude, an accomplishment not replicated until the eighteenth century (fig. 2.3).[9]

The Cherokee may have perpetuated a folk memory of this mechanical marvel in the legend of the Tlanua, or Great Hawk, the name for which is almost exactly the same.

An ancient navigational device discovered at the turn of the century and recently carbon dated to the second century B.C.E. (not long after the expedition of Maui) is just as sophisticated and modernistic. According to a 2006 article in the journal *Nature*, the puzzling bronze construct found in the wreck of a cargo ship off the Greek island of Antikythera almost a century ago is nothing less than an astronomical instrument. The Antikythera Mechanism, as it is known, contains "30 bronze gears and many astronomical inscriptions" and "is technically more complex than any known device for at least a millennium afterwards." A joint British-Greek team reconstructed the instrument based on surface imaging and X–ray tomography and concluded it was a sophisticated predictor for the relative calendrical positions of the sun, moon and planets across any given sector of the earth. The editor of *Nature* calls it "the world's oldest known analogue computer."[10]

Despite mounting evidence, scholars summon all their ingenuity to dismiss ancient testimony that Greeks, Egyptians and other peoples of the Mediterranean could accomplish deep-sea voyages. An acknowledged expert on ancient seafaring, Lionel Casson in *The Ancient Mariners* draws attention to three long-distance feats of navigation but manages for different reasons to belittle their importance.[11] The first comes from Egypt. He recalls the "great state-operated maritime enterprise" to fetch myrrh and other unguents and incenses from a distant land called Punt, identified with lands on the Gulf of Aden or Indian Ocean coast of Somalia and Ethiopia. This was some 2,000 years before the modern era. The Pharaoh Mentuhotep III commissioned his minister Henu to cross the desert with 2,000 men, build a boat on Egypt's Red Sea port and sail south in a ship 180 feet long and 60 feet wide with a crew of 120 to establish a sea lane to the foreign source for precious ingredients used in Egypt's royal mummification process. Two months later, Henu returned home.

Casson goes on to explain, however, that the Punt trade lapsed for a long period in

*Top left:* Fig. 2.3a. *Tanawa* from New Guinea cave. *Top right:* Fig. 2.3b. Modern model of *tanawa.* Illustrations by Christopher C. Vigil.

Egypt, only to be revived 500 years later. He thus implies that Henu's expedition was an isolated occurrence. In a perplexing argument, he assigns the "revival" of Egyptian seafaring to the next piece of evidence that happens to survive. It is one that can hardly be ignored. Its instigator was Queen Hatshepsut, the eighteenth-dynasty ruler who was one of only a handful of female pharaohs. (She wore the royal beard like Cleopatra.) Hatshepsut erected a monument displaying her fleet docking at Punt and leaving under full sail laden with goods that included "ebony, myrrh-resin, live myrrh trees ... various other types of incense, ivory, gold, eye cosmetic, skins, 3,300 head of cattle, natives and their children ... native spears, apes, monkeys, dogs, even 'a southern panther alive, captured for her majesty.'" So much for Egypt's feeble attempt to master the seas.[12]

A third demonstration of seafaring took place, Casson continues, under Pharoah Necho in the seventh century B.C.E. After attempting to dig a canal between the Nile and the Red Sea, Necho commissioned the Phoenicians to undertake the circumnavigation of Africa from east to west to explore an alternative route to the southern seas (Indian Ocean). They were to come home into the Mediterranean through the Strait of Gibraltar.

The Greek author Herodotus gives his own half-credulous, half-skeptical account. The Phoenician expedition sailed into the Indian Ocean and put in at whatever point they happened to be sailing by on the African coast, planted and harvested crops and sailed on the following year. After three years they entered the Pillars of Hercules (Strait of Gibraltar) and made their way back to Egypt.[13] Herodotus adds that in sailing around Africa "they had the sun on their right side, to the northward of them"—proof to some historians that the Phoenicians were indeed in the southern hemisphere for part of their voyage. Although later commentators generally dismiss Necho's report as fiction, Casson concedes that "such a voyage is perfectly feasible." He adds oceanographic details that support the Phoenicians' itinerary.

A final feat of navigation discussed by Casson might better be called a massive colonization effort. It was a Phoenician scheme from about 500 B.C.E. to populate West Africa with 30,000 desert-dwelling Moors from the hinterland of Carthage, the new capital (in present-day Tunisia). The record of its undertaking was cast in bronze and displayed in a temple at Carthage. Numerous ancient authors plainly reported the contents of this monument. One actually transcribed it in a surviving Greek document of 650 words.

The leader of the expedition was Hanno, who commanded a fleet of sixty ships with fifty oars each. The colony of Cerne described by him has been identified by some historians with modern-day Herne Island, lying just north of the Tropic of Cancer off the West African coast. From there, Hanno pushed on even farther south to a land of crocodile-infested rivers and "gorillas" (the first use of the term). After that, Hanno says, "We sailed no farther, owing to lack of provisions."[14]

So it goes. Does Herodotus write that the Phoenicians "were wont to visit ... a nation beyond the pillars of Hercules (Gibraltar)" and trade trinkets with the natives for gold? A fable. Do Sumerian tables of the third millennium B.C.E. describe voyages "beyond the western sea" (the Atlantic) and establishment of colonies in a distant land? Surely, this could not be America, for that land had to wait 3,500 years to be discovered by a European. Never mind that Sumerian tablets with cuneiform writing were found in the nineteenth century in Lexington, Georgia, and a Sumerian tablet once in the possession of Chief Joseph of the Nez Perce tribe is displayed today in the West Point Military Museum. Did Barry Fell find correspondences between Ptolemaic Egyptian and more than 400 terms referring to mariners, navigation, astronomy, meteorology, justice and administration, medicine and economy in the Micmac and Abenaki languages of present-day New England? Coincidence.

The "Anthropological Monroe Doctrine" clearly states that there were no meaningful Old World influences in the New World before 1492 C.E.

Casson does admit the reality of the Egyptian "nautical titans" built in the third century. He devotes several pages to the enormous capacities of the so-called "Forty" of Ptolemy IV (reigned 221–210 B.C.E.). Several recent television programs have also celebrated Ptolemy's Forty, so called because of its length. It was a supergalley over 400 feet long and 50 feet wide with benches manned by 4,000 rowers, eight to an oar, 400 deckhands and other crew and 2,850 marines or warriors. The stern and prow towered 70 feet above the water. The rowers were arranged in three banks with the oars of the uppermost measuring 57 feet long—a length not rivaled in the annals of imperial navies until the ships of French King Louis XVI in the seventeenth century. Most astonishing of all is that the vessel's construction was in the form of a catamaran. "The deck that spanned the two hulls would offer a broad expanse, like that of an aircraft carrier, and this would explain how there could be space for a complement of 2,850 marines, a veritable regiment," writes Casson (131).

The double-hulled construction, of course, allowed the ship to negotiate high seas. It may have been the inspiration for Polynesian–style catamarans. Alternatively, Greek and Polynesian designs may have come from a common source in Tamil Nadu, India. At any rate, it was state-of-the-art shipbuilding. Further, there is every reason to think this was the style of ship commanded by Admiral Maui. But could Maui's expedition really have been a "fleet"? Monarchs of Ptolemy's time had navies of over 300 ships, we learn from Casson (133), many of them supergalleys. These sailed both from Alexandria on the Mediterranean Sea and Berenice, Egypt's Indian Ocean port.

A Boston University archeologist in 2004 accidentally opened a cave on the Red Sea, part of the Indian Ocean, near the town of Mersa Gawasis in Egypt and discovered still-sound nautical gear and wooden oars 70 feet long. The finds were identified as relics of the Pharaonic seaport of Saaw, or Sawu, originally called Massawa, dating from at least 1900 B.C.E. in the Twelfth Dynasty. The Egyptian seaport of Berenice founded to the south by Ptolemy II in 275 B.C.E. surpassed the older Massawa in importance. Berenice may be assumed to have been the point of departure for Maui.

Scholars have long been struck by cultural traits shared by Indonesians, Polynesians and Native American peoples. University of California, Davis, retired geography professor Stephen Jett draws attention to several similarities between Southeast Asians and Native Americans.[15] The inhabitants of Borneo, for example, physiologically resemble Arawak Indians of the Caribbean. Natives in both regions use slash-and-burn agriculture, blowguns and head hunting trophies—customs found also among the Cherokee.

It is possible that the seacoast homeland of the Cherokee subject to floods and notable for its water monsters mentioned in so many accounts corresponds to the Sunda Shelf, a now-submerged part of Southeast Asia joined once with Indonesia and New Guinea. According to Oxford professor Stephen Oppenheim, this fertile and populous region was gradually inundated by rising sea levels beginning with the meltdown after the last Ice Age.[16] Jett believes that migrations to escape flooding began about 3600 B.C.E. and lasted until as late as 300 B.C.E., the time of the first Polynesian voyages. Could this explain why the Vision of the Elohi speaks of an increasingly crowded land? Might it also account for the disappearance of the route taken across the ocean, one described as cut off, visible only in broken fragments on the ocean floor? The rising waters of the earth's new climate would certainly have produced a shifting and precarious new seashore. It makes sense that scattered islands sighted by the first voyagers in the Pacific were sometimes never found again since they could not turn back against prevailing currents and winds. It should be noted that the Libyan fleet never returned home.

*The Book of the Hopi* tells of stepping stone islands that sink into the sea behind the emigrants when they land on the West Coast.[17] The Cherokee story seems to echo this experience in speaking of submerged stones on the old pathway. Confirming a Pacific Ocean link, according to Jett, and others are the Cherokees' lack of pottery making, reflecting passage through clay-destitute islands; their sharing of a peculiar oak-splinted basket style with the Orinoco Indians of South America; and the "flying island" homeland off South America mentioned in several Cherokee myths.[18]

For more pieces of the puzzle, let us turn now to Cherokee author William Eubanks. He was a member of the Keetoowah Society who wrote under the name Unenudi. Eubanks was a translator for the Cherokee Nation and indefatigable contributor to the Southern lecture circuit. Around 1900, he authored a tract titled *The Red Race: Originators of the Ancient Apollo Worship*. In it, he alludes to many of the same mysteries contained in the Vision of the Elohi, which, as we have seen, was published by him and attributed to Sakiyah Sanders. He says that "nearly all writers grappling with the problem of the origin of the aborigines of North America make the same error" when they claim that the North American Indian originally came from the Eastern continent [Asia]." Eubanks argues that "on the contrary, according to the traditions of the Indians themselves, they never came to North America at all, but were placed here in Ah-ma-yedi (in the midst of the waters) by Nel-ho-nu-hi (Elohim) [the Hebrew God] ... in the days of [the flood] of Peleg."[19]

Eubanks lends support to the idea of Greeks, Jews and Egyptians mingling together to form the Cherokee people when he writes:

> While the Cherokee is neither Greek, Hebrew, Egyptian, nor Hindoo [*sic*], he has in his language many words purely Greek, Hebrew, Egyptian and Sanscrit [*sic*], and while his ancient religious custom and rites bear a strong resemblance to the rites and religious custom of the ancient Jewish religion, and his secret religion or mysteries is similar in many respect to the Egyptian, still there is strong evidence that he is neither Hebrew nor Egyptian. His other name, which is also the name of other tribes belonging to the initiated brotherhood, is Ah-ni-gi-too-wah-gi [Keetoowahs], and means lights received from the sun.

He argues further that the Cherokee identity, or their true name, "has never been found out, and perhaps never will be," but it is a designation given to those "initiated as a tribe into the eastern mysteries ... by a wise branch of the tribe known as those who spoke the language of Seg" (Asaga). He mentions the name "Esh-he-el-o-archie" (obviously his way of transcribing the Vision of the Elohi's word Eshelokee) and says that the Cherokee were instructed in keeping the sacred fire at "the seven Sacred Lakes."[20]

Connecting the dots, one can perhaps place the Sacred Lakes in South America, for according to tradition, the Cherokee once allowed their Sacred Fire, the eternal flame maintained in the national heptagon, to go out. They had to send a delegation of Keetoowah priests to South America to bring a new one from the source.

According to Brian Wilkes, Keetoowah traditions relate that the Cherokee once journeyed to learn at the feet of Inca wise men. Could this have been at the famed Valley of the Immortals in south Ecuador? This ancient site is renowned for its seven craterlike lakes, sources for streams that flow into the ancient pilgrimage city of Vilcabamba (Quechua for "Sacred Valley"). The area is now a national park, and its unique mineral waters are reputed to be so healthful that many residents live to be over a hundred. On the other hand, Peruvian *curandero* and *misayoq* Enrique Sanes Neyra told Wilkes in 1998 that the location of the seven sacred lakes was the area around Huascaran in Ancash province. If it seems odd to anyone that the Cherokee were ever in the Andes in the first place, Neyra also said the Quechua elders are safeguarding ancient Cherokee sacred records and objects which will be returned at the proper time. According to Wilkes, the Oklahoma Keetoowahs have verified this.[21]

What about the language Seg? This is an enormously valuable clue for reconstructing Cherokee origins and wanderings. Seg is an Austronesian language of Indonesia, part of the very large language family known as Central-Eastern-Malayo Polynesian, with a western form called Thai-Seg and eastern form spoken in the Madang province of Papua New Guinea known as Sek, or Gedaged. The word points to the dispersals from Sundaland and initial sea voyages of the Melanesians and Polynesians since it is the name of an important non-native clan in New Guinea. There is a village called Sek, or Seg, in the Madang district on the north coast, a town called Segh in the Solomon Islands just east of there (one of the stepping stones of the Polynesians), and also a Seg, or Sag Sag, on the nearby island of New Britain, the spring pad for Polynesian colonizers. There is also a branch in South America.[22]

According to geneticist Stephen Oppenheimer, the north coast of New Guinea acted as an important route for seaborne evacuation from the sinking landmass of Sundaland. In *Out of Eden*, his sequel to the book *Eden in the East*, he postulates that Island Indonesia teemed with life and was the source of new currents of agriculture and navigation. It was the true cradle of civilization, not India or Mesopotamia. Madang was the center for an eastward Polynesian diffusion that began about 500 B.C.E. Modern science associates these Austronesians and Malay people with the Lapita culture that spread a distinctive style of ceramics from Southeast Asia throughout Indonesia, Borneo, New Guinea and Melanesia as far west as Fiji and Samoa during the first three millennia B.C.E. Thus, an advanced, lighter skinned civilization from Sundaland mixed with Papuan–speaking (non–Seg) natives.[23] This information harmonizes well with Eubanks' description of the Keetoowahs as a fair-skinned race. The connection could also explain the recurring statement in the Vision of the Elohi that the leaders of the early Cherokee were "skilled at dealing with floods," or words to this effect. Ever afterwards, say storytellers, the Cherokee have dwelt in the mountains, "because they are afraid of another flood."[24]

Seg appears to be one of the so-called aberrant Oceanic languages spoken by the Children of Kulabob described in Oppenheimer's studies. Several experts, not Barry Fell and his school alone, have drawn attention to Semitic, Greek, Egyptian and Libyan elements in Malaysian, Indonesian, New Guinean and Polynesian languages. These pale strangers occupy the role of the sophisticated double in a widely distributed saga about divine twins propagated all around the Pacific. The twins represent competing cultures. Kulabob is a pale-skinned coastal fisherman fleeing from flooded Sundaland and Manup is a dark-skinned hunter-gatherer. A version is claimed to have traveled to Mesopotamia as the story of Cain and Abel, and another to the Mayas, who tell of Hunapuh and Xbalanque. In fact, legends recount how Kulabob created the lagoon of Madang and Seg, the seat of proto–Polynesian culture.[25] Thus two distinct populations clashed and blended, a light-skinned and dark one.

It is hard to resist the temptation to conclude that the latter, non–Seg natives correspond to the Cherokees' "black race of terrible invaders," who came in boats over the waters. These are presumably Austronesians and Melanesians who waged war against the Malaysian and Indonesian people from Sundaland. Recall that after repeated invasions there was no land to fight over since it all "sank into the ocean." To this day, there seems to be recognizable among Hawaiian Islanders as well as the Cherokees a certain Melanesian type (fig. 2.4).

Plausibly, a distant echo of Kulabob's merchant society may be found today in the so-called Cargo Cult of New Guinea, as well as initiation ceremonies. These feature circumcision and a complete course on living wisely taught to 13- and 14-year-old boys by elders in a community house. The former, of course, reminds us of the Jewish custom of imposing the law of Abraham on newborn males; the latter, of studies at Hebrew School preceding a child's bar mitzvah. It is likely that both the New Guinea educational institution and Jewish rites of passage are related to the ancient Greek concept of *paideia,* encyclopedic learning imparted to the young on the verge of manhood. Eubanks' description of the "wise ones" of Seg evokes the "wise ones of heaven" mentioned in the Vision of the Elohi.

There is evidence other than oral tradition that Polynesians joined the Cherokee. Aside from the Pacific Rim traits and characteristics like blow guns mentioned above, one of the seven Cherokee clans is called Anigilohi, the Twister People. This name should mean something like "people from Gilo" and can be taken as strictly Hawaiian. In Hawaiian, Hilo (there is no *g* in Hawaiian) means "braid, twisted." (Compare Greek *illa,* "rope"; *hilo,* "twist, wrap"; *hilex,* "twisting.") Gi-lolo was the land where the earliest ancestors of the Hawaiians came from, identified by later Spanish, Dutch and English navigators as the Moluccas in the Indonesian Archipelago.[26]

The legend goes that Hawaii's city Hilo got its name from the natives' skill in twisting together plant fibers to make rope. The same root appears in hula, the dance ("twist"). Such a derivation explains why the Twister clan members "were once a proud people who strutted when they walked and twisted their shoulders in a haughty manner." The Anigilohi clan's cultural memory evidently reflects its ancient connection with the Polynesians who accompanied the Eshelokee—the People from Hilo. Such identification may also explain why Twisters were considered by the other clans as extraneous foreigners, a group composed of prisoners of war, captives and refugees who had only a tenuous connection to the Cherokee. Chapter 3 presents several famous Twister Clan lines, often representing female lineage B, the classic Southeast Asian and Pacific Islander type.

Tagwadihi, a Cherokee medicine man photographed by James Mooney in the 1890s, not only physically resembles Native Hawaiians but also seems to bear a Hawaiian name, one that may be derived from the Greek. We have seen how the word *dakwa* means whale or sea monster. Anthropologists note that the word was also used of the Cherokee's enemies, the Cawtabas. They usually translate the medicine man's name as Catawba Killer. But Takea is the name of the shark in Hawaiian folklore, and Shark Killer and the like are common Hawaiian surnames. In legend, Maui's sister is repeatedly helped by Takea and other sharks. It was a common rite of passage for Polynesian boys to kill a shark. Probably the Catawbas are called *tagwa* simply because Catawba, which is Siouan, reminded the Cherokee of a word in their own language, much as an Englishman might call a Frank or Frenchman a "Frog." Curiously, one of Maui's names is Talaga, very close to Tsalagi. Maui's father was Tangaroa or Tanoa (seemingly designating a Danaan or Greek). Tanoa was the father of all fair-haired children and came from a land called Atia.[27]

Atia, which appears to be the same word as Attica, was the ancient Polynesian homeland to the west, full of high alabaster temples. One of them

Fig. 2.4a. Cherokee medicine man Tagwadihi, photographed by James Mooney in 1888. Courtesy National Anthropological Archives, Smithsonian Institution, Neg. 1016.

> was very spacious, and was built as a meeting-place for gods and men; and here after death the spirits of the ancients foregathered with the gods. Here originated different kinds of sports, and games and feasts to the gods Rongo,' Tane,' Rua-nuku, Tu,' Tangaroa, and Tongaiti. Here were meeting-places for the great chiefs of those days.... When appointing rulers, and devising measures for the good of the people. Here, too, originated the wars that caused the people to enter and spread over the Pacific.[28]

One could hardly invent a more fitting folk memory of Greek culture. Athens, the capital of Attica, was the envy of the world for its marble buildings dedicated to the gods of Olympus, its trade, games, amusements, learning, food, luxuries, art, philosophy, military prowess and democratic government. It is estimated that the ancestors of the Polynesians left this land when it was governed by the great king Tu-te-rangi-marama about 450 B.C.E., a date that corresponds exactly with Athens' golden age under Pericles. The Hawaiian word that epitomized this lost world is *karioi*, "leisure, ease," literally the same word as Greek for "amusements."[29] Christian missionaries fought to eradicate Polynesians' pursuit of *karioi*, often translating the beloved concept in English as "lewdness."

The Cherokee Seven Clans are unique, distinctive and unusual. They are Wolf (Ani-Wahiya), Bird (Ani-Tsiskwa), Deer (Ani-Kawi), Twister (Ani-Gilohi), Wild Potato (Ani-Gotegewi), Panther (Ani-Sahoni) and Paint (Ani-Wodi). Before they were codified into seven, considered a sacred number by the Cherokee, there existed clans named raccoon, wildcat, fox, corn, water, Shawnee, crystal, wind, man, tree, tufted titmouse, raven, redbird, bluebird, holly, long prairie, blue, sun, fire, acorn and many, many others. This roster is

Fig. 2.4b. Native Hawaiians from Kona District, Oahu, 1930. Top row: Napahi (Maunalua), Hugo K. (?). Bottom row: Wife Makea and two grandchildren. Courtesy Bishop Museum Archives.

not paralleled in other tribes. The Lenape, for instance, have four main clans—Wolf, Turtle, Turkey and Fish. An eightfold division is found in many Indian peoples—Buffalo, Thunderbird, Turtle, Wolf, Deer, Bird, Otter, and Bear. Although sometimes combined with the Panther Clan, the Bear Clan is usually ignored in the Cherokee scheme.[30]

It seems that the Ani-Gotigewi, or Wild Potato Clan, just like the Twister Clan, exists

### Fig. 2.5. Cherokee Clans and Their Strengths

| | | |
|---|---|---|
| Wolf | Ani-Wahiya | Elders, teachers, warriors, beloved men and women |
| Bird | Ani-Tsiskwa | Speakers, heralds, news bearers, messengers, singers and dancers |
| Deer | Ani-Kawi | Runners, ball players, clothes makers, tanners and intellects |
| Twister | Ani-Gilohi | Workers, priests, teachers and keeps of ancient lore, storytellers |
| Wild Potato | Ani-Gotewewi | Keepers of religious customs, writings and games, scribes |
| Panther | Ani-Sahoni | Medicine people, magicians, herbalists, fire keepers, cooks, sorcerers |
| Paint | Anti-Wodi | Doctors, hunters, peace chiefs, keepers of history and prophecy, masters of protocol and diplomacy, music and ceremony |

only among the Cherokee. This clan seems to reflect the Eshelokees' travels in South America. Potatoes come from Peru and were not grown in North America until their introduction by Europeans. Could it be that the name of this clan in the singular, Gotigewa, pronounced approximately K'tigwa, is a corruption of Quechua, the original name of the Andean people we know today as the Incas? Some people attempt to derive the name from Kituwah, or Keetoowah, but this may be a moot point, since the names Quechua and Kituwah appear to come from the same root.

The word for clan in Cherokee is simply a collective prefix meaning "animate beings" or "people" (*ani*). The Seven Clans are called in Cherokee *gatligwogi itsuniyvwi*, literally "seven types of creatures." The second term evokes the tribal name of the Cherokee, Ani-Yunwiya (Principal People). Anthropologists like James Mooney, Albert S. Gatschet, and Herman J. Viola termed these social units *gentes*, Latin for "people" or "nations," a use that conveys the idea of geographically separate origins. They are not clans in the customary sense. It can't be imagined that a Cherokee of a certain clan could easily find "courtesy kinship" with other clan members while traveling among other tribes. Cherokee and other clan systems are, to a large degree, incompatible.

What about the Paint Clan, Ani-Wodi? "Paint People" seems, without question, to be an ordinary term for Phoenicians, whose name for themselves was *Knai* "Canaanites." This appears to be rendered in Native America as Kanawa, the name of a tributary of the Ohio, and the Conoy Indians mentioned by Adair specifically as a Canaanite tribe. We will examine more evidence for the spread of this name in a later chapter. In the Old World, Phoinikoi, the Greek term, was used to designate people associated with the phoenix (a mythological bird that rose from its own ashes), the date palm and a reddish-blue or purple dye, all emblems of Phoenician or Punic civilization. Phoenician trade was founded on Tyrian purple, a violet-purple dye derived from the Murex sea snail's shell. They also are conjectured to have stepped into the copper and tin trade of the Minoans after about 1200 B.C.E., moving their center of operations successively from Lebanon to Asia Minor to Carthage. After the Third Punic War, the Phoenician state was defeated and destroyed by Rome. Among the Cherokee, Paint Clan members were the doctors and hunters (*kanati*, from Greek *gennadi* "noblemen"), keepers of history (*tikano*, from Greek *tynchana* "events") and prophecy, and masters of protocol, diplomacy, and ceremony. Peace chiefs and Ukus, "owls," or wise men in the Greek model, were often chosen from Paint Clan ranks.

By all accounts, the Panther or Blue Paint clan is almost extinct. Its members were known as "Dangerous Men" and "Night People." Its Cherokee name is Ani-Sahoni or Sakanike ("purple"), which means "They sit in the ashes until they turn blue-gray." Because West African medicine men are distinguished by white or blue face paint created from ashes, one might speculate that this minor clan could represent the African component in the Cherokee melting pot. Tribal traditions emphasize that the Cherokee include black people as well as white, red, and yellow. We will return to clan histories and genealogies later on.

It is significant that the Keetoowah culture-bearers in the Vision of the Elohi are called the "wise ones of heaven." The word for heaven used here is Galunlati, literally "The Up-above Place."[31] When Cherokee storytellers talk about the world before the present one it is either up above in a country called Galunlati or in the far West, sometimes called Elohiyi. It is said that gods and goddesses, people, animals, plants and every other type of being lived there until it became over-populated. This land still exists on the other side of the vault of heaven, which is hard as rock and impenetrable. We are the lesser progeny who came to this place amidst the waters we now call home. The Galunlati are also part of Eloh,' the earth.

Tales of Galunlati, of course, embody myths similar to the cosmogenic "Eurasian themes of watery chaos, separation, cosmic egg, trapped offspring and use of body" assembled in versions from all over the world by Stephen Oppenheimer.[32] They represent faded collective memories that transmute and transmit deep history.

In antiquity, it was only the Egyptians, that is, Ptolemaic Greeks, as well as certain Asian peoples, along with the Cherokee and Hopi, who knew the world was round, not flat. It must have been a difficult concept to accept, even by highly educated and inquisitive minds of the day. Indeed, the theory slumbered in Europe until the Renaissance. For people without a firm grasp of mathematics, astronomy or seafaring, the notion of a spherical earth must have been overwhelming. Through a process of collective internalization, then, it was evidently encoded into myth. The Roman author Seneca calls the inhabitants of the underside of the earth antipodes, literally "those who have their feet upside down." The first "Indians" similarly internalized new information in the only terms they knew. An opposite side of the earth separated from them by water and crowded with superior beings, the homeland of magicians, became a rock-hard hemisphere ("vault"). On the other side was a world to which they could never return. Notably, it was in the west, an indication of the direction from which the Eshelokee, elders of Seg and Keetoowah priests arrived.

A round earth seems to explain another of William Eubanks' peculiar notions of Cherokee history. Turning conventional knowledge on its head, he views the "inventing or receiving from a divine source the great religions of the world, as well as building the greatest structures in the world together with discovering and formulating the grandest scientific truths on record" as originating with the Keetoowahs in the Appalachian Mountains and traveling across the Atlantic to inspire the civilizations of Greece, Egypt, Israel, Mesopotamia and India. Of course, this claim could hardly have been made before the arrival of Europeans in America after 1492. After that, the Keetoowahs began to perceive many similarities of religion, art and language with the newcomers. Their ethnocentric conclusion was that European and Middle Eastern culture had originated with the Cherokee. Today it seems more plausible that all these civilizations had a common source in Oppenheimer's Eden in the East. One offshoot spread east across the Pacific Ocean into the Americas while another filtered westward to Greece, Egypt and related cultures.

The Cherokee-Tuscarora medicine man Rolling Thunder had an illuminating world-view. Brian Wilkes, who studied under him, remembers he gave long talks about the pyramids, the Book of Exodus, Egyptians, Babylonians, Greeks, Jews and other ancient peoples. Finally, Wilkes said, "It sounds like our people were a lot like the Jews, Greeks and Egyp-

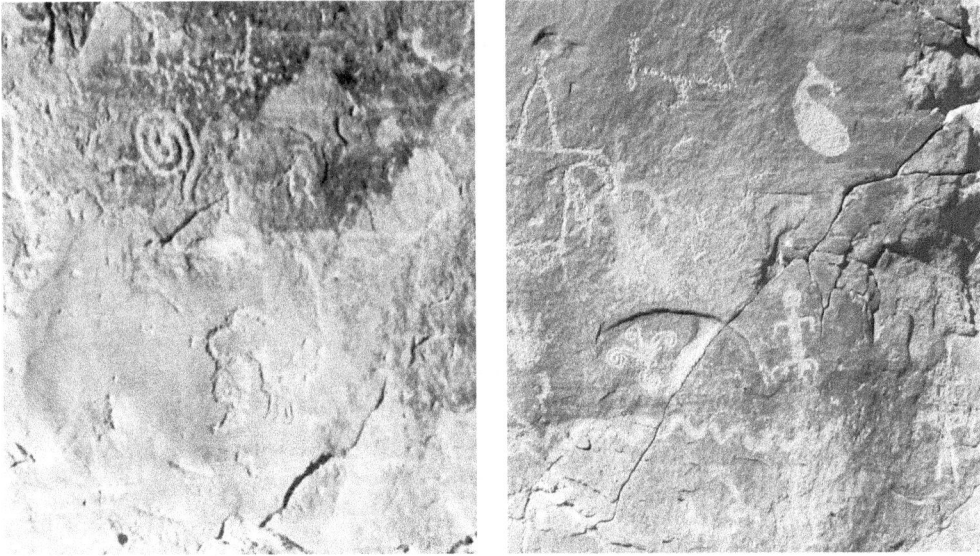

*Top left:* Fig. 2.6a. Distinctive elephant, llama, condor and helmeted soldier at Chaco Canyon fit a migration from North Africa through South America. Author's photograph. *Top right:* Fig. 2.6b. Petroglyph of a whale outside Old Oraibi declares oceanic origins. Author's photograph.

tians." At this, Rolling Thunder looked sternly at him and snapped, "Our people were not *like* the Jews, Greeks and Egyptians; they *were* the Jews, Greeks and Egyptians."[33]

Summing up, we may hypothesize that the Cherokee Nation of American Indians originated as remnants of Ptolemy III's expedition around 230 B.C.E. The mission was to circumnavigate the earth to test Eratosthenes' new concepts regarding its size and shape. Archeological evidence for this comes from cave drawings at Sosorra on McCluer Bay in Western New Guinea depicting, among other things, the *tanawa* navigational instrument used by Alexandrian Egyptian ships. Additional archeological clues are an etching of a Greek hoplite in Tennessee (fig. 2.1b) along with the form and function of the Cherokees' *cahtiyis*, or council house (Chapter 1).

Considered in this context, the Cherokees' migrations and conflicting origins fall into place like pieces of a puzzle. Their early travels through the Pacific beginning as Greeks and related peoples from the East Mediterranean explain the inclusion of Polynesians, Indonesians and blacks in the ethnic mix, a sojourn in South America, abandonment of an original language, and a seven-clan structure with lost tribes and transoceanic migration myths. The first Indian nation's name, Etheloikee or Eshelokee, originally meant colonists.[34]

Yes, but all this is just circumstantial evidence and speculation, one might object. Let's continue now to an examination of Cherokee DNA, which I believe may be the clincher.

# Chapter 3

# *DNA*

*History does not repeat itself. The historians repeat one another.* — Max Beerbohm

Our story begins in a Kansas City hotel room on the morning of June 19, 1977. The previous evening Elvis Presley performed the second gig of what became his farewell tour. He wore the King of Spades suit for the last time and looked puffy, sounding out of breath for most of the show and mentioning he had trouble getting into the suit. That day he was scheduled to appear in Omaha in front of the CBS cameras for the TV special *Elvis in Concert*.

Details are blurry, but people who were there remember the housekeeping staff stripped the sheets off Elvis' bed and whisked them away after he left the hotel room. Carefully preserved, they surfaced at a charity auction following his death two months later, where they fetched a handsome price from an investor in celebrity keepsakes. When the buyer fell on hard times, the sheets and pillow cases changed hands again. They went now to Bobbi Bacha, a plucky Texas private eye played by actress Sela Ward in the movie *Suburban Madness*. This film is based on the real-life story of Clara Harris, convicted February 2003 of killing her cheating orthodontist husband by repeatedly running him over with the family Mercedes. Bacha was an eyewitness. She became perhaps the most talked about P.I. in the world. Her company in Houston, Blue Moon Investigations, enjoyed a meteoric rise to fame.

In 2004, Bacha was ready to authenticate the expensive sheets she owned. She contacted my genetic genealogy company, DNA Consultants. In archival containers on dry ice, properly insured and accompanied by a legal chain of custody, she couriered samples of the blood and semen stains from Houston to a genomics laboratory in Salt Lake City. Though the specimens were nearly thirty years old, the lab director was able to succeed where several labs had failed before. Bacha asked me to evaluate the King's mitochondrial, Y chromosome and autosomal DNA. Whether or not the stained sheets bore bodily fluids from Elvis Presley as everyone believed, their analysis produced a consistent DNA profile of a man with Cherokee Indian lineage, Jewish heritage, a Scottish male line and some interesting ethnic marker anomalies.

It is well known that Presley was not Elvis' true surname, his great-grandmother Martha Rosella Presley having had his grandfather Jessie Dunnan "Dee" McClowell Presley out of wedlock, and having given the child the surname she bore from her father, Dunnan Presley. So it was hardly a surprise that our Elvis Y chromosome type (haplogroup I) matched no Presleys in the available databases. What was surprising was that it exactly matched several males of the surname Wallace. If the blood on our king-sized pillowcase really was from Elvis Presley (it is said he cut his finger on the King of Spades metallic fasteners during the performance), then his grandfather Dee was the child of a man named Wallace in Itawamba County, Mississippi, about 1896.

### Fig. 3.1. Matrilineal Descent of Elvis Presley

White Dove?
Nancy Burdine
Martha Tackett
Octavia Lavenia "Dollie" Mansell
Gladys Love Smith
Elvis Aron Presley

Be that as it may, Elvis' autosomal ancestry markers reveal a picture of his ethnicity that could have been guessed from his appearance and own statements. The results show three Jewish markers (two are those most common in Middle Eastern and Sephardic Jews and suggest he got Jewish genes from both sides of the family), northern European, Mediterranean European, two Native American, an East European, one Sub-Saharan African and one Southeast Asian. The latter is a rare marker tied to Indonesia and Polynesia. Along with these ethnicities there were many indications of Spanish. The top Native American population match was Chole Indians from Chiapas, Mexico, a Maya tribe.

Few people may know that Elvis claimed to be Jewish *and* Cherokee, but our DNA study bore this out, and more. Both of Elvis' assertions were based on the ancestry of his mother, Gladys Love Smith (Fig. 3.1). Growing up in Memphis, Elvis went to summer camp through the Jewish community center. When his mother died, he took care to have her grave marked with a Star of David (since removed). He studied Judaism increasingly in later years and to the end of his life wore a *chai* necklace, symbol of Jewish life. Published genealogies take Gladys' strict maternal line back to great-great grandmother Nancy Burdine, a professed Jewess born in Kentucky, whose mother was White Dove, a reputed full-blood. Since anyone born of a Jewish mother is Jewish, just as anyone born of a Native American mother is Native American, he was a Jewish Indian, an American Indian Jew.

But maybe not. Bracketing for the moment what makes one a Jew, we have to admit that American Indian identity is not simple either. One factor weighing heavily in both claims, however, is DNA.

Paleo-American genetics is fraught with problems. According to a previous director of Tulane's Middle American Research Institute, the field is a notorious "battleground of the theorists," a controversial area "which has snared to their downfall not a few crackpots, mystics, 'linguistic acrobats,' racists and even 'famous institutions' [including] of course the anthropological profession itself."[1] Even population genetics experts are not immune to pitfalls in a landscape strewn with racist bombshells and political dynamite.

About twenty years ago, in a work as revered as it is unreadable, Italian–born geneticist Luca Luigi Cavalli-Sforza at Stanford University unveiled a tree of man based on an analysis of 120 markers from forty-two world populations.[2] Looking solely at female lines, he posited two main limbs, African and non–African. The latter branched off into Europeans (Caucasians) and Northeast Asians (Siberians and Mongolians). Included in Northeast Asians were so-called Amerindians. Amerinds were closest in genetic distance to Northern Turkic, Chukchi and other Arctic peoples. They shared a number of genetic markers with their ancient neighbors, including a similar frequency of female lineages. These came to be called mitochondrial haplogroups A, B, C, and D.

Little did Cavalli-Sforza and his team expect to encounter any snags in their research, much less defunding by the U.S. government and the United Nations, but this is exactly what happened. The genial professor received a letter from a Canadian human rights group called the Rural Advancement Foundation International. The group demanded he stop his work immediately. It accused the Human Genome Diversity Project of biopiracy. The scientists were stealing DNA from unsuspecting indigenous people and mining it for valuable information pharmaceutical companies would use to make drugs Third World people could not afford.

Fig. 3.2. Elvis Presley at Florida Theatre concert, 1956. © Bob Moreland/St. Petersburg Times/ZUMA.

Ever since that slippery slope, geneticists have trodden warily around the issue of Native American demographics and genetics.

But from another perspective, the damage was already done. Theodore Schurr's team in 1990 had matched "Amerindian" changes in mitochondrial DNA over the last 40,000 years with those of Mongolians and Siberians.[3] The lines were indelibly drawn. The scientific community laid down the law that the earliest Native Americans come from four primary maternal lineages. Only female haplogroups A, B, C and D are true Native American types. A fifth lineage, haplogroup X, was admitted, provisionally, in 1997.

Elvis's American Indian mitochondrial type is B. What account can we make of it? Certain critics of the new axiom in American Indian genetics point out that B is not associated in high frequencies with Mongolian populations. Rather, it is Southeast Asian in origin — something borne out by the Elvis sample having a rare Asian ethnic marker. B has a center of diffusion in Taiwan and is common, even dominant, among Polynesians.

Awkwardly, too, haplogroup X smacks of being European or Eurasian, not North Asian. Many believe it may have traveled to America westward across the Atlantic Ocean instead of coming by the assumed route over the Siberian land bridge. In 2011, there were many holes that had been punched in the classic scheme of ABCD haplogroups. Let us glance at a few of those.

Geneticists base their conclusions about ancient migrations on comparisons with population data of living peoples as they have been reported in anthropological and forensic fieldwork. But these are assumptions, pure and simple. Is it certain that populations in places like Mongolia and Alaska in the past — especially far distant past — were the same as they are today? Numerous genetic types become extinct in the course of time. Bottlenecks and genetic drift distort a population's structure and composition. Early migrants can be replaced through competition or changed by gene flow from later arrivals. Genotyping to determine a Y chromosome group from paternal pedigrees or the mitochondrial DNA passed to us by our mother looks at but two lines out of thousands in one's heritage. The current state of genomics cannot test ancestry that crosses from a male to female or vice versa. It cannot isolate the genetic contribution passed to you, say, by your mother's father, or maternal grandfather. Most of our genetic history lies buried in non-sex-linked lines, the province of autosomal DNA.

Using an alternative approach involving human lymphocyte antigens, chemist James L. Guthrie finds no fewer than 28 discrete migration events for settlement of the Americas beginning around 40,000 B.C.E.[4] Peter N. Jones, in a 2002 white paper, notes that "there is ample reason to believe that the genetic history of American Indians is much more complex than the current five haplogroup frequencies lead us to believe." He singled out six limitations in genetics research to date: (1) interpretation of coalescent times (a projection to time of origin of an ultimate genetic mother, much like million-year-old "mitochondrial Eve"), (2) haplogroup fallacies, (3) small sample sizes, (4) use of language groups like the hypothetical "macro–Amerindian" to define population groups, (5) concentrating on contemporary American Indian reservations to infer prehistoric tribal history, and (6) the inconsistent combination of all these approaches to suit preconceived notions.[5] It was a sweeping indictment.[6]

Relatively few ancient samples have been recovered to provide bedrock DNA for population histories. Those that have been usually throw a monkey wrench into the works. One study by Swedish geneticist Svante Pääbo and his team in 1988 proposed the existence of a previously unknown founding lineage on the basis of mitochondrial DNA extracted from a rare specimen of 7,000-year-old human brain matter in Florida. This anomaly was almost immediately dismissed as "of no importance."[7] An analysis of the bone remains of 25 pre–Columbian Mayas by Gonzalez-Oliver's group produced one type of mitochondrial DNA that could not even be classified.[8] The Brazilian geneticist F. M. Salzano has remarked that of the 338 ancient cases investigated to date, over two-thirds could not be assigned to the conventional six "Amerindian" haplogroups.[9] Researchers find that among the remote Cayapa Indians of Ecuador, one-fifth of genetic variation is "other."[10]

Schurr's doctrine of the four ancient founding mothers of Native Americans was based entirely on small Pima, Maya, Ticuna, Mexican and South American Indian samples. A study by D. C. Wallace and colleagues inferred an Asian correlation from evidence taken solely from Arizona's tiny tribes of Pima and Papago Indians.[11] This 1985 article was the source of untold mischief. Four female haplogroups were later "proved" to account for over 95 percent of all contemporary American Indian populations. Geneticists fell into lockstep to show that only a small number of founding mothers migrated from Asia into the New World. In 2004, despite a much shallower time-depth for calculating mutations, scientists decided that it had to be the same for male founders. There was a single, recent entry of Native American Y chromosomes into the Americas.[12]

A dirty little secret about Native American genetic studies is that the sheer technical error rate is likely "large," according to one reviewer, perhaps double that of other laboratory sequencing work. Much of the data is old, and at any rate only 80 out of a total 542 tribes in the United States have been sampled. That represents only 15 percent of the diversity present in Native Americans. No one has studied people of Indian descent who do not live on reservations or have a federal roll number. The Native American Y database taps only 3 percent of all tribes to reach sweeping generalizations about male Q lineage believed to dominate New World populations.

Sometimes as few as two individuals are used to project the population structure of an entire tribe. Outdated results keep being reshuffled, many from decades-old diabetes studies conducted under dubious protocols. The underlying logic goes like this:

All our subjects tested out to be haplogroup A, B, C, D, E or X.

All our subjects were Indians because they were located on reservations.

Therefore, all Indians are haplogroup A, B, C, D, E or X.

It's as though we claimed, "All men are two-legged creatures; therefore since the skeleton we dug up has two legs, it is human." It might be a kangaroo.

Results not supporting scientists' preconceptions are rejected or ignored. One archeologist writes, "Today there is a scattering of both L (African) and H (European) in American Indian populations, but so little that it most likely represents intermarriage since Columbus's time."[13] Surveys of Cherokee DNA have noted the presence of maternal haplogroups H and J, but their authors declare it, *ipso facto*, European. A study of DNA in the peoples of north-central Mexico found significant amounts of European haplogroups H, K, J and U in a sample rigorously restricted to traditional Indios. Researchers were puzzled by the elevated level of African DNA, something corroborated independently by blood group studies and "evident today in the physical appearance and culture of the populations." But they preferred to attribute the anomalous numbers to slavery in the sixteenth and seventeenth centuries. The unsettling incidence of H, K, J and U was assigned to "the presence of European mtDNA haplotypes in Mexican populations" following the Spanish invasion.[14]

Illogically, all European–labeled DNA is factored out when it comes to postulations about the origin of Native Americans. Only 9.5 percent of Native American samples are judged "unmixed" in the first place, and the "Atlantic seaboard and several regions of the Southeastern US have the highest admixture rates, which approximate 50%." According to firmly established genealogies for the Navajo, even this tribe has "not inconsequential numbers of genes of European origin."[15]

Southeastern Indians are particularly under-sampled and under-studied. Out of a total of 1,600 subjects, one major study uses only 37 Cherokee, 35 Creek, 27 Choctaw, and 35 Seminole, most of them from Oklahoma (see Appendix A).[16] Bolnick and Smith's 2003 study of Southeastern Indian mitochondrial haplotypes is similarly limited in its scope.[17] A Y chromosome haplotype survey assigning two-thirds of all Indians to male haplogroup Q3 found that Seminoles formed the exception, having a high incidence of non–Q3 types.[18]

About the time Rutgers professor Elizabeth Hirschman and I were concluding our study of Melungeon DNA,[19] we decided to put together a small sample of Cherokee descendants who could trace their line back to the marriage of a Jewish merchant with the daughter of an Indian headman. Our object was to test the ethnicity of those Cherokee who blended with Melungeons. Those enrolled for the project had to be directly descended from a Cherokee woman strictly through the female line. Only that would give us a picture of ancient mitochondrial lineages. A DNA test was offered to each participant, and detailed genealogies were asked for and received. The raw data generated by the study is shown in Appendix A. Small as it was, Beth and I felt that our study would be an important new step, especially since it was backed up by genealogies. All previous surveys had used anonymous subjects. Genealogies were deemed irrelevant.

To our knowledge, our studies are the first to qualify participants on the basis of their family histories. Invariably, these mention Indian ancestry in the female line, typically Cherokee. Native American chiefs cemented trade agreements with intermarriage of their daughters and other female kinswomen. Early explorer John Lawson wrote about this custom in 1709:

> The Indian Traders are those which travel and abide amongst the Indians for a long space of time; sometimes for a Year, two, or three. These Men have commonly their Indian Wives, whereby they soon learn the Indian Tongue, keep a Friendship with the Savages; and, besides the Satisfaction of

a She-Bed-Fellow, they find these Indian Girls very serviceable to them, on Account of dressing their Victuals, and instructing 'em in the Affairs and Customs of the Country. Moreover, such a Man gets a great Trade with the Savages; for when a Person that lives amongst them, is reserv'd from the Conversation of their Women, 'tis impossible for him ever to accomplish his Designs amongst that People.[20]

The Pennsylvania Jew Jacob Troxell's marriage to Cornblossom, daughter of Double-head, and the marriage of Isaac Cooper at the end of the Chickamaugan Wars to Nancy Blackfox, daughter of Chief Black Fox, are two instances I am familiar with from my own family history.[21] Sometimes the union is formed the other way around. Doublehead's son Tuckahoe married Margaret Mounce (Ashkenazi Jewish surname Munz,[22] "money"). But the classic situation features a merchant (often Jewish), Indian agent (often Scottish) or frontier soldier (often Scottish) receiving the daughter of a local chief as a bride. She then goes to live with him and raises a family in her husband's frontier home. The trader and his half-blood children can return at any time to the Indian town; its doors are always open to them.

Isaac Cooper's grandfather was the pioneer William Cooper. This son of a plantation owner was born on the James River about 1725 and became the guide and scout for Daniel Boone when Boone was hired by the firm of Cohen and Isaacs to survey lands that eventually formed Kentucky and Tennessee. Cooper planted a corn crop in 1775 on the left bank of Otter Creek above Clover Bottom near Boonsboro.[23] He was then employed by Richard Henderson to assist Boone in clearing the Wilderness Road. He died in 1781 in an Indian attack after helping the Cumberland settlers continue the road to what became Nashville, Tennessee.[24] His children lived on Copper Ridge (a corruption of Cooper) in the heart of Melungeon territory, later in Grainger County, Tennessee, and Wayne County, Kentucky. They also took lands in the Cumberland Settlements in Davidson, Sumner and Rutherford counties.[25]

What kind of male DNA did these Coopers carry? Our sample came from Grady Cooper, a cousin of my mother. It belongs to the same paternal lineage of most other males in our Melungeon DNA study—haplogroup R1b. On a narrow basis it matches only two other Coopers out of hundreds. It is a close match with Troy Cooper, who descends from a London branch of the Coopers, and Tom Diaz, whose forbears were Canary Island Jews with the Sephardic Jewish surname Adan (Adam).

Although the Coopers came from England in the seventeenth century and settled on the James River, their more distant origins were clearly Portuguese and Jewish. The Y chromosome of a Choctaw Cooper, Raymond Hurst (his father's adoptive surname) confirms this. His ancestor, also named William Cooper, a son of Boone's scout who settled in Choctaw territory, is mentioned in Spanish records in the General Archive of the Indies in Seville as "a colored man of Portuguese extraction ... working on fort" on the upper Tombigbee River.[26] The word "colored" designates a mulatto, a legal term used in colonial era documents of anyone born of an Indian mother; it does not, as many assume, refer to African ancestry.[27] Now, we know that the wife of William Cooper the elder was Malea Labon and that she was the daughter of John Labon (or Leebow), a land developer who married a Chickasaw or Choctaw woman. Another of William and Malea's sons back in North Carolina, Cornelius, is listed in local records as a free person of color. True to type, William the younger married a Choctaw chief's daughter, and his son, also named William, married Susan King, daughter of principal chief Moshulatubbee.

Thus, the Coopers of early Tennessee and Kentucky seem to be descended from Portuguese merchants, Marranos who became British citizens in the period of the Glorious Revolution of William and Mary immediately following Jews' re-admittance into Britain. This path proves to be a staple feature of Cherokee genealogies.

Only one of the male lines tested proves an Indian type, Q. This was the Sizemore participants' DNA sample. The specific type widely matched American Indian DNA from Panama and other places in the Americas. Paradoxically, some Sizemore lines show R1b (Western European). Exhaustive research by Alan Lerwick of Salt Lake City suggests all Sizemores in this country can be traced to the London merchant Michael Sizemore buried in the Flemish cemetery of St. Katharine by the Tower in 1684. Evidently there was a "non-paternity event" involving Michael's grandson Henry, who grew up in Virginia. Family legends speak of Cherokee chiefs kidnapping Sizemore women. Sizemore descendants tracing back to Henry Sizemore, son "Old Ned" Sizemore (who was hanged by Col. Ben Cleveland on the Tory Oak in Wilkesboro at the end of the American Revolution), grandson George Edward Sizemore (who married Annie Elizabeth Aruna Hart), grandson George "Chief of All" Sizemore (who married Agnes Shepherd) and grandson Ephraim Sizemore (the author's 4th great-grandfather, who came to Sand Mountain from South Carolina), tend to be aware of and proud of their Indian heritage. Descendants of John Sizemore of Pittsylvania County, Virginia, on the other hand, preserved the original R1b lineage of Sizemore males. Many of the R1b Sizemores dispute any Indian heritage without realizing that it can travel down the female lines as well. But these Sizemores, like the rest, were in all probability crypto–Jews in the mold of the Coopers, Harts, Gregorys, Bollings, Greenes, Jacksons, Parkers, Bagleys and Brocks they married with, generation after generation.[28]

Let us now turn to the female side of the project. Gayl Wilson (born Gibson) traces her Wolf Clan line to Sarah Consene, a daughter of Young Dragging Canoe (fig. 3.3). She is an enrolled member of the Cherokee Nation of Oklahoma. Her mitochondrial DNA haplogroup C proves to be one of the leading types among Cherokees. It is found sparsely in Mongolia and Siberia, and its frequency in North America is weighted toward the Northeast rather than Alaska and the Northwest, with a heavy incidence in the lower Appalachians. Wilson's particular type of C matches nine individuals with Hispanic surnames, including Juan B. Madrid (Two Hearts), a California schoolteacher, and 26 anonymous samples from Mexico, Peru, Puerto Rico, Spain and the U.S. This would appear to support the Mexican affinities of the Cherokee, though in which direction the gene flow went is not clear.

Also belonging to haplogroup C is enrolled Cherokee Willora Glee Krapf. Her line derives from Elizabeth Tassel, one of the first Cherokee women to wed an English frontier official, Scots trader Ludovic Grant, about 1726 (fig. 3.4). The marriage produced one daughter, Mary Grant, who in turn married William Emory, another trader. Their issue was prolific, generating many celebrated Cherokee names: Due, Watts, Corntassel, Stuart (from John Stuart, the British agent), Rogers and Waters. Oklahoma cowboy humorist and author Will Rogers (1879–1935) is among the descendants. Elizabeth Tassel was Twister Clan. Samuel Riley, a trader who was one of the founders of Northeast Alabama, married two sisters, Gulustiyu and Nigodigeyu, of this clan. Both were daughters of Chief Doublehead (Paint Clan). That prominent member of the famous Moytoy dynasty married Creat, a cousin, daughter of German spy Christian Priber by a daughter of Chief Moytoy II (Wolf Clan). We see patterns in these connections reflecting the Cherokee taboo against marrying into the same clan. Marriage partners are chosen, instead, from an opposite clan, often that of a grandfather.[29]

DNA that proved to be haplogroup B was contributed by a matrilineal descendant of

### Fig. 3.3. Cherokee Wolf Clan Matriline

1. Sarah Consene, born about 1800, Cherokee Nation East (Hightower/Etowah, Ga.)
2. Peggy Quinlon, born 1830 Cherokee Nation East (Cobb Co., Ga.)
3. Sarah Emma High, born Oct. 27, 1872
4. Bessie Lee Mauck, born Oct. 27, 1898, Wagoner, Oklahoma
5. Emalee Mitchell, born Dec. 2, 1921, Hulbert, Okla.
6. Gayl A. Gibson, born Dec. 1945, Tulsa, Okla.

### Fig. 3.4. Ten generations of Cherokee Long Hair Clan women.

1. Mary Grant (mother: Elizabeth Tassel)
2. Mary Emory
3. Susannah Buffington
4. Mary "Pauline" Beck
5. Julia Ann Hildebrand
6. Willora Cleora Josephine Bee
7. Neel Jewell
8. Neel Von Osdol
9. Willora Glee Krapf
10. Stacy Robin Cooper

Lucretia Parris, halfblood daughter of George Parris and granddaughter of early Cherokee Indian trader Richard Pearis, who died in the Bahamas, April 7, 1794. The Pearis or Parris family is the likely namesake of Parris Island in South Carolina. Their original name was perhaps Perez/Peres. They intermarried with the Dougherty and Cooper families.

U.S. federal Indian agent Benjamin Hawkins describes Cornelius Dougherty's residence near the town of Quanasee and calls him "an old Irish trader."[30] He is said to have been 120 years old when he died in 1788. His original trading post was located at Seneca Old Town on the Keowee River, where William and Joseph Cooper were also situated since 1698. Cornelius' father Alexander was a Jacobite who fled to America after the Glorious Revolution. According to Rogers and Rogers' Cherokee history, it was Alexander who was probably the first white man to marry a Cherokee, in 1690.[31] After 1719, Cornelius became a licensed trader out of Charleston, the British headquarters for the Indian trade, where brothers William and Joseph Cooper were commissioners, and married Ah-nee-wa-kee, a daughter of Chief Moytoy II, thus fulfilling the usual contract. She was of the Wild Potato Clan. Deerhead Cove beneath the brow of Fox Mountain in Dade County, Georgia, and DeKalb County, Alabama, was named for her. The name of the mountain towering over Deerhead Cove honors Chief Black Fox, whose descendants on nearby Sand Mountain are multiply entwined with Doughertys. Another Wild Potato Clan female founder was Susannah or Sonicooie, who married Thomas Cordery. Their descendants include Sarah Cordery, who married John Rogers, and numerous enrolled Cherokees by the names Vickery, Harris, McNair, Mosley and Collins. The Nighthawk Society of Redbird Smith emphasized genealogies and traditions of the Wild Potato. James Vann and Sour Mash were Wild Potato. So was Sickatower, one of the oldest men in the nation around 1800, when he became an important source for ethnographic notes.[32]

Lucretia Parris' form of B loosely matches Panamanian, Huetar, Maya, Nuu-Cha-Nulth, and Yanomana Indians. The ancient Native American woman who heads this lineage supposedly lived as long ago as thirty or fifty thousand years, though we do not know whether to place her in Asia or the Americas at the time.

Elvis' form of B matches Chickasaws, Choctaws and Creeks. But on the basis of one mutation in his profile, his alleged ancient maternal ancestor White Dove must belong to a Cherokee type, which agrees with family oral history. Three other rough matches to the Elvis gene lead to Brazil and Guatemala, locations that agree with migration stories of the Cherokee, but again we do not know the timeframe or direction of genetic flow. Altogether, lineage B accounts for one-half or more of Cherokee DNA and roughly a quarter of all Southeastern Indians. The Maya and Mixté in Mexico are about one-quarter B and one-half A with smaller degrees of C, D and other. The Pima are about half B, half C, with a negligible amount of A. The Boruca in Central America are as high as three-quarters B.

When first described, haplogroup B was believed to be part of a second wave of American Indian colonization from Asia dating to 15,000 to 12,000 years ago. This migration supposedly followed an earlier and larger influx of A. The highest frequencies of B are found along the eastern edge of China in the islands of Taiwan (34 percent) and the Philippines (40 percent). Today, it is more likely to be seen as the trail of early humans following the beachcomber route up through Japan and down the American coast. No Native American B of the exact type discovered in Elvis' DNA is found in Asia, however. By the same token, none of the Asian types of B seems to have made it to the central Asian source of A, C and D in South Siberia. B haplotypes are extremely common in Indians of the American Southwest such as Hopi, Zuni (77 percent), Anasazi (78 percent), Yuman and Jemez Pueblo (89 percent).[33] Significantly, our Elvis DNA sample seems to reflect a lot of this Pacific–facing deep ancestry. It also has specific autosomal (non-mitochondrial, non–Y chromosomal) matches to Sichuan Chinese, Malaysia, Guam, Maya, Colombia, Guatemala, Costa Rica, El Salvador, Venezuela and Central America.

Elvis Presley was born and grew up in Tupelo, Mississippi, on the edge of Chickasaw country. But his maternal ancestor Nancy Burdine came from Kentucky in Cherokee territory. His remote female ancestor could have been either Chickasaw or Cherokee. At any rate, it is an example of a "derived haplotype" within the definition of experts Ripan Malhi and Jason Eshleman.[34] It is, as far as we know, tribally specific to the Cherokee. The Chickasaw and Cherokee had a common border just west of the site of Nashville along the Natchez Trace. They often exchanged female marriage partners in peace treaties and intertribal relations.

Two Cherokee female lines show a connection with the white man who founded the Eastern Band of Cherokee Indians. Col. William Holland Thomas (1805–1893) occupies a special place in the history of the Eastern Band of Cherokee. He went to work at the age of twelve at the Walker trading post on Soco Creek and learned the Cherokee language as he bargained with the natives for ginseng and furs. Drowning Bear, chief of Quallatown, took a keen interest in him. When Drowning Bear learned that the boy had no father or brothers and sisters, he adopted him as a son. Will's best friend was a Cherokee boy who taught him the ancient customs, lore and religious rites.

> When the Cherokee gave up the lands on the upper Little Tennessee River, Will settled his mother on a farm on the Oconaluftee River. His trade with the Cherokee prospered. By the time of the removal, Will owned five trading posts within the Cherokee Nation.... During the Trail of Tears ... Drowning Bear asked the Quallatown Cherokee to accept Will Thomas as their chief.... Thomas went to Washington to argue for many Cherokee claims [and] in 1840 the government Indian Office appointed him to take a census of those Cherokee in the east and to act as the government's disbursing agent. Thomas used the money to begin the purchase of more than 50,000 acres of land for the Cherokee in his own name [and] by 1860 a large block of land known as the Qualla Boundary had been purchased. One of the stories of how the name Qualla came to be applied to this land

### Fig. 3.5. Participant's line of descent from Betsy Walker through Catherine Hyde, Cherokee paramour of Col. Will Thomas (J)

1. Betsy Walker b. abt. 1720 (6th great-grandmother) and husband unknown, parents unknown
2. Elizabeth "Betsy" Walker (5th great-grandmother) married to Edward "Ned" Leatherwood
3. Elizabeth Rebecca Leatherwood (4th great grandmother) married Benjamin Hyde
4. Catherine Hyde (Cline) (3rd great grandmother, sister to Ann "Annie" Hyde), had children with William Holland Thomas and married Michael Cline
5. Josephine Cline Maney (2nd great grandmother)
6. Margarette (Hattie) Maney Pace (great grandmother)
7. Bessie Pace Taylor (grandmother)
8. Shirley Taylor McFadden (mother)
9. Kimberly McFadden Hill (test subject)

is worth telling. Will Thomas's [Cherokee] wife was named Polly. As the Cherokee language did not use words that required the mouth to close, they called her Qualla.[35]

In 1867 Thomas' health failed. The Civil War had ruined him. He eventually went into an insane asylum, where he died May 10, 1893. Without him, however, there would be no Eastern Band of the Cherokee Nation. The 57,000 acre Qualla Boundary is not a true reservation like others. It is held in trust by the federal government as communally owned land, the sole such tract in the eastern United States. Col. Will Thomas was the only white chief of an Indian tribe.

While he was an apprentice for the Walkers, young Will fell in love with Catherine Hyde, a descendant of Betsy Walker, a Cherokee woman from Soco (One-Town) who had been left to Sen. Felix Walker to raise. The project was fortunate to locate a maternal line descendant of the first Betsy Walker, Kimberly Hill, who provided a sample of her mitochondrial DNA (fig. 3.5). What is presumably Betsy Walker's form of mitochondrial DNA proves to be a specific type within haplogroup J. The same haplotype came to light in fellow project participant Sharon Bedzyk, a descendant of Ann Hyde, Catherine's sister (fig. 3.6), and a related haplotype was identified in a late-joining participant with ancestry traced to Myra Jarvis, a Melungeon woman born in 1815 in Georgia.

J is the lineage of the Semitic daughter of Eve, Jasmine. She is the archetypal Jewish mother.[36] Her descendants compose about 10 percent of the entire population of Eurasia. The lineage seems to have originated in present-day Lebanon approximately 10,000 years before present and to have moved north and west into Europe, although views about J are still evolving.[37] The question, of course, arises: Does Betsy's lineage result from recent European admixture or does it go back farther? Suggestively, her precise mutations do not appear in the thousands of Middle Eastern and European samples in standard surveys and concordances. Frequent near-hits are Welsh, English, Cornish and American Caucasian, but none comes very close to matching on all control points. Such rare forms must represent a deeper origin than entry of Europeans into Cherokee country in the seventeenth century. The inescapable conclusion is that Semitic/East Mediterranean maternal lines were part of prehistoric Cherokee society.

A third participant testing as J is Judith Alef, a descendant of Cherokee Myra Jarvis, a Melungeon woman born in Georgia in 1815. And a fourth participant also proves to be J. He is Jerry W. Moore, the father of Michael W. Moore, who traces his father's maternal ancestry to Emily Glover, born in Tennessee in 1837, reputedly Cherokee. Altogether there are five J's in our study.

**Fig. 3.6. Another descent from Betsy Walker**
**through Catherine Hyde's sister, Ann Hyde**

1. Betsy Walker married unknown man
2. Elizabeth Walker married Edward "Ned" Leatherwood
3. Elizabeth Rebecca Leatherwood married Benjamin Hyde, Sr.
4. Ann "Annie" Hyde married Holloman Battle (sister to Catherine Hyde)
5. Nancy C. Battle married John Jackson Wood Jr.
6. Sarah Jane "Sallie" Wood married James David Wiggins
7. Bessie Lillian Wiggins married Fred Johnson Cochran
8. Marian Cochran married Albert Crisp
9. Sharon Crisp (Bedzyk)

Although Col. Will officially married Sarah Jane Burney Love late in life in 1857, he had several paramours. In addition to Catherine Hyde, one was the Polly after whom the Qualla Reservation was named. She bore him Demarius Angeline in 1827. Note that Demarius is a favorite name of crypto–Jews. It is derived from Tamar, Hebrew for "date palm." Here again our project was fortunate. Thanks to the Indian grapevine, a direct female-line descendant of Demarius Angeline Sherrill, nee Thomas, responded to the call. "We were most surprised to learn our Angeline came from the X lineage," said James Riddle. He is literally the last of the line. Since he is male, Angeline's lineage would die out with him. It is an apt illustration of the fragility of haplogroups.

Haplogroup X was first recognized over a decade ago. It was added to Native American lineages A, B, C and D only reluctantly.[38] Its discovery opened the door for more minor founding mothers at the same time that it created a strong push to prove it was Siberian. What is different about haplogroup X is the suspicion it might be an ancient link between Europe and North America. Some view it as a founding lineage that directly crossed the Atlantic Ocean, perhaps with the elusive Red Paint Culture. The detection of X in our study represents the first report of it among the Cherokee. Previously, it was identified only in certain northern tribes. Among the Micmac of the northeastern U.S. and adjacent Canadian provinces, for instance, it attains a level of 50 percent. It is also present in smaller amounts in the West among the Sioux (15 percent), Nuu-Chah-Nulth (11 percent–13 percent), Navajo (7 percent) and Yakima (5 percent).

We have seven instances of haplogroup X. No two are exactly alike, meaning there is a good deal of diversity small as the lineage is in the scheme of things. All the haplotypes examined seem to originate from a Cherokee woman living long ago. Let us now consider the "X Files of the Cherokee" (Appendix E).

In the case of Annie L. Garrett, born 1846 in Mississippi, descendant Betty Sue Satterfield vouches for there being a tradition in the family she was Cherokee.

Michelle Baugh of Hazel Green, Alabama, traces her Cherokee female line to Agnes Weldy, born about 1707. Descendants include enrolled members of the Eastern Band of Cherokee Indians.

Seyinus, a Cherokee woman born on or near the Qualla Boundary in North Carolina in 1862, is the source of a similar X lineage.

Another is the sample taken from Billy Sinor, the son of Gladys Lulu Sutton, born in Indian Territory in 1906. His mother's birth certificate lists her as "Cherokee Indian." Her mother was Olivia McCorkle Walker Ginn, born in West Virginia in 1865. This line matches that of Penelope Greene Fraser, born 1779, in Walton County, according to Sinor.

Finally, an X descendant in the study provides additional evidence for Melungeon link-

**Fig. 3.7. My mitochondrial descent**

1. Cherokee Woman born about 1775
2. Martha Jordan born 1795
3. Lucinda Martha (Patsy) Weaver Lackey born 1815
4. Lovina (Dovey) Adeline Lackey Fossett Shankles 1845–1888
5. Lucinda C. Shankles Goble 1872–1898
6. Dovie Palestine Goble Cooper 1890–1920
7. Bessie Louise Cooper Yates born 1917
8. Donald Neal Yates born 1950

ages within the Cherokee. This participant has documentation of descent from a Cherokee woman who married a Walden/Wallen. Elisha Wallen was one of the first of the so-called longhunters in Tennessee and his name crops up frequently in Melungeon research circles.

My own maternal line goes back to a Cherokee woman in northern Georgia or North Carolina who had children by a trader named Jordan (fig. 3.7). He can be identified as Enoch Jordan, whose Y chromosomal fingerprint is included in the Jordan Surname DNA Project online. Trader Jordan was born about 1768 in Scotland of forebears from Russia or the Ukraine. His Cherokee wife, my 5th great-grandmother, proves to be haplogroup U2, but a form of it with no exact matches in any databases. Given origins in Russia or the Ukraine, and an intervening generation in Scotland, Trader Jordan himself was almost certainly Jewish. The Y chromosome type of his descendants belongs to male haplogroup J, a paternal lineage that contains the genetic signature of Old Testament priests.[39] Here is evidently another case of a Jewish trader marrying a Cherokee woman. But how to account for the Cherokee wife's Old World haplogroup of U?

Haplogroup U is associated with Berbers and Egyptians as well as other early Mediterranean peoples. Professor Bryan Sykes in *The Seven Daughters of Eve* places the sketch of *Ur*-mother Ursula's life he created for his bestseller in prehistoric Greece. The resemblance of family members of my mother Bessie Cooper Yates, who claimed to be one-quarter Cherokee through her female line, to modern-day Berbers and especially Cyrenaic women is striking, down to the hair, eyes, coloring and bone structure.

The initial results of Elizabeth Hirschman's and my Melungeon and Scottish DNA project were released at the Melungeon Fourth Union held in Kingsport, Tennessee, in the summer of 2002. One member in the audience was Phyllis Elliott Starnes of Harriman, Tennessee. Like me, she had a family tradition of being Cherokee in the maternal line (figure 3.9). Astonishingly, her mitochondrial DNA when tested turned out to be very similar to mine. It was another example of U2 with close matches only to other Melungeons. Starnes's characteristic mtDNA mutations produced no exact full matches in any database, although they partially matched my own and had affinities with other U's in the eventual project that developed at DNA Consultants. Starnes traces her maternal line to Susanna Owens, born about 1760, probably in Granville County, North Carolina. The family is Melungeon like the Coopers, and Starnes suffers from a disease common among Melungeons and Sephardic Jews, familial Mediterranean fever. So do her daughters and other female-linked relatives.

Haplogroup U is a complex mega-lineage with an estimated age of more than 50,000 years. It is the oldest European haplogroup that is Homo sapiens rather than Homo erectus or Neanderthal, echoing the first colonization of Europe by its present inhabitants in the Stone Age. U shows up in the archeological record in Delphi and Spain around 50,000 years ago. Today the clade U5 accounts for about 10 percent of matrilineal types in Europeans.

Other clades of U are responsible for about five and a half percent, making U the second largest haplogroup after H. It appears in high frequencies in the Indian subcontinent and at relatively low rates in the Japanese and Senegalese. High proportions of U are found today among Armenians, Georgians, Estonians, Russians and Slovaks, as well as in Finland, Germany, Scotland, France, Gallicia, among North African Berbers and Egyptians and in Portugal.[40] In Finland, a population with a historical bottleneck and relatively small number of founder types, it has been associated with several rare medical conditions, including occipital stroke.[41]

In our study, U covers 13 cases or 25 percent of the total, second in frequency only to haplogroup T. Who are these Mediterranean descendants among the Cherokee?

One is Mary M. Garrabrant-Brower. She belongs to what could be labeled U5a1a. Her great-grandmother was Clarissa Green of the Cherokee Wolf Clan, born 1846. This Wolf Clan woman's grandfather was remembered as a Cherokee chief, as is consistent with what we have proposed earlier about the traditional nature of the Wolf Clan. Mary's mother, Mary M. Lounsbury, maintained the Cherokee language and rituals, even though the family relocated to the Northeast.

Fig. 3.8a. Bessie Cooper Yates, born on Sand Mountain, source of haplogroup U2 for the author. Courtesy Bett Yates Adams.

A Scottsdale, Arizona, doctor in our study, another U5a1a, matches only one other person in the world, Marie Eastman, born 1901 in Indian Territory. Because of the precision of the match, he and the descendant of Marie Eastman who was tested are almost certainly cousins in a genealogical as well as genetic sense. His own descent is documented from Jane Rose, a member of the Eastern Cherokee Band. Her family is listed on the Baker Rolls, the final arbiter of enrollment established by the U.S. government.

Michael Gilbert was given little information about his mother, Wilma Nell Atchison, beyond the fact that she was Blackfoot. This is probably the Virginia/North Carolina tribe by the name, also known as Saponi, Sissipah and Haliwah. His haplotype is U5b2. An exact match leads to Arpahia Finley, born about 1827 in Albemarle County, Virginia. This locale is the traditional homeland of the Blackfoot Indians.

My wife, Teresa Panther-Yates, proves to have mtDNA that can also be designated U5b, the most common "European" subgroup according to genetics journals. It has no exact matches anywhere; it is unique in the world. Teresa traces her maternal line back to Isabel Culver, the second wife of Levin Ellis in Hancock County, Georgia. Isabel died about 1838 at the time of the Trail of Tears. There is a tradition in Teresa's family that this line was Cherokee. One participant who learned of her U lineage claims that her line goes back to Ann Dreaweah, a Cherokee woman married to a half blood Cherokee man.

Another instance of U5a has no close matches at all but appears to have a Cherokee form of it. The subject was adopted in Oklahoma and knows nothing of his mother's ancestry.

### Fig. 3.9. Phyllis Starnes U2 genealogy.

1. Unknown mother in Southwest Virginia
2. Margaret Nelson
3. Martha "Patsy" Quesenberry, born 1821, Mocks Old Field, North Carolina
4. Elizabeth Rutherford, Lee County, Virginia
5. Margaret Fleenor, Lee County, Virginia
6. Sinda Kimbler, Scott County, Virginia
7. Beatrice LaForce, Scott County, Virginia
8. Phyllis Elliott, Scott County, Virginia

Gerald Potterf, U4, traces his mother's line to Lillie C. Wilson-Field, born in 1857, Catawba County, North Carolina. He believes she was probably Cherokee, although her ancestors may have been Catawba, a Siouan tribe from the Carolinas who joined the Cherokee in great numbers during the eighteenth century. U4 is strongly associated with North Africa and the Middle East.

In all U cases where there are Melungeon, Cherokee and Jewish connections in the genealogy, the most frequent clan mentioned is Paint Clan.

Our second phase of testing combined Elvis Presley's DNA with forty new participants (Appendix E). The results blew the lid off Cherokee DNA studies. They were released on the DNA Consultants Blog in August 2009 in a post titled "Anomalous Mitochondrial DNA Lineages in the Cherokee." Among the findings were that most of the Cherokee maternal types are unmatched anywhere else except among other participants. Thus, there proves to be a high degree of interrelatedness and common ancestral lines. Beyond that, it was the Middle Eastern cast of the DNA that shocked. Haplogroup T emerges as the largest lineage, followed by U, X, J and H. Similar proportions of these haplogroups are noted in the populations of Egypt, Israel and other parts of the East Mediterranean.

Maternal lineage T arose in Mesopotamia approximately 10,000 to 12,000 years ago. It spread northward through the Caucasus and west from Anatolia into Europe. It shares a common source with haplogroup J in the parent haplogroup JT. Ancient people bearing haplogroup T and J are viewed by geneticists as some of the first farmers, introducing agriculture to Europe with the Neolithic Revolution. Europe's previous substrate emphasized older haplogroups U and N. The T lineage includes about 10 percent of modern Europeans. The closer one goes to its origin in the Fertile Crescent the more prevalent it is.

All T's in the Cherokee project are unmatched in Old World populations.[42] They do, however, in some cases, match each other. Such kinship indicates we are looking at members of the same definite group, with the same set of clan mothers as their ancestors. So let us briefly introduce some of these descendants of Middle Eastern–originating Cherokee lines.

Jonlyn L. Roberts had a puzzling but typical genealogy that led her to embark on a life-long quest for answers. Her mother, Zella, was adopted by the George and Mary Hand family of Hand County, South Dakota, in 1901. Little information was passed down, but piecing together clues from her childhood, Roberts believes that her mother's original family might have come from the Red Lake Ojibwe Indian Reservation or one of the North or South Dakota reservations. At any rate, her mtDNA haplotype is a unique form of T, one with certain distinctive variations in common with others in the study.

Another T in the study fully matched four other people, all born in the United States. One of these noted their ancestor as being Birdie Burns, born 1889 in Arkansas, the daughter of Alice Cook, a Cherokee. Gail Lynn Dean (T) is the wife of another participant, whose type belongs to anomalous U. Both she and her husband claim Cherokee ancestries. T participant Linda Burckhalter is the great-great-granddaughter of Sully Firebush, the daughter of a Cherokee chief. Sully married Solomon Sutton, stowaway son of a London merchant, in what would seem to be another variation of "Jewish trader marries chief's daughter."

Two cases of T represent descent in separate lines from the historically documented Gentry sisters, Elizabeth and Nancy, daughters of Tyree Gentry, who moved to Arkansas in 1817. The tested descendants are aunts or cousins of Patrick Pynes, a non-registered Cherokee and professor of American Indian studies. Learning of the results of the study, Pynes commented, "The possible connections to Egyptian heritage among these Cherokee descendants are especially interesting. We have a photograph of one of the women in this T* line (a granddaughter of Nancy Gentry, I think), and she is wearing an Ankh necklace. We all thought that was kind of strange. As far as I know, the Gentrys were Methodist Episcopalians."[43]

Three participants with T previously unknown to each other, and living in different parts of the country, turn out to be very close cousins descended from the same Cherokee ancestress. Their mitochondrial mutations exactly and fully match. Two claim Melungeon ancestry — a Yates[44] male-linked cousin of the author and a relative of Phyllis Starnes (U, matching the author's). The third has adoption in the family, so the female ancestry is unknown.

A case of rare T5, Cheryl took not only the mitochondrial test but also our CODIS-marker-based ethnic population test, DNA Fingerprint, to validate "Cherokee or Jewish ancestry" from her mother. The results of the DNA Fingerprint Test show Ashkenazi Jewish in the number one position, followed by assorted American Indian matches. Cheryl says that she is exploring returning to Judaism, but that in the remote Texas town where her family lives there are few avenues or resources to pursue.

As tabulated in Appendix E, our small survey shows a great deal of diversity and relatedness. It includes more than a few participants who discovered they share the same Cherokee ancestry, maybe even the same clan. Unlike a random sample of the U.S. population, they exhibit a mix that turns the conventional numbers on their heads. Haplogroup H, instead of an expected 50 percent dominant position, is one of the smallest, with only 7.7 percent. Haplogroup U, an older lineage representing the Stone Age colonization of Europe before the ascendency of H, contributes 25 percent of the total number. Haplogroup X, marked by an exiguous presence elsewhere, attains a frequency in the Cherokee more than tenfold that of Eurasia or rest of Native America.

Yet the most startling statistic concerns T haplotypes now verified in the Cherokee. At 27 percent, they constitute the leading anomalous haplogroup not corresponding to the types A, B, C, or D. Several of them evidently stem from the same Cherokee family or clan, although they have been scattered from their original home by historical circumstances. So much consistency in the findings reinforces the conclusion that this is an accurate cross-section of a population, not a random collection of DNA test subjects. No such mix could result from post–1492 European gene flow into the Cherokee Nation. To dismiss the evidence as admixture would mean that there was a large influx of Middle Eastern–born women selectively marrying Cherokee men in historical times, something not even suggested by historical records. Mitochondrial DNA can only come from mothers; it cannot be imported into a country by men.

If not from Siberia, Mongolia or Asia, where do our anomalous, non–Amerindian–

appearing lineages come from? The level of haplogroup T in the Cherokee mirrors the percentage for Egypt, one of the only countries where T attains a major showing among the other types. In Egypt, T is three times what it is in Europe.[45] Haplogroup U in our sample is about the same as the Middle East in general. Its frequency is similar to that of Turkey and Greece.[46]

But the most telling evidence in my opinion revolves around haplogroup X. This ranks as the third largest haplogroup. The only other place on earth where it is found at such a prodigious frequency is in the Druze, a people who have dwelt for thousands of years in the Hills of Galilee in northern Israel and Lebanon. The work of Liran I. Shlush and co-authors in 2009 proves that the Druze, because of a high concentration as well as diversification of X, is the worldwide source and center of diffusion for X, bar no time.[47]

In the diffusion of X, however, there is no starlike expansion driving it outward into Europe and to parts of the Middle East and beyond. The lineage spread in discontinuous fashion to the Americas and to places where it is found today such as North Africa, England, South America and Papua New Guinea. It must have arrived by sea. X survives at elevated frequencies in Canaan, New Guinea and Native North America, where it is found with T, U, K, J and other fellow travelers. Its presence is particularly noteworthy in the tribes situated around the Great Lakes and Saint Lawrence Seaway like the Ojibwe and Micmac — and in the Cherokee.

In conclusion, there may be a reason why Elvis claimed to be Jewish and Native American and loved Hawaii. Let us pick up the thread of ancient American Indians in the next chapter with a look at what their own sacred wampum belts and other records tell us about their origins and migrations. We will see that pre-literate Indians were well aware of their diverse roots before white men began to write their history for them. Only one white man, a Jew from the Ottoman Empire, tried to preserve the truth.

# Chapter 4

# *Ancient History of the Indians*

*To be master of any branch of knowledge, you must master those which lie next to it, and thus to know anything you must know all.*—Oliver Wendell Holmes, Jr.

Posterity has not been kind to Constantine Rafinesque. He discovered (or invented, depending upon your viewpoint) the Wallám Olum, regarded by many as the oldest specimen of Native American writing, and published it as part of *Ancient History of the Indians* in 1824.[1] His surveys and fieldwork first brought the mounds scattered through the Ohio Valley to the notice of the scientific world. He developed a theory of evolution predating Charles Darwin by twenty years. But if his name is mentioned today, it is likely to be in tones of disapproval and denigration. The subtitle of a book published in 2008, *Romantic Antiquarians and the Euro-American Invention of Native American Prehistory*, epitomizes the academic consensus on Rafinesque.[2]

Belonging to a formative period of American science, he made wide-ranging contributions to fields that were just emerging. With contemporaries celebrated still today, he published voluminously in geology, stratigraphy, archeology (Charles Lyell, *Principles of Geology*, 1830–1833), linguistics (Grimm's Law, 1819–1837), historical linguistics (Sanskritists A. W. and F. von Schlegel, and W. von Humboldt, founder of ethnolinguistics and linguistic psychology) and bardic literature (Grimm, *Deutsche Sagen*, 1816–1818). It was Rafinesque who petitioned Congress to establish the Smithsonian—which it did, in 1846. A bibliography of his published works contains 983 entries.

Constantine Samuel Rafinesque-Schmaltz was born to a family of Jewish merchants in the Ottoman Empire on October 22, 1783. Educated in Europe by private tutors, he read a thousand books by the age of twelve and studied fifty different languages by the time he was sixteen. From 1802 to 1805, he visited America. Returning to this country in 1815, he was appointed to a professorship at Transylvania University in Lexington, Kentucky. Here he founded a botanical garden, one of the first in the New World. Although details are sketchy, it is here that he seems to have acquired the incised wooden sticks he published as the *Wallam Olum*, or *Red Record*.

Following his Kentucky years, Rafinesque moved back to Philadelphia, where he lectured at the Franklin Institute, continued to travel and pursued his publishing career. Toward the end of his life, he suffered declining health and financial disaster. Altogether, he authored nearly a thousand publications on natural history, philology, banking, economics, the Torah,[3] world civilization and myth. Moreover, he was a skilled draftsman, surveyor, poet, and painter. Sadly, upon his death in September 18, 1840, the much-moved contents of his rented quarters were sold at a hastily arranged auction. His legacy was dispersed or disposed of.

Rafinesque writes in his *Travels* that he explored much of the Ohio valley on "penible foot." He tells us that while the primary object of his researches was the geology of the region, something else began to attract his interest: "I went on foot thro' the whole of Ohio by Chilicothe, Lancaster, Zanesville and Steubenville. It was near Chilicothe that I saw the first great monuments and pyramids or altars, of the ancient nations of N. America; they struck me with astonishment and induced me to study them" (58).[4] The next few pages in his diary show more interest in geology and botany than in ancient monuments, but at the conclusion of a trip to the Cumberland Mountains we read: "Thence I went to Pittsburgh thro' Brownsville. I delivered my map of the Ohio R. to Messrs. Cramer and Spear, who paid me 100 dollars for this labor. I went down the Ohio in a keel boat to Maysville. At Marietta I went to survey the ruins of the ancients town and monuments of the Talegawis" (60).

**Fig. 4.1.** Enamel miniature of Constantine Samuel Rafinesque in a garden before a stand of flowerpots, by William Birch, from the collection of Jacob Schiefflin, an associate. Print Collection, Miriam and Ira D. Wallach Division of Art, Prints and Photographs, The New York Public Library, Astor, Lenos and Tilden Foundations.

Marietta in Washington County, Ohio, with its Great Mound, is the site of one of the most celebrated earthworks in North America. The Great Mound (now a cemetery), Platform A (now a park), Platform B (buried under a public library), and Graded Way (a paved street leading to the river) are generally dated to the middle Woodland period of mound building (500 B.C.E. to 500 C.E.), while the flattened pyramids of the later Mississipian period are considered the farthest point of that culture's northeastward expansion.[5] Rafinesque studied the site before it was built over. Significantly, it is at this point that we first hear of the "Talegewas." From his initial contact with Shawnees to his surveys of Cumberland sites and finally the Great Mound in Marietta, Rafinesque had progressed in his thinking. He was now assigning tribal names to ancient monuments.

Until 1820, Rafinesque concentrated on publishing contributions to ichthyology, botany, zoology, geology, fossils, and geography. In the 1830s, however:

I began to study earnestly American history and Archeology, with the Ethnography and Philology of the American nations. I had seen within a few years the Oneidas, Mohigans, Lenaps, Choctaw, Cherokis, &c. This study led me much further than I expected, it became needful to review the whole of comparative philology and primitive archeology, in order to obtain satisfactory results. About this time began my great historical labors, and my collection of materials for Tellus or the history of the earth and mankind, chiefly in *America*; which I have in 10 years increased to nearly 100 books, mpt. [i.e., manuscript or handwritten] containing 5000 pages and 500 maps or figures. It is there I borrow for all my historical, ethnographical and philological works. I have since for that object explored all the public Libraries of Lexington, Washington, Philadelphia, New York and Boston. My first historical Essay or fruit of this labor, was my ancient history of Kentucky published in 1824 in Frankford [*sic*] as an introduction to Marshall's history of Kentucky. This however was far from being perfect, as I was not yet then sufficiently advanced in this difficult study; but

my account of the ancient monuments of N. American annexed to it is valuable, and has been translated into French [63, 73].

In a peripatetic career, Rafinesque became involved in soliciting subscriptions for his new botanical garden. He traveled all around the region as far as New Harmony in one direction and Harrodsburg in another.

> I went on horseback with Dr. Graham to survey ancient monuments on Salt R. where we dug fossil teeth. I surveyed a stone fort on Dick R. and other remarkable sites. My friend Mr. Ward took me to Cynthiana in a gig, where I surveyed other ancient monuments, and found a fine locality for fossils [74].

This passage is significant because it takes us to New Harmony, a Utopian community still under the sway of the Rappites, and marks Rafinesque's return to Angel Mounds, a Mississipian–era, 603–acre site near Evansville. It contains the only information we have concerning the provenance of the Wallam Olum.

Here is how he describes another visit to the area on which he meets the naturalist Jean-Jacques Audubon:

> At Hendersonville in Kentucky I left this boat too slow, and spent some days with Mr. Audubon, Ornithologist, who showed me his fine collection of colored drawings, which he has since published in England. Thence I went to Mr. Alvis who lent me a horse to follow the Ohio by land. I made an excursion to new Harmony on the Wabash, where dwelt then the sect of Harmonists, and since famous by the vain efforts of messrs. [Robert] Owen and [William] Maclure to establish communities. I saw there Dr. Miller who had a fine herbal and gave me some fine plants: we went together to herborize in the meadows. Crossing the Wabash, I entered Illinois and went to Shawaneetown on the Ohio; whence I made a rapid excursion to the mouth of the Ohio, returning to Hendersonville by Morgantown [56].

Shawneetown had neither geological formations nor flora and fauna to interest him. It was a shabby refugee town inhabited by the defeated members of Tecumseh's Shawnee party, being squeezed westward. Like most other Eastern Indians, they would end up across the Mississippi. However, it had one important citizen whom Rafinesque may have wished to consult. That was Tecumseh's brother, Tenskwatawa, the honored chief and seer. Known also as the Prophet, Tenskwatawa lived to a ripe old age on a succession of reservations allotted to the Shawnee and died in Indian Territory in 1837.[6] The cultural provenance of the Wallam Olum, which he acquired in New Harmony, then, appears to be Shawnee, not Delaware. It is an important point.

The connection with Tenskwatawa was raised previously by William Newcomb, an anthropologist.[7] Newcomb suggested that the Wallam Olum given to Rafinesque by the mysterious Dr. Ward was composed shortly before 1820 by the Prophet in an effort to revive Shawnee traditions and boost their spirits. He wrote that the whole "concoction" was "an account of a Golden Age which never was." We can detect more than a grain of condescension in this view.

We get a different reading from Mèssochwen Tëme, a member of the Eastern Lenape Nation:

> There is great controversy as to the authenticity of the Walam Olum due the circumstances surrounding its discovery. Constantine Rafinesque ... claimed that the Walam Olum was given to him in 1820 by a Dr. Ward. (Rafinesque failed to identify who Dr. Ward was, and even to this day all attempts to identify him have been unsuccessful.) Rafinesque describes the Walam Olum as a collection of "flat sticks with unidentified hieroglyphics of Indian design." In 1822, Rafinesque acquired a collection of verses in Lenape which he claimed went along with the sticks, although he was unable to translate the verses at the time. Rafinesque paid little attention to these items, and,

other than to copy the pictures and verses into a series of notebooks, made no further mention of them. In 1833, he had the verses translated by a man he identified only as John Burns. Rafinesque also claims to have found several centuries of additional Lenape history records and added these to the original Walam Olum. These records he too credited John Burns with the translations of. All attempts to identify John Burns have been unsuccessful — another of Rafinesques' phantoms.[8]

Whether fixed in prayer sticks, wampum belts, totem poles or on hides or birchbark, the underlying writing system is of the same nature and importance, what have been called pictograms or pictographs. These are symbols whose similarity to pre–Shang Chinese bone oracle script have been noted by Chinese scholar Chen Chi-Yun and others.[9] Lest anyone doubt the purpose and high standing of such records, let us look at a newspaper article that came to my attention at the time of writing. One of the keepers of Canadian aboriginal peoples' sacred wampum belts died on August 4, 2011. He was William Commanda. Born November 11, 1913, named Ojigkwanong, meaning Morning Star, he became chief of the Zitigan Zibi First Nation located two hours north of Ottawa in 1951, just like his great-grandfather Pakinawatik before him, who moved the tribe from the Montreal area in the mid–1800s and earned the Commanda. At the time of his death at the age of 97, Commanda "remained the carrier of three wampum belts of historic and spiritual importance: the Seven Fires Prophecy Belt, which represents choice, the 1700s Welcoming Belt, which represents sharing natural resources and values of the First Peoples with the newcomers, and the Jay Treaty Crossing Belt, which recognizes Turtle Island (North America) as a coherent entity."[10] A visiting chief from Tennessee, Paul Russell, who was invited into Grandfather Commanda's tent for a ceremonial exchange of gifts at the Circle of All Nations gathering in August of 1996, remembers that the chief of the Seven Algonquian Tribes said he had heard and read of the Wallam Olum. It was a version of the "old talk" of which he was the present keeper. Who will receive the belts with Commanda's passing is still being discussed, according to the tribe.

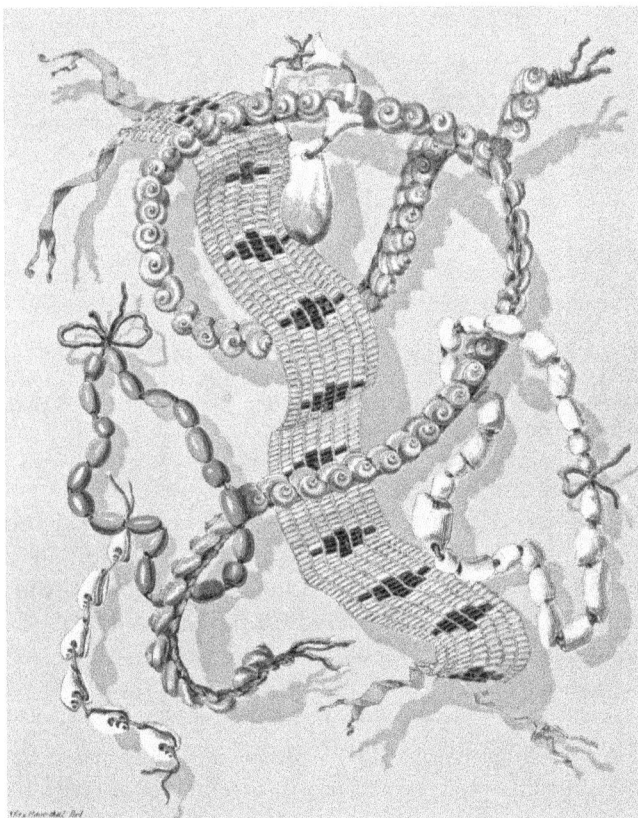

Fig. 4.2. Wampum, by Max Rosenthal, lithography by Louis N. Rosenthal, Philadelphia, about 1850. Emmet Collection, Miriam and Ira D. Wallach Division of Art, Prints and Photographs, The New York Public Library, Astor, Lenox and Tilden Foundations.

Fig. 4.3. Kee-an-ne-kuk (Foremost Man), Kickapoo, chief of the tribe "in the attitude of prayer, as he desired me to paint him," by George Catlin, published in *Souvenir of the North American Indians, as They Were in the Nineteenth Century* (1850). Rare Books Division, The New York Public Library, Astor, Lenox and Tilden Foundations.

A corrupt version of Rafinesque's "old talk" was published in *History of North and South America* many years after the Wallam Olum's discovery. As mentioned, Rafinesque's books and papers were auctioned off upon his death. The original prayer sticks were probably tossed out at this time, but the Wallam Olum notebooks were purchased by Professor S. S. Haldeman of the University of Pennsylvania. They disappeared until 1844, when they were sold to Brantz Mayer, a serious historian and collector in Baltimore. In 1846, he loaned Rafinesque's notebooks to the unsavory E. G. Squier, a newspaper editor who was preparing the Smithsonian series *Contributions to Knowledge*. Squier was an old foe who took credit for publishing many of the Kentucky and Ohio sites first surveyed by Rafinesque.[11] Soon the authenticity of the manuscripts would be contested by another enemy, Henry Schoolcraft, superintendent of Indian Affairs in the Northern Department for the U.S. government and self-appointed dean of American Indian studies. Out of professional jealousy, Schoolcraft had forbidden the foreigner Rafinesque to publish anything on Indian topics. His own curious *Algic Researches* (2 vols., 1839) is now generally acknowledged to have been the work primarily of his half–Ojibwe first wife, Jane Johnston Schoolcraft.

Rafinesque's riffled manuscripts disappeared again for ten years. Racist antiquarian Daniel Brinton acquired them and transcribed them in his book *The Lenâpé and their Legends: With the Complete Text and Symbols of the Walam Olum* (1885).[12] Some of Rafinesque's manuscripts, extremely disordered, are now kept at the American Philosophical Society in Philadelphia, where they continue to attract a sporadic stream of skeptical researchers.

In a passage in the last work he published, *The Good Book*, Rafinesque explains that he had long been collecting the signs and pictographs current among the North American

Indians: "Of these I have now 60 used by the Southern or Floridian Tribes of Louisiana to Florida, based upon their language of Signs— 40 used by the Osages and Arkanzas, based on the same — 74 used by the Lenapian (Delaware and akin) tribes in their WALAM OLUM or Records— besides 30 simple signs that can be traced out of the NEOBAGUN or Delineation of the Chipwas or Ninniwas, a branch of the last."[13]

From these remarks, we can see that after grappling with the problem of the language of the Wallam Olum for nearly twenty years, Rafinesque at last realized that it was not a writing system at all, but an aide-de-memoire. Like wampum belts, it could be interpreted in whatever language the speaker chose.

Of his acquisition of "Lenapian" records, Rafinesque writes:

> Having obtained, through the late Dr. Ward, of Indiana some of the original WALAM OLUM (painted record) of the Linapi Tribe of Wapihani or White River, the translation will be given of the songs annexed to each.... Olum implies a record, a notched stick, an engraved piece of wood or bark. It comes from ol, hollow or graved record. These actual olum were at first obtained in 1820 as a reward for a medical cure, deemed a curiosity; and were inexplicable. In 1822 were obtained from another individual the songs annexed thereto in the original language; but no one could be found by me able to translate them. I had therefore to learn the language since, by the help of Zeisberger, Heckewelder and a manuscript dictionary, on purpose to translate them, which I only accomplished in 1833. The contents were totally unknown to me in 1824 when I published my "Annals of Kentucky."[14]

These remarks prove that the Wallam Olum and what became the *Ancient History of the Indians* are two separate and distinct works. As for the former, from a note in Rafinesque's handwriting, on the title page of his MS. of 1833, it is clear that both he and "Dr. Ward" had examined the wooden sticks and they were not invented. It seems hard to believe anyhow that an original text comprising 687 words and 183 pictograms was fabricated: "This Mpt & the wooden original was [*sic*] procured in 1822 in Kentucky — but was inexplicable till a deep study of the Linapi enabled me to translate them with explanations. *(Dr. Ward).*" We are thus left to puzzle for all time over the meaning of Rafinesque's cryptic annotation "Dr. Ward."[15]

In order to make up our minds about the Wallam Olum we must decide on the basis of what survives, the transcriptions. Lenape expert David M. Oestreicher's recent "exposure" of an "outright fabrication ... elaborate hoax" proves nothing, since it rests on an analysis of a translation Rafinesque worked on and reworked and left incomplete.[16] The charge that Rafinesque translated from English into Lenape (rather than the other way around) is beside the point. Rafinesque's originals were a series of pictograms, not words. The "mistranslations" Oestreicher adduces have no other bearing than to reveal that Rafinesque thought the pictographic symbols of the Wallam Olum should appear in print in an Indian language, and that language must be Delaware.

The original Wallam Olum consisted of engraved and painted sticks that served the same purpose as wampum belts and contained authentic tribal origin and migration stories (fig. 4.2). George Catlin painted a picture of Kickapoo warrior Kee-an-ne-kuk reciting from a prayer stick of this exact description in 1830 (fig. 4.3), and we have seen that the Keetoowah priests maintained similar historical accounts ritualistically recited at the Cherokees' green corn festival each year. A contemporary witness to this form of native record keeping in 1827 writes:

> All treaties among the various tribes of Indians were confirmed by belts or strings of Wampum ... an important use of the Wampum was its substitution for writing.... Thus ... a treaty's terms could be kept in mind, and the various circumstances in the history of a nation could be recorded.... [A]

historian was set apart, whose office it was to record events, and to store up in his own mind the facts recorded by his predecessors, training in turn others to succeed him. Then some, and perhaps all tribes gathered themselves together at certain seasons, and the historian taking a piece of Wampum from the bag, repeated aloud its meaning, and passed to the person who sat next him, who followed his example, and thus each piece was recited at least annually by every member of the tribe, male and female.... The meaning of a belt is remembered by the Indian Tribes in this [the following] manner: The whole body frequently assemble, and being seated, each piece is passed from hand to hand, every person repeating the words as he takes it. Then again the color conveys some idea. A blood-colored hatchet readily gives an impression of something warlike, while white speaks of peace.[17]

A scrupulous and methodical scholar, Rafinesque used the most credible sources he could find for his *Ancient History of the Indians.* He was fortunate to have access to the last generation of traditional seers. In addition to Shawnees like Tenksquatawa, he consulted "Oneidas, Mohigans, Lenaps, Choctaw, Cherokis, etc."

*Ancient History of the Indians* begins with the origins of the human races, which Rafinesque believes all came from one. True to today's model of prehistory, Rafinesque holds that the earliest Europeans and American Indians came from the high plateaus of Central Asia. His starting point for human occupation of North America is about 10,000 years ago, a date not inconsistent with the theories of twentieth century Big Science. "The principal nations of the eastern continent which have contributed to people North America ... were: the Atalans and Cutans, who came easterly through the Atlantic ocean; the Iztacans and Oghuzians, who came westerly through the Pacific ocean" (10–11).

In agreement with modern-day theories, he divides the ethnic groups which colonized the Americas into two types, those who crossed the Atlantic and those who came "through" the Pacific. In his opinion, both these movements were accomplished by transoceanic or coastal navigation. Taking a holistic view, he adopts a relative chronology for the Atalans and Cutans that extends through four periods and seems far more natural than the Archaic-Paleo-Indian-Woodland demarcations of today: (1) from the dispersion of mankind to the first discovery of America, (2) to the foundation of the western empires, (3) to the Pelegian revolution of nature,[18] (4) to the invasion of the Iztacan nations, "including about twelve centuries," and (5) to the decline and fall of the Atalan and Cutan nations, "including about thirty centuries to the present time" (19).

Rafinesque's thinking on catastrophic events goes counter to the uniformitarianism that prevailed in his day. However, it is now generally agreed that ice masses melted very rapidly at the end of the last Ice Age. That was the first flood, about fourteen thousand years ago. In the aftermath of the Younger Dryas cold snap of 11,500 years ago the meltdown of Greenland occurred within as brief a period as 50 years, causing a second world flood. But the most precipitous events occurred in a third world flood about 5,000 B.C.E., possibly the single largest flood of the past two million years, according to numerous authorities.[19] Two large inland seas of glacial formation in North America called Lake Agassiz and Ojibway burst their natural dams and raised sea levels by up to eighty feet instantaneously amid large scale tsunamis and other phenomena never seen before. It appears that this corresponds to what Rafinesque calls Peleg's flood.

Rafinesque writes that after Noah's flood (perhaps about 12,000 years ago when the Ice Age ended),

The nations which peopled the western shores of the eastern continent, were the Gomerians [Cymmerians] in Europe and the Atlantes in Africa. The Atlantes formed a powerful empire in North Africa, which gave laws to many nations, such as the Lehabim or Lybians, the Phyuts [Phoenicians], Naphthuhim or Numidians, the Warbars, Barabars or Berbers, the Darans [Northwest Africa], the Garamans [Garamanni], the Corans or Guanches [Canary Islands and West Africa], &c.

In Europe, the Gomerians divided into many nations; those that occupied the sea shores were — 1st. the Pelasgians, scattered from Greece to Ireland, under the names of Tirasians in Thracia, Arcadians in Greece, Lestrigons in Sicily, Œnotrians &c. in Italy, Tubalans in Spain, Cunetans or Henetans in France; Termurians in Ireland, &c.; — 2nd. The Celts [K-Celts], or Pallis [P-Celts], who became Hellens or Yavanas in Greece, Meshekians, Ausonians and Ombrians in Italy, Sicules in Sicily, Gaels in France, Hesperians and Gadelians [Goidels] in Spain, Direcotians in Ireland, Cumrics [Cimbri] in Scotland, Feans or Feines in England, &c.; — 3rd. the Sacas, who became Magas in England, Saxons and Rasins in Germany, Etruscans or Tuscans in Italy, Sicanians in Sicily, &c.; — 4th. The Garbans, who became Cyclops [literally "ring-eyed"] in Greece and Sicily, Ligurians in Italy, Cantabrians in Spain, Bascans [Basques] in France, &c. [20].

All those nations were intimately connected in languages and manners. The Pelasgians [Sea Peoples] were bold navigators, and ventured to navigate from Iceland to the Azores and Senegal. The Azores, Madera, Canary and Capverd [Cape Verde] islands were then united in one or more islands, called the Atlantic Islands, which have given the name to the Atlantic ocean, and were first populated by the Darans [from the Maghreb] and Corans [Kora, Senegalese] or Western Atlantes. Iceland was called Pushcara [from Sanskrit elements *prush* "ice, frost" and *ku* "earth, land"] and was not settled, owing to the severe climate and awful volcanoes.

Numerous revolutions and invasions took place among those nations, until at last the Atlantes of Africa, united them all by conquest in one powerful empire, which extended over North Africa, Spain, France, Italy, part of Greece, Asia, &c.; and lasted many ages under several dynasties and emperors.

It was during the splendor of this empire, that America was discovered [i.e., perhaps about 8,000 B.C.E.?], by some bold navigators who were led by the trade winds, to the West Indies, in a few days from the Atlantic islands. They called them Antila Islands, which meant before the land, and America was called Atala or Great Atlantes.— Returning to the Azore land, by a north east course, they extolled the new country, and a great settlement was soon formed in Ayati or Ayacuta (Hayti,) [the island of Hispaniola] and the neighboring continent [North America] by the Atlantes.

The Atalans, or American Atlantes spread themselves through North and South America, in the most fertile spots, but the marshy plains of Orenoe [Orinoco River in Venezuela, Guyana and Brazil], Maranon [northern Peru], Paraguay, and Mississippi; as well as the volcanoes of Peru, Chili, Quito, Guatimala and Anahuac [Mexico], prevented them from settling those parts of the continent. Many of the subjects of the Atlantic empire, such as the Tubalans [descendants of Tubal (Gen. 10:2) believed to have populated the region south of the Black Sea from whence they spread north and east], Cantabrians, Cyclops and Cunetans [Canaanites], follow the Atalans in America, and become the Cutan nations [21].

Significantly, Rafinesque's story of the peopling of the Americas is much more complex and inclusive than the accounts provided by modern-day genetics (which, as we saw, may be flawed). At one point, he remarks, "Several other nations, besides the Atalans, Cutans, Iztacans, and Oghuzians, had reached various parts of America, before the modern Europeans, such as the Mayas or Malays, the Scandinavians, the Chinese, the Ainus [white race of Japan, perhaps the same as the Jomono culture in Peru], of Eastern Asia, the Nigritians or African negroes &c." (35).

Kutans, a word Rafinesque takes to mean "the men," from supposed roots *ku* "men" and *tu* "land," appear to be the same as our Keetoowahs. Ki-tu-wa in Cherokee (*kituwa, ani-giduhwa*) cannot be etymologized, nearly always a clue to foreign derivation. The connection with *ga-do-hi* "soil," *ga-du-hv* "town, and *ga-du* "bread" in Cherokee clarifies little, as these all have the same root. This can be traced, I suggest, to a word that appears in Hebrew as K-T-B בתכ, "write," hence "people of the writing." (The Cherokee language has no sound for b and renders it with *wa*.) Based on what linguist Mary LeCron Foster calls the Proto-Pelagian (Early Sea People) phylum of languages, the shared root is *$qw(a)$-

"build/construct," as seen in Egyptian *qs*, *qd*, Quechua *qorikánča*, *qósqo* "Cusco," Hindu *kúta* "walls and houses made in part or whole of cement or mortar," and Iberian *kuta*, "a fortification, a defensive wall." Foster seems to miss the possibility that Quechua itself, the Incas' name for "language," is related.[20] Hence, the Kutans represent a Mediterranean or North African element, those peoples we class together today as speaking Afro-Asiatic languages like Hebrew, Egyptian, Berber and Arabic, and having E, J, T and U genotypes, while the Atlantans are the Atlantic Coast peoples, speakers primarily of Indo-European languages, with typical lineages R1 and H.

> The Allegheny mountains were called Localoca [White Mountains]. Beyond them the country was called Great White Land, (Mahasweta-Bhumi of Hind:) and it became the seat of a great empire or the Western Atlantic Empire. This included of course Kentucky, but extended from lake Ontario in the north, to the Mississippi. The Atlantic shores called Locuta [White Places; cf. Greek *leukos* λεύ-κος, "white"], or Lachacuta [Seaside Places; cf. Latin *lacus*, "lake"] not settled, owing to their arid soil, lately emerged from the sea. This western empire may be called the Atalan empire....
>
> An intercourse was kept up more or less regularly between all the primitive nations and empires from the Ganes [Ganges] to the Mississippi. Crishna or Hercules, and Ramachandra, two heroes of India, visited Atala and the court of the western monarchs, which is called one of the heavens on earth, by the holy books of the east.
>
> The Atalans were civilized like the Atlantes; lived in towns; built houses of wood, clay and rough stones. They worshiped the sun and moon as emblems of the Deity, and built them circular temples. They knew geometry, architecture, astronomy, glyphic signs, or writing; the use of metals, agriculture, &c. They had public games, festivals, &c. Their food was flesh, fish, fruits, roots and corn which they brought from the east.
>
> At the time of their highest prosperity, a dreadful convulsion of nature happened in the Atlantic ocean, and other parts of the world, which is recorded in the oldest annals of many nations, the Hebrew, Hindoux, Chinese, Mexican, Greeks, Egyptians, &c. It appears to have been occasioned by simultaneous eruptions of volcanoes and earthquakes, which sunk, destroyed or convulsed many islands and countries, and among others the Atlantic land, of which the volcanic islands Azores, Madera, Canary and Capverd are the remains.
>
> In America, the Antilan lands were severed, the Carib islands formed, the Atlantic shores inundated by awful tides [tsunamis], and many countries sunk or altered. This cataclysm is the division of the earth under Peleg, the flood of Ogyges [in Greek mythology, the first king of Thebes] or Ogug, the sanscrit [*sic*] convulsion of the White sea or Atlantic ocean.— The terror occasioned by this phenomenon interrupted the intercourse between Europe and America. The Eastern Atlantes thought that the whole American continent had sunk, like the Atlantic and many Antilan islands [Antilles]: and the Atlantes of the interior of America became insulated and separated from the Atlantic empire [23].

From Rafinesque's naming of Atlantes emperors in these pages and his equation of Hercules with Krishna, not to mention speaking of the Ganges, it appears he is not following Greek or Roman sources, but ancient Indic and Hindu. He appends an impressive bibliography to the *Ancient History of the Indians*. Among some of the more unusual works cited in it are Maurice's *History of Hindostan*, Gebelin's *Monde primitif* (which contained one of the first histories of China), Boudinot's *Star in the West*, and "Marsden Sumatra and Malays."

When did Peleg's flood occur? A date of 1645 B.C.E. can perhaps be assigned to this cataclysm, which, as Rafinesque remarks, was much more than simply a flood, but which included earthquakes and volcanic activity. Radiocarbon dating of the ruins of a Minoan colony on the island of Thera or Santorini in the Mediterranean led Danish geologist Walter L. Friedrich and others to suppose that the eruption of a volcano on Thera around these years may have been the source of Solon and Plato's tale of an advanced island civilization destroyed overnight by the wrath of the gods, a story Solon got from Egyptian priests. But studies of ice cores from Greenland suggest that volcanic eruptions were hardly restricted to one island in the Mediterranean. They probably involved the entire Mid-Atlantic Ridge. In his account, Plato says that the entire Atlantic Ocean was so full of pumice and ash that it was closed to shipping for centuries afterwards.[21]

The Poverty Point earthworks site[22] on Bayou Macon in Louisiana overlooking the Mississippi floodplain is usually dated to 1700 B.C.E., about the same time as the Santorini disaster, a date coinciding with the heyday of the Atlans described by Rafinesque. Six concentric rings can be distinguished beneath an artificial mountain shaped like a thunderbird, a plan that resembles that of the capital city of Atlantis as described by Plato. The Portsmouth Works on the Ohio shore of the Ohio River, another one of the oldest mound sites, and visited more than once by Rafinesque, has the exact proportions and design of the so-called cross of Atlantis, or Celtic cross. Brian Fagan, who is certainly no friend of diffusionism, writes,

> The Poverty Point culture of the Lower Mississippi Valley and adjacent Gulf coast [and its] ... more than 100 ... sites form ten regional discrete clusters within natural geographical boundaries apparently grouped around a regional center.... Poverty Point's great horseshoe earthworks are a remarkable contrast to the humble base camps typical of the Eastern Woodlands at the time ... although foreshadowed in ... other enormous Archaic mounds.... Poverty Point took ... a building effort that would not be undertaken again in North America for another millennium ... the Poverty Point site and its associated lesser centers were the nexus of a vast exchange network that helped foster an unprecedented level of cultural complexity ... before the exchange system and the political forces that drove it collapsed.[23]

The function of Poverty Point's layout has puzzled archeologists, who debate whether its mounds were residential or symbolic. Noting the absence of platform constructions, Kenneth E. Sassaman, the contributor of the Poverty Point piece to a recent standard work of North American archeology, believes that such mound building not only required mathematical theory and "esoteric knowledge that was unlikely to be shared by all," but even the oldest Archaic mounds in the Southeast presuppose a long period of antecedents "constructed according to a common plan." He concludes that Poverty Point was a place of pilgrimage where "the entire regional landscape was telescoped down to the place of all origins." Thus, Poverty Point appears to satisfy in almost every respect Rafinesque's description of an American empire which perpetuated the mother culture but went into decline after it was separated from its European and North African counterpart by a cataclysm in the Atlantic Ocean.

The Atalans of North America became now divided in many states and nations, such as

The Apalans or Tlapalans [Appalachee], scattered from Florida to Virginia.
  The Timalans [Timuchua] from Texas to Guatemala.
  The Pocons or Locans [cf. Poconos, Poca, Pocasset, Pokagon, Poquoson "swampy"] from the Allegheny to Panama. These divided again into Golocas [Calusa], Conoys [of Maryland and Pennsylvania], Naticoes [Nanticoke], Zolacan [Tsalagi, or Cherokee], Lomashas, Popolocas, Wocans [Waccamaw of North Carolina and Virginia] and Poconchians [Poconos of New Jersey].
  The Corans [Coras of Mexico] from Missouri to Mexico.
  The Talegans [Talagewi] in Kentucky, Illinois, Ohio, Virginia, &c.
  While the Cutans of North America became also independent, and formed many nations, such as The Ayacutans of Hayti, &c.
  The Lachacutans of Cuba and Alachuans of Florida.
  The Yucutans [Yucatans] of Mexico, and Yucuyans [Lucayo] of Bahama.
  The Arohuans [Arawaks] of many islands and South America.
  The Tunicas of Louisiana, Tepenacas [Tepemaca] and Tononacas [Tonkawa] of Anahuac [Mexico].

The Panucans [Pawnee] of Texas, and Tanutans [Tanasi] of Tennessee.

The Catabans [Catawba] of Carolina and Florida.

The Cuzans [Coosa], Cuzadans [Cusseta] or Quezedans of Tennessee and Alabama.

All those nations were often contending for supremacy; except the Islanders, who became happy peaceful nations, whence the West Indies were called the Fortunate Islands when discovered again.

It appears that the Talegans [Taligewi] of the Ohio, and the Apalans [Appalachee] south of them, were two of the most powerful empires of that period. The Apalans had many provinces or tribes, such as the Apalachis, Apalehen, Tlapan, Alatamaha [Altamaha], Ichiti [Hitchiti, Lower Creeks, Seminole], Opalusas [Opelousa], &c.; and were often at war with the Talegans [24].

To comment on but one of these tribal names, Apalan reappears as the Appalachee, Paloosa and Palachee overrun by Muscogean invaders from the north. All these tribal names seem to mean "from (far) across the water." A more localized meaning in the sense of "on the other side of our river" seems ruled out by use of the name in a generalized way. Many of these tribes did not even live along a river or across a river. Nonetheless, they recognized kinship with one another. The root *apa* can be seen in Gr. απο (*apo*), "far from, down" and German *ab* and is another sign of Indo-European language roots. In 1734, Umphichi, "a Uchee chief from Palachocolas" went with the chief Tomochichi to England at the invitation of the founders of the Georgia colony. Tomochichi was described as a Yamacraw Indian, but he often lived with the "Palachocolas." "These Talegans, which we found named Talegawas or Alleghanys afterwards, had dominion over a large extent of country. Their several provinces were situated in the most fertile regions, such as Kentucky, Ohio, the Kenhaway [Kanawa, Conoy Indians] valley, the Illinois, the banks of lake Erie and Ontario" (24).

It is one of the riddles of American geography whether the Allegheny Mountains were named after the Taligewas or vice versa, since Taligewa in Algonquian languages means "the people over there," and Allegheny means "the over-there mountains." We may cut the Gordian knot by considering that Taliwa and Taligewa are both Algonquian terms for "People from Far Away" and "Land of the People from Far Away." At any rate, those were names given to the existing inhabitants by invading Algonquians. Perhaps the Mound Builders' own name for themselves was something like Apalan or Apalachi (those from the other side, viz. of the sea).

After some centuries, America was visited again by the nations of West Europe and Africa, but neither frequently nor in numbers. A casual intercourse was restored between the two continents. The Azores were visited as well as Madera, but not peopled owing to their active volcanoes; but the Canary or Hesperides islands were; from thence the navigators went to Cerne or St. Jago, and in 18 days to the Carib islands. — About this time the Carib, or Galibis, must have come to South America; they appear of Cantabrian [Celto-Iberian] origin. The great nation of Guarani [the most widely spoken language in South America] which extended all over Guiana, Brazil and Paraguay was of Daran [Mt. Atlas region in the Maghreb] origin and previous arrival.

When the Arcutans [Northern Cutans] or Fermurians of Ireland, were expelled by the Dannans [Tuatha de Danann of Irish myth? Greek Danaans?], a trible of Pallis or Gaels, (after many revolutions in the island,) they fled to Ayacuta, or Western Island of Hayti, and became probably the Arohauc [Arawak] nation [24]....

Rafinesque portrays the successors to the Atlantean civilization in America as weakened and fragmented. He says, however, that the Talegans still retained a united culture and identity. Evidently, these are the Mound Builders of the Adena period in American archaeology concentrated in the Ohio River valley (about 1500–200 B.C.E.). Typically, towns consisted of regional ceremonial centers surrounded by farming hamlets, and there was trade with distant lands. The Talegans later merge with the Cherokee.

Till then all the inhabitants of America had come from the east; but now a great invasion took place from the west or from Asia. Perhaps these Asiatic nations had crossed the ocean before the Pelegan or Ogugan [Ogygian] catastrophe [i.e., before about 1500 B.C.E.]. They are traced to the north west coast of America, and gradually came in contact with the Atalans and Cutans on the Missouri and in Anahuac [Mexico]. I shall call them Iztacan [Aztecan], from their ancestor Iztac [Aztec]....

The wars which happened in consequence of the Iztacan invasions, had the effect to annihilate some nations, and scatter many other, while several were subdued and incorporated with their conquerors. Kentucky was conquered by the Ulmecas [Olmecs], the Hausiotos [Northern Utes] and Taenzas [Taensa, Tensaw], three Iztacan nations. After the successive rule of these nations on the Ohio, the Siberian nations or Oguzian [about 200 B.C.E., Uigur Turk, Algonquian] tribes ... began to appear and wage war on the Iztacans and the Atalans, which they drove away to the south. The last remains of the former Atalans and Cutans, which can be traced to have escaped these conflicts and were still existing towards 1500, were the following: — The Wocons [Woccon and Waccamaw] in Carolina, the Homoloas [cf. Homosassa], Malicas [on De Bry's map, an Indian village located inland from the mouth of the St. Johns River in 1564], Appalachians and others in Georgia and Florida, the Conoys of Virginia, the Nanticoes of Maryland, the Catabas of Carolina, the Cahuitas [Cowetas] and Calusas of Alabama, the Tunicas of Louisiana, the Corans, Coroas or Escoros [Cora of Western Mexico] of the Missouri, Arkansas, Carolina [Corees], California and Mexico, besides many nations of Anahuac, &c.

Before the Christian era ... the Phenicians and Gadesiems [ancient Punic people of Cadiz, Celto-Iberian] traded to America: this continent was known to the maritime nations of West Europe and North-west Africa. The Numidians [Libyans] went there 2000 years ago, as well as the Celts; they frequented Paria [Paraguay] and Hayti principally. The Etruscans, a powerful nation of Italy, who settled there from the Rhetian Alps about three thousand years ago, went to America and wanted to send colonies there, but were prevented by the Carthagenians [about 500 B.C.E.]. This intercourse gradually declined, owing to the numerous shipwrecks and warlike habits of the Caribs, Iztacans and Oguzians, till the knowledge of America became almost lost or clouded in fables and legends [25–26].

In 1957, a small boy in Phenix City, Alabama, dug up a coin and took it to a local grocery store where he traded it for fifteen cents worth of candy. It was "probably minted in the Carthaginian colony in Iberia," according to epigrapher Gloria Farley. She compared it with a bronze coin from a noted cache in Georgia and dated it to around 146 B.C.E., the year of the destruction of Carthage by the Romans.[24] The Phoenicians are believed to have introduced a pre-coinage currency of flat sheet copper in the shape of ox-hides about 1000 B.C.E., a custom that survived into Roman times. This form of money was based in turn on the huge ox-sized ingots of copper ore mined and shipped back to Phoenicia from Cyprus, Bahrain, Spain, Arabia, Britain and elsewhere.[25] Wealth in ancient times was on the hoof. The bull is one of the earliest symbols of the Mother Goddess as increaser and bringer of plenty in Paleolithic and Neolithic societies. Archeologist Clarence B. Moore discovered numerous specimens of this ancient currency in 1913 in Copena mound sites in the Ohio valley (1000 B.C.E. to 500 C.E.) but could not determine what they were. He called them reel-shaped ornaments.[26] The custom of wearing money around one's neck as a sign of power is distantly echoed in the Washington peace medals shown in portraits of chiefs by Catlin and others.

During the decline of the Atalans, some fled to Anahuac [Meso-America] and South America, where they founded new empires, or civilized many nations, such as the Cholulans [Toltec] of Anahuac, and the Muyseas [Muzo of Colombia], Puruays [Paraguayan Indians], Collaos [Aymara of Andean area], Tiahuanacos [Incan] and Cojas [Quechua] of South America, who ascribe their ancient civilization to white and bearded strangers [Quetzalcoatl and feathered serpent myths]. Thus the ancient arts and sciences of North America were transferred to the South [26].

After this overview, Rafinesque next tells the history of the Iztacans, the Indians we know as Uto-Aztecan. He divides their chronicles into five periods of time: (1) from the Iztacan empire of Asia to the Iztacan invasion of the Ohio Valley about 700 B.C.E., (2) to the foundation of the Natchez empire around 200 B.C.E., (3) to the Oghuzian (Algonquian) invasion around 300 C.E., (4) to the expulsion of the Natchez around 800 C.E., and (5) to the present time, including the Chickasaw and Cherokee dominions in Kentucky, "about ten centuries" (27). All these are without doubt Asiatic Indians who settled in Mexico and established a succession of empires in the wake of the previously flourishing Vera Cruz culture (also called Olmec).

> Soon after the formation of the great Asiatic empires of Iran, Ayodhia, Vitora [Turkistan?], China, &c. another was founded near the Caspian sea, on the mountains of Caf or Caucasus and Vipula or Bactria [Afghanistan], which was successively called Aztula, (strong land) Aztlan, Tula, Tollan, Turan [Tarim] &c. The first monarch of it was Iztac–mixcoatl, (strong head snake:) He had six sons, who became the heads of as many nations; they were
>     Xelhua or Colhua, the father of the Colhuans [Cholula Indians], &c.
>     Tenoch or Tenuch, ancestor of the Tenuchs [Tenochas, Tenochtitlan], &c.
>     Olmecatl or Ulmecatl, ancestor of the Olmecans [Olmecs], &c.
>     Xicalancatl or Xicalhan, of the Zicalans [Huichols], &c.
>     Mixtecatl or Miztecatl, of the Tecas [Toltecs], &c.
>     Otomitl, ancester [sic] of the Otomis [Utes, Mexican Otomis north of Aztecs, also Otoe, a Siouan tribe in Wisconsin], &c.
>     From these have sprung all the Iztacan nations, scattered all over North America and part of South America.
>     Many other empires having begun to rise in the vicinity of Aztlan, such as those of Bali [Indonesia, perhaps Oppenheimer's Eden in the East?], Scythia [Russian steppes], Thibet, Oghuz [Lake Baikal area], the Iztacan were driven eastwards, north of China; but some fragments of the nation are still found in the Caucasus, &c. such as the Abians or Abassans, Alticezecs [Altai Turks], Cushazibs, Chunsags, Modjors, &c.
>     The six Iztacan nations being still pressed upon by their neighbours the Oghuzians, Moguls [Mongols], &c. gradually retreated or sent colonies to Japan, and the islands of the Pacific ocean; having discovered America at the peninsula of Alasca [Alaska, a Chinese word], during their navigations, the bulk of the nation came over and spread from Alasca to Anahuac, establishing many states in the west of America, such as Tula [Toltec], Amaquemeca, Tehuajo [Tewa, Tiwa, Tawa], Nabajoa [Navajo], Teopantla, Huehue, and many others.
>     After crossing the mountains, they discovered and followed the Missouri and Arkanzas rivers, reaching thus the Mississippi and Kentucky [26–27].

    With this description of a population expansion from Central Asia into the Americas, Rafinesque appears to draw on Indic histories and Aztec chronicles, harmonizing the two, with some knowledge of Chinese accounts. The people of the Tarim basin and surrounding mountains are greatly diversified and mixed: they include Uigur Turks, Afghans, Huns, Mongols, Chinese, Yueh-chi (in America, the Yuchi), Tibetans, Iranians, and even some Romano-Celtic peoples as shown by the presence of Tokharian, farthest eastern specimen of a *centum* or Western Indo-European language.

> The Olmecas or Hulmees ... came in contact with the Talegans, and not being able to subdue them, they left the country, invaded Tennessee, &c. The Winginas and Westoes of Carolina, as well as the Yamasees of Georgia, may be remains of these Olmecas [Ocmulgees]; but the bulk of the nation went to Anahuac with the Xicalans [Huichols], having made an alliance with them. The Xicalans were another Iztacan nation who had come down the Arkanzas; meeting on the Mississippi with powerful Atalans, such as the Corans, Talagans, &c. they joined the Olmecas in a confederacy against them.
>     After partly settling in Alabama, Tennessee, Georgia and Florida; they were both compelled to go to Anahuac, which they reached from the north-east, and where they became powerful in time.
>     The Otomis [Otomi, Oto Sioux "lechers"] were the most barbarous of the Iztacans, being hunters rather than cultivators; they had spread gradually from the Missouri to Anahuac, in the

rear of the Xicallans, under the names of Mazahuas or Mahas [Omaha], Huashashas or Ozages [Osage], Capahas [Quapaw] or Arkanzas [Arkansas], Otos or Huatoctas [Lakota], Minowas or Missouri or Ayowas [Iowas], Dareotas [Dakota] or Nadowessis [Nakota], Hautanis or Mandans, &c. They began to make war on the Talegans of Illinois, Ohio and Kentucky, and the Otos [Sioux] appear to have become the Sciotos of Ohio, the Huasiotes [Northern Sioux] of East Kentucky, and the Utinas of Florida.

The Colhuans [Cholulas] and Tenuchans [Tenochas as in Tenochtitlan] came the last on the Arkanzas, and settled the kingdoms of Tollan [Toltec word meaning "place of reeds," any city], Tula, Huehue, Copatta, &c. in that region. The Atalans and Iztacans were successively at war or in peace; but the Iztacans prevailed at last in West Kentucky, when all the Iztacans east of the Mississippi formed a confederary [*sic*] against the Atalans; this was the beginning of the Natchez dominion [about 200 B.C.E.].

During these struggles, many peaceful Atalans left the country and went to Anahuac, Ayati [Haiti], Ohohualco and South America, where they became legislators and rulers....

The Natchez empire, or confederacy of Iztacan nations, extended from the Ohio to Florida, and from the Alleghenies to the Mississippi; west of it were the kingdoms of Capaha, Pacaha and Coppatta, (perhaps only one,) also Iztacan. This confederacy consisted of five hundred towns, and many tribes, such as the Natchez, Taensas, Chitimachas [Chichimecs, Dog Men], Movila [Mobile, a Siouan tribe], Yasoos [Yazoo Indians] or Hiazus [Mexican people related to Toltecs], and many more. East of them were the Appalachian and Cataba confederacies, and north the Talegans who had retreated on the north side of the Ohio.

The nations forming this empire or league, were civilized and cultivators; they became polished by their intercourse with the Atalans, and borrowed many customs from them.— They worshiped the sun and fire; but did not build circular temples, erecting instead pyramids and high altars, generally of a square or angular form. Each tribe had a king, each town a governor; but the Natchez kings who were called Suns, had the supremacy over all. Agriculture and trade were well attended to. Many contentions and revolutions happened; but the Oghuzian invasion was the most fatal.

The Siberian nations, which had spread over the north of Asia at the dissolution of the Oghuzian empire, having come to America across the Behring Strait, sought milder climates by traveling south, and coming in contact with the civilized but less warlike nations of anterior origin, began to wage war over them, and drive them gradually further south, towards Florida and Anahuac [27–29].

Rafinesque makes a broad distinction between Atlantic peoples who built round fortresses, as in many of the Adena monuments, and Asiatic tribes concentrated in Mexico who favored pyramids and square temples, as in the Hopewell and Mississipian periods that followed Adena. The Asiatics seem to have settled in a more spread-out fashion and were more often nomadic while the Atlantic people concentrated themselves in towns. Rafinesque postulates two waves of invasion by Central Asian peoples: (1) Turks he calls Iztacan representing the races of the Tarim Basin, Chinese Turkistan, and Mongolia, corresponding approximately to the Uto-Aztecan tribes of modern-day anthropology, and (2) the Oghuzians, who represent other Mongolian and Siberian tribes, including the Algonquian people.

At the Oghuzian invasion [about 300 C.E.], the Taencas, a Natchez tribe, occupied West Kentucky, the Huasiotos [White or Northern Sioux] were in East Kentucky, and some Talegans still held the banks of the Ohio, &c.

The Cherokees or Zulocans, an Atalan nation dwelling west of the Mississippi, being driven by the Oghuzians, came to Kentucky and Tennessee, and settled at last after many wars in the mountains of Carolina, where they became a nation of hunting mountaineers, and gradually destroyed the Hausiota [Iztacan, literally Northern Ute] nation of the Cumberland mountains [29].

The mention of Zulocans (Zolacans) places the entry of the Cherokees in the East at about 300 C.E. in Rafinesque's chronology. They are Caucasian Indians (Atlans) from West of the Mississippi, he says, and were pressed eastward into the Ohio valley by the Asiatic Mexican Indians. Rather than Eshelokee, the Greek colony and Keetoowah's own name for themselves

(Chapter 1), Rafinesque uses a variant of the surrounding tribes' name for them, Tsalagi, in Choctaw trade jargon, *Choloki*, which he relates to the suffix Loca ("white"). Their movement at this time agrees with Choctaw migration stories, which maintain that the Cherokee preceded the Choctaw, Creek and other Muscogean tribes in fleeing Mexico after a political convulsion and eventually crossing the Mississippi River into the eastern parts of the country.

> The Shawanees ["Southerners"], an Oghuzian [Algonquian] tribe, came then in contact with the Natchez and expelled them from Kentucky, which they occupied for a long time.
> The Talegans north of the Ohio, were partly destroyed or driven south, through Kentucky, to join the Apalachian, or down the Mississippi towards Louisiana and Mexico.
> The Natchez confederacy declined gradually, becoming divided into several independent nations, such as the Taenas, Chitimachas [Chichimecs in Louisiana], Alabamas [Alibamu, removed now to Texas], Coosas [Creek], Cahuitas or Cowetas [Koasati], Winginas, &c. spread from Louisiana to Carolina, which however did not wage war together, but were often united against the Cherokees, Catawbas and Oghuzian nations.
> The great Otomi [Lakota] nations, extending from the Missouri to Anahuac, divided into numerous tribes, such as the Osages or Washashas, Missouris, Ottos [Oto], Mazahuas, or Omahuas [Omaha], Capahas [Quapaw] or Arkansas, Mandans, &c.: the Osages, Missouri and Arkanzas, penetrate as far as West Kentucky, the banks of the Wabash, &c.
> A succession of wars and contentions take place between the numerous nations of various stocks scattered in North America, by which they are weakened and prevented from improving their civilization, or uniting against the encroachments of the Europeans.
> The Spanish, French, and English, after the discovery of America by Columbus, settle in North America, and in three hundred years occupy all the land from Canada to Mexico, except a few small spots, acquiring possession of it by various means, conquests, cessions or purchases [aided, as we now know, by plague and disease] [30].

Rafinesque creates a synthesis of Indian history focusing on a succession of antagonistic cultures, beginning with an Atlantic civilization and a less settled one emanating from Central Asia and Siberia. The old becomes new. Tribal identity goes through a number of sea-changes. The Cherokee persist as the oldest group, heirs of the Atalans, Kutans and Talegans. Many anthropologists and historians today believe that the whole dynamics of the Southeast region revolves around the Cherokee and their allies pushing out the Siouan tribes, "the most barbarous of the Iztacans." American Indian history itself in fact revolves around the Cherokee, the bearers of the standard of civilized ways. When the Cherokee first entered Arkansas and Indian Territory in the 1830s, delegation after delegation complained to Congress about the Quapaw and Osage, whom the Cherokee called "wild Indians."

In support of Rafinesque's point about confusion of tribes, the Lumbee Indians of Robeson County, North Carolina, combine today several different linguistic and tribal stocks, including Tuscarora, Eno, Occaneechi, Coharie, Waccamaw, Woccan, Cherokee, Cheraw, Catawba, Yuchi, Shakori, Nottoway, Nansemond, Saponi, and Meherrin.[27] A similar history has been suggested for the Saponi-Haliwa on the North Carolina-Virginia border. The Iroquois Confederacy unites six tribes. The Creek Confederacy brings together three different language groups, Muscogeans, Hitchiti and Yuchis.

The expulsion of the Huichols by the Toltecs in Mexico seems to correspond not only to the beginnings of Southeastern Indians chiefdoms replacing the older Natchez empire during the Mississippian Period (500–1500 C.E.), but also the civilizations that flourished in the American Southwest beginning with the Hohokam and ending with late Puebloan (about 300–1350 C.E.). In both regions Mexican influences brought about great changes. We will follow the thread of these events in the chapter on America's "Middle Ages."

Rafinesque is the first historian to write about the rise and fall of Native American civilizations in a credible, complete and coherent manner. His compilation of Indian history from tribal informants supplemented by Aztec chronicles, Hindu histories and other sources agrees with the picture of prehistory slowly emerging from archeological, ethnographic and genetics research. The first inhabitants of the Americas, the Mound Builders—Rafinesque's Atlans and Kutans—came from Europe, North Africa, the Mediterranean and the Middle East across the Atlantic, not from Central or Western Asia across the Bering Strait. Two subsequent waves did arrive from that direction. They correspond to the influx of Uto-Aztecan peoples (Iztacans), originally from Central Asia, who built empires in Mexico and conquered the "white Indians" of the Atlantic and Gulf shores, followed by the fierce Algonquians or Uigur (?) Turks (Oghuzians), who made war on both their predecessors.

In agreement with the dispersal of some Atlans southward after the arrival of Algonquians, the eighteenth-century Indian agent William Johnson reported that the Delaware Indians told him there were other foreign people besides themselves in America in former times: "It is a prevailing opinion among them that Florida had been inhabited by white people, who had the use of iron tools. Blackhoof [a Shawnee chief] affirms that he has often heard it spoken of by old people, that stumps of trees, covered with earth, were frequently found, which had been cut down by edged tools."[28]

Endemic warfare goes far towards explaining why certain haplogroups perished in the Americas—or at least why they became hidden in the gene pool. It is usually male haplogroups that are extinguished as new invaders come in. Gradually, male haplogroup Q dominates the ruling pedigrees throughout the Americas.

This chapter has examined the ethnographic theories of Constantine Rafinesque against a backdrop of his contact with local Native American sources of information. Combined with his firsthand survey of archeological sites and encyclopedic learning, he was uniquely situated to publish his outline of Indian history in 1824. But it was only part of the whole. One critical component, the Wallam Olum, has been shown to be a Shawnee version of authentic Algonquian annals, not Delaware, or Lenape. An unbiased reading of Rafinesque has to open our eyes to striking parallels with the evidence from genetics, the final arbiter he could hardly have dreamed of.

Rafinesque turns out to be correct about many things. Was he also right in thinking there was contact between the surviving "white Indians" with visitors or new colonists from their trans–Atlantic original homelands? Intriguingly, the indigenous people on American shores were first called "savages," a word whose original meaning is "stranded, to be saved, rescued." Let us continue into "America's Middle Ages."

# Chapter 5

## *America's Middle Ages*

*Anyone undertaking to set himself up as judge in the field of truth and knowledge is sure to be shipwrecked by the laughter of the gods.* — Albert Einstein

Archeology usually presents American Indian prehistory in large periods unfolding in a seemingly unchanging fashion across time and space. But a recent bestseller, *1491: New Revelations of the Americas Before Columbus,* has dramatically altered many people's thinking. Charles C. Mann portrays sophisticated and flourishing civilizations that put medieval Europe in the shade. Pre-Columbian Indians not only developed advanced societies with ingenuous technologies and beautiful works of art but also shaped the land and left their mark on the very geography of North and South America. It was only the ravages of European disease[1] and consequent decimation of Indian populations that created in the minds of the invaders an impression of savagery and primitiveness, one perpetuated by scientific investigations down to our day.

It is as though an "American Middle Ages" does not exist, as Barry Fell noted when he wrote that "fragments of pottery have been made the basis of our interpretation of history." He continued, "Adhering naively to the idea that all new developments are brought from another place by some footloose peoples, we have created a host of different fictitious "Peoples" whose complex comings and goings fill the pages of American archeology texts but tell us absolutely nothing about the languages or places of origin of any one of them!"[2]

With the benefit of Rafinesque's outline of events, let us take a closer look now at some of the native nations inhabiting that chasm of the past, including the Real People or Cherokees. Rafinesque continues his *History of the Ancient Indians*:

> Something like a chronological order can be now introduced. The records of the Mexicans, the traditions of many Oghuzian nations [Uighur Turkic, i.e., the Algonquians' Wallam Olum], and the annals of the Europeans, afford sufficient materials for a complete history; but I must be very brief.
>
> Nearly two thousand years ago [200 B.C.E.], great revolutions happened in the north of Asia; the Oghuzian empire was severed, and a swarm of barbarous nations emigrating from Tatary [Mongolia] and Siberia, spread desolation from Europe to America. In Europe they nearly destroyed the powerful Roman empire, and in North America they subverted many civilized states.
>
> Several of those Oghuzian nations, driven by necessity or their foes to the north-east corner of Asia, came in sight of America, and crossing Berhing [*sic*] Strait on the ice, at various times, they reached North America. Two of them, the Lenap [Delaware] and Menguy [Iroquoian tribes], seeking milder climates, spread themselves towards the south; while another, the Karitit [Eskimo], which came after them, spread on the sea shores from Alaska to Greenland, and some others settled on the north-west coast of America [Haida, Tlingit, et al.] [31].

These events correspond to the first period of the Algonquian people's history as presented in the restored Wallam Olum of David McCutchen. There we read of a multitude "ten thousand strong" crossing "the frozen sea at low tide in the narrows of the icy ocean"

(III, 17).[3] Twenty-four chiefs' reigns pass as they settle for several generations in Turtle Island (North America), migrate to the Snake (Enemy) River (present day Washington and Oregon, where there are still at least two Algonquian–speaking tribes, the Yurok and Wiyots of California, that were apparently left behind) and make their way across the interior to emerge in the Mississippi River valley, defeat the Talegans and settle with them on the Wabash River in Indiana.[4] McCutchen calculates this span of time as one of 500 years on the basis of 13⅔ years per chief. If we take Rafinesque's starting point for the invasion to be around 200 B.C.E., this brings us to around 300 C.E. for the Algonquian army's progression to the eastern shore of the Mississippi. Here the Algonquian armies conquer the Natchez (Iztacans) and Talegans (Atlans mixed with Iztacans). Let us see how McCutchen's chronology compares with Rafinesque's:

The Lenaps [Lenni Lenape, or Delaware Indians, principal Algonquian tribe in the U.S.] after set-tling some time on the Oregon and Multnomah rivers, crossed the Oregon mountains, and follow-ing the Missouri, fighting their way through the Ottomies [Sioux], &c. they reached the Mississippi, nearly at the same time with the Menguys [Iroquois], who had come north of the Mis-souri. They found the powerful Talegans in possession of Illinois, Ohio, Kentucky, who opposed their progress and cut off the first party that ventured to cross the Mississippi. A long war ensued [hence the name Kentucky meaning "Dark and Bloody Ground"], in which the two Oghuzian nations [Algonquians and Iroquois] joined in a confederacy against the Talegans, and succeeded after a long struggle to drive them away to the south.

When the Lenaps had defeated the Talegans, they had to contend with the Natchez of West Ken-tucky, the Huasiotos [Northern Sioux] of East Kentucky, the Sciotos [Siouan] of Ohio, besides many remaining branches of the Atalans, Cutans [of Eastern Mediterranean and Middle Eastern origin], &c. scattered in North America, which they vanquished, destroyed or drove away, occupy-ing all the country from the Missouri to the Allegheny mountains; while the Menguys [Iroquois] settled north of them on the lakes.

The Lenaps were hunters, but lived in towns, and became partly civilized by the prisoners and slaves that they made.—They began to cultivate corn, beans, squashes, tobacco, &c. Their hunters having ventured across the Allegheny mountains, discovered a fine country, not occupied by any nations, in Maryland and Pennsylvania. Many were induced to remove to that country, where they should be more distant from their southern foes.

A settlement was made east of the mountains, and the great Lenapian nation became thus divided into many distant tribes, independent of each other; but connected by a similarity of lan-guage, religion, manners, and acknowledged origin.

The principal of these tribes, which thus became independent nations, were the Chinus [Chi-nook] on the Oregon, the Anilcos and Quiguas on the Missouri, the Utawas [Ottowa] and Miamis north of the Ohio, the Shawanees or Massawomees in Kentucky, the Mohigans and Abnakis in New England, the Sankikans in New Jersey, the Unamis and Minsis [Munsee] in Pennsylvania, the Powhatans in Virginia, the Nanticoes [Nanticoke Indians] in Maryland, the Chipeways [Chippewa, Anishnabe, Ojibwe] and Clistenos [Sauk or Fox?] on the upper Mississippi, &c.

A similar division took place in the Menguys, and the independent nations sprung from them, were the Hurons or Wyandots near lake Huron, the Eries or Erigas on Lake Erie in Ohio, the Tus-cororas in Kentucky, the Senekas [Seneca], Mohawks [Iroquois], Cayugas, Oneidas on the St. Lawrence, &c. That portion of the nation which remained west of the Mississippi [e.g. Blackfoot and Cheyenne, two Algonquian–speaking Plains tribes], became mixt [*sic*] with some Otomian [Sioux] tribes, and formed the great Darcota [Dakota] nation, since divided into many tribes, such as the Sioux, Assiniboils [Assiniboine], Tinton [Teton Sioux], Yanctons [Yankton Sioux], &c.

The Oghuzian nations had united for a long while against their southern enemies; but many Menguy tribes became jealous of the Lenaps when they saw them possessed of the best lands and growing very powerful. Dissentions occurred between the various tribes east and west of the [Allegheny] mountains. The Senekas and Mohawks begin to quarrel with the Mohigans and Lenaps. They endeavour to excite wars between them and the Cherokees. Several wars occur between the Lenaps and many Menguys, in which the Wyandots [Hurons] and Erigas [Erie, or Neutral Indians] take no part [32–33].

This is one of the first explicit mentions of the Cherokee. They are presented as a third force in a power play between the Iroquois (Menguy) and Lenni Lenape, the core Algonquian nation, showing they had probably broken with their allies the Iroquois for the second time. A Lenape legend tells how the Iroquois stirred up a war against the Cherokee by killing a Cherokee child and leaving a Lenape war club on the scene as evidence. This tale may relate to those distant days.

That the Iroquois, like the Cherokee, lived once on the other side of the Mississippi is apparent from several sources. One of these, a Tihanama Indian story, relates that the Iroquois (wherever they may have come from) encountered the Lakota Indians for the first time on the grassy prairies across the Mississippi. "Who are you," the Iroquois asked them. The Lakota replied, "We are hunters of the buffalo. Who are you?" "We are hunters of men," said the Iroquois, challenging the Lakota warriors to a fight on the spot. "You are not men," said the Iroquois, after winning the contest, "but women." They split the Lakota warriors' noses, the mark of an adulterous woman, and sent them on their way. "Tell your people to send men the next time," they said.[5]

The Cherokee (Eshelokee), then, crossed the Mississippi about the same time as the Algonquians and Iroquois, around 300 C.E. All these tribes take up residence in the area along the Ohio vacated by the Talegans, Natchez (Iztacans) and remaining eastern Siouan tribes (Otomi).

In McCutcheon's version of the Wallam Olum, we read that before crossing the Mississippi, somewhere along the south bank of the Missouri, the Algonquians encounter a foreign tribe they call the Stonies under a chief named Strong Stone. The latter is depicted with an angular headdress of five horns unlike any other in the Red Record. "Strong stone" is an apt description of metal. The prominent headdress could represent a Greek hoplite's stallion crest. This style distinguished the Eshelokee warrior and seems later to have been imitated by certain local Plains tribes like the Pawnee and Poncas. Known as a porcupine roach, it is a prized part of Indian regalia today. Hardly any leading man or fancy dancer at a powwow would be without one.

Recall from Chapter 1 that the Cherokee come into conflict with the Iroquois west of the Mississippi and as a concession abandon their non–Indian language and adopt Mohawk. At this stage of their migrations in Rafinesque's history, the Cherokee (Stonies) had clearly already joined with the Iroquois and become Iroquoian–speaking. The Cherokee form part of the alliance of Indian nations that then conquer the Moundbuilders (Talegans).

Meanwhile the Shawanees of Kentucky [a division of Algonquians or Lenapes] have many quarrels and wars with their neighbors; they drive away the Tuscaroras to Carolina, and some Erigas to Florida. They wage war by turns with the Natchez, Tapoussas [Opelousas], Cherokees, and Appalachians to the south, with the Catabas, Wocons and Westos to the east, the Capahas [Quapaws], Ozages, &c. to the west. Not satisfied with the possession of Kentucky, they extend their conquests and settlements as far as lake Ontario to the north, in Carolina and Georgia to the south. The Cumberland river became the centre of their settlements. They were hostile to all their neighbours except those of Lenapian origin, and being in contact with many more than any other branch, were considered as the bulwark of that nation [33].

We are now in the second period of Lenape history, comprising thirty-six reigns of their chiefs from their settlement along the Ohio to a figure known as Lekhihiten the Author, in other words about 800 C.E. The Cherokee, Iroquois and Lenape thus inhabit the former territory of the Mound Builders for about 500 years. Another thirty-six generations will pass until the Lenape arrive in their ultimate home along the Delaware River. A special black wampum belt was made to commemorate this event. When the beads were counted in historical times, the belt showed that the Lenape arrived in their easternmost home-land in 1396.[6] Eastern North America was swept by many new migrations beginning about 1375.[7]

Let us continue with our comparison between McCutcheon and Rafinesque:

In order to resist their numerous enemies, they formed a general confederacy extending from the Lakes to Florida, which soon became formidable even to their former allies, under the name of Massawomees or Wassawomees. The branches of this great alliance were known by the names of Sakis [Sauk] and Kicapoos [Kickapoos] in the west, Uchees [Yuchis] and Chowans [Chowanac] in the east, Satanas in the north, Savanas in the south, &c.

The Utawas [Ottawa] were a branch of the Lenaps, settled north of the Lakes, and holding supremacy over the Northern Lenaps; being driven south of the lakes, by their wars with the Men-guys [Iroquois], they assumed a superiority over the Miamis of Ohio, whom they defeated in bat-tle; but they had more difficulty in their contentions with the powerful Shawanees [*sic*]. A long war was the result; the Utawas conquered part of central Kentucky, and compelled at last the Shawanees to acknowledge [26] them as superiors and entitled to hold the great council fire in the west, as the Lenaps did in the east.

During this struggle many revolutions had occurred around Kentucky. The Conoys had become powerful in the Kenhaway [Kanawa] valley, and the Illinois on the Wabash. The Shawanees enter into an alliance with them. The Chicasaws begin to grow powerful in the south-west, and wage war with the Shawanees, &c.

The supremacy of the Utawas was acknowledged gradually by all the Lenapians west of the mountains, and the chief of that tribe was considered as the greatest chief [later, Pontiac, an Ottawa, who united the same tribes]. They settled in many parts of lake Huron and Michigan, on the Mississippi, and left Kentucky to the Shawanees.

Towards the discovery of America by Columbus in 1492, the situation of the nations residing in Kentucky or the immediate neighbourhood was nearly as follows:

The Massawomees or Shawanees had possession of the greatest part of Kentucky, the Cumber-land valley in Tennessee, nearly all the banks of the Ohio, and they had settlements or colonies in Illinois, Georgia, Carolina, Gennessee [Tennessee], &c. They had nearly one hundred towns, many of which very populous.

The Chicasaws claimed by conquest the west of Tennessee and Kentucky, and resided southerly of the Ohio.

West of the Mississippi near Kentucky, the most powerful nations were the Capahas [Quapaw], Ozages, Anileos [Fox], Quiquas [Kickapoo], &c.; the two last of Lenapian origin, and extending east as far as the Wabash.

In Ohio were the Miamis, Erigas [Erie], Tongorias, &c.

In Virginia, the Conoys, Monacans, Chugees or Ichias [Yuchis], &c.

On the St. Lawrence, five tribes of Menguys—the Senekas, Mohawks, Oneidas, Cayugas and Onondagos, had united into a league [Iroquoian Confederacy], which soon became formidable (under the name of Iroquese [*sic*] or Five Nations,) to all the Oghuzian nations.

On the Atlantic shores the Lenapian tribes had divided into numerous nations, often at war with each other for supremacy or dominion [34–35].

The millennium between 300 and 1300 C.E. witnesses the breaking off of the Iroquois to migrate onward to their historical locations concentrated in Upper New York State along with the formation of the Shawnee dominions southward and the Lenape advance eastward. Sometime during this era, corresponding approximately to the Mississippian Period of archeologists, the Cherokee break for the second time with the Iroquois. The Cherokee migrate to the southern Appalachian mountains in East Tennessee, where they wrest a new homeland for themselves from the assorted Muscogean, Yuchi and Natchez tribes inhabiting the area.

The Muscogean tribes apparently preceded the Algonquians in settling the Eastern U.S. as part of a wave of Iztacan invaders from the south following an even earlier Natchez migration. As Rafinesque writes,

When the Toltecas of Mexico drove away the Xicallans [Huichols, about 100 B.C.E.], the bulk of that nation came to the Mississippi, and settled on both sides of it, above the Natchez; many nations have sprung from that stock, all intimately connected in language and manners, such as the Chicasas [Chickasaw], Choctaws [Choctaw], Yazoos or Tapousas, Muscolgees [Muskogee], Cofachis [Cofitachique], &c. spreading north and east of the Natchez, they formed a bulwark between them and the northern invaders; the Chicasas [Chickasaws] extended their conquests to the banks of the Ohio in Kentucky.

Horatio Bardwell Cushman's *History of the Choctaw, Chickasaw and Natchez Indians* was first published in 1899. The son of missionaries, its author spent his entire life among the Choctaws, first in Mississippi and then in Oklahoma. Because of the work's long period of gestation, its length, its depth of scholarship and the numerous interviews it contains with chiefs and other leading men of the nation, it is prized not only as an original source for Choctaw history but also as a valuable introduction to southeastern Indians in general, one that could only have emerged from a single opportune moment in history. Cushman derives the origins of the Choctaws from Mexico. The Choctaw and Chickasaw long ago crossed the Bering Strait ("'Big Waters' far to the northwest") in boats ("canoes") and migrated down the Pacific coast "the same as the Cherokees," he says.[8] (We can assume these were not the Eshelokee but an Asiatic people they later fused with, the source of lineages A, C and D.) Like the Cherokee and Creek Indians before them, the Choctaws were forced out of Mexico by political upheavals, which we can now identify as the struggle between the Huichols and Toltecs about 200 years before the Common Era. The Choctaw crossed the Mississippi River "with a force of ten thousand warriors" and followed their "warrior-prophet" Chahta to Nanih Waiya, the mound near present-day Philadelphia, Mississippi, which they regard as their mother town (p. 18).

What kind of Indians lived in the territory the Choctaw and Chickasaw carved out for their new home? According to their traditions, reports Cushman, as confirmed by excavations of bones in Tennessee, it was a "race of white giants":

> The tradition of the Choctaws ... told of a race of giants that once inhabited the now State of Tennessee, and with whom their ancestors fought when they arrived in Mississippi in their migration from the west, doubtless Old Mexico. Their tradition states the Nahullo (race of giants [literally, wizards]) was of wonderful stature; but, as their tradition of the mastodon [which used to be found on the Great Plains], so this was also considered to be but a foolish fable, the creature of a wild imagination, when lo! Their exhumed bones again prove the truth of the Choctaws' tradition [151].

These giants could have been Rafinesque's Atlans.

Cushman then recounts the discovery in 1880 at a burial mound site near Plano, Texas, of human bones "of enormous size ... the femoral bones being five inches longer than the ordinary length, and the jaw bones ... so large as to slip over the face of a man with ease." Cushman goes on to identify them with the older occupants of North America called Allegewi or Taligewi (Talegans). Many historians, moreover, speculate they were the builders of the Adena mounds.

As for the Chickasaw, Cushman notes that they have no record of their history before the colonial period, although it is assuredly "the same as the Choctaws, being one tribe and people until the division made by their two chiefs Chikasah and Chahtah many years after their arrival and location east of the Mississippi River" (p. 358). Of the Natchez, Cushman records that they, "if tradition may be believed, also came from Mexico where they had lived for centuries" (p. 440).

A story was told by the Comanches in 1857:

Innumerable moons ago, a race of white men, ten feet high, and far more rich and powerful than any white people now living, here inhabited a large range of country, extending from the rising to the setting sun. Their fortifications crowned the summits of the mountains, protecting their populous cities situated in the intervening valleys. They excelled every other nation which was flourished, either before or since, in all manner of cunning handicraft — were brave and warlike — ruling over the land they had wrested from its ancient possessors with a high and haughty hand. Compared with them the palefaces of the present day were pygmies, in both art and arms. They drove the Indians from their homes, putting them to the sword, and occupying the valleys in which their fathers had dwelt before them since the world began. At length, in the height of their power and glory, when they remembered justice and mercy no more and became proud and lifted up, the Great Spirit descended from above, sweeping them with fire and deluge from the face of the earth. The mounds we [i.e., the speaker Chief Rolling Thunder and his Spanish listener] had seen on the tablelands were the remnants of their fortresses, and the crumbling ruins that surrounded us all that remained of a mighty city.[9]

The word Nahoolo or Nahullo "is now emphatically applied to the white race and no other.... The Nahullo were of white complexion, according to Choctaw tradition, and were still an existing people at the time of the advent of the Choctaws to Mississippi," concludes Cushman (p. 153). In agreement, the Indian trader Adair often refers to the *Nani Ishtahoolo* as departed white ghosts vested with spiritual powers whose descendants were priests and magicians. Their cries and magic spells could still be heard in the mounds like those at Ocmulgee.[10] These references contribute to the suspicion that the "Indians" who preceded Asiatic tribes from Mexico were, as we would say today, Caucasian.

The evidence for ancient Greeks in America is sparse, but compelling (Appendices G, H). Traces of the Greeks may explain the migrations of the Eshelokee through Mexico and are borne out by Keetoowah traditions, as we have seen. It is clear that after the Cherokees' exodus with the Huichols from Toltec Mexico they lived for several centuries in the Oklahoma-Arkansas-Missouri region, remembered in legend as The Land of Sorrows. Finds of a bronze Athenian medallion along with two examples of a coin from the Athenian colony of Thurium on the Red River in Oklahoma suggest one tarrying place where they stayed.[11] Here they must have clashed with the Iroquois and adopted the Iroquoian language as a peace concession, for when the Algonquian army arrives around 300 C.E., they join it as the Stonies (Armored Men). The three nations cross the Mississippi, defeat the Natchez and Talegans and live together in a state fluctuating between friendly and hostile for a thousand years until the Shawnee begin to build up their hegemony over all tribes. Although legends handed down among the Iroquois set the second break on the part of the Cherokee in the Finger Lakes District of New York, the Iroquois must not have arrived there until shortly before the Lenape south of them in 1396. The fact that the Tuscaroras broke away at the same time as the Cherokees, and were also living in Kentucky according to Rafinesque, lends support to the notion that the split occurred in the Talegan region along the Ohio, not in the northeastern part of the country.

The Cherokees, Iroquois, and Algonquians, including the Shawnee, did not build mounds; only the Iztacan Indians from Mexico raised these monuments. Principal among the Iztacan or Uto-Aztecan Indians were the Natchez, who, as reported by Rafinesque, were forced out of the Ohio Valley by the incoming Algonquians and Iroquois (called by him Oghuzians). By the time of recorded history under the Europeans in America, the domains of the Natchez recede within the surroundings of the city named for them on the lower Mississippi. Only the Natchez Trace and its continuation, the Avery, remained to show that their empire once stretched into Kentucky. It is documented fact that they built their last mound in 1712 shortly before being subjugated by the French.

In the late 1700s, the Indian agent Benjamin Hawkins took several Cherokee leaders to see the Etowah mounds situated just north of present-day Atlanta. They told him these were not the monuments of those who now held the land, the Creek, but of Indians who came before the Creek. We may identify these as Iztacan tribes like the Natchez. Hence, one of the important mound sites in Georgia is Ocmulgee, the name also of a major river. Rafinesque records this culture as a branch of the Mexican Olmecas or Hulmees.

The Atlantic shores of America were not unknown to the ancient Greeks, just as they were visited by the Minoans, Egyptians and Phoenicians before them. In Strabo's *Geography* of about 25 B.C.E., America is called Epeiros Occidentalis, the Western Continent. Writing in the first century C.E., Plutarch describes the northern sailing route and records that the Western Continent lay 5,000 *stades* beyond Greenland. He also mentions a southern route beginning in the Canary Islands followed of old by Phoenicians. This information seems to be based on the earlier writer Diodorus Siculus (1st century B.C.E.). Plutarch writes also that Greeks founded a colony among the indigenous peoples across the Atlantic. A Greek tetradrachm found in Cass County, Illinois, dating to between 175 and 164 B.C.E. seems to indicate that Hellenistic–era Greeks navigated up the Mississippi at that time. There is an abundance of other signs for Greeks in the Americas (Appendix H).

As we have seen, archeologists are just beginning to develop a chronology for the Mississippian Period, conventionally set in the years 1200–1600.[12] Occasionally, however, a random window opens up on these blank centuries. The Rocky Creek Stone is just such a testimony. It is, I propose, a record of the Cherokee conquest of their new territories in the Cumberland and separation from the Shawnee. The 19 × 15 inch engraved limestone tablet was exhumed in 1870 in a Mississippian Period mound on Rocky Creek near Castalian Springs, Sumner County, Tennessee. It is now in the possession of the Tennessee Historical Society and sometimes on exhibit at the Tennessee State Museum in Nashville. Engravings were published and partially elucidated in 1890 by Gates P. Thruston in his *Antiquities of Tennessee* (fig. 5.1).[13]

I will go further than Thruston and say that the Rocky Creek tablet probably commemorates a peace treaty concluding a war between the newly arrived Cherokee and the Shawnee, whose stronghold by then was in Middle Tennessee. History reveals that the Cherokee waged continual warfare against the Shawnee. Finally, in 1715 they joined in an alliance with the Chickasaw in West Tennessee and drove the Algonquian tribe northward across the Ohio, planting a wedge between it and remnants of subjugated and associated tribes like the Yuchi to the south.

The tablet shows us a Cherokee with a war club, far left, identified by his distinctive topknot, four scarification marks across his face, the traditional sign of a chief, and sun symbols on his skirt. (The Cherokee were so proud of their topknots that a silver cylinder to hold them in place was one of the most popular trade items bartered to them by English traders out of Charleston in the 1600s and 1700s.) He battles a Shawnee warrior distinguished by Mohawk hairdo, feathers, spear and large square shield with "sky-serpent" design. The Cherokee side evidently carries the day. The Shawnee sue for peace. The two tribes smoke the peace calumet in a longhouse of the Shawnee hung with checkered wampum belts (bottom center).

The two chiefs are reprised on the right, dressed now in ceremonial attire, the Cherokee wearing a horsehair crested helmet and carrying spear and shield of a Greek hoplite, the Shawnee clasping hands in a wedding ceremony with a Cherokee woman bearing wampum belts as a pledge of peace. She has her hair in a bun, the sign of maidenhood, and wears a

Middle Eastern–style plaid kilt displaying a large six-pointed star on her breast. The groom has brought the requisite blanket and bag of meat to exchange. Thanks to the union of the two, the Cherokee and Shawnee people are now on the path of peace (symbolized by the horizontal lines beneath them) rather than warpath (indicated by a 90-degree angle at the feet of the Cherokee chief). A V–shaped sign of concord, a common Indian symbol, joins the married couple and shows that they and their people have come together.

Fig. 5.1. Rocky Creek Stone. From Gates Thruston, *Antiquities of Tennessee,* 1890.

The Cherokee chief has a gorget about his neck in the shape of a crescent moon, below it a sun, and there are sun signs also on his skirt and shield, a similar configuration of quarter moon and sun was depicted on the posts of the Cherokee council house, the *cahtiyis*.[14] The early Cherokee — like the ancient Greeks, Egyptians and Libyans— were sun-worshipers, calling themselves "a great nation known as the Eshelokee of the half-sphere temple of light" (*Vision of Eloh'*). The Shawnee man, on the other hand, is identified by a double serpent design on his shield. Above him and going through his head is a longhouse or village with a serpent and other clan symbols over it, encoding, doubtless, its name — perhaps Turtle Town? These pictograms resemble those of the Wallam Olum, while the Cherokee writing system, on the other hand, appears to be ogam, a Mediterranean script. Letters in this alphabet seem to act as captions to the various scenes. The words in front of the Cherokee's mouth in his warrior guise on the left are probably a speech taunting his adversary. A whole cluster of words appear in the upper right, but because of the wear of the stone they are not clear.

Obvious to those who are informed about such things are numerical annotations within what I have called the longhouse or village in the upper left. Their glyphic shapes come from a base-five numbering system which the Cherokee brought with them from their sojourn among the Indians of Central America, and which remained in use with the Maya.[15] These could represent a tally of some sort or a date.

The six-pointed star adorning the Cherokee woman seems to me to be a star of David, emblem of Judaism. In my experience, no other type of star like it can be adduced from Indians of this time period. She wears a skirt of woven cloth and bracelets, both exotic touches. Of the skirt's pattern, it may be pointed out that Thruston found numerous instances in the same area of what he calls the "familiar Greek key or classic fret pattern." Citing his predecessor Conant, he also notes that human figures from nearby excavations are shown "clad in flowing garments gathered by a belt around the waist and reaching to the knees"— a perfect picture of the tunics and chitons of ancient Greeks. Cave murals discovered in 1883 by the archeologist Priest in Ohio tell the same story: Their location now unknown, they depicted Indians with Greco-Roman toga-like costumes. Further, an Egyptian–style mummy with Greek writing on the wrappings was untombed on the Cumberland River near Carthage, Tennessee, in 1815 — not far from Castalian Springs. As described by the antiquarian Haywood, it was a young woman with blonde hair wearing a silver clasp on her wrist. All these clues seem to lead back to the original Eshelokee.

The Rocky Creek tablet was probably kept in the chief's dwelling in this town on the Avery Trace at the western gate of Cherokee lands to show other tribes the legitimacy of their claim. The mummy was found not thirty miles eastward in Carthage. If one were to continue along the Avery Trace, one would arrive at the so-called Standing Stone in a state park by the same name that marked a division between Cherokee territory and that of the Shawnees to the north in Kentucky. At the heart of this new domain is the Sacred Dog monument in Monterey. Originally, an eight-foot-tall sandstone carving out of living rock stood guard over the homeland of the Cherokees on the Avery Trace, facing westward in the direction from where they originated.[16] In the centuries before the arrival of Europeans, the Cherokee extended their possessions into East Tennessee and Western North Carolina as well as down the Savannah River in Georgia at the expense primarily of the Creek and Yuchi Indians.

Speaking of ogam, I must relate the following story. When my wife and I moved to New Mexico, we made a beeline for Bandelier National Archeological Monument twelve miles southeast of Los Alamos, birthplace of the atomic bomb. The general impression it gives is one of a Greek or Roman or Tunisian ruin. How did the people who lived there dress all those blocks of sandstone, slate, and even granite and basalt? Tens of thousands of squared-off stones were required to build Bandelier, and hundreds, if not thousands, of metal tools. "Obsidian," the ranger informed us. But obsidian, volcanic glass, shatters on stone. Nor can stone easily be used to chop stone. An archeological experiment attempting to do just this produced an 80 percent degradation of tools within a few hours.[17]

After being pointed onto the path to what the ranger called Quetzalcoatl's Cave, we stood face to face with a classic example of ogam. Peeking into a cliff-dwelling down the way, we saw examples of Tifanag, a Berber script, in the painted plaster ceiling. Ogam (pronounced OM, also spelled ogham) has been known in the British Isles and Spain for several centuries, but it was Barry Fell who first studied its remote origins.[18] A key document is the short Ogham Tract added to the end of a medieval Irish manuscript kept today in the library of Trinity College, Dublin. This treatise in the great Book of Ballymote contains specimens of ogam arranged geographically with Gaelic and Latin translations beside them. Its rediscovery proved to be the Rosetta Stone for ancient North African writing. Fell was able through this link to decipher different versions in Libyan, Egyptian, Punic, Ibero-Celtic and a welter of other languages. For instance, a script called African by the Ballymote scribe is an Iberian variety used by Phoenician Semitic speakers in southern Spain during the first millennium B.C.E. Fell published a chart comparing the oldest styles with the fully developed and more familiar Irish style of the Middle Ages.

Predictably, Fell's discoveries were ridiculed. Archeology students are still cautioned by their professors not to speak of *anything* that appears to be prehistoric writing in America. The stricture against finding any script among indigenous Americans goes back to the era of Indian removal. In 1820, Caleb Atwater of the American Antiquarian Society wrote: "In one word, I will venture to assert that there never has been found a medal, coin, or monument, in all North America, which had on it one or more letters belonging to any alphabet, new or ever in use among men of any age or country, that did not belong to Europeans or

Fig. 5.2. Ogam: Often-Overlooked American Indian Writing System. Author's photograph.

their descendants, and had been brought or made here since the discovery of America by Christopher Columbus."[19]

Ever since Major Powell directed the Smithsonian's Bureau of Ethnology, there has been a ban on the subject. I was not surprised to discover upon my return to Santa Fe that among the hundreds of books, surveys and dissertations written about Bandelier, not one mention was made of the marks at Quetzalcoatl's Cave.[20] One of my friends suggested they were grooves where the Bandelierian Indians sharpened arrows.

The Bandelier inscription is a garden-variety specimen of Old Ogam. It was unquestionably produced with the aid of metal tools. From right to left, in the fashion of Hebrew, it reads: Q-H-T-Z-H-L C-TL-H-TL-H (fig. 5.2). The marks are in a style similar to a specimen discovered on Manana Island, near Monhegan Island on the coast of Maine. Sometimes called Hinged Ogham, this is a variety of Bronze Age ogam quite common in America, similar in fact to no. 16 in the Irish Ogham Tract. The Manana stone states: "Ships from Phoenicia, Cargo platform."[21]

The old-time Cherokee unashamedly glorified their bodies. Their athletic orientation can perhaps be explained by the original Spartan and Dorian Greek cast of their society. David Sansone, in his study of athletics in the ancient world, notes correlation between Cherokees and Greeks in this respect without suggesting any historical link. He points to "numerous and striking parallels between the practice of the Greeks in connection with athletes and that of the Indian ball players," although he remarks that there is "no question of direct contact" between the two.[22] Ascribing the coincidences to a common origin in the magical practices of prehistoric hunter societies, Sansone explores repeated correspondences between the Greek rituals surrounding the Olympic Games and Cherokee athletes' preparation for ball play, a form of lacrosse. They extend to "prohibitions against specific foods," a taboo against intercourse with women for a period of one month before and seven days following an event, disqualification if the athlete's wife is pregnant, bathing before and after in a nearby river, and a fire ritual.

Both Cherokee and Greek athletes scraped their skin before the pre-game bath. The Cherokee scored it "with an implement designed to produce parallel superficial gashes" just before a ballgame. Greek athletes used a toothed sickle, replaced later by a smooth-edged strigil, to scrape and scarify their muscles. Cherokee men submitted to having a comb with teeth of turkey spurs or some other sharp object (*canuga*, "scratcher"; compare Greek *kanon*) dragged across their bodies before plunging seven times in a stream. The scoring of skin was supposed to strengthen athletes and help them win. The sickle or strigil, "with which we may compare the Cherokee turkey-bone comb," says Sansone, opened the surface of the skin to allow the purifying waters of the bath to soak in and any weakness or illness to escape: "The function of the strigil was analogous to ... that of the turkey-bone instrument used in the Cherokee scratching ordeal. The pain thus caused was considered an act of sacrifice."

Archeologists have noted the distribution of so-called chunkey stones from 600 C.E. in a southward pattern.[23] Their spread exactly fits the time and direction of the Cherokees' travels before they settled in the southern Appalachians. The prized heirlooms (from the root *tlan-*, meaning "swoop down, fall") were housed in Indian temples and clan houses, and they seem to be the same as the Greek *diskos* ("thing to pitch"), one of the events along with the javelin in the Greek pentathlon, the main contest of the Olympic Games. Indian chunkeys come in many sizes but are usually round, flat, polished stones about twelve inches in diameter. They were used in a contest between two men on a sandy playing field. Bets were wagered by the spectators. One player hurled the stone so that it rolled as far as possible in a direct line while the other ran forward a few yards to a line and threw a javelin at the traveling chunkey. The first player then threw his javelin. Whichever came closest to the chunkey when it came to rest determined the winner. Chunkey stones were often of venerable antiquity and were owned by the religious hierarchy of the town, not individuals. Like the Greek discobolus depicted in a familiar ancient Greek statue by Myron, Cherokee athletes competed in the nude, or at least bare but for breechclout. Curiously, it was a tradition recorded by the first pioneers in Abingdon, Virginia, that the Indians used to have intertribal sporting events at Blackmore's Fort every four years; the custom was discontinued shortly after the English arrived.

Finally, let us consider the figure of Stoneclad, or Stonecoat. This culture hero must come from the Cherokees' Stony Tribe past. He is a fierce warlock "responsible for bestowing on the Cherokees specific medicinal formulas and knowledge, hunting songs, the crystals [*ulungstata*, cf. Greek *ouluntata* "judged healthy"] used for divining, and the red clay used for face and body painting."[24] His "whole body is covered with a skin of solid rock."[25] He is a flesh-eating warrior with a long sharp instrument he uses for killing people, and he is called an *askili* or *tsasgili/tchaskili*, "witch," a name for one of the types of Cherokee spiritual practitioners which can also mean owl.[26] I suggest *tchaskili* or *tchaskiri* in the Lower Cherokee dialect, with its telltale foreign *ts-* sound, from Greek. It appears to be a corruption of Θρηικιος, Θρηξ, "Thracian."

The Thracians were a people of non–Greek speech and mysterious origin to the north of Greece in what is now Bulgaria. They were known for their encasing metal armor and characteristic sharp knives or pole-arms, particularly a single-edged blade that was the terror of the ancient battlefield, the *rhomphaia*. They were famous also for their music and magical arts. Both of these qualities are summed up in the ancient Greek mythic cycles centering on the figure of Orpheus, a representation of Thracian culture in all of its wild and savage aspects, including tales of cannibalism. Stoneclad is the very epitome of a practitioner of the dark arts to the Cherokee.

When Stoneclad dies he is given a funeral pyre. He sings forth all of his magical charms and storied knowledge for everyone to hear and bequeaths to the seven clans a firm foundation for the Cherokee Nation.[27] Ever afterward it is taboo for any Cherokee to add to the stories and songs of old (*tikano*, cf. Greek *tynchano*, "to come to pass").

According to musicologists, the Cherokee greatly favor "anhemitonic scales." One of these five or six note scales is built into every Southeastern Indian flute made today. It can be simulated by playing all the black notes on a piano keyboard. One hears it in the harmonies of many country music songs, an industry that originated in the Cherokees' former homeland of Tennessee. The "harsh" but harmonic Dorian mode of country music pickers and the Southeastern flute underlies much of American Indian music, particularly that of the Hopi, Zuni, Pima and Cherokee. To get an idea how it sounds, think of the song "What Shall We Do with a Drunken Sailor," the Beatles' "Eleanor Rigby," or the Doors' "Light My Fire." Most of the Doors' songs, in fact, are in the Dorian mode.[28] Cherokee stomp dance songs have melodies in the slow sections that are anhemitonic.[29] The closest analogs in Native America appear to be Hopi, Zuni and Pima music.[30] Cherokee music is also noteworthy in featuring water drums and leg rattles, instruments with a deep history in Egypt.

Up to this point, we have attempted to let the keepers of the Old Talk speak in their own words, even if it is through the medium of early outsiders who recorded those histories. In the mid-eighteenth century, a Scots-Irish trader by the name of James Adair became one of the first Europeans to cross the Cumberland Gap and gaze into the mountain stronghold of the Cherokee Nation. While he interpreted what he experienced with the eyes and attitudes of a British man of parts, his resounding shock of recognition remains indispensable to an understanding of the Cherokee, who would never be the same.

# Chapter 6

# *James Adair and the Lost Tribes of Israel*

*O could their ancient Incas rise again,*
*How would they take up Israel's taunting strain!* — William Cowper, "Charity"

The Eshelokee kept searching for five missing clans out of the original twelve. It seems a scenario reminiscent of the lost ten tribes of Israel, and many people have jumped at the opportunity to draw comparisons. Based on Biblical history, there were ten "lost" tribes— Reuben, Simeon, Issachar, Zebulon, Gad, Asher, Dan, Naphtali, Manasseh and Ephraim. All were deported by the Assyrians when they conquered the northern kingdom of Israel between 740 and 700 B.C.E. The two tribes of Judah and Benjamin in the southern kingdom fared somewhat better but eventually they also were led into a Babylonian captivity with the fall of Jerusalem to Nebuchadnezzar in 697 B.C.E.

Throughout history, lost tribes have been "discovered" all over the world, from the Khazars and Shindai Tribe of the Japanese to the Ibos of Nigeria and Masai Tribe of South Africa. The American version of the theory came into being with Spanish and Portuguese writers. Its godfather was Bartolomé de las Casas, a rare advocate for native rights who wrote the earliest and largest compendium on American Indians. Other Spanish writers ascribing to the theory were Francisco López de Gomara, Diego Gonzalo Fernández Oviedo, Diego Duran in his *Historia de los Indios de Nueva España* (1585), and Gregorio García. French Calvinists also endorsed it. But it was in England that the hypothesis truly blossomed. There it rapidly became a Puritan article of faith.[1] In 1650, Thomas Thorowgood published *Jews in America, or Probabilities that those Indians are Judaical*, prefaced with a report by the preacher John Eliot. Thorowgood's arguments are these: (1) The Indians wear robes like Jews and go barefoot, (2) They constantly anoint their heads with oil, (3) They pierce their ears and wear jewelry, (4) They take frequent baths, (5) "They delight exceedingly in dancing...." (6) They call uncles and aunts Father and Mother, (7) They eat no pork, (8) They wash strangers' feet, and (9) They compute days from sunset to sunset.[2] Only with the Enlightenment of the eighteenth century did the theory decline in popularity and yield to other explanations. Thomas Jefferson thought American Indians were Turks and Tartars coming across the Bering Sea from Asia,[3] while his contemporary John Filson believed them to be Phoenicians.[4]

The Lost Tribes theory is generally now relegated to the outer fringes of forbidden history. "Today it is viewed as taboo and blasphemous in many circles despite a conclusion never really having been reached," points out one writer, Daniel T. Pasher.[5] Quite aside from whether such an interpretation might be true, however, it may be instructive to look at who developed the theory in the first place, and why, and to consider what made it so appealing to certain people.

In 1650, Amsterdam rabbi Menasseh Ben Israel wrote the influential book *The Hope of Israel*. Born Manoel Diaz Soeva in Lisbon in 1604, he belonged to the upper echelons of Spanish-Portuguese Converso families. He married into the illustrious Abravanel family. Under his religious name, Ben Israel wrote his first work of scholarship at the age of eight. He eventually spoke eight languages. Like others before him, he soon escaped the Iberian Peninsula and relocated to Amsterdam, the Jerusalem of the North. Here he became the leader of its large Sephardic congregation, Neveh Shalom. In 1649, after a successful diplomatic mission to London, he petitioned Oliver Cromwell to readmit Jews into England. (Notably, Cromwell himself was a descendant of Jews, as Elizabeth Hirschman has documented.)[6] The main arrow in Ben Israel's quiver was a pamphlet titled "How Profitable the Nation of the Jewes Are." In January 1650, he followed up with publication of the lengthier study, *The Hope of Israel*. This was originally written in Castilian Spanish and addressed to the Parnassim (leaders) of the synagogue Talmud Torah. It was later rendered into Latin, and from the Latin translated into English, somewhat lamely, by Moses Wall. The title comes from Jeremiah 14:8: "The hope of Israel, the saviour thereof."[7]

Ben Israel's plea was officially denied by the England. In 1656, he responded with another tract, *Vindiciae Judaeorum*. Parliament would never formally endorse any new policy, but through his efforts Jews did gain the government's tacit agreement to be able to reside there and live openly as Jews for the first time since 1290. With the celebrated case of a Marrano merchant named Robles, Whitehall suddenly lifted the ban against Jews. Ben Israel died November 20, 1657, before seeing the great influx of Dutch Jewish merchants into London. Ben Israel's eloquent plea for the rights of Jews and Indians as related peoples was in reality a masterstroke of public relations. It was widely read, and misread. According to his biographer, Cecil Roth, "The Sephardic Messianic manifesto beat a royal way through the steppes, forests, and villages of the Ashkenazi Jews."[8] The name Mikve Israel became a favorite choice for the first Jewish congregations in the New World, Curaçao (1654), Savannah (1733), and Philadelphia (1773), among others.

In treating of the origins of Indians, Ben Israel relied heavily on Garcia's *Origen de los Indios del Nuevo Mundo e Indios Occidentales* (Valencia, 1607), but he also introduced a new theme. He had a brother in Brazil, as well as numerous business contacts in the Spanish colonies. A central argument of his came from fellow Sephardi Aaron Levi, also known as Antonio de Montezinos. Guided by an Indian named Francisco, this Jewish merchant set out from Cartegenas for the interior of Colombia. Francisco led him to Rio Cauca. It is there that de Montezinos claimed to hear Indians reciting the Shema in Hebrew ("Hear, O Israel, the Lord our God is One"). They were of the lost tribe of Reuben. King Solomon's mines were nearby. The Indians were now to be embraced as fellow Jews. It was one thing for Europeans to project Jewishness onto Indians but quite another for Jews themselves to promote a family likeness.

Despite laws against emigration to the New World, many Portuguese and Spanish Jews did manage to escape persecution and flee to the Americas.[9] The Inquisition followed close behind them. There were *autos-da-fé* and widespread arrests in Mexico City and Antioquia, Colombia, well into the eighteenth century. The grisly machinery of the Holy Office was not shut down until the 1820s.[10] Perhaps because they believed Ben Israel's message on a literal level, or perhaps because they wanted a common ground vis-à-vis the Christians, Jews often associated and intermarried with Indians.

Today, the most famous group of these Mestizo Jews is in Venta Prieta in eastern Mexico. Rick Aharon Chaimberlin, writing in the magazine *Petah Tikvah* (*Door of Hope*), describes them as follows:

> They look like American Indians, but have "reconverted" openly to Judaism. Unfortunately they have for the most part received much rejection by the ethnically "pure" Jews of Mexico City. A notable exception was Rabbi Samuel Leer [Lerer], a Conservative Rabbi who arrived in Mexico City in 1968, and became their spiritual advisor. He performs marriage ceremonies for them once they formally convert to Judaism, and helps their sons through the Bar Mitzvah process. He performs the conversions [he said], "not because they need to but in order not to antagonize the other rabbis here...." Every couple married since 1968 as well as the children born to these couples are now incontestably Jewish.[11]

I confirmed this story with Rabbi Lerer personally when he gave the keynote address at the annual conference of the Society for Crypto-Judaic Studies in San Antonio, Texas, in August 2003. He would tell prospective converts, "You are Jews, crypto–Jews, but now I'm going to open you up!" Even though many of these were returning to Judaism after a lapse of five hundred years, Rabbi Lerer considered their conversion "merely symbolic." They had always been Jews. The congregation in Puebla, Mexico, is named Beth Shmuel after him.

Occupying an unusual position in Jewish and American history is the Spanish-Portuguese grandee Luis Moses Gomez. Born in Spain in 1660, he escaped the Spanish Inquisition to live in France and England, where he was denounced as a Judaizer. He made his way to New York City in 1703. There he purchased 6,000 acres of land on the Hudson River, at a spot where several Indian trails converged. The location was later known as Jews Creek. He built a stone house with walls three feet thick into the side of the hill. Continuously occupied for more than 280 years, Gomez Mill House, located just off Highway 9W, five miles north of Newburgh, New York, is today the oldest house in Orange County on the National Register of Historic Places. It is also the earliest surviving Jewish residence in North America.

In 1729 Gomez used the right of British citizenship granted him by Queen Anne to purchase a plot of land in lower Manhattan. This site became the first cemetery of Congregation Shearith Israel, the synagogue founded by Dutch and Caribbean Jews in 1645. Both his sons, Daniel and David, also became traders with the Indians.

> It was said that other merchants were hesitant to venture into Orange County because of the many stories they had heard about the Indians. However, the Gomez family and the Indians had a good relationship at a meeting place near their home, where the Indians brought them valuable furs and traded them for other goods. At that time Sephardic rabbis of New York and Newport issued responsa (judicial opinions) enjoining Jews not to mistreat Indians, on the possibility that they might be descendants of the Ten Lost Tribes of Israel. American and Caribbean Jewish law condoned marriage between Jews and Indians, and the progeny of such unions were ruled to be Jewish.[12]

Like papal bulls, responsa are not issued lightly. They are one of the pillars of halakic, or traditional Jewish, law. These rulings were an indirect result of Menasseh Ben Israel's campaign for Jewish (and Indian) rights. Although Gomez did not marry a native woman, many other Jewish merchants of the time did. They did so apparently not so much out of convenience as from a desire to keep both business and religion safe within the same family.

Let us now turn to that other famous trader among the Indians, James Adair. In Scottish legend, the Adair family name is linked to that of Currie (Arabic Khoury, Kori). A Currie seized the castle of Dunskey on the southwest coast of Scotland and was declared a rebel, robber, and pirate. A proclamation was made that whoever should produce Currie, dead or alive, would be rewarded with his fortunes. An Adair presented Currie's head to the king.[13] He got the lands and the family was known ever afterwards as the Adairs of Portree. When a castle was built on the spot in Dumfrieshire where Currie was struck down in the early sixteenth century, it was called Kilhilt. The beheading of the pirate Currie appears in the Adair crest, which depicts "a man's head couped and bloody."

The origin of the name Adair is usually explained as Gaelic. It is said to be cognate with Edzaer, meaning "the ford of the oaks." But the Celtic etymology of the name from Gaelic *ath* "oak" and *dare* "ford" may cover up an original Hebrew one. Edzaer does not even sound like Athdare or Adare. Adairs proper do not appear in Scottish history until the fourteenth century, long after Gaelic ceases to be the language of the land but has mostly been replaced by Scots, a dialect of English.

After taking part in the Ulster Plantation movement in the seventeenth century and establishing themselves in northern Ireland, the Adairs were quick to branch out into America. Their piecemeal emigrations over a period of years illustrate a common path pursued to the extreme western frontier by settlers landing in Maryland. Elizabeth Hirschman has termed this the Great Melungeon Migration.[14] The reasons for this rush to the wilderness do not seem to be the same as those offered commonly by historians— desire of a small freeholder to avoid taxation by moving gradually beyond the reach of the authorities.[15] Instead, we see a pattern of landing, often illegally, on the sandy shores of Maryland or swampy inlets of Chesapeake Bay and making a beeline for Kentucky and Tennessee, stronghold of the Melungeons. Here breakaway Carolinians had gone so far as to establish the semi-independent Watauga Country, and later, State of Franklin.

John Adair, Sr., comes to Baltimore with his family in 1760 from Ballymena, County Antrim, Ireland. The family heads straight for the westernmost English settlement, in Augusta County, Virginia (later Botetourt, briefly called Fincastle). In this strange frontier enclave, Adair joins the militia and signs a series of petitions that are today celebrated as precursors to the Declaration of Independence.[16] As soon as the way is clear, we find the entire John Adair family in East Tennessee. A few years later, they have moved to the Boone Settlement in Kentucky. John Adair, Sr., eventually builds Adair Station near Knoxville, the fort that becomes a leverage point for removing the Cherokee Indians to their new Lower Towns in Georgia and Alabama. John Adair, Jr., follows in the footsteps of his father, helping defend the frontier around the mouth of the North Fork of the Holston near present-day Kingsport. In 1789 the North Carolina legislature establishes a storehouse for provisions for the Cumberland Guard, poised to extend European settlements to Middle Tennessee. The storehouse is in the home of John Adair. The Wilderness Road bypassing and outflanking disputed Cherokee territory in the tribe's heartland is forged through Kentucky by William Cooper. John Adair III marries William Cooper's great-granddaughter, granddaughter of Cherokee Chief Black Fox, Sarah Cooper.

The Adairs are among the earliest Wayne County pioneer families. Others are Adkins, Burnetts, Barnes, Barriers, Bells, Burks, Blevins, Coopers, Denneys, Davenports, Dobbs, Dolens, Elams, Gregorys, Keetons, Kogers, Lovelaces, Parmleys, Parkers, Phipps, Rices, Ryans, Scotts, Sallees, Sanduskys, Smiths, Sharps, Vaughns and Youngs.[17] Most of the younger generation intermarry with those of their same background, often cousins, or else with Cherokee Indians, whom they see as being of the Tribes of Israel. There is even a rudimentary Jewish congregation or minyan gathered at one time around Isaac Cooper (about

Fig. 6.1. Public mural in Darien, Georgia celebrates friendship between Indians and Scotsmen. Author's photograph.

1775–1845), who married a daughter of Black Fox. Marriage — and presumably other religious — services are held in his home on Beaver Creek. The names of the leaders of this congregation, the first west of the Alleghenys, are commemorated in a number of courthouse documents in which the parties cite each other as character witnesses. John Adair, Jr.'s, Revolutionary War pension, for instance, names Isaac Cooper, Fleming Gregory, John Bell,

Lewis Coffee, Martin Beaty, and William Hardin, all of whom lived in the neighborhood and bear crypto–Jewish surnames.

DNA analysis demonstrates that James Adair, the Indian trader and author, who was probably a cousin of our John Adair, belongs to male lineage J2, a fairly common Mediterranean and Jewish genetic type. Possibly, he came from Sephardic stock. Transplanted to Scotland and Ireland from the lands of the Mediterranean, and thence to America, he and his kinsmen were perhaps in the process of getting back in touch with the family's Jewish past. If so, Adair's observations on Hebraisms in his book *History of the American Indians* are fully understandable. They result from ethnic recognition.

This long, encyclopedic work published in London in 1775 is divided into twenty-three arguments, ranging from common purification practices and similarity of Indian chants like Yo-he-va to the name Jehovah. It is a work that has been lauded and reviled, sometimes by the same critics. Many modern scholars like Charles Hudson see Adair as a praiseworthy forerunner of anthropological methods.[18] Others accuse Adair of having "tormented every custom and usage into a like one of the Jews, and almost every word in their language [into] a Hebrew one of the same meaning."[19]

Adair's approaches to the problem may be listed from his table of contents to show that not all of his arguments are linguistic, and thus so easily dismissed: I. Their division into tribes, II. Their worship of Jehovah, III. Their notions of theocracy, IV. Their belief in the ministration of angels, V. Their language and dialects, VI. Their manner of counting time, VII. Their prophets and high priests, VIII. Their festivals, fasts and religious rites, IX. Their daily sacrifice, X. Their ablutions and anointings, XI. Their laws of uncleanness, XII. Their abstinence from unclean things, XIII. Their marriage, divorce, and punishment for adultery, XIV. Their cities of refuge, XVI. Their purification and ceremonies preparatory for war, XVII. Their ornaments, XVIII. Their manner of curing the sick, XIX. Their burial of the dead, XX. Their mourning for the dead, XXI. Their raising seed to a deceased brother [Levirate law], XXII. Their choice of names adapted to their circumstances and the times, XXIII. Their own (historical) traditions. Adair cites many contemporaries who agreed with his views. One of these was his fellow trader Abraham Mordecai, the founder of Montgomery, Alabama, "an intelligent Jew, who dwelt fifty years in the Creek Nation [and] confidently believed that the Indians were originally of his people" (p. 50n.).

Other leading thinkers of the day had similar points to make, among them Cotton Mather, Roger Williams and William Penn. But Adair introduces new material in what was becoming a well-worn theme. His apparent familiarity with Jewish life and customs is particularly striking, for he delves into the precise meaning and significance of cities of refuge, Levirate law[20] and "their festivals, fasts and religious rites." We will return to these observations in a later chapter.

But exactly who *was* James Adair? Until the year 2000, no one really knew. Before that, the sum total of knowledge concerning his life, writings and exploits was little.[21] He was born in Ireland around 1709 and is believed to have emigrated about 1735 to South Carolina, where he became a deerskin trader among the Catawbas, Cherokees, Chickasaws and Choctaws. He dabbled in frontier politics. For the rest, he is an enigma.

New information on Adair surfaced about ten years ago.[22] Genealogists on the Internet brought to light a forgotten historical marker on Highway 710 near the town of Rowland in Robeson County, North Carolina, the traditional homeland of the Lumbee Indians. The marker noted that James Adair, Indian trader and historian, was buried nearby. Persistent searching turned up paydirt: a lost will preserved in an old genealogy compilation, *Kinfolks*, the work of great-great-great-grandson William Curry Harllee. It was written September 21, 1778, filed in Elizabethtown, Bladen County (parent county of Robeson) and probated in 1787. Later destroyed by a courthouse fire, it named a wife plus three daughters, no sons.

Several important facts about Adair's life emerge from the will. First, kinsman Robert Adair is remembered with the not-insignificant bequest of ten pounds. This is surely Sir Robert Adair (1763–1855), illegitimate son of "Dr. Robin Adair" and Lady Caroline Keppel (b. 1735). Our James Adair's middle name was Robert, although within the family he was known as Robin, a form of Reuben. A popular ballad of the nineteenth century, "Robin Adair," tells the story of an English lady who had a romantic adventure with a dashing and witty young man rejected by her family.

> What's this dull town to me?
> Robin's not near.
> What was't I wished to see,
> What wished to hear?
> Where's all the joy and mirth
> Made this town
> a heav'n on earth?
> Oh, they're all fled with thee,
> Robin Adair!

Adair accords his daughter Agnes rather harsh treatment in the will. He leaves her and her husband John Gibson the nominal sum of only one shilling. If he had left her nothing, she could have protested to the court that he simply overlooked her. John Gibson is one of the "mulatto" Gibsons of the Great Pee Dee river valley in the Carolinas. A relative, Gideon Gibson, plays a leading role in the Regulators Revolt. When members of the well-to-do Gibson family first move to the state in 1731, representatives in the House of Assembly complain that "several free colored men with their white wives had immigrated from Virginia." Governor Robert Johnson summons Gibson and his family and reports:

> I have had them before me in Council and upon Examination find that they are not Negroes nor Slaves but Free people, That the Father of them here is named Gideon Gibson and his Father was also free, I have been informed by a person who has lived in Virginia that this Gibson has lived there Several Years in good Repute and by his papers that he has produced before me that his transactions there have been very regular. That he has for several years paid Taxes for two tracts of Land and had several Negroes of his own, That he is a Carpenter by Trade and is come hither for the support of his Family.[23]

The Gibsons are obviously of Sephardic Jewish derivation. Quite rightly, they are discussed as Melungeons in Brent Kennedy's 1996 book and explicitly as Sephardic Jews in Elizabeth Hirschman's 2005 historical study.[24] Melungeon Gibsons take their origins from the Chavis family, one of the oldest Portuguese-Jewish names in America.[25] It is more hilarious than any Yiddish skit in redface by Fanny Brice or Eddie Cantor[26] that historians continue to parade forth these Sephardic Jews as African Americans owning land and marrying white women.[27]

The emigrant figure in the Adair family is Thomas Adair, born of a long pedigree in Scotland and Ireland in 1680. According to family recollections, he migrates to America in 1730 with three sons. The second son, Joseph, is a soldier in the Revolutionary War. The third son, William, "the pioneer," is the grandfather of Gen. John Adair (about 1753–1815), who distinguishes himself at the Battle of New Orleans and later becomes the eighth governor of Kentucky. Son James Adair is the eldest. According to sources that have never been verified, he has two sons, John and Edward. It is the children of Edward and some of the children of John who marry native women and start the long line of Adairs in the Cherokee Nation. There is a Lucinda Adair on the rolls who claims descent from James Adair through Edward. The comedian-politician Will Rogers is a descendant of this branch.

The Adair family first settles in Chester County, Pennsylvania, as part of a Scots-Irish group "with not much love for the mother country." In other words, they are Jacobites. Later, after James begins trading with the Indians with Charleston as his base, they obtain a large grant of land from King George II. The tract lies beyond the frontier deep in Indian country on Duncan's Creek in what is now Laurens County, not far from where James later died.

According to family remembrances, in going from the settled part of Pennsylvania to see this land in South Carolina, they found no roads, no surveys, no white settlements. They cut out a way as they went. After examining the land and selecting their homestead sites, some went to work to build houses and clear land for cultivation, while others went back to Pennsylvania for their livestock. Their corn mill they brought along and set up for operation by nailing it to a tree. This colony obtained corn the first year by trading with the Indians.

Shortly after the Adairs become established in this swampy corner of South Carolina, another Scottish pioneer group joins them to found the large Waxhaw Colony to the east. Both the Adairs and their Waxhaw clansmen become ardent patriots when the War of Independence breaks out in the American colonies.

No picture survives of James Adair, but family recollections remember him as "splendidly muscular, fine-looking, broad-shouldered, bearded man of a little more than medium height."[28] Could Adair, honorary chief of the Chickasaws, actually have been an Irish, or Scottish, Jew? The surname is suspiciously close to Hebrew *Adar*, the name of a month in the Jewish calendar.

Passages in Adair's book seem to strengthen the supposition he is Jewish. Disingenuously, he assures us he is just "an Indian trader, who professes but a small acquaintance with the Hebrew, and that acquired by his own application" (p. 40). Hebrew was not well known in the eighteenth century except by Jews. Its use had been proscribed in the Iberian Peninsula since 1492. If it was studied at all it was outside Spain and Portugal, usually in secret. Significantly, it continued to be used by Jewish merchants in private letters and trade correspondence.

Adair surprises us by quoting the Talmud, "The best physicians go to hell" (p. 201). Equally Talmudic seems to be, "The divine care extended itself from the horns of the unicorn to the very feet of the lice" (p. 36). At one point he notes that the Hebrew heard today is more guttural than the dialect of the American Indians, suggesting that he has attended Jewish services at some time, somewhere (p. 65). He pronounces Yom Tov, the Hebrew form of congratulation, as Yoma Tobe (p. 47), which sounds too idiomatic for him to have gleaned from printed sources. Additionally, he uses a number of proverbs of evident Jewish provenance: "For they who serve at the altar must live by the altar" (p. 51) ... "to carry a thing to Canaan," meaning to be dead (p. 56) ... "burial of a Jewish ass" as a euphemism for a suicide (p. 155) ... and "pouring out salt tears before God" (p. 61). Finally, he mentions "rabbins," and cites as a source the seventeenth-century French Jewish antiquarian Samuel Bochart (p. 39). At last, Adair drops the disguise entirely and speaks of Hebrew greeting customs as "our method of salutation" (p. 47). This is an allusion to the Jewish formality of greeting others at temple services with the Ashkenazi Hebrew word *Shabbos*.

Another indication of Adair's Jewish identity may be his hostility toward idolatry, particularly varieties of it common in Spanish Catholicism.[29] He admires the chaste form of monotheism he finds among the Indians. These attitudes are in keeping with those of Marranos.

> They [Indians] pay no religious worship to stocks, or stones, after the manner of the old eastern pagans; neither do they worship any kind of images whatsoever. And it deserves our notice, in a very particular manner, to invalidate the idle dreams of the Jesuitical fry of South-America ... that none of all the various nations ... has ever been known, by our trading people, to attempt to make any image of the Great Divine Being, whom they worship. This is consonant to the Jewish observance of the second commandment ... and their conduct is a reproach to many reputed Christian temples, which are littered round with a crowd of ridiculous figures to represent God, spurious angels, pretended saints, and notable villain [p. 24].

Besides turning tables on the Spanish and labeling them, not the Indians, "pagan," Adair pillories "half-savage Europeans who are become their [the Indians'] proselytes" [p. 34], meaning the Catholic French traders.

A letter kept in the extended family and made known to me by a cousin in Kentucky seems to unscore that the Adairs long appreciated they were Jewish, at least until about the middle of the nineteenth century, when the document was composed. It is written from John Adair in Arkansas to his brother-in-law John Lovelace in Kentucky.

> Crooked Creek, Arkansas, U.S.
> Jan 2, 45
> To Mr. John Lovelace
> Wayne County
> Monticello P.O.
> Ky
>
> State of Arkansas, Newton County
> December the 29th, 1844
>
> Dear Brother and Sister,
>
> I avail myself of the present opportunity of writing you a few lines to let you know that myself and family are at this time through the favor of God enjoying the great blessing of health, and I truly hope that these few lines may find you and yours in the enjoyment of the same blessing.... I have sent you a letter since I got home but I have got no answer, but I got one from you since I wrote. Now, my jew-lark, I want you to write to me as soon as you get this letter and let me no whether you intend to come to this country in the spring or not — and I don't want you to say "I am not coming" for I want you to come.
>
> Now, John, I will tell you what I want you to do for me: I want you to go and get what money is coming to me yet from my father's estate, and I hearby authorise you when you get all the money that is coming to me from the estate to give me a clear receipt — and if you come out to this country next spring I want you to bring my money with you, if you don't come I want you to send me word of the amount of the sales and how much is coming to me, for if you can't come and see us and fetch my money, I shall of course have to try to come after it, so no more —-. Your friends and connection in this country are some sick and some well. Jonathan Burks [married to a third sister, Nancy Cooper] and his family have all been sick, and John, Nancy, Pete, and Ben, that is, still got the chills, but they are not very bad. James Cooper [a brother, married to Lucretia Blevins] and his family are all well.... I will now come to a close by wishing to be remembered by you all ... so I add no more.
>
> I am, with respects, your most humble servant,
> John Adair
>
> Sarah Adair

What is striking about the letter is Adair's reference to his brother-in-law as "Jew-lark."[30] They were both married to daughters of Isaac Cooper and Nancy Blackfox.

Clarified as coming from a Jew, Adair's reporting takes on new meaning and credibility.

Observing that "several old American towns are called Kanāi" (p. 56), he suggests that the Conoy Indians of Pennsylvania and Maryland are Canaanites and their tribal name a corruption of Canaan. Most modern readers of Adair would be inclined to dismiss this detail as another example of his bending of the facts to suit his theory. But Adair had no way of knowing that the Phoenicians' name for themselves was not Sidonian, Carthaginian, Punic or the like, but Chnai, "Canaanites."[31] The Conoy are the same Indians William Penn describes as resembling Italians and Greeks.[32] By about 1735 Adair says they had dwindled to a "remnant of a nation, or subdivided tribe, of Indians."

Adair believes the Saponi are also strictly Middle Eastern, specifically Egyptian. To the Saponi can probably be added the Cheraw Indians, with whom they blended, known to the Spanish as the Judah Indians, as well as the Coree, whose tribal name is Arabic, *Koury*. Even today the Coree include Muslims among their numbers. Intriguingly, the same name appears as that of the mother of Adair's descendant and biographer, Col. William *Curry* Harllee.

James Adair has a strong connection to the Chickasaw. Around 1745, he established operations in Piomingo in north Mississippi, then a mixed Choctaw and Chickasaw town. Most of his book is based on information he received from Chickasaws, not Choctaws or Cherokees. The bulk of the manuscript was written there in the 1760s. "I have the pleasure of writing this," he says, "by the side of a Chikkasah female, as great a princess as ever lived" (447). Elsewhere, Adair notes there were already adults in that country who were octoroons, one-eighth Indian. The Indian–white intermarriage necessary to produce a mixed-race progeny of this description must have occurred at least three generations before, about 1720.

The date 1720 leads us to what I believe is the smoking gun in the mystery of America's first Jews. Both the French and English call the Chickasaw the Halfbreeds. This name appears as early as 1720 in the records of the Board of Commissioners of Indian Trade in Charleston. It is the only official tribal Indian name that specifically recognizes white intermixture. About 1735 the tribe was invited to settle in the hinterland of the new colony of Savannah. They eventually owned thousands of acres in fee simple on both sides of the Savannah River around Augusta, particularly in North Augusta on the South Carolina side. One reason they enjoyed such a favored status in the eyes of the English was evidently their resolute anti–Spanish and anti–French orientation. It is likely some of them were Jewish or crypto-Jewish.

The story of the Mississippi Bubble seems very apposite here. In Europe at this time, a Scottish Jew, John Law, became French finance minister. Historians are divided in their opinion as to whether he was a "knave or a madman." Born in Edinburgh in 1671, he first carried on his ancient Fife family's business of gold smithing and banking before turning international gambler and having the ill luck to shoot a rival dead in a duel. He was arrested, but he somehow managed to escape to the Continent, where, after a checkered career, he ended up at the court of the Sun King. A reward for his apprehension describes him as "Captain John Law, a Scotchman, aged twenty-six; a very tall, black, lean man; well shaped, above six feet high, with large pock-holes in his face; big nosed; and speaking broad and loud."[33]

Law has the dubious credit of being the first to print paper money to rescue a bankrupt state treasury. One of his schemes along these lines was the Mississippi Bubble of 1718. This venture involved rounding up the poor of Paris and Jews of Alsace, along with stray Gypsies and beggars, and sending several shiploads of them up the Mississippi to colonize the interior of France's new American territory. Law's land agent was Elias Stultheus, a fellow Jew. The project goes down as the first effort of a European power to plant a Jewish colony in the New World, even if it was unintentional. The public madly bought bonds on speculation until the scam was realized and Law fled the country. The hapless settlers were left stranded among the Indians.

At this same time, the Old Settlers in what became today's Northern Cherokee Nation of the Old Louisiana Territory left the Lower Towns of South Carolina for points west under their chief, Dangerous Man.[34] Beginning with some 600 families, they became known to their kinsmen who stayed in the east as the Lost Cherokees. One of the first was a Cherokee family headed by a William Cooper.

The original landing was in Chickasaw territory around Memphis, a barricaded point along the river-long a bone of contention with the British (probably the ancient mound town of Chiska where De Soto met his downfall and the French later built Fort Prudhomme).[35] When it was realized back in Paris that the shares in the company were worthless, and that unarmed Jews in any case did not make good guardians of the frontier, the colonists were left to shift for themselves. Many of them threw themselves on the mercy of the Natchez and Chickasaw. Stultheus's Gypsies, one of the sources for the new colonists, seems to account for the fact that Gypsy magic is widely practiced today among the Choctaw. Gypsies emerging from among the Chickasaw made North Augusta the Romany capital of America while Memphis remained their sacred burial place.

The *Encyclopedia of Southern Culture* confirms that the oldest Jewish communities in the South were not on the Atlantic or Gulf coast but in the middle Mississippi river valley.[36] The first Jews lived on the St. Francis and Arkansas River in outposts originally Spanish or French and in Natchez, New Madrid, Kaskaskia, Cape Girardeau and Memphis. These are all Jewish ghost towns now, like the ruins on Caribbean Islands that mark the first synagogues in the New World. Today there are only twenty-five Jews in Natchez. The city's Museum of the Southern Jewish Experience stands as a lonely tribute to Mississippi's Jewish pioneers.

By 1800, after the area around Memphis and Natchez had returned to Spanish rule, there was just one town of Halfbreeds left. It is mentioned in the memoirs of a steamboat captain as still in a sort of pitiful existence below the fourth bluffs on the Mississippi: "Fort Pickering ... stands on the left side of the river, in the Mississippi Territory. The United States have a factor here, but the settlement is very thin; it generally consists of what is called the half breed, which is a mixture of Indians and whites."[37]

Significantly, the earliest name given to this region by the Cumberland settlers was Moro District — the "Moorish District." It may be this colony that Choctaw chief Apunkshunnubbee refers to in the 1790s when he tells the Indian agent: "You Americans were not the first people who got this country from the red people. We sold our lands, but never got any value for it."[38]

Finally, let us briefly consider some of the Cherokee clan connections of the Adairs. James Adair's son John married Gahoga of the Deer Clan. Another Scotsman, John Bell, married a Deer Clan woman in the same district, and his only known child married Charlotte Adair, John and Gahoga's daughter, also Deer Clan. Nancy Ward's first husband, Kingfisher, was Deer Clan. We find a lot of within-the-clan and cousin marriage in these half and quarter blood families. Major John Ridge (The Ridge) and Oowatie or David Watie were brothers, the children of Oconostota or Tatchee (Dutch), of the Paint Clan, and a woman of the Deer Clan, so they were both Deer. Major Ridge married Susannah Wickett of the Wild Potato Clan, and David Watie married Susannah Reece, daughter of Nancy

Adair (hence Deer). David and Susannah's children included Buck Watie (who adopted the name Elias Boudinot, and who married out of the tribe) and Gen. Elias (Stand) Watie, who had wives from the Fields, Miller, Looney and Bell families.[39]

Unlike the Wolf, Paint, Bird and Wild Potato clans, the Deer Clan does not have a very settled history or origin. Its members were supposed to be good intellects—something true of Elias Boudinot certainly, the editor of the Cherokee newspaper *The Phoenix*. What strikes me as a common element in the Deer Clan is its Arab and Middle Eastern component. We will return to that theme later.

All of the historical Indian groups reviewed in this chapter—Halfbreeds, Conoy, Saponi, Cheraw, Coree, Old Settler Cherokee—were lost communities, if not lost tribes. How old their Jewish roots were can only be a matter of speculation. But it is certain that incoming Jews and crypto-Jews easily fell in with them from the moment they reached American shores. The hotbed of Judaization was in Cherokee territory. In the next chapter, we will come face to face with some of these admixed Cherokees who sit for their portraits at the court of king George II.

# Chapter 7

# *The Crown of Tennessee*

*Dedicated to the memory of my ancestor Attakullakulla*

British colonial governors recognized the expediency of having natives visit England as soon as possible. There they might be overawed with the mother country's wealth and impressed with its formidable military might. Between visiting the Tower of London and going to plays and catching shows, such delegations had their official portraits painted by court artists. As recounted in the book *Indians Abroad,* they then returned home with news about the teeming numbers of Englishmen and hopeless odds involved in fighting King George.[1] They also acquired a taste for English goods. The Cherokee peace chief Attakullakulla ordered a pipe organ to be delivered to his home in the Tennessee wilderness so his wife might learn to play it. He had been impressed by the one he saw in St. Paul's Cathedral.

One of the records of these visits by Indians to Europe is a large oil painting titled *An Audience Given by the Trustees of Georgia to a Delegation of Creek Indians (1734–35).* It is now owned by the Winterthur Museum in Delaware but used to hang in the trustees' offices in London.[2] The sponsors of the new colony of Georgia are assembled at their London headquarters receiving a visiting party of Indians usually identified as Creek.[3] The painting is the work of William Verelst, a Dutch master who worked for the court. The occasion is the 1734 state visit of Tomochichi (d. October 5, 1739). Tomochichi was the Yamacraw Indian who befriended the colony's founder, General James Edward Oglethorpe. Tomochichi opened many doors for the English settlers in Savannah. This painting was displayed in the Whitehall offices of the trustees as long as they continued in existence. To this day, reproductions can be found in museums and offices across the state of Georgia and beyond. Upon dissolution of the trustees in 1752 and conversion of Georgia to a royal colony, the original passed to Anthony Ashley Cooper, fourth Earl of Shaftesbury. It remained in the Cooper family until acquired by the industrialist Henry Francis du Pont in the 1930s. In 1926, the ninth earl presented to the state of Georgia a copy painted by Edmund Dyer in 1826.[4]

Despite the original painting's notoriety, not much is known about it. Art critics assume it was based on preliminary studies, either live sessions or renditions, and that the work was completed over a period of several years following the Georgia Indians' visit to London in June to October 1734. Of the painter, Edgar P. Richardson writes, "William Verelst belonged to one of those transplanted families of artists whom the English think of as Dutch and the Dutch think of as English and who are, in consequence, ignored by both."[5] Art reference books contain scant mention of him. Another Verelst, Jan, probably a cousin, is better known. He painted official full-length portraits of the five Iroquois Confederacy chiefs who visited Queen Anne in 1710.[6]

If the artist is mysterious, his subjects, at least the Indian ones, are even more so. All the Englishmen are identified. These include the president of the trustees, Viscount Percival,

Earl of Egmont, the Earl of Shaftesbury and Oglethorpe.[7] But of the Indians, only Tomochichi is named. He appears prominently in the center of the scene handing a devotional book to an Indian boy. The Indians fill the right half of the canvas, in a formal diptych opposite the white men, with an interpreter identified by some as John Musgrove interceding between them and the British. On the frame of a later copy of the painting the Indian boy is identified as Toonahowi, Tomochichi's nephew. The sole female figure is Senauki, his wife. A portrait or study by Verelst of Tomochichi and his nephew verifies these identities.[8]

The other five Indians, including the conspicuous young man in the foreground with a Mohawk hairstyle, have never been identified. In most reproductions they are simply labeled "Indians," "Creek Indians," or "Yamacraw Indians." I will demonstrate they are not Creek, but Cherokee.

Our first clue is the small-framed Indian holding a fan in the foreground (fig. 7.1). This is fairly obviously Attakullakulla, who visited England with a party of Cherokees in 1730, four years before the Creek mission. Investigation of the diplomacy of the delegations of 1730 and 1734 supports this identification. French Algonquian Indians were prominent in the affairs of the Cherokees in this period.

The scene depicted purports to show an actual meeting between trustees of the Colony of Georgia and a delegation of Yamacraw Indians under their chief, Tomochichi. It is supposed to record an event that took place on July 3, 1734. Six Indian men, an Indian boy, and an Indian woman are being introduced to the body of trustees assembled in the Georgia Rooms in Whitehall, the seat of British government, with clerks and an interpreter present. Though rendered in oil, on a colossal scale, it thus captures a small moment of time. The interpreter has just finished speaking and gestures toward Tomochichi, the clerk's pen is momentarily raised from his minute-book, and a bear cub held on a leash by the Indian in the foreground has just jumped up playfully to clutch the young man's knee.

Court painters often painted such events, much as official photographers today snap summit meetings and corporate mergers. The museums, castles and palaces of Europe are full of such ceremonial paintings. But while this event was of great solemnity, nothing vouches for its absolute faithfulness to what actually occurred. Presumably, no crowd of observers from the public could have confirmed the actual appearance of the subjects or even who was present. It was a private affair. The meeting took place behind closed doors and William Verelst was later commissioned to make a pictorial record of it.

Of the three-hundred-plus representations of American Indians in Lila Fundaburk's catalog of images of Southeastern Indians, none is quite like Verelst's sumptuous, detailed portraits counterpoising Europeans and American natives. Here is a vital source for physical anthropology, one containing a wealth of information on Indian lifeways, including hairstyles, tattoos, dress, animal mascots, ceremonial objects, weapons, individual physiognomy, musculature, gestures and expressions. But what tribes and cultures are we viewing?

The Spanish, Portuguese, Dutch, English, and French had radically different ceremonies of possession by which they legitimized their claims in the New World.[9] The English method was normally to make surveys and treaties and mark their possessions with houses, gardens and fences. Often a twig or piece of turf was presented from the old owners, the Indians, to the new ones. Colonies were thus imagined as plantations, plantings of English agrarian society in a foreign setting. As early as the reign of Elizabeth, Sir Francis Bacon advised rulers to treat the so-called savages "justly and graciously ... and send oft of them over to the Countrey that plant, that they may see a better Condition than their own, and commend it when they return."[10]

Ogelthorpe, too, spoke of planting and "cultivating" in words that probably inspired the trustees to bring the Georgia Indians over to England for a visit in the first place:

And here I can't omit saying, that it is a Policy of considerable Benefit to our Colonies, and an Expence well laid out, at proper Distances of Time to persuade some of the chiefest Savages, both for Authority and Understanding, to visit Great Britain. That awed with the high Idea which our Metropolis gives them of the Grandeur of this Empire, and propagating that Idea among their Tribes, our Planters in their several Neighbourhoods may enjoy uninterrupted Peace and Commerce with them, and even Assistance from them, for at least one Generation. Such was the Journey of the Irroquois Chiefs in the Reign of Queen Anne, and such was lately the Visit from our Indian neighbors of Carolina. The good Effects of these Visits are well known to the Planters of those Colonies respectively, and probably will be felt with Pleasure for an Age to come.[11]

Oglethorpe's comments refer to the visit by Iroquois sachems in 1710, a delegation of seven Cherokees brought over to England by Sir Alexander Cumming in 1730 and the visit of Tomochichi, his wife, nephew and war captains in 1734. All were part of the English diplomatic strategy. One of the last such delegations was the Cherokee visit arranged by the Virginian Henry Timberlake in 1762. Its purpose was to cement the recent peace concluded between England and the Cherokees. Again, official portraits were made, including one of Ostenaco by Sir Joshua Reynolds.[12] After the establishment of the United States and Treaty of Paris, England had no further use for visiting Indians except as exotic curiosities.

France employed a different approach. If the English concept of plantations was grounded in a national love of gardens and *le confort anglais*, the French rite of possession rested, according to historian Patricia Seed, on a flair for drama. It was staged, specifically, along the lines of the *joyeuse entrée* featuring a French monarch or lord entering a free city. Key elements were elaborate costumes, dancing and music. Amid festivities, the people gave their open consent to receive the visitor in hospitality and friendship. A French explorer describes his expedition as "conquest not by arms, but by the cross, not by force, but by love which has sweetly led them to donate themselves and their country to the king of France."[13] As a consequence, the French enjoyed better relations with the Indians.

Certain elements in the *Audience* painting reflect a French model of diplomacy. This should not surprise us at a time when Parisian court life and opera set the tone for other countries. The English, it must be remembered, were at this time were trying to woo Indians away from the French. And so the overall scene is one of stately entry, festivity and joy. Tomochichi is painted with a definite if artificial smile, reaching out the hand of friendship.

The Indians are shown in native dress. When they arrived in the English capital considerable discussion ensued on how to dress them for official audiences. "Suitable garments were ordered for them so they might make a proper appearance at court. They wished to wear their native dress, but Oglethorpe insisted on a combination of civilized and savage costume."[14] In Verelst's painting, Senauki and Toonahowi wear complete English dress and some of the other Indians have vestiges of European–style adornments, but the stark contrast between naked Indians and civilized Englishmen could not be more pronounced. In the actual formalities, however, the Indians wore the "shirts we gave them over their covering, which is only a skin that leaves their breasts and thighs and arms open." They refused to put on breeches or boots. Some of the delegation is in festive, native attire to underscore the exotic nature of the scene.

Not only did Verelst take liberties with the clothing of the Indians, but he was also less than literal about their real appearances. We read in a contemporary magazine account: "The war-captain and other attendants of Tomo-cha-chi were very importunate to appear at court in the manner they go in their own country, — which is only with a proper covering round their waist, the rest of their body being naked, — but were dissuaded from it by Mr. Oglethorpe. But their faces were variously painted after their country manner, some half black, others triangular, and others with bearded arrows instead of whiskers."[15] Verelst did not include half-black faces and triangular face paint in his painting. Such differences between the Indians' reported appearances and his presentation of them suggest he used other models.

So what models did he use for the five remaining Indians? Why were these not identified? There are several possible answers to these questions: (1) the English did not know the Indians' names, (2) their names have been lost through an accident of history, (3) the five Indians were not thought important or (3) they are not whom we suppose them to be.

According to records and accounts kept on the Indians' visit of 1734, the English certainly knew the names of the chiefs attending Tomochichi. They are "Hillispilli the war-chief of the Lower Creeks, four other chiefs of that nation, to wit: Apakowtski, Stimalchi, Sintouchi and Hinguithi, and Umphichi a Uchee chief from Palachocolas."[16] One of the six, Senauki's brother, died of smallpox at his lodgings in Little Ambrey, Westminster. He was buried in the churchyard of St. John the Evangelist with his regalia and possessions.[17] Umphichi, the Yuchi chief, is therefore absent from the painting. Accordingly, the Yuchis did not have any direct representation in the transactions, a failure that was to create difficulties for Tomochichi with the other chiefs when he returned to Georgia, as the Yuchis had not formally entered into any of the agreements. Hillispilli and Stimalchi were very familiar names and faces to the colonists, having been among the first greeting party encountered by Oglethorpe.[18]

It is hard to believe that the English would have thought these chiefs important enough to bring before the king and immortalize in a painting but not important enough to identify later. Each of them spoke for a tribe of the Lower Creek confederacy, just as Tomochichi, albeit something of a renegade, spoke for the Yamacraws. The identity of the five chiefs was vital to validation of the treaty. Tomochichi needed to present the terms to a plenary council of Creek chiefs for ratification when he returned to America, something in the course of things he only partly accomplished.

The last alternative is our best explanation. The Indians are not who we might think they are. The trustees had good reason to omit the names of Tomochichi's attendants and simply lump them together with no tribal identity if they were actually substitutes from a previous delegation. Significantly, the Creek Indians returned to Savannah before their portraits could be done, except for Tomochichi and his family. No Indians were available in London as live models during the years Verelst worked on the painting from 1734 to 1735. The representations of Creek chiefs Hillispilli, Apakowtski, Stimalchi, Sintouchi, and Hinguithi are facsimiles. Attaching their names would have been a transparent fiction.

Let us consider next what the true identity of these Georgia Indians might be by looking at a previous attempt at British treaty-making. In 1730, a scapegrace Scots laird by the name of Alexander Cumming traveled to the Overhill Towns of the Cherokee and captured what he later called the Crown of Tennessee. Originally intending to bring back the "king," Moytoy, he persuaded instead seven countrymen, mostly younger Cherokees, to meet George II in London. His main contacts in Cherokee country were the brothers William and Joseph Cooper, traders based at Keowee in South Carolina. We have encountered the Cooper name before. Evidently William and Joseph Cooper belong to the same Marrano family as Robert Cooper, a London merchant. The Cumming adventure resulted in an unofficial alliance between the Cherokee and English, though the board of commissioners ended up giving little credit to him. Later, any treaty was repudiated by the Cherokee chiefs. An outraged war party looted and burned the Coopers' trading post.

In 1734, someone at Charleston sent the authorities at Savannah the following complaint:

> The Principal actors in this Affair was those Indians that Sr. Alexander Cummings carried over lately to England; we find notwithstanding the good Treatment they met with there that they are more insolent than the others and say that we are all Slaves to the Great George, and all the Goods carried to their Nation are his and he sends them over as Presents to them.... I am sure it will be for the Service of this Province never to Suffer any more of them to go there; the Treaty of Alliance Settled between them and the Lords of Trade they now despise.[19]

The famous Crown of Tennessee was tossed aside in a royal closet at Hampton Court and never seen again.[20]

The Scottish baronet from Aberdeen responsible for this fiasco is described by modern-day writers with words like "bizarre," "madcap" and "eccentric." In and out of debtor's prison, he died in ignominious circumstances. One of his more audacious schemes was the establishment of a stock company that would settle 300,000 "honest and industrious" European Jews among the Cherokee Indians. This white elephant may have been inspired by John Law's Mississippi Bubble. Cumming also claimed to be the "deliverer of the Jews." That he himself was a Jew seems more than likely from all the circumstances of his life and career.[21] Moreover, "He was called by his mother, a few days before her death, both Jacob and Israel."[22]

If we ask how Cumming even *knew* of the existence of 300,000 Jews, a fairly accurate estimate of Ashkenazi Jews in Eastern Europe at the time, some surprising connections emerge. Like many Aberdeen crypto–Jews, he spent the first part of his career as a merchant and soldier in Russia and Lithuania. He may have retained connections with eastern Jewry, for "wild as his projects were, some of the most learned Jews seem to have given him several patient hearings on the subject."[23] One can infer that Sir Alexander was an Aberdeen crypto–Jew. The family name comes from the Flemish nobleman Comyns, a knight who accompanied William the Conqueror to England and boasted of being directly descended from Charlemagne. The Cumming clan's association with Gordons, Sutherlands and Setons supports Jewish roots.

While the seven Cherokee were in London, their movements were followed closely in the press. A popular engraving was made of them in the clothes that had been presented to them by the king. This etching is said to have been done by Isaac Basire "after a painting by Markham," now evidently lost.[24] Shown in St. James's Garden, they are identified as Onanconoa, Skalilosken Ketagustah, Kollannah, Oukah Ulah, Tathtowe, Clogoittah and Ukwaneequa. The last mentioned, Uk-uk-u-ne-ka (White Owl), is small of stature, slender of frame and boyish-looking. He wears his hair in a Mohawk, a sign he is a Northerly, or Algonquian. As suspected at the outset of this inquiry, he can be none other than Attakullakulla (Ata'gul'kalu, "leaning wood"), supreme peace chief of the Cherokee 1760–1775. The engraving (and painting) captures him at about the age of 20. Since there is no mention of a youth among the visiting Creek and Yamacraw Indians other than the boy Tooanahawi, this must be Attakullakulla. The 1730 etching shows him carrying the eagle feather wand that the Cherokees presented to King George. In the 1734 painting he has the same feather wand. The Quaker naturalist Bartram described him as "a man of remarkably small stature, slender and of a delicate frame, the only instance I saw in the [Cherokee] Nation; but he is a man of superior abilities." [25] In later life, Attakullakulla often mentioned his trip to England and offered to go back and see "the Great King George."

The fact is that the eight Creek chiefs brought to England by Oglethorpe were widely heralded in London as Cherokees even though they came from non–Cherokee Savannah. The designation Creek Indians was not yet well established for Muskogean tribes. Moreover, as we have seen, the 1730 treaty was in a state of limbo. The English were eager to revalidate it with the new group that accompanied Tomochichi. It would seem that whatever paintings or studies were prepared in 1730 must now be unpopular, though they might nonetheless serve as good models of the "noble savage," a concept then capturing the popular fancy thanks primarily to French philosophers like Montesquieu and Voltaire.

So who are the other Cherokees in the painting? Tathtowe (Tistoe, a ceremonial title meaning "smoke maker") is the tall figure with dangling side locks. In the 1734 grouping, he is evidently the headman of Keowee remembered as the fifth to join Cumming's party in 1730. The Cherokee title Tistoe distinguished an official responsible for smudging or producing the sacrificial smoke in the assembly house. Today it refers to Santa Claus, bringer of firecrackers during holidays. The word probably comes from Greek τυφω (typho) "to raise smoke."

The short figure on the extreme right in the 1734 painting is Clogoittah ("gun carrier," another title). He was from Tenase, the home of the Crown, fourth to join Cumming's party. The older man behind Tomochichi in the 1734 painting, second from the left in the 1730 etching and labeled Skalilosken (Speaker) Ketagustah (Second in Command) are the same persons. The Cherokee title *skalilosken*, which cannot be analyzed into Cherokee elements, seems to come from Greek *kerux*, "herald." In both instances, it is a title borne by the man responsible for summoning an assembly, delivering "talks" and making diplomatic contact with the enemy. Our Kittagusta, in reality, was probably the son of French Huguenot trader John Beamer and a Cherokee woman named Quatsis/Quatie ("Patsy/Patty").[26] Appropriately, Kittagusta the Speaker was chosen by the 1730 delegation to make a ceremonial speech in response to the treaty drafted by the British.

The muscular war chief in the foreground of the 1734 painting is the same figure as the one in the background of the 1730 etching. He is Collanah (The Raven) of Settico, brother of the same Quatsis/Quatie. That this is Collanah of Settico, not the Creek/Yuchi war chief Umphichi, follows from the facts as we have established them, namely, that Umphichi died before the audience with the Trustees took place. The brother of the mother, or maternal uncle, was considered the head of the household, according to Cherokee custom. Hence Collanah stands behind the Speaker Kittagusta and Mankiller, his sister's children in the 1730 etching.

The remaining two Cherokees from the 1730 delegation do not appear in the 1734 painting. They are: (1) Outacite (Mankiller) Skiagusta (Great Warrior), headman of Tassetchee, the second to join Cumming's party after Attakullakulla, and brother of Skalilosken Kittagusta, called Ukah Ulah (Principal Chief to Be) by the English, and (2) Ounakannowie (White Deer), second from the right next to Attakullakulla, a last minute addition to the Cummings party from the Upper Towns. Thus, three of the seven are members of Quatie's family, situated at the time in the Cherokee town of Tassetchee. One might speculate that Verelst omitted the chiefly figure of Outacite since the role of a headman in the 1734 scene was filled by Tomochichi.

Summing up, Verelst's graphically realized details hint there was a lost painting or study upon which his portraits were based. Markham's painting (and the engraving inspired by it) depicts the Cherokees in English clothes, but the Trustees painting has them in native dress. Perhaps an intermediary picture from 1730 was discarded after the Cherokees revoked the treaty, but used out of convenience as a mold for the Trustees painting in 1734.

Two members of the 1730 delegation, Kittagusta the Speaker and Collanah the Raven of Settico, previously of Tassetchee, are evidently mixed, not full bloods. Collanah exhibits a muscular build untypical of American Indians, more like black slaves or Europeans. Cherokee historian Brent Cox says Collanah, brother of Quatie, married Nancy, who was "one half white."[27] It was unusual at that time for an Indian male to marry a white or part-white woman; the inference is perhaps that he also bore some non–Indian genes. There could have been African ancestry in his parents' makeup. The names Quatie (Patty) and Nancy (Nanheyi), moreover, are not originally Cherokee names.

John Beamer (Beamor, French Benamour, Sephardic surname Benamor) was a French Huguenot of an Iberian Jewish family fleeing from the Spanish Inquisition. His father came to the Carolina colony soon after the foundation of Charles Town. Beamer met Quatie in 1699; he was thus one of the first white men, along with Alexander Dougherty and Joseph Cooper, to intermarry with the Cherokee. She was his Indian wife; he had a series of white wives back in the settlements, one of them the daughter of the governor. On the frontier he received the name Beaver, Cherokee *Amadohiyi*, English Moytoy. Cox regards this as a clerical error but why should we not take it at face value? One meaning of the word is "beaver," another is "mariner."

We know that John Beamer's grandson, Thomas Beamer, was called a Mustee, proof of some degree of African blood.[28] Derived from Mestizo, this term is confined to admixtures of the Indian and Negro races. In the Beamer-Moytoy family, then, we can trace — genealogically and pictorially — a tri-racial mixture later known as Melungeon, the white constituent in which is Sephardic Jewish.

Another of the children of John Beamer and Quatsis/Quatie was Oconostota (Ground-hog Sausage), known as the Great Warrior. A descendant, Narcissa Owen, claims he also was part of the 1730 delegation although not under his true name, rather a title. Brent Cox demurs about this and suggests that the British uniform Owen claims Oconostota brought back was actually passed to him by his uncle, Collanah, who, as we saw, certainly did participate in the delegation. Quatie later married Jacob the Conjuror, of Settico, previously of Tassetchee, another player in the Cumming mission. Jacob, like Oconostota, may also have been mixed since he bears an English, originally Hebrew name.

By the year 1730, there was a significant degree of admixture among the Cherokee, including French, English, Portuguese, Spanish, Moroccan, Scottish, African and Jewish strains. This admixture appears to be concentrated in the ruling families of the largest Overhill Towns, Tellico, Echota and Settico, located primarily in what is now Monroe County, Tennessee. English, Scottish and French merchants out of Charlestown, typically Sephardic Jews, were the first to intermarry with the Cherokee.

It has often been maintained that the office of principal chief was not introduced among the Cherokees and other southeastern tribes until the British created it, wishing to have a single authority to deal with on matters of trade. English policy was to appoint headmen to sign treaties for all towns in their "nation." As R. S. Cotterill, for instance, says of the 1721 treaty at Congaree, the British "created, on [Gov. Francis] Nicholson's suggestion, the new office of principal chief, elevating thereto a chief whom the Carolina writers have effectively disguised as Wrosetasatow [a form of Outacite, Mankiller, from the Lower Town of Estatoe]."[29] The historian Charles Hudson agrees that principal chiefs did not come into fashion until the mid-eighteenth century, when a breed of Indians who might be termed "Fort Indians" gathered around the trading posts built on the southeastern frontier.[30] Moytoy, Old Hop, the "non-entity" Amascossite, Attakullakulla and Oconostota thus serve as treaty chiefs for the Cherokee. In the same way, Tomochichi and the "Emperor" Brim function as puppets manipulated by the English in Georgia. Conchak Emike (Chief Skunk-Hole) fulfills the same role among the Choctaws until the French have him killed.

Such a picture of tribal government may not be completely accurate. The principal actors in the Cherokee Nation at this time were Jews. The Stuart monarchs had long favored Portuguese and Scottish Sephardim because they knew that Jews harbored an abiding hatred of the Spanish. If captured, Marranos and New Christians would be burned at the stake as heretics. They knew it. For this reason, Savannah Jews of Sephardic background fled to nearby Charleston during the brief War of Jenkins Ear when it seemed the Spanish might invade Georgia. Only Ashkenazi Jews like the Sheftalls remained behind. How much of Jewish participation in Cherokee politics was opportunistic and how much was borne out of the traders' recognition of genetic and religious ties cannot be known, but the official titles used by the Cherokee delegation of 1730 confirm the story of the Elohi and Eshelokee. Most of them are Greek and military in inspiration, from Moytoy (Admiral) to Skalilosken (herald) and Kolanu (*karanos*).

The ancient equivalent for the proverb "carrying coals to Newcastle" was the adage "sending owls to Athens." Athens was the home of philosophers, and the owl with its huge eyes, nocturnal habits and ability to turn its head and look all around was the emblem of the wise man, or scholar. The Cherokee called their peace king Uku, which has been translated "owl," but the fact that they also had a word for his feathered counterpart (*huhu*) as well as one for owls in the sense of witches (*skili*) tells us something. Most Indian tribes regard the real owl as a bird of bad omen and death. Only the Cherokee and Hopi seem to make an exception, for in the Hopi language the words for owl and chief are also the same, *mongwau* and *mongwi* (both evidently built on an Egyptian root *mn* "exalted").

The true origin of the Uku explains the significance of the Crown of Tennessee, for the Uku traditionally wore an otter headdress.[31] After nearly two thousand years, and in their own way, the Cherokee retained many of the customs of the original Eshelokee. No ordinary colonists these. They appear to have been handpicked for intellectual standing and superior knowledge. One leader was a philosopher-king. Another was called the Admiral.

# Chapter 8

## *She Who Walks with the Little People*

*Stars we cease to believe in grow pale.* — Heinrich Heine

Nancy Ward is one of three or four women in the history of Indian nations to be given the title Beloved. In Cherokee, she was called the Ghigau, the Beloved, Red, Honorable, or War Woman. She received this honor in 1755 attending her husband Kingfisher on a war party against the Creeks in Upper Georgia. She performed tasks customary for women, such as cooking, carrying water and gathering firewood. But when Kingfisher was slain before her eyes, she took up his bloody tomahawk and helped rout the entire Creek army. She fettered the captives, cattle and slaves and drove them home. In Chota, the Cherokee seat of government, she was elevated to the highest position a woman could hold. As the Ghigau, she decided whether or not a captive taken in war would be killed or adopted into the tribe.

Following the defeat of her people in the Chickamaugan Wars, Nancy retired to the Amovey District near the Ocoee River at her brother Long Fellow's home. Louis Philippe, duke of Orleans, destined to be king of the French from 1830 to 1848, called on her there during his travels in America. He remarked she lived in "barbarian splendor."[1] She died in 1822.

Nancy came from the Moytoy family examined in the previous chapter. Her mother was Tame Doe and her father Sir Francis Ward, a Scottish laird at the nearby British outpost of Fort Loudon.[2] A close relative of hers was Nionee, wife of Attakullakulla and mother of Dragging Canoe, the last great Cherokee general.[3] Another of her names was Tsistuna-gis-ke, "Rose." This seems to be what Muslim Indians called her, perhaps the Creeks, for the surname Ward in Arabic means "rose." One of her relatives, John Ward, was a Tunisian pirate who converted to Islam and became known in Muslim annals as Wardiyya ("of the rose"). A Jacobean play lambasted Ward, whose flagship was manned by an Anglo-Turkish crew of 400 pirates.[4] This Barbary connection, like the Deer Clan of her grandfather, the Algonquian Indian White Owl Raven, seems to relate to the presence of Arab and Muslim culture in the eastern United States at the time, how old or extensive it is difficult to say.

Years after Nancy's death her memory was still alive. Someone carved a life-sized statue out of native granite and placed it over a grave in the Arnwine Cemetery overlooking the Clinch River, near Liberty Hill in Grainger County, Tennessee. In the 1970s, the unusual memorial was stolen by grave-robbers who spirited it away in a brown Chevy never to be seen again by the locals. Fortunately, D. Ray Smith, a descendant, had photographed it (fig. 8.1).[5]

In Cherokee tradition, heroes and heroines are often associated with, and typified by, a mascot or namesake animal they capture, save or domesticate. In some cases, a woman would suckle a fawn or cub. It is no longer remembered how Nancy's mother, Tame Deer, received her name but it may have been for such a reason as this. The name of the powerful Uktena-slaying magician Oconusti of Cherokee legends means Groundhog Mother and was given to him because he showed a tender heart to an orphaned baby groundhog. The question is: What animal does Nancy Ward hold in her arms and foster, and why?

The statue shows Nancy displaying a coat of arms with her name on it along with the words "Watauga 1776." The Watauga Country was a bold experiment in government established by the followers of Daniel Boone in their attempt to carve out a free state in what is now East Tennessee. Elizabeth Hirschman has shown that there were religious as well as political motives behind the establishment of Watauga and has suggested that many of its leaders were crypto–Jews.[6] It is Nancy's dealings with the Wataugans that make her career inscrutable. Over and over, she commits daring betrayals of her people, sends secret warnings to the enemy and engages in risky reversals of war council policy.

The settlements she alternately aided and thwarted began in 1769 when

Fig. 8.1. Nancy Ward Statue. © D. Ray Smith. Used with permission.

William Bean of Pittsylvania County, Virginia, followed the first trail blazed into Cherokee upper country by white men. Bean built a lonely cabin on the Watauga River near present-day Elizabethtown. He became the first settler to put down stakes in what would become the State of Tennessee. Tradition says he hunted with Daniel Boone and that was why he chose Boone's campsite to build his cabin on—a hillside at the mouth of Boones Creek, whose entrance was guarded by a waterfall. According to Tennessee's earliest deed book, Bean formally entered his land shortly after the treaty of Sycamore Shoals on April 3, 1775. Later that year he recorded deeds for nearly 2000 acres on Boones Creek and elsewhere in Watauga.[7] He established Beans Station on the road from Carters Valley over Copper (Cooper) Ridge to the Clinch River, a landmark tavern and fort through which almost every traveler to and from Natchez and Washington City passed in the early days of the frontier. His closest neighbors in both locations were the Coopers, Portuguese Jews associated with Boone.

The Watauga Association that Bean and others formed to run the pioneer government was a precursor of the independent State of Franklin that encompassed much of present-day Kentucky and Tennessee. After the collapse of the Regulator movement in the Carolinas, landowners led by James and Charles Robertson[8] established their homes farther west and joined the fledgling community. They drew up a charter for a secret, separate state in 1772, claiming to have a ten-year lease from the Cherokee. Other settlers along the Holston and Nolichucky rivers threw in their lots with them. In 1775 the Wataugans negotiated with Cherokee chiefs, primarily Attakullakulla, to annex a vast tract stretching into Kentucky, never precisely surveyed. The Henderson Purchase sparked Dragging Canoe's rebellion and the withdrawal of the disaffected southward, where they founded the new Lower Towns in Georgia and Alabama and became known as the Chickamauga Confederacy.[9] Dragging Canoe's policies are now generally understood as a nativist ghost-dance movement that eventually failed. The Chickamauga leader is widely viewed as a prophet-warrior who preceded Tecumseh. At any rate, it was the beginning of the end for the Cherokee Nation.

One tale from many will illustrate Nancy Ward's habitual knack for incensing the rest of the Cherokee by perversely favoring the Wataugans. When the American Revolution broke out, the tribe leaned strongly toward the British cause under their agent John Stuart, a Scotsman, who had been formally adopted into the Wolf Clan by the Moytoy family. Cherokee warriors in the Overhill Towns could not wait to join their Lower Town and Middle Town brothers in striking back at the white settlements. Impetuously, they mounted a skirmish on the eve of the planned attack and outside Beans Station captured Lydia Bean, William's wife, along with 13-year-old Samuel Moore. They intercepted Mrs. Bean as she was making her way from her home on Boones Creek to Sycamore Shoals. The warriors marched the white female and boy to the Overhill Towns and strapped them to a stake. At this juncture, Nancy Ward called a stop to the proceedings. She told them that they could use Mrs. Bean's knowledge. In this decision, the Beloved Woman was exercising her right to spare a condemned captive's life. But she went much further. She took the injured Mrs. Bean into her own home and nursed her back to health. Samuel Moore was freed.

Mrs. Bean, like most colonial women, wove her own cloth. At the time, the Cherokee were wearing a combination of traditional animal skin clothing and loomed cloth purchased from traders. Cherokee people had rough-woven hemp clothing, but it was not as comfortable as that made from linen, cotton or wool. Mrs. Bean taught the Ghigau how to set up a loom, spin yarn and weave cloth. This skill would make the Cherokee people less dependent on traders, but it also Europeanized the Cherokee in ways little fathomed at the time. Women came to be expected to do the weaving and house chores. Men took over duties in the cornfields and became settled farmers. The females became dedicated housewives.

Another side of Cherokee life that changed with the two women's friendship was animal husbandry. Lydia owned dairy cattle which she moved to Nancy's house at Chota. There she taught Nancy to prepare and use dairy foods. Cattle were soon slaughtered to supplement the traditional fare of deer meat, making the Cherokees less dependent on hunting. In 1780, when the Virginia militia arrived to help the Tennesseans strike back at the Cherokee, Nancy Ward reciprocated Lydia Bean's gift. As a gesture of peace, she drove a small herd into the Wataugan camp to feed the hungry troops.[10] Because of Ward's introduction of cattle among the Cherokee, her people would soon begin to amass large herds and farms, requiring more and more manual labor. This led them to rely on slaves. Ward herself had been awarded the black slave of the Creek warrior she had felled.

These innovations were to have far-reaching effects. Not only did livestock, European clothing and slavery give the Cherokees the appearance of being civilized, but these institutions also carried some real advantages in treaty making. Instead of the usual trinkets, guns, and whisky, the Cherokee began to ask for and receive farming tools and spinning wheels from the U.S. government. By 1820, the chief of the Nation, Charles Hicks, reported:

> The growth of cotton, the use of the wheel and cards, and the manufacturing of their own clothing, and the advantages of the labor and aid of the horse and plough, have also been found in the enlargement of their farms.... The arts of weaving and knitting have become part of the female attention of this nation.... It is believed that there is not more than one eighth or ninth part of the families, but has either horses or cattle; and perhaps there is none without a stock of hogs.... There are six grist and two saw mills owned by natives, and fourteen or fifteen grist and two saw mills owned by white men who are married into native families.[11]

According to a federal official named Jedidiah Morse, the Cherokee in 1809 numbered 12,395 people, half of whom were of mixed blood, besides 583 slaves. They had 65 villages and towns with "property in horses, cattle, sheep, plows, mills etc. estimated at about $571,500."[12] They also had schoolmasters, blacksmiths, millers, saltpeter and gunpowder manufacturers, ferrymen, turnpike keepers and a range of "mechanics."

The design of the Nancy Ward statue focuses on her protection of the white settlers, and this connection may also explain the young cub or kit in her arms. Plainly not a lamb, or bear cub, or panther's kitten, it is rather a blackfox (*Martes pennati*). This animal was evidently chosen to allegorize the new leadership promoted by the Beloved Woman's actions.

When Nancy hastened to the settlements to warn the Wataugans of an Indian attack, it was along the so-called Black Fox Path, named for Dragging Canoe's nephew, Enola (who became principal chief of the Cherokee in 1801). The historic Black Fox Crossing is on the Clinch River between Claiborne and Grainger counties in Tennessee, now covered by Lake Norris. Several other places bear the name Black Fox in Bradley County and White County, Tennessee. There is also a noted Black Fox Camp Springs near Dilton and Murfreesboro in Rutherford County on what was then the edge of the Cumberland Settlement in 1793. A story told about the chief when he was a young warrior goes that he often hunted and camped at this magnificent spring on the Stones River. "Once he was pursued to this place, and rather than be caught by the soldiers, sprang into the water and disappeared from sight. The soldiers believed him to be lost, but by an underground channel, he came to surface again at Murfree's Spring, two and one-half miles below."

Enola is not a Cherokee word — usually a clue to foreign roots. It does crop up among the Choctaw and Chickasaw but its true origin lies in the diminutive of a girl's name for Hebrew Hannah, meaning "gracious."[13] Its most notorious occurrence is in the *Enola Gay*, the plane that dropped the atomic bomb on Hiroshima in 1945. Enola was the name of the bombardier's mother. Chief Black Fox was the first to bear the name outside of Choctaw and Chickasaw territory, and it may have been suggested by the name of his former seat at Eustanali (either "small blackfox" or "place of the river rocks"). Whatever the connections, *enola* became the Cherokee word applied to the mysterious, sleek long-tailed animal known as blackfox in the fur trade, actually not a fox at all but type of ferret. Enola in and of itself does not "mean" blackfox. The animal's appearance on the Nancy Ward statue is thus the perfect emblem for the Cherokee people in their transformation to mixed bloods. It made sense not only because of its associations with the Black Fox trail but also because of the blackfox's traits and qualities. It is a fierce fighter, lives in caves and, uncannily, disappears in self-defense. According to Indian tradition, the blackfox knows the paths of the spirit world. As noted in the story about Black Fox above, the blackfox has anomalous characteristics and supernatural powers. When Chief Black Fox died, he was buried Egyptian-style with a treasure of lead ingots and flint points in an earthen pyramid in a valley of kings located in Blount County, Alabama.

Nancy Ward's counterpart among the Choctaws is the trader Hardy Perry. This pioneer of probable Jewish or crypto–Jewish origin operated a trading post as early as 1767 near present-day Tupelo, Mississippi. He came to the territory from Georgia. The Perrys are a Sephardic family whose name (Perez) stands for the pear tree of the Land of Israel.[14] As we have seen, they are probably also the namesake of Parris Island, where the last of Juan Pardo's Portuguese settlers disappeared off the map of history. Richard Pearis, a partner of Nathaniel Gist, became the first interpreter among the Overhill Cherokee.

Hardy Perry introduced oxen to the Choctaws, bringing the animals north from Mobile. Curiously, the name of his Choctaw wife from near present-day Grenada, Mississippi, was Anolah, the same name as Enola. Possibly, this is a sign that chief Black Fox's mother was Choctaw, like William Cooper's wife Malea Labon. Did she come from the mixed descendants of the abandoned French colony of 1720? Perry also had a wife in the neighboring Chickasaw Nation of Halfbreeds, as did certainly his son, Chief Isaac Perry. Three Perrys signed the first Choctaw treaty of 1805, and it was their land that included what became the Eliot Mission site, located in the present-day town of Holcomb, Mississippi. Chief Isaac Perry was one of the signers of the Treaty of Dancing Rabbit Creek in 1830, whereby Choctaws were removed beyond the Mississippi. In Indian Territory, the Perrys became important witnesses in the landmark tribal enrollment case of *Nancy Cooper v. The Choctaw Nation.* So we see in this culture-bearer, too, a connection with the Coopers.

One of Nancy Ward's other names is Nunnehi, which may be translated One Who Goes Where She Pleases, a reference to a fairylike folk called by the same name. These figures in Cherokee folklore are also called Anetsageta, a word related to *anetsa*, "games"[15] and clue to their deep ancestry. The likely Doric Greek root is *neika*, "game, play." Anetsageta would of old have been understood to mean something like "The Playful or Mischievous Ones." The various terms are conventionally rendered as Little People in English. Literally, though, the term Nunnehi means "living, going anywhere." It can also be taken as "people of the paths." It is this designation that recalls their distant origins, for these Immortal Ones of Cherokee legend are descendants, anthropologically speaking, of the Fates of Greek and Roman religion. In Hebrew folk belief, they are the *hadas*. In Celtic mythology they are usually known as fairies. But all are one and the same.

The folklore of other Indians includes Little People. The Makiawisug among the Mohegan and Geo-lud-mo-sis-eg among the Micmac are their equivalents. But none of these myths quite matches that of the Cherokee. Instead of fulfilling the role of benevolent ancestral ghosts, these other Little People seem to be nature spirits, diminished gods, totemic forces or memory of aboriginal races of smaller stature.

Like their antecedents in the Old World, the Nunnehi are generally heard but not seen. They are oddly perverse and do things backwards. They live in caves and abandoned mounds but also have a council house under the water of lakes and rivers.[16] Sometimes a beautiful Nunnehi woman will steal a young man away from the dance and take him home to their subterranean dwelling, exactly as in the story of Thomas Rhymer and the Fairy Queen.

They can also help lost travelers. If they take a pot or other utensil from the household they always pay the owner back for what they "borrow."

All these characteristics recall the *lares viales* (gods of the roads) and *compitales* (gods of the crossroads) of the Romans, magical spirits who guard roads and protect wayfarers. The celebration of *compitales* in ancient Rome came at the end of the old year and beginning of a new year. Certain members of the household were believed to be better suited than others to befriend and propitiate the fickle nether beings. These shadowy beings dwell in the country and are especially fond of crossroads. The meeting of two roads is a magical place presided over by their queen, Hecate (the crone incarnation of the triple Mother Goddess, later reduced to a witch-figure). All these ancestral ghosts are to be propitiated by sacrificing a crust of bread or pouring out a bowl of milk for them. Several stories about Cherokee fairies include the act of a member of the household leaving a crust of bread for them overnight, often against the will of the others. The fairies then repay the respectful one with kindness and punish the non-believers with spiteful accidents.

In addition to the Nunnehi, who are of normal size, the Cherokee believe in a second type of fairy being. These are creatures about three feet tall called Yunwi Tsundsdi (literally, "people, little"). They inhabit laurel patches, broom sage patches, caves behind waterfalls, mountaintops and, especially, rockslides. Although their activities imitate those of the Cherokee — they hunt, plant corn, and hold dances — they do not look like the Cherokee. The men are elderly with beards, mustaches and long gray hair, their complexions ruddy, their heads crowned with caps. The Choctaw, too, have their little men, Bohpuli, about two feet tall, who live in the deep woods and play tricks on people. Although most scholars today are probably inclined to attribute both types of fairy folklore to the influence of late-arriving Europeans among the Cherokee and Choctaw, it seems more likely that such universally held traditions have deeper roots.

Modern–day Cherokee beliefs based on "actual reports of encounters" with the Little People are recorded in a book published in Cherokee, North Carolina, in 1998.

> When the Little People visit Cherokee homes, the kitchen seems to be their favorite room of the house. They like bright things such as silverware, pots and pans or shiny appliances. According to many stories one can often hear these items being moved around and afterward find them out of place. They seem to come to play with these things or to look at themselves in the mirror surfaces. They don't usually take anything unless they are hungry.
>
> Since the Little People seem to especially enjoy it, the Cherokee women often leave cornbread for them on the kitchen table. Frequently, the ladies report, the cornbread is gone the next day with crumbs left on the table or trailing across the room to the kitchen door.[17]

If we compare these accounts of Indians' Little People with a study by authority Katharine Briggs, we see that the Cherokee versions incorporate, story by story, all the stock motifs of European fairy tales: brownies or house spirits making noises like poltergeists, pixies and pouks misleading travelers, will o' wisps, the supernatural passage of time in fairyland, shape shifting, the power of bestowing good or ill luck, caves as an entrance to fairyland, changelings (one of the earliest traditions), stealing food (or at least sucking nourishment out of milk and bread — a memory of the Homeric offering to ghosts), levitation (but no wings, a Victorian and very late invention), bargaining and exchanging items of trade, trooping and inflicting illness or helping with miracle cures.[18]

Where do fairies come from? In their ancient Mediterranean form, they have been traced to the spirits of the dead, vapid and furtive beings that continue to live in the imagination of the common people. The Greeks and Romans knew them as underground figures variously called Moirae, or Fates, Parcae (Sparing Ones) and Eumenides (Kind Ones). Hesiod turns them into the trinity of Clotho, Lachesis and Atropos, sisters who appear at a child's birth. The first spins out the newborn's thread of life, the second measures it and the third cuts it off. All these nebulous visitors from another world were considered remnants of pagan (literally, "rustic") mythology, hence their association with the countryside. The word "pagan" has connotations of "backward, countrified." Both the Olympian religion of the Greeks and Romans and later the Christian faith relegate all such beliefs to the domain of superstition and ignorance. But as Briggs shows, these "old wives' tales" are very persistent. The three weird sisters Shakespeare's Macbeth encounters at a crossroads (*pagus*) are of the same lineage. True to form, they bestow on him his destiny.

In the Middle Ages the Fata of Greco-Roman belief systems recur as the Fées of France, *hadas* of Iberia (a word derived from *fata*) and fays, or fairies, of the British Isles. As before, "they visited the house where a child was born, with gifts of good and evil fortune" and in "sophisticated fairy tales ... they became fairy godmothers."[19] Among the Jews of Spain, a widespread custom is to celebrate all night with a *veula* or vigil prior to a boy-child's circumcision in order to bring good luck and ward off evil from the baby. This ceremony is the origin of the practice of throwing a gold or silver coin into a male infant's first bath to bring riches, a custom still practiced by Melungeons. The *hadas*, as Jews call the festivity, is a vestige of the Roman celebration of the Fata. The Sephardim of Spain also practiced a *fadamiento* for female children, which took place on the occasion of their naming dinner. As Judaic scholar David Gitlitz describes the celebration, the extended family would wait seven days before feasting and then shower the baby and its mother with presents.[20] According to Cherokee tradition, if one wishes to join the Nunnehi, one must fast for seven days before going to them.

Old World belief in fairies most likely came to America with the Greek, Jewish, Phoenician and Egyptian Elohi, not with later Spanish and Portuguese Jews or people of British Isles background. Cherokee traditions about fairies are little influenced by Christianity. Everything we know about fairy lore among the Cherokee stamps it as being either pre–Christian or non–Christian.

Nancy Ward was not actually called "She Who Walks with the Little People" but Nunnehi, one of the fairy folk themselves. With this name, she recalls the familiar figure of the Fairy Bride or Fairy Queen. She is a changeling as well as change agent. Her erratic actions in sometimes aiding the Wataugans against the war party's better judgment and sometimes shrilly denouncing them gave her a certain aura of the anomalous and other-worldly. She acquired a powerful influence. Nearly every Cherokee alive can find a connection to Nancy Ward in their family tree. It has been estimated that her known descendants number over 6,000. She left a dual legacy as the peaceful Beloved Woman and fierce War Woman, an ambiguity masterfully captured in the design of her funerary monument. She was not only a tribal mother. She became one of the immortals. And with good reason. Nancy's clan, Wolf, are the Dodewah, elders, teachers, people to carry on beliefs. Wolftown on the Eastern Cherokee Reservation in North Carolina is named after this clan. Its foundation goes back to the beginning of the Ani-Yunwiya, or Principal People. Here is the Cherokee origin story as I heard it from a Tennessee elder in the 1990s.

## Story of the Sacred Dog

When the pioneers came through the Cumberland Gap into Tennessee, they stumbled onto the Cherokee stronghold. They followed what was known as the Avery Trace. On its northern end, this went to Kentucky and joined the Great Warrior Path to Iroquois lands. On its southern end, it continued on through Nashville and became the Natchez Trace. These roads once connected empires. They went from capital to capital, sacred place to sacred place. The Cherokee had their sacred place on Monterey Mountain. It was marked by a stone monument to their national hero, the dog. The people had carved a large dog out of the top of the mountain in gratitude for their deliverance in the long-ago times.

Before the Great Flood there lived a man and his wife in a land now below the waters called Lami. There were no Cherokee at that time. The people of that place were a single nation with one tongue. Many had become wicked. They turned to witchcraft to satisfy their desires. This man and his wife kept to the old ways and were faithful. They had a dog that was loyal to them that they loved very much.

The dog spoke to the man and his wife in their dreams. One night it told them the world was going to be destroyed. They should make preparations to save their family. The man did not want to believe this. When he saw the dog in the morning, he asked the animal what he meant. The dog whimpered and cowered. The man shook his head. He petted the dog, but the dog was not to be comforted. Finally, the dog took the man down to the river and jumped into the rushing water. To show the man what he meant, he tore his arm and leg muscles with his teeth and drowned. The dog gave his life to save the lives of his people.

The man now knew what he was to do. He began building a boat. He put food and other necessities on it. The neighbors laughed at him because the ocean was far away even though they lived on an island. The stream was too small to carry his boat. When the man tried to warn them, they made fun of him for talking with dogs! It began to rain, and they ridiculed him all the more. The man quietly gathered his family and loaded their things on the boat.

The flood waters swept them down the river to the sea. It rained for many months. There were earthquakes, and the entire earth was covered with water. Finally, their boat came to rest on Monterey Mountain [in Putnam County, Tennessee]. This is why the Cherokee still live in the mountains, because they are afraid of another flood. They do not like to live where there are no cedar trees either.

The man and his wife had children, and the children had children. The Cherokees spread out to the east and settled the outlet to the sea along the Savannah River. They are called the Principal People [*ani yunwiya*] to show they are all descended from this couple. The original Wolf Clan is still the most common.

What happened to the stone monument, the Dog? The settlers in the Cumberland chipped away at it. Soldiers dynamited it. The atrocious Bledsoe brothers built their fort in the middle of the Avery Trace overlooking sacred ceremony ground. They took potshots at the Indians who came to trade and worship there. By the end of the century after they had left the region, the Cherokee Dog had dwindled to a foreleg. This was removed by some civic group. Eventually, it was placed on a pedestal in a park in the nearby town of Monterey, where you can see it today, although the fragment is not recognizable as part of a dog.[21]

The Wolf Clan is a vital part of the Warrior Society of the Cherokee, their Dog Soldiers, the Eshelokee. Clan members are known for their fierce loyalty and protection of family. Nancy Moytoy, Tame Doe's mother and Nancy Ward's grandmother, named one of her sons Big Dog and another White Dog. Naturally, chiefs Motoy II and Old Hop belonged to the Wolf Clan. Charles Hicks was another. Names like Nita (Pup) are common in Wolf Clan families.

The Algonquian Indians also have a Wolf Clan. The Cherokees' claim to be called the Dog People may have something to do with the Chichimeca (Dog Lineage) tribes of Mexico associated with the barbarian north. They are remembered as predecessor peoples to the more civilized Toltecs and Teotihuacanos. The Chichimeca in turn may be related to the Chickamauga, the militant faction of the Cherokee.

Up to this point in our narrative, we have heard more of men than women. Besides Nancy Moytoy and Nancy Ward, are there other well-known Cherokee women? Is there a significant cult of the female among the Cherokee? James Adair claimed the Cherokee had "petticoat government."[22] Along with the Iroquois and Hopi, Cherokee are often mentioned as a people who placed a special emphasis on matriarchy. But the word matriarchy gives perhaps a false impression. As Riane Eisler reminds us in her book *The Chalice and the Blade*, "matriarchy" means "rule by mothers," whereas early societies before the institution of domination by patriarchies seem to have been egalitarian. "To describe the real alternative to a system based on the ranking of half of humanity over the other, I propose the new term *gylany*," she writes, going on to explain that her coinage comes from the Greek words for man and woman, linked neutrally.[23] Once in our sights, gylany seems in abundant evidence as a worldwide societal phenomenon before about 3000 B.C.E., when it, together with the Mother Goddess religion underpinning it, yielded universally to the blood-and-thunder sky-gods of warrior societies. Did anything like gylany ever exist in the ancient Cherokee world? Was there a time when, as archeologist Marija Gimbutas, archeo-psychologist Erich Neumann, classical scholar Jane Harrison and a host of other writers suggest, both Cherokee men and women worshiped a Mother Goddess as the bringer of life and supreme deity?[24]

We can start with the recent past and have a look at the sacred formulas of the Cherokees collected by James Mooney around 1900. We note that in love charms, the lover prays to the spider or the moon. The spider has several aspects, in the north, east, south and west, and is in fact the heavenly spider invoked in several cures as the most powerful healer.[25] Oddly, the moon is conceived of as a woman, whereas the Cherokee usually regard the moon as masculine. "The prayer is addressed to Age'yaguga, a formulistic name for the moon.... The shamans can not explain the meaning of the term, which plainly contains the word *age'ya*, 'woman'.... The ordinary name is *nunda*, or more fully, *nunda sunnayehi*, 'the sun living in the night.'"[26] In one prayer, the ruler of life is called the Terrible Woman "most beautiful" and described as residing with the Elohi of legend in the Far West. "There in Elahiyi you are at rest, O White Woman. No one is ever lonely when with you."[27]

If we should search for a source for this Moon Goddess we can do no worse than to quote from *The Golden Ass* by the Berber Apuleius (1st cent C.E.). Here is how the picaresque anti-hero in this romance describes his reconciliation with the Great Mother Isis and regains his human shape after having been turned into an ass.[28]

> When midnight came that I had slept my first sleepe, I awaked with suddaine feare, and saw the Moone shining bright, as when shee is at the full, and seeming as though she leaped out of the Sea. Then thought I with my selfe, that was the most secret time, when the goddesse Ceres had most puissance and force, considering that all humane things be governed by her providence : and not onely all beasts private and tame, but also all wild and savage beasts be under her protection. And considering that all bodies in the heavens, the earth and the seas, be by her increasing motions increased, and by her diminishing motions diminished : as weary of all my cruell fortune and calamity, I found good hope and soveraigne remedy, though it were very late, to be delivered from all my misery, by invocation and prayer, to the excellent beauty of the Goddesse, whom I saw shining before mine eyes, wherefore shaking off mine Assie and drowsie sleepe, I arose with a joyfull face, and mooved by a great affection to purifie my selfe, I plunged my selfe seven times into the water of the Sea, which number of seven is conveniable and agreeable to holy and divine things, as the worthy and sage Philosopher Pythagoras hath declared.
>
> Then with a weeping countenance, I made this Orison to the puissant Goddesse, saying : O blessed Queene of heaven, whether thou be the Dame Ceres which art the originall and motherly nource of all fruitfull things in earth, who after the finding of thy daughter Proserpina, through the great joy which thou diddest presently conceive, madest barraine and unfruitfull ground to be plowed and sowne, and now thou inhabitest in the land of Eleusie; or whether thou be the celestiall Venus, who in the beginning of the world diddest couple together all kind of things with an ingendered love, by an eternall propagation of humane kind, art now worshipped within the Temples of the Ile Paphos, thou which art the sister of the God Phoebus, who nourishest so many people by the generation of beasts, and art now adored at the sacred places of Ephesus, thou which art horrible Proserpina, by reason of the deadly howlings which thou yeeldest, that hast power to

stoppe and put away the invasion of the hags and Ghoasts which appeare unto men, and to keepe them downe in the closures of the earth : thou which art worshipped in divers manners, and doest illuminate all the borders of the earth by thy feminine shape, thou which nourishest all the fruits of the world by thy vigor and force; with whatsoever name or fashion it is lawfull to call upon thee, I pray thee, to end my great travaile and misery, and deliver mee from the wretched fortune, which had so long time pursued me.

Apuleius falls asleep and the Mother Goddess appears to him. He describes her as having "in the middle of her forehead ... a compasse in fashion of a glasse, or resembling the light of the Moone, in one of her hands she bare serpents, in the other, blades of corne, her vestiment was of fine silke ... sometime (which troubled my spirit sore) darke and obscure, covered with a blacke robe in manner of a shield, and pleated in most subtill fashion at the skirts of her garments, the welts appeared comely, whereas here and there the starres glimpsed, and in the middle of them was placed the Moone, which shone like a flame of fire, round about the robe was a coronet or garland made with flowers and fruits." The Goddess tells him:

> Behold Lucius I am come, thy weeping and prayers hath mooved mee to succour thee. I am she that is the naturall mother of all things, mistresse and governesse of all the Elements, the initiall progeny of worlds, chiefe of powers divine, Queene of heaven! the principall of the Gods celestiall, the light of the goddesses: at my will the planets of the ayre, the wholesome winds of the Seas, and the silences of hell be diposed; my name, my divinity is adored throughout all the world in divers manners, in variable customes and in many names, for the Phrygians call me the mother of the Gods: the Athenians, Minerva: the Cyprians, Venus: the Candians, Diana: the Sicilians Proserpina: the Eleusians, Ceres: some Juno, other Bellona, other Hecate: and principally the Aethiopians which dwell in the Orient, and the Aegyptians which are excellent in all kind of ancient doctrine, and by their proper ceremonies accustome to worship mee, doe call mee Queene Isis.

Finally, she instructs him how to escape his ass's shape and be restored to his human self.

I have given the text at some length, in what many consider the version most true to the original, not just because it may not be familiar to readers but because Apuleius' detailed picture of the Mother Goddess epitomizes a whole belief-system. It sums up all the symbolism, mythology, attributes and associations surrounding a cult whose origins are lost in our Paleolithic past. In the pagan author's vision, the Goddess appears in all her glory, before Christianity, Judaism or Islam have robbed her of any power. We are reminded that she was the first divinity, "the principal of the celestial gods," who now lives with spirits of the blessed in Eleusie, "adored throughout the world in diverse manners, in variable customs and in many names." In her triple aspect of maiden-mother-crone, she rules the heavens, earth, sea and underworld. Under various guises, she is the mistress of animals, increaser of crops, bringer of love and happiness, and protector against evil spirits. We are told how to recognize her by the moon on her forehead, serpents and corn in her hands, black cloak and rich, "plaited" costume. In saying that "the Phrygians call me the mother of the Gods," and in mentioning Ephesus, Apuleius acknowledges that the birthplace of the Mater Magna is Asia Minor, where modern-day archeologists have traced her worship in excavations such as Çatal Hüyük (7500–5700 B.C.E.).

Has anyone detected the presence of the Mother Goddess in America? Not to my knowledge. Erich Neumann adduces female figurines from Peru which he compares to Neolithic representations of her from Thrace. He also discusses Mother and Child effigy vessels from Peru in the context of the Goddess with Dead Young God, a cult that appears in the Cybele-Attis religion as well as Christianity with its Virgin Queen of Heaven and her divine child.

But images of the goddess, we suspect, are overlooked in most books and articles about American Indians. The Spider Medicine we glimpse in Cherokee healing prayers and love charms makes no appearance in explications of the ubiquitous spiders and swastikas of Mississippian "iconography," where they are analyzed as "motifs" of martial accoutrements.[29]

A recent study of Southeastern Indian religious objects includes a contribution on the enigmatic and arresting humpbacked Old Woman effigy vessels that have attracted the attention of archeologists and antiquarians since the earliest white settlement of Tennessee in the 1790s. One typical of the genre was excavated in the Campbell Site in the 1960s; it shows a red and white painted, covered ceramic bottle in the shape of a corpulent woman with her mouth open, squatting, with no arms.[30] A figurine in the same tradition comes from Noel Cemetery in Sumner County, Tennessee, five miles south of Nashville off Franklin Turnpike on Browns Creek.[31] "Among the numerous human effigies of the hooded-bottle form throughout the Southeast — and especially in the three most productive regions: northeastern Arkansas, southeastern Missouri, and central Tennessee," observe Carol Diaz-Granados and James R. Duncan, "humpbacked figures are extremely common."[32] These experts present hooded female effigy bottles uncovered in pristine condition from the Averbuch site in Davidson County in the late 1970s, of a type they call "without doubt the single most important subject in the pottery of the Middle Cumberland Culture" (178). But their interest is especially aroused by the Woman in the Patterned Shawl variant of the Old Woman, a humpbacked, kneeling female figure with prominent breasts and bun hairdo folding her hands in her lap and wearing a boldly patterned dark cloaklike garment and fancifully trimmed knee-length woven skirt. They reach the following conclusions:

> Overall, the characteristics of these female effigy vessels — and numerous additional examples from these same counties and others nearby that require further study — united them as representations of the same possibly supernatural personage who was venerated or invoked in the practices of a mortuary cult complex across the Cumberland River basin.... No one has yet made a case for a single interpretation of the identity of the Cumberland female effigy figure, but these lines of investigation suggest that the quest may not be fruitless [195–96].

I am going to make a case for a single interpretation. I propose that the Old Woman is the same as the Mother Goddess. The humpback that baffles Americanists like Diaz-Granados and Duncan has been amply documented in the work of Marija Gimbutas and others. Like the exaggerated hips and enormous rump of the Stone Age Venus of Willendorf, the humpback symbolizes the mysteries of the female body, a vessel that swells with pregnancy and the milk of nourishment.[33] Images of the fertility goddess or earth mother abound in the literature wherever we look, provided we look. Often a pregnant woman holding belly with hands with breasts emphasized and masked face is shown. The mystical and abstract transformational aspect of the goddess (Apuleius' Juno or Hecate) can be traced back into the Middle Stone Age. Innumerable masked figurines in the publications of Gimbutas show M signs, V–shaped necklaces and butterflies symbolizing the waters of life, milk, nourishment and regeneration. Many of these exhibit the Bird Goddess' open mouth and closed eye motif, found on both sides of the Atlantic. Tri-lines represent the triple aspect of the goddess (birth, marriage, death), and the double swirl stands for the deity's forces of transformation — woman's powers of bringing to birth and taking away into death. Both in America and the Middle East and Europe, the Goddess is Mistress of Game and Livestock, with the deer, panther, fox and bear her magical companions. Universally, she is Giver of the Crafts of spinning, weaving, metallurgy and music.

By way of concluding, let us return to the name invoked to call out to the moon goddess in Cherokee prayers. As we saw, Age'yaguga could only be partially explained by white anthropologists. They recognized the first element in it as Cherokee for "woman" but could not determine what the second part meant. Well, *guga* is Cherokee for "bottle." When the Cherokee first came to Indian Territory, they dubbed Bartlesville Gugu-i because the English place-name sounded to them like Bottlesville.[34] Accordingly, the name of the supreme Cherokee deity must be Bottle Woman.[35]

# Chapter 9

# *Yom Kippur with the Cherokee*

*On Rosh Hashanah it is written, on Yom Kippur it is sealed; how many will pass on, how many shall come to be? Who shall live and who shall die? Who shall live to see ripe age and who shall perish?* — Jewish Yom Kippur Service

The Cherokee, Choctaw and Chickasaw enthusiastically embraced intermarriage with British and French traders and soldiers — especially, as we have seen, with any who happened to be Jewish or crypto–Jewish. The Civilized Tribes were among the first to benefit from the resulting acculturation. But Cherokees, like others, were hardly open-armed toward Christian missionaries arriving in the wake of the traders and soldiers. Among the Cherokee, pockets of traditionalists resisted the "white man's religion" down to the present day, notably in the Keetoowah Night Hawk Society, and as late as 1900, the religious leader Inoli, or Black Fox, outwardly a Methodist preacher, died "in the ancient faith of his forefathers."[1] The old religion held on for a long time. But what exactly *was* that religion?

The first official Cherokee conversion to Christianity occurred on August 13, 1810. The convert was Peggy Scott of the Wolf Clan, one of the several wives of the richest man in the nation, Chief James Ti-ka-lo-hi Vann of the Wild Potato Clan.[2] A niece of Chief Charles Hicks, she joined the Moravian church at Spring Place in Georgia shortly after her husband was murdered (or assassinated) in a tavern brawl. The Moravians remembered her as the "First Fruit" of their efforts. They had been active in north Georgia for a decade but had made little inroads on their Cherokee hosts, who maintained "Christianity was necessary for white people only ... that the Indians could get to heaven without it."[3] They were about to give up and go home before Peggy and other members of the ruling Wolf Clan converted. "Over the next two decades only a tiny minority of Cherokee sought Christian baptism," writes William G. McLoughlin, an expert on Cherokee religion of the nineteenth century.[4] Few Indian souls were won over by the Brainerd Mission of the American Board of Commissioners for Foreign Missions. It was founded near Creek Path, Chief Black Fox's former seat on Sand Mountain, in 1816, but had little success. Anti-mission sentiment lasted to the bitter end in the old Eastern Cherokee Nation, according to McLoughlin.[5]

H. B. Cushman, the historian of the Choctaw, mentions that the earliest convert in that nation came with the short-lived Elliott mission in 1817.[6] The Choctaws' first permanent missionary, Cyrus Byington, did not begin work among them until 1820. Notoriously, the Methodist preacher John Wesley failed in efforts to bring Christianity to Indians in Savannah in the 1730s. The heathens he attempted to bring to church conceived the wrong idea about baptism and wanted to do it each Sunday. They saw nothing wrong with being saved over and over again. Adair notes Indians' skepticism toward various forms of Christianity throughout his book. Indian agents affirmed in 1802 that their religion was "as good as that of Mahomet" and just as proof against proselytization.[7]

By all accounts, the Cherokee did not observe the sort of animistic-shamanistic spirituality practiced by many of their neighbors. They were scornful of the "barbaric" rites of the sweat lodge, sun dance and coming-of-age rituals of the Siouan tribes, as reported by eighteenth-century explorer John Lawson.[8] Mexico, they said, was inhabited by six tribes of cannibals. They had hardly a better opinion of the cruel sutees and grisly boneyards of the Natchez.

In a series of articles about the religion of American Indians appearing in 1862, Cherokee newspaperman John Rollin Ridge wrote that they, in general, rejected the preaching of the missionaries. As evidence, he reprinted the famous speech of Red Jacket. When questioned whether Christians worshiped the true God, the Seneca chief replied that he would wait and see if their religion made them behave any the better. Ridge held that the Cherokee took their religion from the ancient Greeks, Persians, Jews and Chaldeans. They were superior in this respect, as in many others, to "the Athabascan, the Algonquin, the Iroquois, the Decotah, the Appalachian, the Chicorean, and the Natchez."[9]

According to Mahir Abdal-Razzaaq El, a practitioner of Islam belonging to the Northeastern Band of Cherokee Indians, although "many people are not aware of the Native American contact with Islam that began over one thousand years ago by some of the early Muslim travelers who visited us ... there are many documents, treaties, [laws] and resolutions that were passed between the 1600s and 1800s that show that Muslims were in fact here and were very active in the communities in which they lived."[10] He believes that Cherokee clothing basically replicates the kimah and long dresses for women and turban and knee-length tunics for men of the Arab world.

John Rollin Ridge (1827–1867) seems to have come from a Muslim–affiliated Cherokee family. He left the Cherokee Nation after the assassinations of his father, grandfather and cousin Elias Boudinot in 1839 to become the defiant exile, Byronic poet and biographer of California's bandit hero, Joaquín Murieta. His uncle was Stand Watie (1806–1871), the last Confederate general to surrender his troops in the Civil War. Gen. Stand Watie's Arabic or Spanish Jewish name was Ramadhan Ibn Wati. His father, David Oowatie, was the son of Tah-chee (Dutch), a member of the Beamer/Oconostota/Attakullakulla family. In Arabic, *wadi* means "ridge, crest." Watie's brother Maj. John Ridge took the name in English translation. A look at the Ridge-Watie family tree shows some unusual naming practices. Saladin Watie was named for the Egyptian general who repulsed the Crusaders in the twelfth century. Another of Stand's sons was named Solon, after the philosopher-ruler of ancient Athens. One of Stand Watie's four wives is Eleanor Looney, great-granddaughter of Chief Black Fox. Cousin marriage with other Sephardim runs true to type. Toward the end of his brief life, John Rollin Ridge dreamed of publishing a hidden history of the Cherokee Nation, the "impartial account," as he wrote to uncle Stand Watie, "of the treatment they have received at the hands of a civilized and Christian race."[11]

Important sources for Cherokee religion are the papers of Presbyterian missionary Daniel S. Butrick (1798–1851) and pamphleteer John Howard Payne housed in the Newberry Library in Chicago.[12] John Payne was an indefatigable activist on behalf of Indian rights who is often remembered only as author of the song "Home Sweet Home." Of a Long Island Jewish family, he became an adopted Cherokee tribe member. In later years, he served as American consul to Tunis.

The Payne Papers include accounts of the seven Cherokee festivals and other aspects of the history, culture and religion of the tribe. One striking feature in them is the weight given to stories of Wasi (Cherokee for Moses). Wasi is more important than Jesus for the

Cherokee, notes Butrick. Most commentators see this as evidence that the Cherokee learned Bible stories from traders. Given what we now know about the Eshelokee, however, could these stories possibly predate Jewish traders of the eighteenth century? Could they, like the name Elohi, actually be vestiges of the Cherokees' Mediterranean origins?

If Jews were not on board from the beginning, they certainly had arrived in Cherokee country by Roman times. In the 1960s, Minna Arenowich was working in her flowerbed on Cedar Street in Columbus, Georgia, when she dug up a bronze Roman coin. It bore the image of Antoninus Pius (emperor 135–161 C.E.).[13] Archeologists often dismiss such finds because they do not come to light in the course of an official excavation. Who is to say someone did not plant a Roman coin in Minna Arenowich's garden? Perhaps it was a souvenir brought over by early settlers?

Fig. 9.1. Bat Creek Stone. Catalogue No. AB4902, Department of Anthropology, Smithsonian Institution.

The same criticism, however, cannot be leveled at the Bat Creek Stone. This small stone engraved with Hebrew was exhumed in a mound containing the skeletons of an East Tennessee chief and eight retainers by the Smithsonian Institution in 1889. Bat Creek is a tributary of the Little Tennessee River in Cherokee country about thirty miles southwest of Knoxville.

Cyrus Thomas, who headed the Smithsonian's mound survey project, at first thought the inscription on the stone was Cherokee writing, in Sequoyah's syllabary. He published it — upside down — in 1894.[14] The stone was then tossed in a back room of the Smithsonian and forgotten. Not until Semitics professor Cyrus Gordon of Brandeis University studied it was interest rekindled. Gordon identified its letters as Paleo-Hebrew in square capitals from the second century c.e, reading from right to left: דוחי ל קר RQ L'YHWD, "a comet/*roq*/phoenix for Judea."[15] The Bat Creek Stone is now on indefinite loan from the Smithsonian to the McClung Museum of the University of Tennessee in Knoxville (fig. 9.1).

After Gordon's identification there ensued a storm of controversy over the Bat Creek Stone. In an all-out campaign (perhaps not entirely devoid of anti–Semitism), anthropologists lined up to prove it was a fake. An exposé by Robert Mainfort and Mary Kwas appeared in the journal *American Antiquity* in October of 2004.[16] Their attack was answered, and I believe refuted, by Ohio State University professor Hugh McCulloch. McCulloch disproved a key argument, Mainfort and Kwas's comparison of the stone's Hebrew writing to that printed in a Masonic treatise of 1870. He reminded us that radiocarbon tests performed on wooden ear spools found with the skull of the individual laid to rest with the stone yield a secure date "significantly pre–Norse, not to mention pre–Columbian ... consistent with Gordon's first or second century A.D. paleographic dating of the text."[17] McCulloch observed that the Bat Creek inscription contains peculiar letter forms and punctuation that would have been unknown to casual students of Hebrew in nineteenth century America and cited other examples of Square Paleo-Hebrew. "The fact that Cyrus Thomas, the Smithsonian's chief debunker of alleged Old World inscriptions, did not see this glaring similarity, demonstrates, if nothing else, that he was incompetent for this task," McCulloch added. The Bat Creek Stone appears to have been reinstated as an authentic Hebrew inscription in ancient Native America. A recent review in *Pre-Columbiana* lays to rest Mainfort and Kwas's charges.[18]

The stone's reference to the Jewish hero Simeon Bar Kokhba also seems genuine — a connection, again, first made by Cyrus Gordon. Discovered directly beneath the skull of the dignitary whose burial it marks, it proclaims, "Comet for the Jews," a slogan of the revolt against Rome in 132–135 C.E. This final bid for nationalistic sovereignty in ancient times was led by Simeon Bar Kokhba, whose name means "Son of the Star." It is a short leap to wonder whether the elite personage of the tomb was either a relative or leader of survivors from Bar Kokhba's revolt.

Who interred these warriors? From the elaborateness of the entombment it must have been their own people. An enclave of compatriots? That the burial is not an isolated instance of Jewish settlement in the region seems clear from coin finds:

> Coins struck during Bar Kokhba's regime have been extracted in Kentucky — Louisville 1932, Clay City 1952, Hopkinsville 1967 — and in southeastern Missouri from the St. Francis, a tributary of the Mississippi, 1922.... They read in Hebrew *Simeon* lower right around to lower left on the obverse and "Year Two [133 A.D.] of the Deliverance of Israel" on the reverse.[19]

A tablet inscribed with an archaic version of the Ten Commandments in Hebrew was found in 1860 beneath a forty-foot high pile of stones near Newark, Ohio. Cyrus Gordon also studied this Jewish artifact. He describes it as a mezuzah from the ancient Middle East.[20]

A Cherokee chief of the present day, Beverly Northrup, not only links Bar Kokhba and the Cherokee but speaks also of earlier Jews "who refused to bow down to Caesar, saying that they would bow down to no one but God, the King of the Universe":

> This group of Jews was known as Sicarii [literally, "those with daggers, thugs"]. During their fight with Rome, the Sicarii took refuge at Masada, a mesa near the southwestern shoreline of the Dead Sea. At the time of the Roman siege at Masada, Eleazsar [*sic*], a man of influence with the Sicarii, held the command there. He was a descendant of Judah of Galilee.... The Roman general advanced [and kept] the Sicarii from having an easy escape route....
>
> Josephus' writings ... report some of the Sicarii were able to flee to Egypt [they went mostly to Cyrene]. The Romans were intent to get an apology from the Sicarii. Yet the Sicarii still refused to acknowledge Caesar as their lord....
>
> The story has been kept alive among our Cherokee people that the Sicarii who escaped from Masada, are some of our ancestors who managed to cross the water to this land, and later became known as Cherokees.... It is interesting that Josephus [actually, a Continuator, since Josephus died before 135 C.E.] reported that some did escape. To me this is more evidence that not all the Sicarii killed themselves at Masada.[21]

All these clues to the mystery lead to Melungeon territory. A similar lead comes from the Ramey family of Tennessee — an unrecognizable type of writing that turned up in the family's North Carolina attic in the 1990s. The script was written by Thomas Ramey, a circuit preacher and spy, in coded messages during the Civil War in Tennessee (fig. 9.2). It stymied most experts until identified as a variety of a demotic Coptic "cipher" script similar to ones long used in Alexandria in Egypt. The samples I have seen come from a rather substantial horde which the family continues to guard out of fear their contents might get them into trouble.

Fig. 9.3 Latter-day Jewish-Egyptian-Cherokee multigenerational family group photographed in Hazel Green, Alabama, 1916. Clockwise from bottom left: Elzina Grimwood (baby), Etalka Vetula Goode Grimwood (mother), Redema Elizabeth Ramey Goode (grandmother), Mary Ann Elizabeth Jean Ramey (great-grandmother). Courtesy Teresa A. Grimwood Panther-Yates.

Ramey is a well-known Melungeon family, one that stems from a single emigrant figure, Jacques Remy, a Frenchman who came to Westmoreland County, Virginia, in 1654.[22] Ramey genealogies include the rare given names Redema (converso), Vetula ("old woman," a Latin amulet name), La Vera (all Judeo-Hispanic), Etalka (Ashkenazic pet name for Adela) and Elzina (Arabic "beautiful"). Cousin and Levirate marriage is common. Elder members of the family tell of origins in ancient Israel, with branches spreading to Alexandrine Egypt and later Rome, Spain, Portugal, France, England, Virginia and Tennessee. In autosomal DNA studies of Melungeons, Teresa Panther-Yates, a Ramey descendant whose father was probably Cherokee Bird Clan, and whose mother's matriline goes back to a Lower Cherokee "anomalous" U5, produces a top match of Egyptian. In six other cases in the same study, Middle Eastern populations rank as No. 1 in the participants' results.[23]

The Rameys, like many others mentioned in this book, were evidently Marranos. The origin and meaning of this term is disputed, but it appears to have first gained currency in the mid-fifteenth-century anti–Jewish riots in Toledo and Cordova. Its heyday for usage was the sixteenth century, when Jews escaping Spain and Portugal to other Catholic countries were denounced as "judaizers" by the Inquisition and Spanish crown. According to an entry in the *Jewish Encyclopaedia,*

> The wealthy Marranos, who engaged extensively in commerce, industries, and agriculture, intermarried with families of the old nobility; impoverished counts and marquises unhesitatingly wedded wealthy Jewesses; and it also happened that counts or nobles of the blood royal became infatuated with handsome Jewish girls. Beginning with the second generation, the Neo-Christians usually intermarried with women of their own sect. They became very influential through their wealth and intelligence, and were called to important positions at the palace, in government circles, and in the Cortes; they practiced medicine and law and taught at the universities; while their children frequently achieved high ecclesiastical honors.[24]

None of the usual explanations given for the origin of the term Marrano seems compelling, least of all the suggestion that the word is derived from Spanish *marrano,* "wild pig." Certainly over-ingenious is Hebrew scholar B. Netanyahu's claim that it comes from "a haplologic contraction of the Hebrew *mumar-anus* (which caused the omission of the first syllable), effecting the transformation: mumaranus, maranus, marano, marrano."[25] If we look it up in Latin dictionaries before the modern period we find nothing about pigs, only a definition in civil jurisprudence of *maranus* as "privileged Jewish administrator who feigns to be Christian."

I suggest a different origin: the Mariannu mentioned in Egyptian annals. They were Ramses III's "only trustworthy allies" against invading Persians, according to the Elephantine Papyri. The word was introduced into the Egyptian language from the Aramaic Mareinu, meaning "noblemen," and applied to the Semitic "princes" who garrisoned the Jewish military town of Elephantine, located on an island in the Nile opposite Aswan. This important colony guarded Egypt's southern frontier and maintained several synagogues along with a "temple in exile" perpetuating the memory of the one built by King David in Jerusalem destroyed by the Assyrians.[26] According to Immanuel Velikovsky, who has made a study of the surviving documents of Elephantine:

> The very first words [of one letter] are *el-maran,* which means "to the sir," and the word *maran* is repeated again and again in this and in others of the Elephantine papyri [dated to the 5th to 4th centuries]. The word *maran* or *marenu* ("our sir") was put before the name of the satrap [provincial governor] in Jerusalem when the chiefs of the colony wrote to him; they themselves were

addressed as *mareinu* ("our sirs") by the ordinary members of the colony in their letters. The singular and plural possessive forms, *marenu* and *mareinu*, are used profusely in the papyri of Elephantine.[27]

Evidently, the Egyptian title *maran* may have been carried by the conquering Arabs to Spain and retained for use in their civil administration. It then gave birth to Spanish *marrano* and survived in common Jewish surnames Moran, Morene and Moren as well as in Marianne, a favored name for girls in Jewish, Cherokee and Melungeon families. One doubts that the Moran and Moreno families of France, Scotland and Italy are embarrassed by the thought that their name might mean "pig" in Spanish. The true Egyptian origin of the word is also alluded to in the surname Elphinstine, an important crypto–Jewish family in Aberdeen, Scotland.[28]

How, and why, did Bar Kokhba's faction go to Tennessee? Dr. Robert Stieglitz, a scholar of Middle Eastern history and culture at Rutgers University, believes that in the revolts against the Romans, various bands of Jews went to the western Mediterranean "and then later, either through accident or by connection with Mediterranean sailors who were acquainted with deep-sea navigation, they reached the New World."[29] According to Josephus, after their suppression "the Hebrews fled across the sea to a land unknown to them before." A Continuator writes that it was called Epeiros Occidentalis, the Western Continent.[30] A modern historian writes that after the "devastating defeat of the Second Revolt under Bar Kokhba in 135, the Jews virtually abandoned Judea.... Others left for faraway places in the Diaspora where they knew Jews were living or welcome."[31] Some rabbis considered Bar Kokhba to be the Messiah. Could the Bar Kokhba party have known they would be well received by the Cherokees? Is that why they went into exile where they did? One can only speculate about the answers to such questions. Barry Fell believed, "Evidently some Hebrews were already here in 69 A.D. when the First Revolt of Jerusalem against the Romans occurred." On the evidence of coin finds, he places Jews in Tennessee and Greeks in Arkansas.[32]

Whatever the antiquity of a strain of Judaism in Cherokee religion, it is clearly pre-rabbinical and pre–Diaspora. It is reminiscent of a state religion like that practiced by the Jews in their homeland before the destruction of Jerusalem by the Romans in 70 C.E. James Adair reaches a similar conclusion:

> The Indian system is derived from the moral, ceremonial, and judicial laws of the Hebrews, though now but a faint copy of the divine original.— Their religious rites, martial customs, dress, music, dances, and domestic forms of life, seem clearly to evince also, that they came to America in early times, before sects had sprung up among the Jews, which was soon after their prophets ceased, and before arts and sciences had arrived to any perfection; otherwise, it is likely they would have retained some knowledge of them, at least where they first settled [227].

These words indicate he thought that the Cherokee Jews belonged to the time of the First Temple (ca. 1000 B.C.E.) or even before. Yet on the basis of a detailed comparison of religious rites it is really not necessary to place their origins earlier than the inauguration of the Second Temple in Jerusalem in 516 B.C.E. and reorganization of Jewish religion under Ezra beginning in 458 B.C.E. Jewish customs could have been planted in the Appalachians as late as the first and second centuries C.E., to judge from the Bat Creek Stone. The Cherokees' celebration of the new year seems to reflect Jewish practices in the style and fashion of the Second Temple.

The Cherokee reckon the start of the new year on the first new moon of the first month of autumn, Tishri in the Hebrew calendar. For the Brooklyn Jew as well as an Oklahoma

Cherokee, this falls sometime between September 5 and October 5. Ever since the Second Temple this date inaugurates the Days of Awe, or Repentance, and it ushers in the most holiday-intensive period of the year, a season focused on purification and renewal. According to first-century C.E. Jewish philosopher Philo of Alexandria, an old name for Rosh Hashanah (Head of the Year) is the Day of the Sacred Moon. In Cherokee, this holiday is called the Great New Moon Festival. In both cultures, the New Year is followed after exactly eight days by a second holy day considered the most important of the entire yearly cycle. Yom Kippur (Day of Atonement) in the Jewish faith and the solemn Propitiation Festival in Cherokee religion bear the same approximate name. Both follow the new year by a week.

The similarities do not end there. The Jewish conception of the New Year is a time of reflection, of coming to terms with the past year, of purification, resolutions and predictions. Jews of old believed that the Almighty One maintained books in which he wrote the names of those who will live and those who will die in the coming year. Hence the greeting of temple congregants to each other, "May you be inscribed and sealed for a good year." Hence also the passage in the Yom Kippur service, "What was written on Rosh Hashanah is sealed on Yom Kippur."

During Rosh Hashanah, devout Jews eat tongue to symbolize the *head* of the year. So also on the Cherokee New Year hunters present the tongue of the first-killed buck deer to the Uku. This he uses for a sacrifice while the priests conduct divinatory exercises with crystals to determine which of the people are to die before the first new moon of the following spring.

In Jewish observance the afternoon of Rosh Hashanah is occupied by a second ceremony associated with the New Year, Tashlikh ("casting away"). This involves going to water and casting away the sins of the previous year. The Cherokee engage in a remarkable enactment of the same rite:

> Two hours before sunset, the Uku's principal assistant ordered everyone to go to the water.... As they waded in, the men went upstream and the women and children went downstream. Everyone quickly faced east [the direction of Jerusalem] and plunged entirely under the water.... Some people followed the custom of wearing old clothing, and while in the water, they disrobed and let the old clothing float away. This carried all their impurities away with it.[33]

Between the first and second holy day, Cherokees fast on the fourth day — an apparent echo of the Jewish Fast of Gedaliah on Tishri 3. In Cherokee practice, their Day of Cementation is preceded by a 24-hour period of fasting. It has a special liturgy with a unique melody, just like the Kol Nidre ("all vows") of Yom Kippur.[34] Adair notes the similarity of the music in both cases. This is also the time, Adair says, when the ancient hymn *Ye ho waah* was sung. Of this hymn, informants observed:

> The Chief Supreme Being ... was both God and king [whose] name was to be spoken only on an appointed holy day. It was *Ye ho waah* [i.e., Jehovah], and he gave a certain hymn to the Cherokees that could only be sung by selected persons on "occasions of the greatest solemnity." The hymn played a special role in the exciting Cementation Festival [Day of Reconciliation, i.e. Yom Kippur].... The words ... were described as being part of "the old language."[35]

The Cherokee Propitiation Festival seems to reflect a third holiday of the Jewish high holy days, Sukkot, the Festival of the Tabernacles. Other parts of this very old holiday seem to be incorporated in the harvest celebration called the Exalting, or Bounding Bush, Festival. Like Jews today with their myrtle boughs, the Cherokee shake white pine sprigs to all the directions. In the Propitiation Festival they sing the Great Hoshanah noticed above ("please save us") and purify their dwellings, both important aspects of the Jewish Sukkot observance.

Cherokees sanctify the whole town by beating sycamore wands against the eaves of buildings. At the end of Sukkot on the seventh day, Jews make seven circuits about their tabernacle and then beat willow branches against the floor after singing the hosanna.

One relic of their ancient religion the Cherokee have been careful to preserve is the *ecacate* or Urim and Thummim, as they are called in the Vision of Elohi. In the portion of the text that follows the third invasion of black men, we read: "The wise men then came home and after consulting the *e-ca-ca-te*[36] or Urim and Thummim told the people that these warriors would not come any more for seven years."[37] At another point, the Eshelokee people face the invasion of white people. They are helpless, as they have lost the secret of the Uktena's poison. A solemn war dance of the clans attempts to revive the Cherokee's secret powers, housed in the half-sphere temple of light, but

> the wise men after entering found that it could not be lighted with light that emanated from the spiritual light or from the wise men. Seeking the cause of the failure of the temple to light up, the wisest of the wise, the Koola clan,[38] answered and said: Our temple, ancient and sacred, has been neglected; the original fire, the eternal and primitive, has been allowed to become extinct by destroying the wise oo ca-te-ni or the tanian, the wise of the tribe. He can never be found again until the other clan be found and the tribe reunites. We can do nothing only to employ a substitute to illuminate our temple and which shall be the outer body of the eternal fire. When the substitute for light, the fire, was kindled, the wise men looked upon their e-ca-ca-tis and could behold nothing in them but images, as a brilliant light appeared in them originally.

Finally, the *ecatate* appears in the prophecy that concludes the vision, where it is referred to as "the stone of truth containing the image." After being subjected to the religion of the white man, the Eshelokee are

> to remain under his influence to the close of the seventh period of the Sa-ho-ni clan[39] when the red race will move from under his power. When the race will, at that time, according to the oracle of the stone of truth containing the image, be driven to the seashore, where they will cross the water and landing in the old country from whence they came will find the five lost clans, become reunited into twelve clans, into one people again, will become a great nation known as the Eshe-el-okee of the half sphere temple of light.

We see in each of these turning points in the history of the Cherokee people an attempt to reestablish contact with their founders and their founders' religious beliefs. The founders possessed higher powers and knowledge and are, in a significant passage, named as the Tanians. I believe this is a specific reference to the Greeks. Horace's line about the Greeks' ruse of the wooden horse at Troy comes to mind: "I am afraid of Greeks (Danai) even and especially when they come bearing gifts." Danaoi was the term used throughout antiquity for the earliest of the Greeks, who were believed to have originated in Thrace and settled in the Peloponnese in the dim past. Danauna was the name the Egyptians used for the Sea Peoples.[40]

Hebrew priests of the Temple in Jerusalem carried crystals about their necks called *urim* and *thummim* ("lights" and "protections"). Known as the Perfect Light, these crystals were carried in the breastplate of the Hebrew high-priest.[41] They were consulted on decisions of war and peace and borne into battle as well as used to divine God's will on crucial occasions in a ritual held before the Holy of Holies. Cherokee priests entrusted with carrying their ark took the *ecacate* on war parties. At home, they wore the divinatory crystals about their necks and looked to them on the most solemn occasions to foretell the future. At the New Moon Festival, the Cherokee equivalent of the High Holy Days, people approached the priest after purification to discover whether they would live for another year. The priest gazed into his crystal, another name for which is *oolungtsata*. If he saw the supplicant's figure upright they would live. It the shape was cloudy, they may fall sick, if broken, they may be injured, and if prostrate, they would die before the next New Moon Festival. The alternative name of the divining crystal seems to be Ionic Greek, from the aorist participle for the verb ουλω, "to be well," used in the same sense as the Latin salutation *salve.*

The Cherokees' Green Corn Festival seems to be the same as Shavuot (Pentecost), the feast of first fruits held fifty days or seven weeks after Pesach or Passover.

Whatever other Jewish customs the Cherokees may have preserved, they did not have Hanukkah or Purim. The first Hanukkah (Festival of Light) was celebrated in 145 B.C.E. at the end of the revolt of the Maccabees against the Seleucid rulers in Palestine. The events commemorated by Purim — Queen Esther's triumph over the evil Persian viceroy Haman — are set in the fifth century B.C.E., and carnival-like Purim with its costumes and noise making did not become popular until the Middle Ages. It was especially beloved by the Sephardic Jews. If Cherokee Jewish customs are due to the influence of Spanish-Portuguese or Scottish Jews in the seventeenth or eighteenth century, one would expect to find some echo of the two most popular holidays. The *terminus post quem* of 145 B.C.E. for Hanukkah puts the likely arrival of Jews among the Cherokees before the second century B.C.E. This timeframe fits with our trans–Pacific expedition of Cyrenaic Greeks, Jews, Libyans, Phoenicians and Egyptians in 231 B.C.E.

Like the ancient Romans and Greeks and Jewish people with their *mikve*, the Cherokee of old set great store in ritual bathing. They were so fond of "going to water" (*amo': hi atsv': sdi*) that they have even been called "hydrocentric." Here is how ethnographer Raymond Fogelson describes the national passion, so ingrained that Christian missionaries had to select another word to translate "baptism," *agawo':da*, meaning "washed clean":

> In the past, steam baths were taken in small earthen sweat lodges and followed by plunges into a nearby stream, after the proper recitation of prayers for health and long life. This seems to have been a regular ritual that was observed throughout the year, regardless of season.... The presence of this rite in Cherokee culture may also help explain why Free Will Baptists, with a similar rite, have been so successful among the Cherokee.[42]

Traditionally, the Cherokee were obligated to dip seven times in running water facing the rising sun each day. No other Indian tribes seem to have the same obsession. Nor does any other tribe possess a sweat-bath like the Cherokee *asi*. This is a rectangular log cabin with meeting times for men separately from the women, resembling the ancient social institution of public baths or today's Jewish *mikve*. According to one expert on Jewish culture in Greco-Roman Palestine, Judaism "made purity of the body a central element of everyday life, especially for priests." Ritual baths (*mikva'ot*) were installed in many, if not most, Jewish households. Even if fetched from a distance, pure water from a stream was essential.[43]

Much of Cherokee religion was under the control of the Bird Clan. We saw in Sakiyah Sanders' version of the Vision of Elohi that during their difficulties with the white man the clan elders appealed to these "wisest of the wise" for help in restoring the temple rituals. They were in charge of the powerful Eagle Dance as well as the sacred fire and crystals.

The Bird Clan is without doubt one of the core clans of the Ani-Yunwiyah, or Principal People. Its original name was Red Flicker, Sapsucker, Woodpecker or Ani-Tsaliena or Tsunilyana, meaning Deaf Clan. Both the Wolf and Deer clans are offshoots of it.[44] Birdtown in North Carolina is one of its important communities, though there are more Wolf Clan members in Birdtown than Bird Clan. Traditionally, Bird Clan members are regarded as the tribe's sacred keepers of religious knowledge. Many chiefs, particularly peace chiefs, have been Bird.

Bird Clan members were also considered to be the messengers or communicators, as we would say today. They made excellent speakers, heralds, seers and bearers of news. Typically, a speaker sat or stood on the principal chief's left-hand side on formal occasions, particularly in the council house. The war chief was to the principal chief's right. If a stranger or foreigner approached the village, a herald, often an elder of the Bird Clan, would be sent to greet him. Only Bird Clan members were allowed to catch eagles and harvest their feathers.

Chief John Ross (1790–1866) was Bird Clan, descended in the strict female line from Ghi-goo-ie, wife of William Shorey, a Scotsman. Shorey was probably a crypto–Jew. His surname is Hebrew ("bull," a sobriquet used for Joseph). Ross's boyhood name was Cooweescoowee, a rare water-bird infrequently spotted in the Cherokee homeland. In Ross's honor, a judicial district in Indian Territory was named Cooweescoowee. Quatie Conrad was also Bird Clan. She married Alexander Brown, Archibald Fields and John Benge. These are some of the better known members of the ancient Bird Clan.

# Chapter 10

## *Sequoyan Syllabary*

*In Memoriam Gloria Farley* — Oklahoma Epigrapher

The Cherokee syllabary is conventionally credited to Sequoyah (fig. 10.3), the only person in history to single-handedly invent a system of writing. It seems like sacrilege to doubt the story, engrained in American memory. But there is evidence Sequoyah did not invent it.

According to rock-art experts, the state of Kentucky possesses the largest number of sites within the entire Ohio River valley.[1] A cave entrance overlooking the Redbird River, a tributary of the South Fork of the Kentucky River in Clay County, Kentucky, in the Daniel Boone National Forest, harbors some of these little-known bits of American history. They are part of the extensive Red Bird River Petroglyph Site. A nearby cave is identified as the burial place of a Cherokee man known as Red Bird, also called Aaron Brock.[2] The style of pervasive "well-preserved linear carvings" on flat, vertical sandstone surfaces is "different from any of the previously reported Kentucky petroglyphs," write the authors of the guide published by the Kentucky Heritage Council and State Historic Preservation Office.[3]

Kenneth B. Tankersley of the University of Cincinnati believes our cave entrance "carvings" display a nineteenth-century example of writing in the Cherokee syllabary. "The earliest writing in the system developed by the Cherokee known as Sequoyah, has been found in a Kentucky cave," announced accordingly the Archaeological Institute of America.[4] Tankersley told *The New York Times* the linear incisions consist of 15 Cherokee characters and dated them 1818 "or 1808," but they "don't spell any words—they read like ABCs."[5]

Testing of the Y chromosome DNA type of a male claiming descent from Aaron Brock reveals Brock, or Red Bird, together with all his forefathers, apparently carried the Cohen Modal Haplotype. This is the genetic signature of high-priests going back to the Jewish patriarch Aaron. The Brock descendant who tested his DNA is J12f2.1+, an ancient form of the Cohen haplotype, which mutates over time (the plus-sign stands for one-step mutations).[6] Chief Red Bird's Y chromosome is not matched in exact particulars by males living in Europe or the Middle East or from families originating there, only by other Cherokees. Since his father, from whom he received his Y chromosome, was a tribally identified Cherokee born about 1700, the appearance of the Cohen Modal Haplotype in America would appear to exclude the possibility Red Bird was the son of English, French, Spanish or Portuguese Jewish settlers. As we have seen, the first European to marry a Cherokee was Cornelius Dougherty. Most intermarriage occurs after 1750.

Chief Red Bird's mother is unquestionably Cherokee, reportedly Paint Clan. Marriage and naming patterns are consistent with Cornell, Sizemore and other Jewish Cherokee or Melungeon or Black Dutch families. The paternal line of this rare Cherokee Kohane can be traced in historical and genealogical records back to Moytoy I, born about 1640. He married

Quatsi (Patsy) of Tellico, a fullblood Cherokee of the Wolf Clan. Before 1680, the Cherokee had little contact with Europeans, so it is unlikely Moytoy's father was a European. If he had been, it seems strange that he or his male descendants would have been promoted into positions of leadership in the tribe. His line includes Moytoy II, Red Bird, Raven of Hiwassee, Tathtowe, Bad Water, Old Hop, Old Tassel, Doublehead, Tuckahoe and other Cherokee chiefs. Although most male Cherokee pedigrees were extinguished through warfare following European contact, the survival of the Red Bird or Moytoy line in Brock Y chromosomal DNA is an exception (as is the Sizemore case examined in Chapter 3).

Part of the Red Bird rock-art group called Marked Rock has been preserved in Rawlings-Stinson City Park in Manchester since 1994, when a 60–ton chunk of sandstone cliff collapsed on the hillside and fell onto Kentucky State Highway 66. While in place, it was listed as #89001183 on the National Register of Historic Places and marked with a plaque by the Kentucky Historical Society. There are allegedly inscriptions in Old Arabic, or South Semitic,[7] and ogam[8] covering it and scattered elsewhere in the area, in our cave in particular. The Red Bird Petroglyphs lie on the ancient, heavily-traveled Great Warrior Path of the Cherokee that is an extension of the Natchez Trace and Avery Trace in Tennessee running north up the Appalachian mountain chain to the lands of the Iroquois. It was a heavily-trafficked spot.

A local resident calls our cave entrance inscription (fig. 10.1) Christian Monogram #2 and dates it to the 1st to 2nd century C.E. He reads, in Greek letters: σωτηρος ιήσούς υιος του θεου πατηρ [sic] χαι [sic], and translates: *The Saviour, Jesus, Son of God the Father, lives.*[9] Though this reading is unsatisfactory for a number of reasons, the language may have been correctly identified. We have sent it round and received several expert opinions. It "could very well indeed be Greek," writes Klaus Hallof, who heads a project of the Berlin Academy of Sciences to publish all the inscriptions of ancient Greece. "We think we can discern the word TOPOS. That suits the context extremely well in that it means, 'This is the place of....' It would be expected that there would also be a name above TOPOS in the genitive case. TOPOS inscriptions are a widespread occurrence in Greek epigraphy. According to the letter forms (sigma has the form [ ), the inscription belongs in high or late Augustan times, i.e. 2nd-3rd century after Christ."[10]

Many people miss the fact that there are two inscriptions here, not just one. The top line is of one age and character — Greek, not Cherokee — and the bottom line is of an older age and different alphabet, unquestionably Semitic. The letter-forms of the Semitic alphabet resemble the proto–Hebrew script on Maccabee coins. As we saw in the last chapter, several of these coins have been found in the region.[11] Some were struck in honor of Simeon Bar Kochba, the Jewish hero who led the revolt against Roman rule during the reign of Hadrian in 132–35 C.E.

Both inscriptions come long before Sequoyah (b. *c.*1770) or Red Bird or Aaron Brock. Evaluations by epigraphers place their Greek and Hebrew in the 1st to 3rd century C.E. The engraving, furthermore, was produced with metal scalpra and maul, whence its striking appearance.

If Greek cannot be Cherokee, could Cherokee be Greek? We pose this question because of another enigma, the Possum Creek Stone. "It was first reported to me in January 1975," writes Gloria Farley, "by Elaine Flud and her friend Jeanna James, who had slipped and fallen over it near the creek bed. It lay at the edge of the old main channel of Possum Creek, a tributary to Brazeal Creek, the Poteau River and the Arkansas River, near the town of Calhoun. The exact location was 200 yards to the NW of the center of the SW quarter of

Section 5, Township 7 North, Range 24 East, Le Flore County, Oklahoma." She adds, "The Possum Creek stone is pecked with four eroded symbols, 3½ to 6 inches tall. They are in a straight line and have mostly curved lines, which is not typical of most inscriptions. The flat stone measures 5 feet long, 30 inches wide, about 5 inches thick, and weighs about 300 pounds."[12]

Gloria shared her discovery with Barry Fell of Harvard University. Fell agreed that the writing was Cherokee and classified it with other ancient East Mediterranean syllabaries like Linear A and Linear B and certain Cypriot scripts. He read the inscription as saying, "Place of Invocation"—an inspired guess, as it turns out.[13] "The discovery of a carved stone in my own Le Flore County, Oklahoma," writes Farley in volume two of *In Plain Sight*, "led me to an in-depth study of Sequoyah, the Cherokee genius, who is believed by most

*Top:* Fig. 10.1. Ancient writing at Clay County cave entrance. Courtesy Phyllis Starnes. *Bottom:* Fig. 10.2. Possum Creek Stone. Photograph by Gloria Farley courtesy Bart Torbert. © Gloria Farley Publications Incorporated.

people to have invented the Cherokee syllabary." She goes on to investigate the historical figure known as Sequoyah and conclude that he was really a fictitious person to whom a pre-existing writing system was conveniently, and politically, attributed.[14] She stops at transliterating the inscription or translating it. That is done for the first time by me in this book.[15] The stone is in the collection of the Robert S. Kerr Museum in Poteau, Oklahoma.

The four letters etched in relief on this monumental inscription are, as Farley and Fell recognize, identical to Sequoyah's syllabary. Farley reads SO-NI-WI- SA,[16] and Brian Wilkes, a Cherokee language expert, KE-NI-WI-SA (or HO-NI-KA-SA or LUN-NI-O-SA).[17] None of these readings makes any sense in the Cherokee language. If we read the inscription as Greek, however, it clearly says HO-NI-KA-SA, or ℟hⱭℍ, or 'ο νικασα, i.e., "This is the one who has taken the prize of victory." This is a common formula for the inscription on a dais upon which victors are crowned at ancient games. The use is Homeric, although the spelling is Doric, not Ionic, the main dialect found in Homer. The proportions, size and type of inscription of the Possum Creek Stone approximate those of a number of ancient Greek victory altars or victors' pedestals. A good example of one in Greece's National Archeological Museum comes from Athens and dates to the 5th century B.C.E.[18]

Cherokee writing, then, does not appear to be the invention of Sequoyah but represents an ancient East Mediterranean script similar to Linear A, Linear B and other Cypriot and

Minoan syllabaries. Only one other sample of ancient Cherokee epigraphy has been reported: a brief inscription in Cherokee characters published in the *Jefferson* (N.C.) *Times* newspaper in June of 1983.[19] It is likely that more will be found once people know what to look for. The two known examples are both pre–Columbian and prove that the Cherokee writing system was practiced before Sequoyah in Oklahoma and North Carolina.

A different account of the syllabary emerges in Traveller Bird's *Tell Them They Lie.*[20]

Fig. 10.3. Sequoyah, a lithograph in *Indian Tribes of North America*, McKenney and Hall, 1836, from the portrait painted by Charles Bird King in 1828. Courtesy Hargrett Rare Book Room and Manuscript Library, University of Georgia Libraries.

Published in 1971, it is a curious book. Without citing any evidence, and in fact, defiantly refusing to do so,[21] Traveller Bird makes several unusual claims. First, the Sequoyah of the history books never existed, only a man named George Guess (1766–1839) or Sogwali (Horse), warrior-scribe of his people. Sequoyah's true father was not Christopher Gist/Guess, or as others would have it, a German peddler, but Young Warrior (Gvlihuanida) of Sogwiligigagei (Red Horse Place, now in Rutherford County, North Carolina). Sequoyah did not invent the syllabary associated with his name. It had been used by the Cherokee (whom he calls Talagi) since 1483 and before. In other words, it was not devised from English, Hebrew and German letterforms in the years between 1809 and 1822, as frequently claimed.[22] Finally, there was never any painting of Sequoyah, or George Guess, or George Gist, because the true Sequoyah had been disfigured. The famous portrait by McKenney (fig. 10.3) is of Thomas Maw.

Traveller Bird obviously has an animus that colors his work. He calls the white traders "traitors," and the Indians "red sons-of-bitches." He lambasts "sainthood stories" and "made-up information" about Sequoyah at every turn. But is Traveller Bird's biography any "truer" than the versions he attacks? As scholars point out, there are as many Sequoyahs as there are biographers. Neither his parentage nor birth date seems to be known with certainty. The famous letter to the U.S. government reporting his mysterious death while in Mexico on the trail of lost Cherokee, it has recently been suggested, was a forgery.

Most other sources on Sequoyah contradict Traveller Bird. For instance, "The Life of George Gist" was dictated to John Howard Payne in 1835 by Major George Lowrey, Sequoyah's cousin; Mike Waters, Sequoyah's brother-in-law; and The Bark, another relative associated with Sequoyah since his youth. In it, Gist's age is given as about 60 and he is said to have left the Cherokee Nation with the Arkansas immigrants about eleven years before. In 1843, he was reported to have died on a trip undertaken on behalf of the tribe in San Fernando, Tamaulipas, Mexico. A Sequoyah descendant, Molly Running Wolf, maintains that the place of Sequoyah's death is a town called San Fernando just south of San Miguel de Allende, and that there are "blond-haired, blue-eyed Cherokee" of the family name De Luna living there at present.

One detail of Traveller Bird's account does ring true. According to him, Sequoyah's people came from the West and after encounters with the Americans returned to the West. An origin in the West explains the location of the Possum Creek Stone in Oklahoma, while the return of the Keetoowah to the same area provides the reason for the United Keetoowah Band's presence across the Mississippi today. When one of Constantine Rafinesque's friends, naturalist Thomas Nuttall, visited them in 1819, the Keetoowah were already partially removed and living in Arkansas. In fact, Chief Beverly Northrup maintains they were present in the Old Louisiana Territory since 1721, and perhaps before that, as Lost Cherokees. The Possum Creek Stone was found just where we would expect to find it considering the Eshelokees' migrations through Oklahoma and Arkansas.

From family records and the John Howard Payne papers, we get a coherent biography of the Sequoyah who was the son of Cherokee trader Nathaniel Gist.[23] Perhaps the conflicting accounts can be reconciled if there were actually two persons who went by that name, a scribe-warrior and the half-breed son of the trader. Proof of the latter's existence is in the form of a letter preserved by the Gist family stating that Sequoyah visited his father, Nathaniel Gist, in Kentucky and was acknowledged as his natural son.[24] Whatever the solution, it is evident that the "Sequoyan" syllabary greatly predates its alleged modern inventor. Despite what Traveller Bird says, it goes back far beyond 1483.

Mention of the Lunas and Gists brings us again to Sephardim. Both are crypto–Jews. Sequoyah's parentage is another instance of a Jewish trader marrying the daughter of a Cherokee chief. His mother is Wurteh (Gurty or Gerty, a diminutive of Margaret). A contemporary of his father is the Virginian Samuel Gist, partner of George Washington. Samuel Gist became one of the first admiralty insurance brokers in London. He lived for nearly a hundred years, helped start Lloyd's Bank of London and owned the first stud racehorse to come to America, an "Arabian Turk." The horse, Bulle Rocke, was foaled about 1718, and out of him sprang some of the most valuable of U.S. racing stock. In *The Fabulous History of the Dismal Swamp Company*, Gist is explicitly called "an old Jew" by son-in-law John Anderson.[25] By blood or marriage, he was related to the Smiths, Andersons, Coopers, Ashleys (Arabic and Hebrew for "honey seller"), Howards (dukes of Norfolk, originally *Norman* Hereward "guards of the Army"), Boleyn/Bollings (Hebrew "bath keeper"), and Masseys (from Sephardic surname Mazza), an Edinburgh and Aberdeen mercantile family.[26] There is a small town on Sand Mountain, a Melungeon–populated place, named Guess, and when Joseph Gist died, his manumitted slaves were granted land in Ohio. They went there *en masse*, becoming the so-called Brown County Melungeons.

The origin of the Gist surname seems to be Altaic Turkic GWSTṬ/Gostaṭā, *Heb.* אטטטוא, the name of a line of Khazar rulers in the Caucasus who adopt Judaism after holding a contest between the three major religions. Its Byzantine form is Κώστας. The same dynasty later spearheads a migration of Khazar converts to Kiev and the Ukraine, where their name is rendered in Latin letters as *Gostou-n/s*.[27] In Spain, the family adopts the name Da Costa, which they derived from "God's rib" (Hebrew Abravanel). Acosta is a variant. This becomes Kist in Ashkenaz (*Ger.* "coast," through a pun on *costa*, which can mean either "rib" or "coast"). From all accounts, then, it appears that the Da Costa, Abravanel and Gist families of Spain, Italy, the Low Lands and the British Isles were originally Khazar Turkish converts. The same name occurs in the Ragusan/Croatian/Venetian Gozzi family of traders, explorers, admirals, and physicians who are active in Elizabethan London and the Ottoman Empire.

Contemporary references to Christopher Gist, deputy Indian commissioner to Gov. Edmond Atkin of Maryland and agent of the Ohio Company, describe him as exceedingly tall, dark-complexioned and hairy, with a full beard. George Guess's half-sister, Maria Cecil Gist, married Benjamin Gratz of Lexington, Kentucky (1792–1884), son of the frontier merchant Michael Gratz, who endowed the Spanish and Portuguese synagogues in Philadelphia and New York and established communities in Lancaster and Lexington. The Gratz family came to Philadelphia from Inquisitorial Spain, where their name was Gracia, or Garcia, via Silesia. They intermarried with the Hayses, Howards, Frankses, Ettings and Levys.[28]

Could these roots explain why the portrait of George Guess, or Sequoyah, shows him in a Turkish turban and distinctly Mediterranean clothing? And why he was a silversmith, a rare occupation for an American Indian at that time?

Both the Red Bird inscriptions and Possum Creek Stone offer solid evidence for the Greek origins of the Cherokee. Together with the syllabary's connections with Phoenician tablets and the Cherokee's discarded base-five Meso-American numbering system, the rock-art record captures the trail of the Eshelokee from South America through Mexico to Arkansas and Tennessee. In all the locations where they have resided and settled and migrated, Cherokee have welcomed Sephardic Jews into their society.

# Chapter 11

## *Phoenix Rising*

*There are many humorous things in the world, among them the white man's notion that he is less savage than the other savages.* — Mark Twain

In Robert Conley's *The Dark Way*, the Ani-Kutani priests are overthrown by their fellow Cherokee tribesmen, who accuse them, among other things, of privileged behavior out of control and of trying to revive the ancient practice of human sacrifice. Although the Kutani promise this act will propitiate the angry spirits and revive the tribe's failing crops, the other Cherokee men and women rise up against them when a young warrior returns home and discovers his beautiful wife raped by one of the priests. The rulers had become "haughty, insolent, overbearing, and licentious to an intolerable degree." The outraged people kill every Kutan, young and old. In the aftermath, Cherokee society takes on a different cast. The Kutani retreat into the background, where they remain to this day. A curse is placed on them forever:

> You *Ani-Kutani,*
> I've just put you under the ground.
> They, not you, will be successful.
> Your souls will be wandering
> Aimlessly in the Ghost Country.
> They will never rest.[1]

We have met these Kutani before. They are Rafinesque's Kutans, "who came easterly through the Atlantic ocean," Mediterranean peoples who appear to have spoken Afro-Asiatic or Proto-Pelagian languages. Their counterparts, the Atlans, who seem to belong to Indo-European language groups for the most part, settled the hinterlands of Eastern North America with them, where they built the imposing mounds at Poverty Point, Newark and other centers. Following the cataclysms that "interrupted the intercourse between Europe and America" and left both the Atlans and Kutans to pursue their own course of development, a tribe named as Tsalagi appears on the world stage for the first time. They are heirs of the Atalan civilization, which has gradually disintegrated to produce the Zolacans, as Rafinesque refers to the Cherokee, as well as the Appalachee, Calusa, Conoy and Talegans. During the same period, the Kutans fragment into the Maya, Pawnee, Catawba, Coosa, Cusseta and "Tanasi of Tennessee."

We saw how the "Cherokees or Zolucans, an Atlan nation dwelling west of the Mississippi, being driven by the Oghuzians [Algonquian Indians from South Siberia], came to Kentucky and Tennessee, and settled at last after many wars in the mountains of Carolina, where they became a nation of hunting mountaineers." The Cherokee gather up remnants of the Atlan–affiliated Talegans and part company with their old allies in the Ohio Valley,

the Lenape, Iroquois and Shawnee. In Tennessee, the fair-skinned Cherokee blend success-
fully with the Yuchi, Coosa, Catawba and Cusseta — smaller-bodied, Semitic and darker-
skinned — while keeping the fierce Asiatic Indians and Northerlys at bay. During the
Mississippian Period, a balance of power evolves as the Cherokees amalgamate with southern
mound-building Kutan tribes and enjoy on-again, off-again friendly relations with the
Natchez and Muskogean tribes to the south. The next great transformation does not come
until they revolt against the Kutan priesthood.

One consequence of the eradication of the Kutans by the Cherokee was that "all religious
ceremonies" and "priestly functions" were "assumed thereafter by individual doctors and
conjurors."[2] Another was that any unified political organization they may have had before
that now fell apart.

> Each Cherokee town was autonomous in those days. Each town had its own government and was
> not tied to the government of the other towns in any way. In other words, in those days, there was
> no Cherokee Nation as we know it today. There were simply many Cherokee towns. Perhaps we
> could say (ignoring anthropological definitions) that there was a Cherokee tribe, in that all of the
> Cherokee towns were populated by people who spoke the same language, followed the same cere-
> monial life, and shared the same seven clans, so that, in theory at least, every individual Cherokee
> had relatives in every Cherokee town.[3]

We do not know for sure when this ethnic cleansing took place — Chief John Ross
thought it was in the early eighteenth century[4] and Adair places it in a similar time frame —
but clearly, it had enormous repercussions for the Cherokee people.

What was the Cherokee form of government before the Kutans and what new forms
evolved in the vacuum created by their massacre? There are few observers to record what
Cherokee government was like before about 1800. Benjamin Hawkins, the first agent of the
American government, spent most of his time among the Creeks, paying little attention to
the Cherokee. Before him, the Cherokees were in an almost permanent state of war with
the white Tennesseans, Carolinians and Virginians. The workings of their government were
effectively closed to outsiders. British agents Ludovic Grant, Anthony Deane, Alexander
Long and John Stuart resided at Chota and had the necessary access and longevity of office
not only to observe the Cherokees' political machinery but even to influence it. All had
Cherokee wives and were held in high regard. Their scanty reports, however, do not include
much useful information.

As soon as the Revolution broke out, the main agent, John MacDonald, was cut off
both from the British and Americans. Little was heard from him. A virtual blackout occurs
in knowledge of Cherokee affairs during these critical years. Earlier witnesses like the trader
Eleazar Wiggins, active among them since 1708, Joseph and William Cooper and Cornelius
Dougherty are of no help for the very early period. And as for James Adair, his observations
are focused on the Chickasaw. They can be applied to the Cherokee only as generalizations.

In the absence of much to go on, most historians and anthropologists assume that the
Cherokee were like other Indians of the region and had no central government to speak of.
Raymond Fogelson, in his article on the Cherokee in the *Handbook of American Indians*,
writes: "Although they constituted a people with a shared language and culture, the Cherokees could hardly be regarded as a tribe, in the sense of a unified polity with superordinate
system of authority, until the mid-nineteenth century, when pressure from the Americans
forced the establishment of a unified government."[5]

The narrative outlined by William McLoughlin in his book *Cherokee Renascence in the
New Republic* tells the story of halting and confused acquiescence to the overtures of U.S.

presidents Jefferson, Madison, Adams and Jackson. When the National Council in New Echota finally passes legislation establishing a "new republic," McLoughlin claims, the laws simply "overlay aspects of Anglo-Saxon jurisprudence on Cherokee customs."[6] This move "risked alienating [a] conservative people in order to prove to the white man that the Cherokees could understand and manage a republican form of government ... and [had] considerable appeal to the missionaries whom the Cherokees were eager to have on their side." Such framing with little credit given to Indians for their own contributions to a synthesis or process of acculturation is common among U.S. academic historians.

In reality, it was probably Jewish merchants like the Coopers and Gists who first nudged the Cherokee into nation building, not New England Christians. Both Jews and Indians had a lot in common. Some of the Indians' ancient Greek and Egyptian institutions from their long Kutan and Atlan pasts may have still been in makeshift operation. We have seen how the Eshelokee added a decidedly Greek tone to Cherokee life. More importantly, though, the Cherokee, like their neighbors the Creeks, absorbed a large infusion of Muslim customs. At the time of contact with the English and Americans, there were upwards of eighty-five Cherokee towns. Each had its own Greek–styled assembly hall and Muslim–styled police force. As a city of refuge, Chota fulfilled the same role as Delphi or Jerusalem, although not a political capital until the Jewish traders made it one. The towns were only loosely confederated, in the fashion of Greek city-states. Outside them were bands of Cherokees under leaders who behaved much like independent sheiks. Out of this ancient and multilayered system, arriving Jewish and crypto–Jewish traders, interpreters and agents forged an office of "principal chief" for treaty-signing purposes. They were America's earliest diplomats to conquered peoples. Even before the Cherokee Nation was fitted out with all the accoutrements of sovereignty, indeed before it existed on paper, it had representatives at large in Charleston, Pensacola, Philadelphia, New York, Havana, Amsterdam and London.

How old are Jewish and other Mediterranean and Middle Eastern influences among the Southeastern Indians? When the American painter John Trumbull sketched Creek chiefs visiting New York in 1790, contemporaries were astounded by what they saw. Indians were said to resemble Roman senators "for their dignity of manner, form, countenance and expression."[7] The public was shocked to find out that Indians wore Turkish turbans and Islamic crescents. The Creek chieftain Hol-te-mal-te-tez-te-neek-e or Sam Perryman possesses regalia consisting of a fez, *imama* and *kaffiy*, as sketched by George Catlin.[8]

Choctaw half-breed Israel Folsom told the historian Cushman that all Indians believed themselves to be of Jewish extraction. This opinion was held also by Jewish trader Abraham Mordecai, founder of the city of Montgomery in Creek Alabama. The same belief was shared by Cherokee traders Cornelius Dougherty and James Adair, both whom were probably of Jewish descent themselves. Many of the first white pioneers among the Choctaw and Chickasaw — Pitchlynn, Colbert, Cooper, Gunn, Nail, Stuart — had Melungeon surnames and are believed to come from crypto–Jewish families.

Perhaps, as critics claim is true of Adair, these beliefs were only projections. Yet there is ample testimony from the Cherokee people that they viewed themselves as "white" and fair-skinned by origin. When the Cherokee Ghost Dance erupted in 1811, a traditionalist called The Elk told Moravian missionaries in Spring Place that he was "really a descendant of the family of the first inhabitants on this side of the sea" and "the brothers on this side were originally white like those over the sea."[9] As we have seen before, Keetoowah priest William Eubanks espoused the same theory.

Muslim traders appear to have been very active on American shores. Al-Masudi's *His-*

*torical Annals* of 942 C.E. records a sea voyage when a ship under the command of Captain Khashkhash (probably a Babylonian) set sail from Cordova, Spain. After a long journey west across the Atlantic, it returned laden with treasures. Al-Idrisi in his world geography, *Nuzhet al-Mushtaq* (1154), tells of a similar voyage undertaken by the Brothers Al-Mugrurim, who embarked from Lisbon seeking islands in the western Atlantic. They sailed for about a month and brought back a report that the opposite lands were inhabited by Berbers and thick with sheep.[10] Over the centuries, Arab–speaking visitors or settlers seem to have penetrated far into the interior. Islamic coins, Arabic trade tokens and Kufic writing remain as the signs of their activities from Massachusetts to Tennessee.

The Kutans, as we have seen, had deep roots in North Africa. Islamic scholar Ivan Van Sertima refers to a thesis published by the French commandant Jules Cauvet in Algiers in the 1930s, who examined the origins of seventy-seven tribes on both sides of the Atlantic. Van Sertima summarizes Cauvet's work as follows: "The ethnic names of certain Berber groups were the same as those of certain American Indian tribes.... Certain American ethnic names are only duplicated among the Berbers and are not found anywhere else in the world; certain other names have undergone Berber transformations; the origin of a number of names is attested by the grouping of names of collectivities in the vicinity of their point of origin."[11] One example is the Guales of South Carolina, who appear to be the same as the Guellaïa of the Rif in North Africa. I have noted the North African origins of the Coree in a previous chapter. Colonization efforts evidently also went in the opposite direction. A study by the anthropologist Harold Lawrence appearing in 1962 demonstrates that certain tribes living in the Sahara possess American Indian traits with similar names and naming methods. The Berber "Indians" live in tents rather than the mud-brick houses of their neighbors.[12]

Of all sites in North America, Tennessee has the best-known and longest inscriptions in Kufic Arabic writing. According to Barry Fell, Arab traders in the Southeast contributed the core vocabulary to the language we now call Mobilian Trade Jargon. As well as providing the basic form of intertribal commercial contract and system of credit, the *commenda*, Islamic institutions also played a role in the development of civil administration and military organization for Indian tribes.[13] Jewish and Muslim models of civic life both come from the world of the Mediterranean and Near East. These models were fundamentally different from the feudalism of Northern Europe brought over by the British and French.

Cherokee chieftains living in the hills and hollows away from town life very much evoke Muslim *shaykhs*. In the words of Albert Hourani, an Arab historian, these are de facto leaders who "had little effective power except that which was given them by their reputation in the public opinion of the group."[14] The British found it exasperating to deal with their equivalents among the Indians. Some bands were so furtive they even escaped the dragnet of removal that came later with the Americans. Tsali and his tribesmen in North Carolina held out defiantly after the Trail of Tears and their group eventually became the Eastern Band of Cherokee Indians. A multitude of other Eastern and Southeastern Indian groups are still fighting today for federal recognition.

In a Cherokee town, just as in Islam, there existed structured government, a developed administrative system and a sense of history and cultural traditions. Its leaders were military officials in the pattern of dynastic rulers in charge of Muslim cities, the *sayyids* or *sharifs*. These descendants of the Prophet ran the affairs of the *shari'a*, assuring implementation of a social code in compliance with the dictates of religion, exactly the same role played by the Kutan priesthood. In the same way, the government of the Cherokee state was essentially military in nature, with headmen given titles that were martial in origin. Like Muslim appointees, members of this elite corps moved between towns as governors. The same crypto–Jewish half-breed families held control of the Cherokee state from its formal beginnings until its extinction in 1900. After that, the U.S. government dissolved tribal government and allotted communal land in severalty under the Dawes Act. But the age-old patterns of public life continued. There has always been constant friction between admixed town-dwellers with their wealth and guarantees of law and order and the mostly full-blood country folk with their clan system and notions of summary justice.

The ancient office of *qadi* is peculiar to Arabs and their neighbors. The word itself probably has the same root as the name Ani-Kutani, and it too finds an echo in Cherokee society. As

Fig. 11.1. Tuskatche Mico, or the Birdtail King of the Cusitahs, 1790, by John Trumbull. Emmet Collection, Miriam and Ira D. Wallach Division of Art, Prints and Photographs, The New York Public Library, Astor, Lenos and Tilden Foundations.

historian Albert Hourani describes it, the *qadi* represents the urban elite placed in charge of guarding "a system of learning, values, modes of behavior and ideal types of personality."[15] A similar function is performed by the Keetoowah and Seven Scribes' Society of the Cherokee. In the acculturation process, these traditional roles are gradually usurped, and improved upon, by the half-breeds. The mixed bloods rekindle a public-spirited model inspired by the Islamic idea of the *waqf*, or foundation, for the property-less. In the Muslim world, the *waqf* is "an assignment in perpetuity of the income from a piece of property for charitable purposes, for example, the maintenance of mosques, schools, hospitals, public fountains or hostels for travellers, the freeing of prisoners, or the care of sick animals. It could also be used, however, for the benefit of the founder's family."[16] In this same spirit, the Vanns endowed the Moravian school at Spring Place, where they had their own children and relatives educated. It was the same story at the Brainerd Mission at Creek Path. Doublehead and others established large plantations along the same principles. On Sand Mountain, the Burns, Lowrey and Davis families even sought a special section of land from the U.S. government to build a self-sustaining college.

Many of these Arab–styled leaders among the Cherokee belonged to the Deer Clan, the third of the original clans. Deer Clan members were supposed to be good intellects. Anawaika or Deerhead Cove at the foot of Fox Mountain between northern Georgia and Alabama, near Lookout Mountain, was one of their traditional territories. Part of Paint–town in North Carolina was once called Deer Place. The Cherokee clans were suppressed by the reforms of affluent half-breed planters and Deer Clan members and brought under a new judicial system. The Light Horse Brigade introduced by Maj. Ridge (al-Wadi) is, unsurprisingly, modeled on the institution of the *qadi*. Henceforth, Cherokee marshals, not clans, had the power to punish acts like illicit sexual intercourse, theft, drunkenness and murder.

A formal decree abolishing clan law was signed at Eustanala, April 18, 1810, "by order of the seven clans."[17] A reactionary Ghost Dance Movement flared up briefly in 1811, but by the time of removal in 1838, clans were little more than a memory. Government rolls largely ignored them, emphasizing patriarchal credentials and father's surname rather than mothers and female-linked relationships. Marriage within one's clan, formerly punishable by death, eventually became a non-issue. Probably few Cherokee today can recite the clan history of their parents and forebears with any great degree of confidence. Descendants with little Cherokee blood, even those who may preserve a direct female line, are often completely in the dark.

When they resettle in Oklahoma, the Cherokee seek to transplant many of these ancient institutions. The same leading families help found orphanages, schools, libraries, assembly halls, stomp grounds and even interest-free lender banks. In more than one respect, the Cherokee at the time were far in advance of the rest of American society. Whether they knew it or not, they emulated Marrano ideals of community. Jewish history is replete with the stories of Sephardim who establish their own "nations" in exile after 1492. Typically, as in the case of Livorno, Bayonne, New Amsterdam, Savannah and the Caribbean islands, the parnassim or leaders move quickly to set up a widows' pension fund, orphanage, cemetery society and other charitable organizations.

It can be argued that Muslim courts of justice are also replicated in the new Cherokee state in Georgia after 1820. The elected officials at New Echota take great care to establish a Supreme Court with Superior and Inferior Courts. These courts were quite different from those of the United States, despite the similarity of names. Men like George Lowrey and Richard Keyes served the people without drawing a salary, in the same way as Muslim leaders discharged their duties in the upper 'ulama of a Spanish or Turkish city. The Cherokee judges cooperated with local law enforcement officials like the Light Horse Brigade. Hourani's characterization of the qadi applies equally well to the assistant chiefs and National Council representatives of the Cherokee: "The qadi was a central figure in the life of the city. He not only administered the law, but was also responsible for the division of a property after a person's death in accordance with the laws of inheritance, and could have other powers of supervision given him by the ruler."[18]

Let us turn now to external relations in the new Cherokee state. Whereas the old model of treaty making revolved around notions of kinship, with Indians addressing colonists as "our brothers" and the English or French king as "our father," the new leaders around 1790 adopt an approach based on egalitarian principles in negotiating with the white man. Thanks to Attakullakulla (who calls himself "president," not "chief"), Nancy Ward, Trader John MacDonald and Chief John Ross, the Cherokee are often able to treat with Washington on a parity. Undoubtedly, this turn of events betrays the counsel of half-breeds of Portuguese Jewish or Scottish Jewish extraction. Suddenly, the Echota chiefs begin to deliver written copies of their "talks," a practice unparalleled in any other Indian tribe. These expanded charters and dispatches developed a notion of justice and just relations. And they acted as a durable record for arguments that might otherwise be swept aside and ignored. The half-Sephardic Oconostota even wrote letters to the editor of the Knoxville *Gazette* published after his death in 1792, if we are to credit one account.[19] Eventually, the Cherokee were able to send embassies to Washington City, hire lawyers and accountants and retain lobbyists for their cause.

At the center of all these developments are the Ridges, Lowreys, Waties, Hickses and Rosses. Elias Boudinot (1800–1838), first editor of *The Phoenix* newspaper, was actually the brother of Stand Watie. Known originally as Buck Watie (Gallegina), he took his name from Elias Boudinot, the Yankee lawyer who served as the first president of the Continental Congress. The elder Elias Boudinot wrote *Star in the West,* an exposition of the Lost Tribes of Israel theory about American Indians. The Cherokee *Phoenix* was published in English and Cherokee from 1828 until 1834. As evident from its first issues, its overriding purpose was political: to unite Cherokees scattered in isolated pockets across eight different states in the East and four in the West. The first number contained the Constitution of the Cherokee Nation along with a proud display of Sequoyah's syllabary.

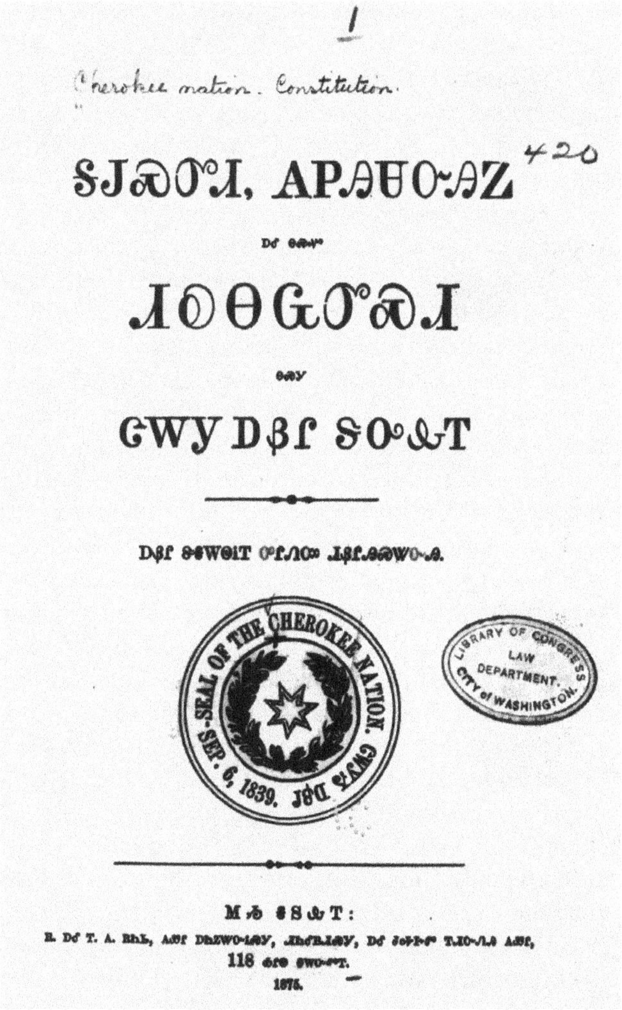

The symbol chosen for the national newspaper was an image of the phoenix, a fabu-

Fig. 11.2. *The Constitution and Laws of the Cherokee Nation,* or *Tsalagihi Ayeli,* published in Cherokee, 1875.

lous beast from Greek folklore and Jewish mysticism. Prehistoric Cherokee have many stories about this mythic bird. It was said to be the largest in the world. Adair gives its name as Sinnawah, although others call it Tlanuwa, Tsalnuwah or Tlaniwa the "Great Hawk." Adair's rendering of the name seems to be the original form. Taking a broad view, the Cherokee phoenix is the same as the Sina, or Saena, of Persian stories, S'yena in Sanskrit, all of which mean "raptor," as does Cherokee *tlanu,* "swoop down." The fabulous Senmurw (Saena Bird) was known to all peoples of the Middle East. It is the basis of the Arab people's roc, phoenix of Greek legend and Simorgh ("Sina-bird") of Judeo-Persian folktales.

The symbol of the phoenix served Marranos in Amsterdam, Livorno and Salonika as an emblem of state. True to its meaning in both Cherokee and Jewish usage, it stood for the resurrected spirit of a chosen people. Portuguese Jews went by the name "gentes de naçao," People of the Nation. Although they paid lip service to their Portuguese citizenship, their secret meaning of the term was the Hebrew Nation. A Judeo-Spanish prayer book of

1612 displays the phoenix as the special badge for the Amsterdam congregation Neveh Shalom, with the Hebrew verse "Who is like thee?" (Ex. 15:11).[20]

The case of *Euchella v. Welsh* in 1824 brought an ambitious bid by intermarried Jewish landowners to create a national reservation for the Cherokee in the East. Like the *Phoenix* newspaper, it would mark the Cherokees' arrival into an elite circle. Soon there was talk they might receive a seat in Congress. Public sympathy for them was fanned by converted Jews like John Howard Payne.[21] In the end, they never won the promised representation in Washington. But they did secure a permanent place in the story of America.

On the legal front, a battle of words that broke out during these years between Tennesseans and the Cherokee over the meaning of "tribe" and "tenant at will," "claim" and "right" boiled over into *The Cherokee Nation v. The State of Georgia*, 30 U.S. 1 (1831) and *Samuel Worcester v. The State of Georgia*, 31 U.S. 515, 550–56 (1832).[22] Chief Justice Marshall ruled that Indian tribes are "domestic dependent nations" and defined the "trust" the United States owes them. Before this, men like John Stuart, John MacDonald and Chief John Ross had temporarily turned the tables on the Tennesseans and Georgians and begun citing the same law books as the white men. One of them was Vattel's *The Law of Nations*.[23] These moves are not unlike Menasseh Ben Israel's strategy for winning rights for the Jews. The Cherokee relied on arguments "invoking claims of justice, assistance, equality, and autonomy along with Federalist notions of paternalism that contributed to the trust arrangement," according to political science analyst Cynthia Cumfer.[24] The concept of limited sovereignty and wardship has benefited all Native American tribes down to the present. It is part of the Cherokee — and Jewish — gift to other Indians.

The Cherokee nation was inspired by and patterned on the Sephardic experience, but it has never been Zionistic. It was born as a nation in exile. The full meaning of exile would become plain when the Cherokee, after being driven out of Tennessee into Georgia, were removed to Arkansas, then to Oklahoma, and when even these lands were taken from them. The Cherokee Nation, like world Jewry, has been repeatedly destroyed. But in the process, it has always risen again like the phoenix. The ancient heritage of the Ani-Kutani could not be laid to rest as easily as story and song might have it.

Let us turn now to the final chapter of the Kutans and Eshelokee, which is set on a remote Appalachian ridge in Alabama called Sand Mountain.

# Chapter 12

# *Sand Mountain*

*A human life is like a single letter in the alphabet. It can be meaningless, or it can be part of a great meaning.* — Jewish Theological Seminary of America

Sand Mountain is an extension of the Cumberland Plateau and Waldens Ridge about a hundred miles long flanking the Tennessee River in the tri-state area formed by Tennessee, Georgia and Alabama. Its twin ridge, Lookout Mountain, lies across the valley. Between them now runs Interstate 59. The two mountains are broad and flat on top, with streams and even rivers. They stretch from Chattanooga, Tennessee, to Fort Payne and Boaz, Alabama, near Blountsville. In ancient times, a mixture of Cherokee, Yuchi, Koasati, Creek and other Indian tribes inhabited the area. The Spanish explorer Hernando De Soto visited its towns in 1539–1540.

Jackson County constituted the first white county formed in Alabama. It was carved out of the Cherokee Cession of 1816. Not all its settlers apparently were white, though. Today we would call many of them mixed race or brown-skinned people. In the census of 1950, Jackson County had 70 persons identified as Melungeon, making Sand Mountain an important location for the ethnic group. In this chapter, we will survey the genealogies of some of these Cherokee and Melungeon families and follow their fortunes down to the present. Among surnames are Adkins, Black, Blevins, Brown, Burke, Cooper, Fields, Gunter, Justice, Keys and Lowrey.

My own odyssey of discovery[1] started when I came across an Isaac Cooper who served as a witness in a famous legal case. The records showed the grandson of William Cooper, guide and scout for Daniel Boone, giving a series of depositions in the home of James Cooper in newly-formed Jackson County, Alabama, in 1820. The case concerned the Great Salt Works of the Big South Fork of the Cumberland River in Wayne County, Kentucky:

The Big South Fork of the Cumberland River empties into the Cumberland River in Pulaski County East of Burnside. Today, the River is mostly in McCreary County KY, and then crosses the border into Scott and Fentress Co's. TN. Years ago, before McCreary County was formed, the West/North bank of the River was Wayne County KY, and Fentress County TN. The East/South bank (the River runs mostly North to South, with a large bend near Bear Creek that turns the flow East to west for a few miles, then it turns South once more), was Pulaski and Whitley County KY, and Campbell and then later on Scott County TN. In the 1900's, this was a coal mining area, and today, it is a National Park. It is stunningly beautiful place, with large bluffs along the River canyon.

In 1807, John Francis first reported the discovery of saltwater along the Big South Fork of the Cumberland River. This initial discovery was reported to be "near the mouth of Bear Creek, where Richard Slavey now lives." (I believe that Richard Slavey and John Francis were in laws, as both married a woman named Mounts.) Francis and Slavey petitioned the State Legislature, and in 1811, received a Grant for 1000 acres, conditional upon their production of 1000 bushels of salt. The time limit for this production was later increased, due to the War of 1812. By the time the 1000 bushels were produced (around 1818), several other items of interest occurred: John Francis received another Grant just South of the 1000 acres for the same purpose; Marcus Huling, working with Col. James Stone, sank another saltwater well, on the sight of Francis's other Grant; Stephen F. Conn, Martin Beaty, and a host of other people became involved in these enterprises in several different ways. This activity started a series of Law Suits, lasting up into the 1830's, as well as the accidental sinking of the world's first oil well.[2]

A flash in the pan in the business of ancestor hunting? Yes, but this dispute decided the fate of an important area claimed by the original Eshelokee. There are Greek–style fortresses and cave paintings nearby at Yahoo Falls. The litigation over mineral rights involves the familiar Melungeon names of Slavey, Cooper, Francis, Mounts, Stone, Conn and Beaty.

The outcome of these drawn-out suits and countersuits need not be told here. I am sorry to say the first question that came into my mind was *Where did all that money go?* What became of the Melungeon families in Boone's first settlement in Kentucky so active in the first land sales, mineral prospecting, manufacturing, ferry and mill operations, trade, merchandising, banking and law of the region? Did they throw in their lot with the Cherokees and go west? Did they hide in the hills? Were they ever able to build a community elsewhere? Did their unusual heritage of Jewish and Native American create any strains within families? How much of this heritage was discarded over the years and how much of it remembered? Sand Mountain genealogies offer some answers.[3]

The **Adkins** (also spelled Atkin, Atkinson, Aiken) family is heavily intermarried with the pioneer Coopers, Blevinses and Burkes from Wayne County, Kentucky. They came from Pittsylvania County, Virginia, an important staging area for the movement of Melungeon families along the northern and eastern boundaries of the Overhill Cherokee. The family is traced to a James Atkinson, a Quaker who came to Philadelphia in the 1600s, probably from a seaport in Wales. His great-grandson William Adkins left a will dated Jan. 22, 1784, probated March 15, 1784, detailing an accumulation of wealth, and was buried near Cooper's Old Store, Pittsylvania County. William's son Owen was born about 1750 in Lunenberg County, Virginia (parent county of Pittsylvania), and died in Watauga, Hawkins County, Tennessee, about 1790. He married Agnes Good/Goad, from the same family that provided a spouse to Valentine Sevier (1701/02–1803). Good is the English equivalent of Yom Tov, Buen, Boone, Le Bon and other names for those bearing the "good name" of King David.[4] Valentine and Agnes were the parents of John Sevier, the first governor of Tennessee. One of his sons, Valentine, married Sarah Cooper. The Seviers can be traced to Don Juan de Xavier of a Sephardic family who took refuge in Navarre during the Spanish Inquisition.

In 1836, Benjamin Adkins built a log mill on the Little South Fork of the Cumberland near Parmleysville, Kentucky, made of huge squared logs. This mill, with rifle slits on two levels, is still standing. He left a will in 1839 showing $10,000 in debts owed him and an estate of great value. Numerous family members moved first to Sequatchee (Marion County, Tennessee) and subsequently to Sand Mountain and to a hidden cove at the foot of Fox Mountain (named after Black Fox) called Anawaika, or Deerhead, on the Georgia state line. Some proceeded west to Arkansas. William E. Adkins (about 1828–1862) married Susan E. (Sukie) Cooper (about 1831–1901), the daughter of Isaac and Mahala Jane (Blevins) Cooper, April 20, 1847, in Henry County, Tennessee, and descendants filed unsuccessful applications to be enrolled as Cherokee in Indian Territory. Memories of their Cherokee ancestors ran thin, but Steve Adkins of Arkansas recalled in 2001, "When I was little my Great Grandma Adkins (Virgie Stanley) use to tell me stories about my Great Grandfather's (Arthur 'Aud' Adkins) Grandmother. She said her name was Sukie and she was a Cherokee Indian. I later found out that 'Sukie' was a nickname for Susan. She also mentioned the name Mahala Blevins."

The Atkins surname seems to come from Aix/Aachen, the capital of the Frankish empire under Charlemagne and an important Jewish mercantile center.

Proceeding in alphabetical order, **Black** is a Scottish name associated with clans Lamont, Macgregor and Maclean. About 1790, Mary Ann Black married William Davis, a Revolutionary War soldier born in Virginia in 1753. Davis died in 1848 and was buried in Maynards Cove on Sand Mountain near the former Chickamauga capital of Creek Path. Mary Ann was a daughter of Black Fox, who at the time she was born served as a lieutenant in Dragging Canoe's Chickamauga army fighting the Tennesseans.

Black Fox signed the Holston Treaty, July 2, 1791 (but not the stipulation of February 7, 1792), and delivered the funeral oration for his brother-in-law Dragging Canoe. He was originally chief of the lower town of Ustanali. He became principal chief of the Cherokee after the death of Little Turkey in 1802. He signed the October 20, 1803, agreement for opening a road through the Cherokee Nation, as well as the Oct. 27, 1805, Jan. 7, 1806, and Sept. 11, 1807, treaties. On March 3, 1807, the U.S. Senate and House of Representatives enacted a statute at large giving "the Cherokee chief, called Black Fox" a life annuity of $100, allegedly for helping to arrange peace with the Illinois tribes, a mission in which he was aided by Robert Looney. He sided with Chief Doublehead during the rebellion of 1806–1810 and was deposed for it, with Pathkiller taking his place. On April 18, 1810, he and others signed an act of the Cherokee Nation abolishing clan revenge. After this he was reinstated as principal chief. He last received his $100 stipend, by proxy, on July 11, 1810, when the agent, Return J. Meigs, referred to him as "Black Fox Cherokee King."

Chief Black Fox had his nation formally cede 7,000 square miles of land to the government, presenting a ceremonial wampum belt to Col. Meigs as a token of faith. This sale transferred Muscle Shoals with its rich iron ore deposits to American ownership. He is believed to have died in 1811 and to have been buried at a spot lying on the boundary between Cherokee and Creek lands in Blount County, Alabama. This location, named Browns Valley, might better be called the Cherokee Valley of the Tombs because of its numerous pyramid-shaped mounds. The dead chief's name was carried on by the Black Fox, who signed the treaty of 1828 and emigrated west.

Some descendants remained in the East around the chief's former residence of Creek Path on Sand Mountain. There are rumors that Black Fox did not die in 1811 but changed his name to Henry White and moved from Alabama to Ohio.

As we have seen in the Nancy Ward chapter above, blackfox in English designates the medium-sized fur-bearing animal known as the fisher, a very elusive type of marten that lives in caves and feeds primarily on bats. Cherokee names of this era often punned on words in translation. A Chickamauga mixed blood chief, Thomas Glass, who signed the treaty of Tellico next to Black Fox, was known as The Glass, or Tunnquetihee. His residence was Nickajack Town opposite the end of Sand Mountain near Chattanooga. Glass is a Scottish clan that originated in France. It is remembered for producing the religious sect known as Glassites, who taught that every meeting of worshipers constituted a church in itself. Chief Glass appears to have begun life as Thomas Glass in the white settlements in South Carolina, for he served in the home guard in 1779 and 1780. A William Glass then bought land in Watauga near John Sevier and James and Charles Robertson.

A description of Black Fox's tomb in *An Account of Some Creek, Cherokee and Earlier Inhabitants of Blount County* mentions a horde of valuable iron ore, smelted lead and other metals that was buried with him. From these notes it is apparent that Black Fox was involved in mining and trading metals, an unusual activity for an Indian.[5]

The **Blevinses** were an old Welsh family who immigrated in the 1600s to Rhode Island. They became one of the first to venture into the future states of Tennessee and Kentucky. William Blevins, a longhunter from Pittsylvania County, married Agnes Walling/Walden, the sister of Elisha Walling (for whom Walden's Ridge is named). Blevinses were among the signers of the Watauga Purchase on March 19, 1775. Jonathan Blevins (about 1763–about 1830), like his twin brother Richard, was a Revolutionary War soldier in the Upper New River Valley. During the shift of the Cherokee population southward in the 1820s and 1830s, the two brothers bought land in Marion County, Tennessee, like the Coopers. Elections were held in Jonathan's house on the stage road between Sequatchie River, Walden's Ridge and Cumberland Mountain.

Jonathan was married to Charlotte Muse, the daughter of Richard Muse (English Mews came from Musa, Arabic for Moses), a wealthy land agent who disposed of over 2,400 acres of land in Montgomery/Wythe/Grayson County, Virginia, before settling in what became Campbell County, Tennessee. Most of Jonathan and Lottie Muse's children avoided the Trail of Tears. Two sisters Lucretia (Creecy) and Mahala Jane (Linny) married two brothers, James and Isaac Cooper. Throughout all their moves, the Blevinses were careful to support other members of their circle. For example, Richard Blevins served as character witness for Jacob Troxell in Marion County, Tennessee, in 1832, before Jacob too moved on to DeKalb County, Alabama. William Blevins gave an affidavit in 1850 for his widowed sister Jane Cooper in Dade County, Georgia. Jonathan (Jont) Blevins (1779–1863) married Catherine (Katie) Troxell, the daughter of George Jacob Troxell and his Cherokee wife Cornblossom (his brother Tarleton married her sister Mary Polly Troxell). He was the commander of road work near the Little South Fork River in Wayne County, Kentucky.

During the Civil War, many of the Blevins men, most of them railroaders like their Cooper cousins, joined the U.S. Cavalry of Tennessee. Afterward, they and their Cooper relatives were forced to leave Deerhead Cove and move to New Hope across the state line on the other end of Sand Mountain. The men are usually described as having been fairly tall, lean, of dark complexion, with dark hair and either blue, green or yellow eyes–a physical type similar to North African Jews. Many Blevinses are buried either in Cagle Cemetery in Deerhead Cove or New Hope Cemetery on Sand Mountain.

Blevins DNA is E1b1b, especially common in Berbers, Egyptians and Tuareg in North Africa. E1b1b is the second most common Hebrew male lineage after J.

With the plain-sounding **Browns** we may actually be dealing with the common Converso name Pardo. "The whole business of 'Jewish' names is quite confusing," writes Colonial American Jewish historian Jacob Marcus. "There was a definite tendency on the part of the immigrant Jews in those days to drop their Spanish and their German Jewish names, as they passed through England, and to appropriate English names. Thus it is that we find them in the seventeenth and eighteenth centuries with such names as Phillips, Brown, Rice, Hays, Henry, Laney, Simson, Jones, and the like ... Saul Pardo ('brown') blossomed forth as Saul Brown."[6] The Jewish origins of this Cherokee family can be seen in the names they favored for children (Alexander, Alice, Rebecca, Cassie, David, Eli, Ephraim, Goldie, Hulda, Isom, Julia, Minnie, Nely, Sarah, Silas, Sylvia, Violet, and Zachariah), as well as in marriage partners' surnames (Barton, Burke, Cooper, Craze, Fields, Frazier, Gilbreath, Guess/Gist, Harris, Hearne, Jean/Jane, Lowrey, Proctor, Ross, Ruth, Sizemore, Vann, White and Yates). There are at least seven Chickamauga chiefs of the name Brown, most associated in some way with Creek Path. The Browns supplied so many soldiers for the Creek War that their contingent was called "Brown's army." After the Battle of Horse Shoe Bend, they were granted extensive lands in western Alabama. They operated Brown's Ferry across the Tennessee River near Chattanooga as well as the military road that came in later. They were also involved in ironworks.

The **Burkes** were French Sephardic Jews who settled in Virginia, North Carolina, Pennsylvania and Kentucky. John Burke emigrated from Cork, Ireland, to Pennsylvania and his descendants proceeded south to Virginia and North Carolina and west to Kentucky. Their name may come from Burgos, the city in Portugal. The Burke coat of arms shows a French name DeBurque with a knight and a panther with a chain around its neck. A Benjamin Burges is mentioned in trade documents of South Carolina in 1751, and a James Burges appears in Hawkins around 1797. James Burke, born in County Limerick, Ireland, about 1705, discovered Burke's Garden located in Tazewell County, Va., in 1753, and is frequently mentioned in local histories of that region. John Burke signed a petition from North of Holston against the so-called Fincastle Petition in 1777. Benjamin Burke (1765–1828) married Elizabeth Troxell (1752–1851), the sister of trader-spy George Jacob Troxell (1758–1843, DeKalb Co., Ala.), and they are buried in the Smith-Kidd Cemetery, Great Meadow Community, Rock Creek, McCreary Co., Ky. Surnames of favorite marriage partners include: Anderson, Bane, Brown, Blevins, Byatt, Coil (Coyle), Davis, Gregory, Hatfield, Lewellan, Millican, Orr, Smith and Steele.

A photograph of Jonathan Burke, whose wife, Nancy Cooper, was a granddaughter of Chief Black Fox, depicts what might be taken as a model of the Jewish Indian of the period. The family Bible says he was "one-third Choctaw."[7]

Another Jewish Indian in the region was Cornelius Benjamin **Cooper** (1801–1886), Georgia state senator. He and his mulatto father lived in what was part of the Cherokee Nation, present-day Gilmer County, Georgia. Many of these half-breed Cherokees moved to Rusk County, Texas, between 1840 and 1865, in order to get away from the bitter infighting between Indians favoring moving to the Indian Territory (Oklahoma) and those who wanted to stay in Georgia. The ones who moved to Texas were mostly Treaty Party supporters, of the same persuasion of the Ridges, Waties and Elias Boudinot. The opposite faction at the time was the Ross Party.

Exploitation of Choctaw country zoomed in the generation of Henry Labon Cooper (about 1745–after 1830), a planter, road builder and land developer. His name appears as Enrico Labon Cooper of San Esteban de Tombecbe (Tombigbe, St. Stephens) in Spanish records. He took an oath of allegiance and served as corporal together with another Enrico, probably Houston, his son, and Samuel and William (Guilielmo), probably his brothers. The oath was recorded on a 1787 Spanish census of Second Creek. He and his brothers and cousins were all tobacco growers in Second and Sandy Creek, now the tri-state area between Tennessee, Mississippi and Alabama traversed by the Natchez Trace. In one season alone, they grew 21,200 pounds. Before settling in Kentucky and Tennessee, Henry Cooper had lived in Bute County, a crypto–Jewish settlement, where he was a member of the Masonic Temple,[8] and Caswell County, N.C., where he was overseer of roads and a wheelwright. When the Wataugans founded the Cumberland Settlement in Nashville, he bought 640 acres in Sumner County on the west side of the Harpeth River at the mouth of the South Harpeth. This land was conveyed to him by an in-law with "all advantages, ways, water courses, *mines and minerals*"–another indication of industrial interests.

A son of Henry's, Isaac Cooper (about 1775–about 1845), is first attested in the "List of Taxes and Taxable Property" in the bounds of Capt. William Bean's Company in 1799. This was in Cherokee country along the Holston River and Clinch Mountain in Tennessee, later Grainger County, variously known as the Watauga Settlement and State of Franklin. William Bean, Sr., built the first white cabin in those parts as well as Bean's Station located on a saddle of land leading over the ridge of Clinch Mountain called Copper Ridge (after William Cooper, Isaac's grandfather). The tavern there was one of the most visited road-houses between New Orleans and Washington. It was in this heavily forested hunting ground, through which ran the Black Fox Path, that Isaac must have met his future wife, Nancy Blackfox.

Isaac Cooper, Jr. (about 1804–1847), was a mixed blood Cherokee-Choctaw-Jewish railroader from Kentucky who died during the Mexican War in Vera Cruz, Mexico. He is buried in the Church of San Francisco near the Plaza de la Reforma. His brother, William, also served in Gen. Winfield Scott's army of conquest.

According to Isaac's grandson Peter Cooper, "My grandmother Jane Cooper said that the Indian Chief Fox always claimed to be akin to Grandfather Isaac Cooper." Peter Cooper reported that Jane Cooper said, "They, Father and Grandfather, were recognized as white folks when they lived. They lived with white people. Never heard of them living with the Indian tribe except that they were in this state when the Indians left. They did not leave when the Indians left. I don't know why the Indians left." Isaac was called Zack by the family and his wife was known as Linny. The clan most commonly recalled by descendants in North Carolina was Paint.

The dividing paths of the Coopers are illustrated by the career of John Cooper (about 1771–1839), plantation owner and a captain of the Choctaw Indians. In 1836, he lived in Perry County in Tennessee on the west side of the Buffalo River near the town of Linden. His family went over the Trail of Tears several times. A descendant remembers him as follows:

> A man who cultivated his land, raising food for his family and livestock, Captain Cooper was surprised and shocked when the soldiers came in midwinter, January of 1836, and commanded an immediate removal of his family to the Indian Territory. They had only time to gather and pack a few necessities which the soldiers allowed to be tied on their horses' and mules' backs. They rode away toward their new home leaving behind their house, a structure of four rooms, a verandah separating the house from the smokehouse. They also left six cribs of corn and other important foods for their survival.
>
> When they arrived at the Mississippi River the ship or boats which they had been promised in writing were not there to take them across this very cold water. The soldiers, who were driving them had not been told of this promise. They used their only means of crossing, riding their swimming animals across. Many of their party drowned and they also lost most of their food and other necessities.
>
> [Capt.] Cooper's wife [Nancy Ann Piles], who was ill when forced to start on the perilous journey, was physically unable to continue. A few miles from the Mississippi River in the state of Arkansas, the soldiers permitted the sick woman and their old mother [probably Molly Huston Cooper, wife of Henry Cooper] to be left in the wild and rugged country with her two daughters, Delitha and Narcissa [both names are favored by European Jews]. Gen. [sic] Cooper and his son and sons-in-law were made to continue their journey westward, driving their remaining cattle. There remains today a crossing in southeastern Oklahoma called Cooper's Landing, which was named for the courageous and faithful Choctaw husband and father. As soon as possible they escaped from the soldiers and made their way back to where the old mother and daughters were left. The mother had died two days after being abandoned. Delitha and Narcissa had survived by eating bark of trees and other plants and animals.
>
> John Cooper was an educated Indian — spoke and wrote the English language. He fought in the war of 1812 with Andrew Jackson. The two men made a gentlemen's agreement that the Choctaws

of Perry and Maury County, Tennessee were not to be moved to the Indian Territory until the spring of 1836. The two men continued to correspond and Andrew Jackson verified 'their promise in writing.' Our grandfather, John Cooper was deceived by this Democrat. He asked [*page torn*: that no one in the family would ever vote for a Democrat again. They became staunch Republicans].[9]

To list but one surviving record of Cooper property, James Cooper of Jackson County, Alabama, had a home and improvements "on Wills Creek across the ridge from Copelands Mill." Adjoining the Eli Cooper place, it was assessed in accordance with the 1828 treaty with the Cherokee Nation. It consisted of one house (18 x 16) made of hewn logs with a board roof and plank floor "neated and sealed with boards nailed on inside ... 1 door well cased and faced with plank, small window faced, joists and board loft ... chimney well walled with Stone and Stone hearth." Outbuildings included a log kitchen, smokehouse, corn crib, two other cribs, hog lot, yard lot and garden lot "well fenced." During the ensuing Trail of Tears (over which he, too, went more than once) he led his family through Marion and Rutherford County, Tennessee, Kentucky, West Virginia, Ohio, Indiana, Illinois, and Missouri before coming to rest in Marion County, Arkansas.

Many of the family members who managed to stay in the East drifted at later dates to Indian Territory. Nancy Cooper (1803–1880), third daughter of Isaac Cooper and Nancy Blackfox, married Jonathan Burke, separated from him in 1850, and was widowed in 1876. "In the 1880's Peter Burke [their son] loaded an ox wagon and took his mother Aunt Nancy and went to Oklahoma. They were nine weeks on the road. Aunt Nancy rode through on a little bay mare whose name was Teen. I can't forget how she looked when I last saw her. Her last words ... were, and I quote, 'Farewell, we'll meet again.'" Nancy never made it to Indian Territory, where she had Choctaw relatives. She is believed to be buried in the town of Temple, Bell County, Texas.

William Labon Cooper, who also fought in the Mexican War, married Sarah Glass, daughter of Thomas Glass and granddaughter of Chief Glass. The family moved to Wilkes County, North Carolina. After his brother Isaac's death, William took care of widow Mahala Jane Cooper in Anawaika (an example of fulfilling Levirate law). On one of his trips to visit her, he was shot and killed by outlaws in July 1860.

Jackson Cooper (1824-about 1879) was my great-great-grandfather. According to Lily Wigley, nee Cooper, in 1907, "Grandfather Jack Cooper was enrolled, so I am informed. He, it is said, was of Cherokee blood." John Floyd Sizemore, Mary Ann Cooper's brother, mentions his brother-in-law in a letter written to William C. Sizemore from Camp Springs, Tennessee, May 7, 1863, during the Civil War: "Tell Stoner and Jackson Cooper to write to me and not be so dull no more." Jackson Cooper cannot be found in the 1860 census, though his large family does appear in the Alabama 1866 census, living in Fractional Township 4, Range 9 E, in Jackson County. Simultaneously, they were also counted in the same township in DeKalb County as J. Cooper. Their neighbors were Henegars, Thompsons, Sizemores and Shraders. Their land straddled the county line on Sand Mountain. Lily Wigley's ECA 42035 (Eastern Cherokee Application), along with those of her siblings and cousins, was denied. Jackson Cooper lived with his wife, Mary Ann Sizemore, and others, including Blevinses and Holloways, in Shellmound, Tenn. He is listed as blind[10] on the 1870 census.

Jackson Cooper's son was John Cooper (1847–1905). John Cooper bought 80 acres of land in Jackson County, 2 October 1885, E½ of NE¼ of Section 29 T4S R9E, 7 acres residue part of SE¼ of SE¼ and 37 acres part of NE½ of SE¼ of the same section, altogether 124 acres, plus on the same date a residue in S30 of DeKalb County. On March 20, 1886, he bought more acreage in Sec. 30 Tsp. 4S Range 9E. All this lay between Rosalie in Jackson County and Pea Ridge in DeKalb. Some of the land was apparently purchased under the Homestead Act; Cooper's certificate was #3967. He deeded 40 acres to his son James J. Cooper on November 4, 1901. His neighbor was Daniel Shrader. Other land owners were Zilmon Williams (his son's brother-in-law), William B. Kerby (his step-son) and Henry Blevins (cousin). This area was called Fractional Township and straddled the county line. Shrader's mill was located there, near the source of Bryants Creek, which flowed into Johnson Creek in nearby Pisgah, and the Wills Valley Railroad came through after the Civil War. Rosalie was the closest "place." It was a combination of meadow land and sandy loam, perfect for farming. On August 20, 1894, John Cooper deeded 80 acres in DeKalb County for $100 to his wife, Nancy E. Cooper (E½ NE¼ S30 T4S R9E — Reverse Deed Book 3, page 69). Nancy Cooper had bought 40 acres in the same Section on June 2, 1884, and other land there under the Homestead Act on Nov. 20, 1884. John Cooper had entered into ownership October 2, 1885 (certificate 3967). She died shortly after the reverse deed. In 1891, some, if not all, the Cooper land was repossessed by the government (Suspended Land Entries Vol. II, page 2284 — 78 acres Sec. 20 Tsp. 4N Range 9E).

A link between Sand Mountain and Arkansas is provided by the career of Capt. John Cooper (about 1824–after 1886). While serving in the 3rd Arkansas Union Cavalry, he married Susannah (Dockery) Sizemore in DeKalb County, Alabama, September 6, 1869. This was in keeping with Jewish Levirate law, as she was his widowed sister-in-law. They then moved to Arkansas. They may have kept their marriage secret in order not to complicate Susannah's widow's pension on behalf of her deceased husband, William Sizemore. He is probably the John Cooper of John Cooper Associates who had previously bought land in S 10 T5s R4E (Sand Mountain) on Oct. 9, 1852. John Cooper was known in later life as a Baptist minister who, according to Steve Adkins, performed marriages for many of Ezekiel Adkins' children. He was still alive in April 30, 1886, when the Yellville (Ark.) *Mountain Echo* reported from the Hampton Creek community: "J. C. Cooper, by an accident, had most of his fence destroyed by fire the other day." He suffered from deafness and blindness.

John Wesley Monroe Dolphus Cooper (1881–1960) was the full name of my grandfather. Known as J.W. or Dolphy, he was a farm worker in cotton and corn in early life for Dee Vault (Valt?) in the Ft. Payne/Valley Head area of Alabama. In later years he worked for the railroad and did sharecropping. Unlike other Coopers, he never managed to own land. He did woodworking and carving on the side and made fiddles, banjos, and cedar chests, among other things. He had blue eyes and jet-black hair. On June 22, 1907, he filed an application docketed with the Sizemores (kiss of death) to become enrolled as a member of the Eastern Band of Cherokee Indians (Guion-Miller Roll No. 42018). He gave his age as 26 and usual place of residence as Henegar, Alabama (now Long Island). All the Sizemore applications were rejected.

Mary Cooper was the daughter of a chief and married one as well (about 1809–1834). She married Thompson Sinard, great-grandson of full-blood Cherokee woman known as Leek and James Sinard of North Carolina. Sinard was a descendant of the Huguenot religious dissenter Chevalier de Sinard, who came to America via Ireland. The name may have been originally Sinor, a Sephardic Jewish surname. The Sinards were lapsed Quakers and among the first settlers of Buncombe County, North Carolina. James Thomas Sinard died in Collinsville, DeKalb County, Alabama, about 1850. Harriet L. Sinard married William Henry Atkins. There was a connection with the namesake of Big Wills Valley, Little Wills

Fig. 12.2. Mixed blood Cherokee family in North Alabama, about 1906. Shown are James J. Cooper and wife Frances Missouri Williams with their children (clockwise from youngest) John Vester, Luther Granville, Essie, Bessie and Verdie. From the author's collection.

and Little Wills Creek outside Valley Head. Both the north branch and the south branch meander across Little Wills Valley and through the town of Collinsville. William Webber, also called Redheaded Will, was the son of a Cherokee woman. She was the mother also, by Kittagusta, of Ostenaco, and a British officer named Webber. Chief Big Will came from Nequassee in North Carolina. His half-sister was Margaret Siniard, who married a Lamb. Some researchers have Margaret as the daughter of Anawaika (Deerhead). His brother may have been Archibald Webber. He was related to Blackheaded Cooper, Mary Cooper's father, recorded as a Chickamauga chief. The Webbers intermarried with the Vanns as well as other crypto–Jews. Sarah Webber married John Brown. Chief Will's daughter Betsy Webber married Chief John Looney. Their daughter Eliza Abigail Looney married Daniel Rattling Gourd. Another daughter, Eleanor, married Gen. Elias (Stand) Watie. Yet another daughter, Rachel, married John Nave, the grandson of Daniel Ross and Mary McDonald.

William Davis and his home at Maynards Cove are familiar to many Cherokee descendants on Sand Mountain today, although few know about his connection with Black Fox and the Melungeons in Tennessee. He was born about 1753 in Hanover County, Virginia, and fought in the Revolution. He filed for a pension, cert. #31986, issued by the Alabama agency, Sept. 18, 1842, under the act of June 7, 1832. In 1787, he signed the State of Franklin petition as William Daves, and he appears on the 1790 tax list in Hawkins County, Tenn. Around that time, he married Mary Ann Black, a daughter of Black Fox, who had briefly been married to a trader by the name of Pogue. Gen. John Sevier, governor of Tennessee, 1796–1801, mentioned "Davis" as a prominent Chickamauga chief. His son William Alexander Davis also became a chief, marrying the daughter of Chief Arthur Burns about 1830.

On William Davis' tombstone in Proctor Cemetery, Maynards Cove, Jackson County, Ala. is: Alabama Pvt. Lindsy's Va. Regt. Rev. War. According to the records, "In his pension application William Davis stated that he was acquainted with Col. James Lewis in Albemarle County, Va., who resided later in Franklin Co., Tenn. A letter from Col. Lewis stated that he and William Davis were boys in the same neighborhood. The history of Albemarle County, Va. gives the location of Col. James Lewis' residence as being on the western part of the present University of Virginia. William Davis also stated in his pension application that he lived in Albemarle County, Va. at the time of his enlistment." William Davis lived to be 95.

William Alexander Davis was born about 1790, probably in Tennessee. He married Susan Morgan, a white woman, about 1810. A daughter by his first wife is said to have disavowed her father because he later married an Indian woman (Mary Burns). In 1817, he signed the treaty of July 8 as Young Davis, between Charles Hicks and Saunooka. He signed the treaty of New Echota as William A. Davis (1835). After the death of Chief Arthur Burns, his father-in-law, William Alexander Davis became chief of the Cherokee in Jackson County, inheriting the North Sauty reservation near Blowing Cave, comprising 640 acres, an entire section of land. On October 19, 1837, he sold this to Jesse French for $1.00 an acre (Jackson Co., Deed Book A, p. 172). At this time, he was a medical doctor, schoolteacher and planter, and his property on Sand Mountain was evaluated at $3,887.00, as printed in the Acts of Congress ( p. 277). The loss was devastating. In 1838, the family went over the Trail of Tears to Oklahoma. They are listed on the Drennan Roll of 1851. Son John Lowrey Davis married Nancy Turkey. Son William Henry Davis married Eliza Lowrey (Emmet Starr, Oolootsa 1–1–1–7–1–5, p. 368). Daughter Mary Elizabeth Davis married Robert Harrison Akin. Two other daughters married Mayes brothers.

Davis, Davie, Dow, Davidson and their various forms constitute one of the most common Levite names in Scotland.[11]

One-time partners of Black Fox and the Coopers were the **Fields** family, originally from England. In 1837, when most of the Cherokees around Creek Path were forced into a stockade in Fort Payne, Richard Fields's farm was evaluated at $2,611.00, as published in the Acts of Congress. His grandfather had married Susannah Emory, a mixed blood descendant of Ludovic Grant, one of the first Scottish traders in Cherokee country. She was Twister Clan. Father Richard Fields left for Texas in 1821, becoming chief of the Texas Cherokees.[12]

A Welsh trading family, the **Gunters**, after whom Guntersville and Lake Guntersville were named, married into the Holly (Sahoni) and Paint Clans.[13] They became split between east and west during Indian Removal. Augustus Gunter (1815–1894) became agent for the Nashville Chattanooga & St. Louis Railroad in Bridgeport, Alabama. According to the *Cherokee Advocate* of 19 October 1844, George Washington Gunter erected a cotton gin on the Arkansas River, fifteen miles from Ft. Smith, the first in the Cherokee Nation.

The **Keys/Kee** family was evidently Sephardic Jewish in origin. They were heavily intermarried with the Rileys. Many were noted as "bright mulattoes" or "other free" in Virginia and North Carolina records. They appear to have been mixed with Indian early on. In 1817, when an option was offered to the Cherokee to settle on a reservation in the east for life or emigrate west, Samuel Keys and his three sons, Isaac, William and Samuel, chose reservations on Sand Mountain. Isaac Keys was married to Elizabeth Riley, William, to Sally Riley, and Samuel, to Mary Riley. The Riley sisters were all granddaughters of Chief Doublehead (Chuqualatague) through the two sisters Ni-go-di-ge-yu and Gu-lu-sti-yu Doublehead (Twister Clan). During Indian Removal, some Keyses managed to stay in Alabama. Others went on the Trail of Tears. Richard Keys (Chapman Roll 1686) lived for a while in Fabius on Sand Mountain before moving to Indian Territory with his large family. He died February 6, 1892, and was buried in Paw Paw Bottoms, Muldrow, Sequoyah, Indian Territory. Richard Riley Keys (1813–1884), a cousin of Chief John Ross, was married to Minerva Nave (Bird Clan) and served as judge on the Cherokee Nation Supreme Court. Samuel Riley Keys, born 1819 in Fabius, married Mary Hannah Easter, a Choctaw.

The fate of the **Lowreys, Rileys** and **Justices**, all prominent political families of the nation, was not unlike that of the Fieldses and Gunters. Riley is a corruption of Raleigh/Ralegh.[14] Lowrey may go back to Luria, a rabbinical line.[15] It comes from the town of Loria in Italy.[16]

Major George **Lowrey**, Jr., also known as Rising Fawn, Agin'agi'li was assistant principal chief of the Cherokee Nation and member of the Executive Council. He descended from the "terrible" Sahoni or Panther Clan; he became a courier, banker, soldier, translator, law enforcement officer, planter, breeder, and political leader. He was depicted in a painting attributed to George Catlin wearing a turban, saltire sash, and the medal he received from the president of the United States. In the painting he holds a wampum belt symbolic of high office in tribal government. The silver nose and ear ornaments are of a Jewish design, probably workshop of Francis. His father came from Scotland.

One of Lookout Mountain Town's conjurors and a powerful chief was Dick **Justice**. In 1788, he fought with Dragging Canoe against the forces of Gen. Joseph Martin in the Battle of Lookout Mountain in Tennessee. Justice, like many of the Chickamaugan leaders, made peace with the settlers after Dragging Canoe's death in 1792. He became a respected businessman. In 1802, he operated Justice Ferry near the mouth of Lookout Creek. This he sold in order to "voluntarily" relocate to Arkansas with his people. On May 28, 1818, at the age of 65, with ten family members, he emigrated to Indian Territory. The new owner of Justice's Ferry was Thomas Fox Baldridge, also Cherokee. He operated it until 1838, when he was forced to move. There are family stories of Chief Dick Justice having at least three wives and twenty-four children.[17]

Dick Justice was associated with the Coopers, Troxells, Black Fox and The Glass. He signed the 1805 and 1819 treaties. According to *Old Frontiers* by John P. Brown, his Cherokee name was Uwenahi Tsus'ti, "he who has wealth." The word "Justice" is a corruption of Cherokee "Tsusti" or vice versa. In *Folklore of Romantic Arkansas* by Fred W. Allsopp, he is called High Priest Dik-Keh, the Just ... lived to be over 100 years old ... had white hair."

Some Justices, like the Coopers, stayed in the East. Their descendants still live on Sand Mountain. For instance, John Alfred Justice, son of Abraham Justice, was born December 06, 1874, in Alabama and died April 30, 1955, in Crossville, DeKalb County, Alabama. Russell Ruck Sizemore was the last known successor to medicine man Dick Justice. Although they passed for white, the Sizemores carry an American Indian Y chromosome type in the male line.

A large ironworks had been established by Daniel **Ross** and Company in Hawkins County, Tennessee, in the heart of the Watauga Country near present-day Rotherwood. John Ross was captured by the Chickamaugans in Francis Mayberry's boat on the Tennessee River in 1785. John McDonald, the British Indian agent, a Scotsman from Inverness, retained him to help start a trading post and he afterward married McDonald's daughter, Mary, whose mother was a half-blood Cherokee of the Bird Clan, the daughter of a former interpreter. John's son, also named John Ross, the future chief, became McDonald's heir. Like many others from the Watauga Country and Boonesville in Kentucky, McDonald and Ross moved from Sequatchie Valley to what became Rossville, Georgia, at the foot of Lookout Mountain around 1800.

This rather random and much abbreviated listing of Sand Mountain families contains some revealing statistics. Taken all together, there are 24 untimely deaths, 6 murders, 2 hangings, 1 rape, 4 divorces, 4 instances of congenital deafness or blindness, an average migration rate of 4.2 moves per lifetime and 6 cases of lost fortunes. There are uncounted examples of theft, assault, imprisonment, legal sanctions, denial of government benefits and civil rights, law suits and disinheritance. Families were split down the middle, with many members simply disappearing. A high number of sons and daughters chose never to marry. The average lifespan for a female in my mother, Bessie Cooper's, line, of the mitochondrial DNA type U2, is 32 years.

Small wonder when a Cooper married a Brown on Sand Mountain in the 1930s, the two families hired the Pinkerton Detective Agency to protect those who came to the small home wedding. The neighbors knew Coopers and Browns were of Choctaw, Cherokee and Jewish descent.

Such were the material dispossessions and depredations suffered by Sand Mountain Melungeons. But what of the psychological losses? Elders were mostly unwilling to speak of these. In the face of twofold (and perhaps fourfold) prejudice in the surrounding society, the families described in this chapter maintained whatever they could of their heritage, but in a secretive fashion. The decades from the white supremacist Nativist movement of the 1860s to the heyday of the Ku Klux Klan in the 1920s seem to have been the worst. Knowledge faded as the years and generations went by. In the end, many gave up. Some, veritably, became mysteries to themselves. Others angrily denied any such background. But still others, if but a tiny few, continued to be what they had always been: Jewish Cherokees.

# *Epilogue*

*Who can tell the dancer from the dance?* — William Butler Yeats

It is no accident that key pieces of the puzzle proving Greek, Libyan, Egyptian, Jewish and Berber settlement in ancient native America have been forgotten. In 2006, word reached me that the Los Lunas Decalogue Stone was vandalized. The alleged Phoenician version of the Ten Commandments on a boulder in the Isleta Indian Reservation in New Mexico was defaced by someone who took a hammer to it and obliterated the top two lines of Hebrew writing, including the name of God. These acts of destruction are very thorough and deliberate. We lose a little of our national cultural patrimony every time such things happen. The closing of minds in their aftermath often becomes hermetic and final.

The proofs and refutations of history sometimes hang by slender threads. On excellent authority, Constantine Rafinesque showed that the first inhabitants of North America came from Europe, the Mediterranean and Middle East. The Americas underwent a transition to town life and agricultural production not unlike the rest of the world. Yet on the basis of two anthropologists' articles, Rafinesque's history is categorically rejected today.

In my opinion, the genetic story of the Americas has been botched. Not only are samples flawed but geneticists' times to coalescence are forced into the Procrustean bed of outdated theory. Many haplogroups are ignored, while haplotypes and genealogies are never investigated.

There is a reason why Columbus and other explorers called the natives they discovered savages. That word applied originally to those who had been cut off and reduced to a primitive condition. Evidently, Arabs, Romans, Jews and others who came to the shores of America recognized people who were their own.

American history is usually presented as a clash between Old and New World cultures. There is room in the textbooks for only one "peopling," one discovery, one *entrada*. It's Them vs. Us. As we learn more, though, the Christian colonial powers had their own Indians at home, in pagan Europeans, Irish, Saracens and others they had vanquished before setting out for the Western Hemisphere. The "Indians" over here already had European, North African and Middle Eastern connections. The shock of recognition went both ways. The saga of America's melting pot takes on a different meaning if we emphasize similarities rather than differences and study all the instances of trade, cooperation, intermarriage and interchange of ideas.

The Cherokee are the largest Indian nation in the U.S., and for that matter, the world. They lay claim to the longest continuity of any people outside India and China, older than the Greeks, Romans, Jews, Egyptians, Persians, Turks, Arabs and any European country. It is ironic if they turn out, as I have argued throughout this book, to have significant Greek and Jewish roots. Greco-Roman civilization and Judeo-Christian ideas and traditions are seen as high points in man's cultural achievements. This type of idealization has been denied to Native Americans, who are perceived as fundamentally un–European, un-modern, un-progressive. With a fresh look, perhaps some of the same qualities we admire in Greek philosophers and heroes of the Bible can now be glimpsed in American Indians and their descendants.

If the Cherokee practiced Judaism before the arrival of Protestant missionaries, not due to the influence of Jewish traders, they retained an ancient form of it. Their public and private observance of Judaic law was never subjected to the persecutions and disturbances suffered by European Jewry. Mixed with other elements, it was, to judge from eighteenth century observers, part of the state religion. Modern–day Jews can perhaps derive a sense of pride from its unexpected survival on the opposite side of the globe from Jerusalem.

Certainly, no one any longer needs to wonder where many Cherokee get their blond hair and blue eyes, or their Polynesian looks— why they are as diverse as the rest of us. From around the world, they *are* the rest of us.

Fig. 13.1. Lenni Lenape chief Tishcohan in a painting by the Swedish artist Gustavus Hesselius, 1735. His name may mean Chief Cohen, or High Priest. Courtesy of the Philadelphia History Museum at the Atwater Kent, The Historical Society of Pennsylvania Collection.

# Appendices

*Containing A. Melungeon Male Data; B. Melungeon Mitochondrial Results; C. Surnames; D. Cherokee DNA Haplogroup Data; E. Anomalous Cherokee Haplogroups; F. Anomalous Cherokee Haplogroup Distribution; G. A Ptolemy in Uruguay; H. Ancient Greeks in Native America*

## A. Melungeon Male Data

The following table gives participants' Y Chromosome values and associated surnames from the Melungeon DNA Project undertaken by Elizabeth C. Hirschman. About this study, Hirschman wrote in 2010, "I think the Melungeon DNA Project started with my male ancestor data with surnames Caldwell, Carter, Cooper and the rest during the early 2000s and then grew as people wanted to join it. This would have come about largely as a result of my presentations at the Melungeon Unions from 2002 onward."[1]

The first data incorporated into the project were the 12 marker Y-chromosome results of N. Brent Kennedy, Nov. 8, 2000. Male results were used to illumine certain Scottish clan histories in the book the book by Hirschman and Yates, *When Scotland Was Jewish* (2007).

When the project was concluded, there were 102 members, most with Y chromosome and mitochondrial reports. The bulk of those were tested before 2005 are listed in this appendix. From focusing on Scottish clan and Melungeon surnames (i.e., male lines), the project increasingly broadened its scope.

Hirschman commented in 2010, "Initially, many people in the genetic genealogy community were frustrated that the incoming Jewish DNA results were not originating in the Middle East, as they had strongly believed and hoped (some as Zionists), but were showing a lot of Khazar, Central Asian, Eastern European and Western European/Spanish/French input. Certain researchers besides ourselves had been saying this was the case. Critics were not happy that the data were confirming it. We just followed the DNA trail."

| Kit | Name | DYS Haplo | 393 | 390 | 19 | 391 | 385a | 385b | 426 | 389 | 439 | 389 1 | 392 | 389 2 | Notes |
|-----|------|-----------|-----|-----|----|----|----|----|----|----|----|----|----|----|-------|
| 6659 | Gordon I | J2 | 12 | 23 | 14 | 10 | 13 | 17 | 11 | 15 | 11 | 13 | 11 | 30 | Scottish |
| 6546 | Gordon II | J2 | 12 | 23 | 14 | 10 | 13 | 18 | 11 | 16 | 11 | 13 | 11 | 31 | Scottish |
| 14885 | Carter | R1b | 13 | 21 | 14 | 11 | 11 | 14 | 12 | 12 | 11 | 13 | 13 | 29 | French |
| 2220 | Sizemore | Q3 | 13 | 23 | 13 | 10 | 14 | 16 | 12 | 12 | 11 | 13 | 14 | 30 | Cherokee (?) |
| 1814 | Blevins I | E3b | 13 | 23 | 13 | 10 | 17 | 18 | 11 | 12 | 12 | 13 | 11 | 30 | Welsh |
| 1815 | Blevins II | E3b | 13 | 23 | 13 | 10 | 17 | 18 | 11 | 12 | 12 | 13 | 11 | 30 | Welsh |
| 6532 | Bowles | J2 | 12 | 24 | 15 | 11 | 15 | 17 | 11 | 15 | 11 | 12 | 11 | 28 | Scottish |

157

| Kit | Name | DYS Haplo | 393 | 390 | 19 | 391 | 385a | 385b | 426 | 388 | 439 | 389|1 | 392 | 389|2 | Notes |
|---|---|---|---|---|---|---|---|---|---|---|---|---|---|---|---|
| NQHG8 | Adair* | J2 | 12 | 24 | 17 | 10 | 14 | 16 | 11 | 15 | 11 | 12 | 11 | 29 | Scottish |
| 10005 | Adkins | R1b | 13 | 23 | 14 | 10 | 10 | 14 | 12 | 12 | 13 | 13 | 13 | 29 | Welsh |
| 14175 | Phillips | R1b | 13 | 23 | 14 | 10 | 11 | 14 | 12 | 12 | 12 | 14 | 13 | 30 | English |
| 2258 | Wallen | R1b | 13 | 23 | 14 | 11 | 11 | 15 | 12 | 12 | 11 | 13 | 13 | 29 | Danish |
| 3059 | Alexander | R1b | 13 | 23 | 14 | 11 | 11 | 15 | 12 | 12 | 12 | 14 | 13 | 31 | Scottish |
| 7802 | Vaughan | R1b | 13 | 23 | 14 | 12 | 10 | 13 | 12 | 12 | 11 | 13 | 13 | 30 | Welsh |
| 14071 | Morgan | B | 13 | 23 | 15 | 11 | 11 | 12 | 11 | 10 | 13 | 14 | 11 | 33 | Welsh (?) |
| 2823 | Boone | R1b | 13 | 24 | 14 | 11 | 11 | 13 | 12 | 12 | 11 | 13 | 13 | 29 | English |
| 2933 | Houston | R1b | 13 | 24 | 14 | 11 | 11 | 14 | 12 | 12 | 11 | 13 | 13 | 29 | Anglo-Norman |
| 1780 | Cooper | R1b | 13 | 24 | 14 | 11 | 11 | 14 | 12 | 12 | 12 | 13 | 13 | 29 | Portuguese |
| 3214 | Stewart I | R1b | 13 | 24 | 14 | 11 | 11 | 14 | 12 | 12 | 12 | 13 | 13 | 29 | Scottish |
| 1110 | Caldwell | R1b | 13 | 24 | 14 | 11 | 11 | 14 | 12 | 12 | 12 | 13 | 13 | 29 | Scottish |
| 3051 | Stewart II | R1b | 13 | 24 | 14 | 11 | 11 | 14 | 12 | 12 | 12 | 13 | 13 | 30 | Scottish |
| 12006 | Justice | R1b | 13 | 24 | 14 | 11 | 11 | 14 | 12 | 12 | 13 | 13 | 13 | 29 | English |
| 1609 | Leslie | R1b | 13 | 24 | 14 | 11 | 11 | 14 | 12 | 12 | 14 | 13 | 13 | 29 | Scottish-Hungarian |
| 158 | Kennedy | R1b | 13 | 24 | 14 | 11 | 11 | 15 | 12 | 12 | 12 | 13 | 13 | 29 | Scottish-Turkish |
| 35532 | Brown | R1b | 13 | 24 | 15 | 11 | 11 | 15 | 12 | 12 | 12 | 13 | 13 | 29 | Scottish |
| T043570 | Hurst/ Cooper | R1b | 13 | 24 | 14 | 11 | 13 | 14 | 12 | 12 | 11 | 13 | 13 | 29 | Choctaw |
| 1897 | Perry | G | 14 | 22 | 15 | 11 | 14 | 15 | 11 | 13 | 11 | 12 | 11 | 28 | Unknown origin |
| 6922 | McAbee | I | 14 | 22 | 16 | 10 | 16 | 18 | 11 | 15 | 11 | 14 | 13 | 30 | Scottish |
| T044002 | Looney | I1a | 13 | 21 | 14 | 10 | 13 | 14 | 11 | 14 | 11 | 12 | 11 | 28 | Isle of Man/Portugal |
| 6923 | Flores | R1b | 14 | 24 | 14 | 10 | 11 | 14 | 12 | 12 | 11 | 13 | 14 | 29 | Portuguese |
| 1812 | Austin | E3a | 15 | 21 | 16 | 10 | 16 | 18 | 11 | 12 | 12 | 14 | 11 | 31 | Anglo-Norman |
| 3037 | Forbes | R1b | 13 | 24 | 14 | 11 | 11 | 14 | 12 | 12 | 11 | 14 | 13 | 30 | Scottish |
| 6514 | Rogers | R1b | 14 | 24 | 14 | 11 | 11 | 14 | 12 | 12 | 12 | 13 | 13 | 29 | Anglo-Norman |

*The project's Adair participant did not return his sample. These scores come from an online resource. It is believed that all Adairs in the United States ultimately descend from a single Scots male of the same surname.

## B. Melungeon Mitochondrial Results

In November 2002 a subproject titled Southern U.S. Native American DNA was added to Hirschman's Melungeon DNA Project. This study looked at both male and female lines, especially those that began with an Indian trader and Native woman in the Southeast. Usually Cherokee lineage was involved, as can be seen from the table. A preliminary analysis was presented at a meeting of the Society of Crypto-Judaic Studies in San Antonio, Texas, in the summer of 2003.

| ID | Name | Haplo | Mutations | Ancestress | Notes |
|---|---|---|---|---|---|
| 6283 | Wilson | C | 223T, 298C, 325C, 327T | Cherokee Sarah Consene, daughter of Young Dragging Canoe | Wolf Clan, Quatsi-Moytoy line |
| 6317 | Hill | J* | 069T, 126C, 172C | Cherokee Betsy Walker, born ca. 1718 | Jewish, Cherokee |
| ZZEDJ | Alef | J* | 069T, 126C, 311C, 366T, 368C, 519C, 073G, 093G, 185A, 188G, 228A, 263G, 295T, 309.1C, 315.1C, 462T, 489C, 522–, 523 – | Myra Jarvis, Melungeon, born 1815 in Georgia | Jewish, Cherokee |

| ID | Name | Haplo | Mutations | Ancestress | Notes |
|---|---|---|---|---|---|
| 82302 | Bedzyk | J* | 069T, 126C, 172C, 73G, 228A, 263G, 295T, , 315.1C, 426T, 482C, 489C | Cherokee Betsy Walker, born ca. 1718 | Jewish, Cherokee |
| 6483 | Krapf | C | 223T, 241G, 298C, 327T, 519C | Cherokee Elizabeth Tassel, wife of Ludovic Grant, Scotsman | Long Hair Clan line of Rogers, Bowles, Watts |
| KXTV5 | Mahar | B | 183C, 189C, 217C, 519C | Cherokee Lucretia Parris, daughter of George Parris, Scotsman | Cruz match |
| On file | "Elvis Presley" | B | 182C, 183C, 189C, 217C, 519C, 73G, 159C, 263G, 309.1C, 309.2C, 315.1C | Nancy Burdine, Jewess, daughter of French Huguenot of Kentucky/ Tennessee, mother unknown | Jewish, Cherokee |
| 6407 | Van Horn | H | 183C, 189C, 519C | Mariah Cornell, relative of George All Sizemore, Jewish-Indian | 1 Karelian match, 2 Caucasians in TWGDAM |
| 6898 | Wilkins | H | 362C, 519C | Cherokee Anna Thomas of Buncombe Co., N.C., daughter of Welshman Scottish | Cherokee Recent European |
| 6912 | McKee | H | 519C | | |
| 7011 | Farmer | H5a1 | 304C | Cherokee wife of Thomas Waters, Scots-Irish | Recent European |
| 7802 | Vaughan | H | 519C | English/Welsh/Scottish | Recent European |
| NA | Riddle | X | 189C, 192T, 223T, 278T, 519C, 528T | Cherokee Demarius Angeline Thomas Sherrill | Mother was wife of Col. Thomas |
| 1691 | Sinor | X | 189C, 223T, 271C, 278T, 519C, 73G, 153G, 195C, 225A, 226C, 263G, 309.1C, 315.1C | Cherokee woman married to Indian trader | Prehistoric Native American |
| 41804 | Wallen | X | 189C, 223T, 278T, 519C | Cherokee woman married to Longhunter | Prehistoric Native American |
| T025287 | Yates | U2e* | 051G, 129C, 145A, 182C, 183C, 189C, 362C, 519C; 73G, 152G, 217C, 263G | Cherokee wife of Jewish Trader named Jordan, born about 1775 | Prehistoric Native American |
| T024945 | Starnes | U2e* | 051G, 075C, 092C, 129C, 183C, 189C, 362C, 519C; 73G, 152C, 217C, 263G | Cherokee | Prehistoric Native American |
| 578X5 | Modrall | U2e* | 051G, 092C, 126C, 129C, 183C, 189C, 362C, 519C; 73G, 146C, 152C, 195C, 217C, 263G, 309.1C, 315.1C | Unknown | Prehistoric Native American |
| T024937 | Thornton | H | 162G, 172C, 209C, 519C | | |

# C. Surnames

This appendix lists surnames with their origins and meanings from the Melungeon DNA Project.

**Adair.** Scottish. Hebrew *Adar*, the name of a month in spring. Another etymology derives it from Gaelic Edzaer (?) meaning "the ford of the oaks."

**Adkins.** Scottish. Apparently the same as Akin and Aitken. "One from Aix/Aachen." An alternative explanation is "kin of Arthur."

**Alef.** English and Dutch. Hebrew "aleph," the first letter of the alphabet.

**Alexander.** Scottish. From the ancient Greek hero, a common Hebrew surname.

**Austin.** Norman. From Augustine (?).

**Blevins.** Welsh *Ap+Levin*, "son of Levite."

**Boone.** English. Compare Boen (Dutch), Bon or Le Bon (French) and Buen (Spanish), all meaning "good." Some branches Jewish.

**Bowles.** Scottish. From Bowell; see Riddle.

**Brown.** Scottish. From reference to founder's dark skin.

**Caldwell.** English or Scottish. From Ashkenazic Kahlwil, a place-name.

**Carter.** French, as Cartier, "cartwright, transporter."

**Cooper.** French (Ashkenazic). From "copper, metallurgical worker." A Hebrew form of Jacob (meaning "merchant").

**Farmer.** English. Farmer.

**Flores.** Portuguese. From "flower."

**Forbes.** Scottish. From Phoebus "Sun-god." See Phillips.

**Gordon.** Scottish. Corruption of Hebrew Cohen.

**Houston.** Norman. From "Hugh's Town."

**Justice.** Borderlands Scottish. Probably an English translation of original Norman title.

**Kennedy.** Scottish via the French. Canada, Candia, Candy, Gandy, Candiano (in turn from Turkish "place of the Khan"), the capital of Crete, English Candy, modern-day Greek Iraklion.

**Krapf.** German and Moravian. Baker.

**Leslie.** Scottish. From Hungarian Ladislaus, eleventh century.

**Looney.** From Spanish-Portuguese Luna. Orig. Hebrew Yareakh "moon."

**Mahar.** Variant Meagher. Supposedly derived from the Irish word *michair*, which means hospitable or kindly. This could be a folk etymology, however. The origin may lie in Anglo-Norman Mayer, Meyer ("estate manager").

**McAbee.** Scottish. Same as MacBeth, McBee. From the initials M.K.B.I. (יבכמ), standing for the Hebrew prayer "Who among the Mighty is like unto thee, Jehovah" (Mi cha-mo-cha ba-ei-lim, A-do-nai), which the antiquary Blair explains as the origin of the name Maccabeus, the equivalent of MacBeth, first king of Scotland.

**McKee.** Scottish and originally Norman. Son of Kay.

**Modrall.** Anglo-Norman. Originally Modrell. Meaning unexplained. See Riddle.

**Morgan.** Welsh. "From overseas."

**Perry.** Norman, originally Iberian Perez, Peres, from Hebrew for pear, a fruit grown in the land of Israel and traditionally eaten at Jewish holidays, as were also olives and dates.

**Phillips.** Scottish. Same as Forbes, Febos (Spanish), Forbush, Frobisher, Pharabas (Moroccan), Ferreby, Federbusch (German). Ancient and popular Hebrew surname from Phoebus "Sun–god."

**Presley.** Scottish, originally Anglo-Norman. Variant Priestley. From "priestly," perhaps related to Hebrew Cohen and Ashkenazic Katz ("righteous priest"). Andrew Presley, the earliest known male ancestor of Elvis Presley, came from Aberdeen and fled Scotland after the battle of Culloden in 1745 to settle in South Carolina.

**Riddle.** Same as Riddel. Norman and originally Hebraeo-French. From Arabic *ridh* "judge" + *el*, the name of God. Many, if not most, Hebrew names were formed with this suffix, e.g., Samuel, Nathaniel and the like (Jacobs). Medieval Jews were often ignorant of Hebrew and hence combined with it a word or title in their local vernacular.

**Rogers.** Frankish. From "wagoner."

**Sizemore.** Portuguese. From Hebrew Sismai, "sower."

**Stewart.** Scottish, originally Norman. Altered by royal branch to Stuart in sixteenth century to Stuart. "Keeper of the Kingdom."

**Starnes.** German. Star (of David).

**Van Horn.** Dutch. One from the Horns. Horn is a common Jewish surname, coming from the *shofar* or ram's horn sounded on Yom Kippur.

**Vaughan.** Welsh. The same as Bychan or Vychan, little, small in stature. Compare Klein, Kurz, Petty, frequent Jewish surnames.

**Wallen.** English. Same as Walden, Waldon, Walling "foreigner."

**Wilkins.** Welsh. Kin of Will, Williams.

**Wilson.** English and Scottish. Son of Will.
**Yates.** Anglo-Norman. Hebrew anagram צ ג Ger Zedek meaning "righteous convert."[1]

## D. Cherokee DNA Haplogroup Data

This table summarizes all available DNA studies that include data from Southeastern Indians, with percentage of haplogroups A–D and X.

| *mtDNA Haplogroup* | *n=* | *A* | *B* | *C* | *D* | *X* | *Other* |
|---|---|---|---|---|---|---|---|
| **Cherokee** | | | | | | | |
| Oklahoma Stillwell (Malhi 2001) | 37 | 10.8 | 45.9 | 43.3 | 0.0 | 0.0 | |
| Oklahoma Red Cross (Mahli 2001) | 19 | 21.1 | 21.1 | 52.5 | 5.3 | 0.0 | |
| Smith, et al. 1999 (and Schurr 2000) | 4 | 0.0 | 0.0 | 25.0 | 0.0 | 0.0 | H=50.0 J=25.0 |
| Total | 60 | 13.3 | 35.0 | 45.0 | 1.7 | 0.0 | |
| **Choctaw** | | | | | | | |
| Weis 2001 (and Bolnick & Smith 2003) | 27 | 74.1 | 18.5 | 3.7 | 0.0 | 0.0 | |
| **Chickasaw** | | | | | | | |
| Bolnick & Smith | 8 | 12.5 | 75.0 | 12.5 | 0.0 | 0.0 | |
| **Creek** | | | | | | | |
| Weis; Lorenz & Smith; Bolnick & Smith | 39 | 35.9 | 15.4 | 20.5 | 28.2 | 0.0 | |
| Merriwether & Ferrell; Bolnick & Smith | 71 | 36.6 | 15.5 | 9.9 | 38.0 | 0.0 | |
| Total | 110 | 36.4 | 15.5 | 13.6 | 34.5 | 0.0 | |
| **Seminole** | | | | | | | |
| Huoponen (1997), incl. Bolnick & Smith | 40 | 62.5 | 25.0 | 7.5 | 5.0 | 0.0 | |
| DNA Consultants study 2003 | 12 | 0.0 | 16.7 | 16.7 | 0.0 | 8.3 | U=33.3 J=16.7 H=8.3 |
| **Grand Total** | 257 | 36.6 | 23.7 | 19.1 | 16.0 | 0.5 | 4.0 |

## E. Anomalous Cherokee Haplogroups

This table lists participants in DNA Consultants' Phase I "Anomalous" Cherokee DNA Project by haplogroup and genealogy.[1]

| | *Hg* | *Genealogy* |
|---|---|---|
| 1 | H | New England Indian, Norse? |
| 2 | X2 | Annie L. Garrett, b. 1846, Miss. |
| 3 | J* | Native American |
| 4 | H | Native American |
| 5 | X2 | Native American |
| 6 | H | Cherokee |
| 7 | X2 | Agnes Weldy b. ~ 1707 |
| 8 | H | Canadian? |
| 9 | J* | Cherokee, Emily Glover 1837–1903, Tenn. |
| 10 | X2 | Seyinus from Qualla Boundary, N.C., b. 1862 |
| 11 | U2e* | Cherokee paramour of Lithuanian-Scottish trader Enoch Jordan, b. ~ 1790 NW Ga. |
| 12 | U2e* | Susanna Owens, Cherokee, b. 1760, Granville Co., N.C. |
| 13 | U2e* | Rosannah Alexander, b. ~ 1749, Mecklenburg Co., N.C., Cherokee (?) |
| 14 | U2e* | Susannah Wallen or Waldon |
| 15 | U5b* | Eliza Ann Ellis, wife of George Culver, b. ~ 1775, d. ~ 1830, Hancock Co., Ga. |
| 16 | U2e* | Cherokee, N.C. |
| 17 | U5a1a | Ann Dreaweah, Cherokee |
| 18 | U5* | Adopted, Okla. |
| 19 | U5a1a* | Jane Rose of the Eastern Band of Cherokee Indians |

|      | Hg      | Genealogy |
|------|---------|-----------|
| 20   | U5a1a*  | Clarissa Green, wife of John Hodge, b. 1846, Cherokee Wolf Clan, Okla. |
| 21   | U4*     | Lillie C. Wilson-Field, 1857–1937, b. Catawba, N.C. |
| 22   | U5b2    | Wilma Nell Atchison, wife of Gilbert, Blackfoot (?), b. Kansas |
| 23   | K2      | Sarah Ann Rose, b. Rock Creek, N.C. |
| 24   | T1*     | Ann Houston, b. Va., mother of Susannah Walker; Melungeon |
| 25   | T1*     | Native American (surrogate mother?) |
| 26   | T1*     | Melungeon and Cherokee |
| 27   | X2      | Mother of Ollie McCorkle, b. Ohio, Native American, descendant b. 1906, I.T. |
| 28   | T*      | Melungeon |
| 29   | T2*     | Native American |
| 30   | K       | Mother of Linna Mitchell, born 1779, Choctaw Nation |
| 31   | T2*     | Cherokee |
| 32   | T*      | Sully Firebush, daughter of a Cherokee chief |
| 33   | Unknown | Unknown Bermuda |
| 34   | T5      | Choctaw-Cherokee |
| 35   | T*      | Zella Hand Rogers, adopted 1901 by Hand family, S.D.; Red Lake Band of Chippewa |
| 36   | Unknown | |
| 37   | Unknown | Hurley Choctaw or Pitchlynn on Armstrong Rolls (?) |
| 38   | L1b1    | |
| 39   | T4      | Choctaw-Cherokee |
| 40   | Unknown | |
| 41   | T*      | Cherokee |
| 42   | L1c2    | Subject identifies as Native American |
| 43   | L3      | Juanita Pratts, b. Mexico 1885; Comanche or Mexican |
| 44   | J*      | Betsy Walker, Cherokee, adopted by Sen. Felix Walker |
| 45   | J*      | Myra Jarvis, Melungeon, b. 1815, Ga. |
| 46   | J*      | Betsy Walker, Cherokee, adopted by Sen. Felix Walker |
| 47   | X2      | Polly, Cherokee mother of Angelina Demarius Thomas by Col. Will Thomas |
| 48   | X2      | Cherokee woman married to Longhunter Wallen (Walden) |
| 49   | U2e*    | Jane Campbell, b. 1828, Choctaw Co., Miss. |
| 50   | T*      | Native American |
| 51   | T*      | Cherokee Gentry sisters |
| 52   | T*      | Cherokee Gentry sisters |

# F. Anomalous Cherokee Haplogroup Distribution

This table compares the frequency of Anomalous Cherokees' haplogroups with populations in Europe and other parts of the world.

| Hg     | N=   | %    | Europe  | Middle East | Egypt  | Druze  | Eastern Mediterranean |
|--------|------|------|---------|-------------|--------|--------|------------------------|
| H      | 4    | 7.7  | 53.5    | 36.8        |        |        |       |
| J      | 5    | 9.6  | 9.5     | 11.4        | 6.3    | 7.0    | 12.7  |
| X      | 7    | 13.5 | 1.5     | 3.5         | 1.6    | 27.9   | 4.8   |
| U      | 13   | 25   | 22.2    | 26.3        | 7.8    | 11.6   | 16.4  |
| K      | 2    | 3.8  | 5.8     | 6.2         | 3      | 16.3   | 3.6   |
| T      | 14   | 26.9 | 8.4     | 11.9        | 25     | 4.7    | 6.0   |
| L      | 3    | 5.8  |         |             |        |        |       |
| Unk.   | 4    | 7.7  |         |             |        |        |       |
| X? H?  | 1    |      |         |             |        |        |       |
| J?     | 1    |      |         |             |        |        |       |
| H?     | 1    |      |         |             |        |        |       |
| A?     | 1    |      |         |             |        |        |       |
| Total  | 50   | 100  | n=1021  | n=2736      | n=64   | n=43   | n=165 |

Source: Suppl. data from Richards, et al. (2000); this study.

# G. A Ptolemy in Uruguay

It seems that American scientists have cited evidence of the Greeks in the New World for a long time. This report comes from John McIntosh, *The Origin of the North American Indians* (New York: Nafis & Cornish, 1843) 313–4.

The following article appeared some time ago, in the *United States Journal*, in reference to the Greek antiquities which have been recently discovered in South America:

> A recent discovery seems to afford strong evidence that the soil of America was once trodden by one of Alexander's subjects. A few years since there was found, near Monte Video, in South America, a stone with the following words in Greek upon it: "During the reign of Alexander, the son of Philip, king of Macedon, in the 63rd Olympiad, Ptolemy"— the remainder of the inscription could not be deciphered. The stone covered an excavation, which contained two very ancient swords, a helmet, a shield, and several earthen amphorae of large capacity. On the handle of one of the swords was a portrait of a man, and on the helmet there was sculptured work representing Achilles dragging the corpse of Hector round the walls of Troy. This was a favorite picture among the Greeks. Probably this Ptolemy was overtaken by a storm in the great ocean, as the ancients termed the Atlantic, and driven on the coast of South America. The silence of Greek writers in relation to this event may easily be accounted for, by supposing that on attempting to return to Greece he was lost, together with his crew, and thus no account of his discovery ever reached them.

How these Greek antiquities came to America, we cannot at all conjecture; and it is equally dubious, whether such things have been discovered or not. It would, however, appear presumptuous on our part to contradict it, when we can prove nothing to the contrary.

# H. Ancient Greeks in Native America

This descriptive list of evidence has been assembled from various modern reference works, with the ancient textual source or find-site indicated.

| Type | Source | Reference |
|---|---|---|
| Continent called Epeiros Occidentalis | *Geography* by Strabo, 25 B.C.E. | McGlone & Leonard, 1986 |
| Cattigara in *Terra Incognita*= Peru | Ptolemy's world map, 140 C.E., based on antecedents | Iberra-Grasso, 1991 |
| Antipodum=South America | Eratosthenes, 3rd cent. B.C.E., via Macrobius | Thompson, 1994 |
| Fourth Part of World inhabited by natives | Pomponius Mela, 44 C.E. | Thompson, 1994 |
| Two "Indians" wash up on shore of northern Germany | Pomponius Mela, 44 C.E. | Thompson, 1994 |
| Atlantic Isles, red-skinned natives with horse manes | Greek sailor Euphemus; Pausanias, 150 C.E. | Ashe, 1962 |
| Hesperides, isles in Western Atlantic | Euphemus; Pliny, 2nd cent. B.C.E.; Martianus Capella | Ashe, 1962; Mertz, 1964 |
| Continent on far side of Atlantic Ocean | Aelianus, 3rd cent. C.E.; Egyptian records in Proclus | Trento, 1978 |
| Isles 5000 miles west of Greenland | Plutarch, 75 C.E. | Fell, 1982; Thompson, 1994 |
| Greek goddess of spring motif on club | Caribbean | Thompson, 1992 |
| Assorted coins | North Carolina, Ohio, Georgia, Tennessee and Oklahoma, 50 C.E. and later | Fell, 1980 |
| Cave murals with Greco-Roman costumes | Ohio | Priest, 1883 |
| Pottery figures in toga-like costumes | Tennessee | Conant, 1880 |
| Bronze sword | Maya ruins, Merida, Mexico | Marx, 1992 |

| Type | Source | Reference |
|------|--------|-----------|
| Bronze Athenian medallion | Red River, Oklahoma | Covey, 1991 |
| Greek *theos* "god" | Nahuatl *teotl* "god" | Gordon, 1971; Fell, 1989 |
| Greek *kalia* "shrine" | Nahuatl *calli* "shrine" | |
| Greek *paillio* "butterfly" | Nahuatl *papalot* "butterfly" | |
| Greek sun charioteer | Mexican snake-footed diety | Walker, 1988 |
| Greek goddess Aphrodite | Aztecs' *Coatlicue,* "Lady of the Serpent Skirt" | Gardner, 1986; Walker, 1988 |
| Athenian owls | Mexican codices, 14th cent. | Sorenson and Johannessen, 2009 |
| Greek double flute (aulos), 200 B.C.E. | Colima, Mexico, 100 C.E. | Parsons, 1980 |
| Greek oil lamp, 200 B.C.E. | Colima, Mexico | Thompson, 1994 |
| Pineapples on bronze mirrors | 3rd cent. B.C.E. | Thompson, 1994 |
| Peruvian garden bean | Aristophanes; Hippocrates | P |
| Corn (maize) | Theophrastus; Pliny | Parkinson, 1640 |
| Roman clay pipe with tobacco stains | 100 B.C.E. | Cook, 1925; Brooks |
| Egyptian architecture, aqueducts | Rodadero, Peru | Du Pouget, 1800s |
| Syracusian bronze coins, about | Waterbury, Connecticut | Gastonguay, Fell, 1980 |
| 325 B.C.E. | | |
| Carthaginian sailing routes to America from old MS | Plutarch, d. 120 C.E. | Fell, 1980 |
| Greeks settled among peoples across Atlantic | Plutarch, d. 120 C.E. | Fell, 1980 |
| Satyr masks carved in rockface | Wichita, Kansas | Kellogg; Fell, 1980 |
| Carthaginian coins about 325 B.C.E. | Arkansas River | Fell, 1980 |
| Gold plate of zodiac in Cypriot syllabary | Cuenca, Ecuador | Crespi; Fell, 1980 |
| Greek roots of Micmac language | Maine, Nova Scotia and New Brunswick | Rand, 1880; Fell, 1980 |
| Canary Island route to the Americas | Diodorus Siculus, 1st cent. B.C.E. | Fell, 1980 |
| Greek fret design in petroglyphs | Colorado | Steward, 1930s |
| Bilingual Arabic and Greek warning petroglyph | Nevada | Fell, 1980 |
| Geometric style pottery, swastikas, frets, mazes, Greek letters | Snaketown, Arizona, Santa Cruz time period | Gladwin, 1937 |
| Proclamation of Massinissa on gold tablet, 148 B.C.E. | Ecuador | Crespi; Fell, 1980 |
| Libyan stone tholos or beehive tomb | Upton, Mass. | Fell, 1980 |
| Drawing of Greek hoplite | Sumner Co., Tennessee | Thruston, 1890; Fell, 1980 |
| Labyrinth | Oraibi, Arizona; Cuenca, Ecuador; Colorado | Fell, 1980 |
| Minotaur petroglyphs and labyrinth | Texas | Fell, 1980 |
| Petroglyph of Ursa Major constellation ("The Bear") | New Mexico | Fell, 1980 |
| Zodiac petroglyph | Inyo County, Calif. | Steward, 1929 |
| Zodiacal inscription on tablet | Davenport, Iowa | 1880; Fell, 1975 |
| Greek letters identifying petroglyph of Taurus | Cimarron River, Oklahoma | Farley; Fell, 1980 |
| Greek inscriptions, 1000 B.C.E.–1000 C.E. | Hohokam region, Arizona | Steward, Renaud, Heizer, Baumhoff; Fell, 1980 |
| Attic Greek designs, 3rd–2nd cent. B.C.E. | Hohokam region, Arizona | Steward, Renaud, Heizer, Baumhoff; Fell, 1980 |
| Greek artifacts in mounds | Eastern U.S. | Fell, 1980 |
| Libyan and Iberian carved stone money; Greek letters | Ohio, Tennessee | Thruston, 1890; Fell 1980 |
| Greek slogan *phthaei* "first to come" engraved on tile | Castle Gardens, Wyoming | Fell, 1980 |

| Type | Source | Reference |
|---|---|---|
| Greek tetradrachm of Maximianus, 288 C.E. | Cherokee land in Robeson Co., N.C. | Maynor, 1951; Fell, 1980 |
| Tetradrachm of Antiochus IV (175–164 B.C.E.) | Cass County, Illinois | 1882; Fell, 1980 |
| Grave stele, Byzantine period | Cripple Creek, Colo. | Farley; Fell, 1980 |
| Petroglyph map of Pacific & Americas, 200 B.C.E. | California or Nevada | Fell, 1980 |
| Alphabet stone in Greek, Libyan, about 200 B.C.E. | Allen Springs, Nevada | Fell, 1980 |
| Arithmetic petroglyphs | Clark and Mineral Co. & Nevada | Fell, 1980 |
| Obit inscribed on rock to "Askholos" | Serra de Parentin, Brazil | Da Silva Ramos; Fell, 1980 |
| Greek letters carved on rock | Churchill Co., Nevada & Lagomarsino | Fell, 1980 |
| Greek mummy in cave with silver clasp and yellow hair | Cumberland River, Carthage, Tenn. | Haywood, 1815, 1823; Farley, 1994 |
| Minoan Trident Ship rock carving | Hicklin Springs, Colo. | Farley, 1994 |
| Greek letters inscribed on boulder | Turkey Mountain, Tulsa, Oklahoma | Wells, 1968; Farley, 1994 |
| Limestone bas-relief face | Noel, Missouri | Farley, 1994 |
| Warrior petroglyph | Castle Garden, Wyoming | Renaud; Farley, 1994 |
| Egyptian/Phoenician pipe with image of goddess Tanit | Knoxville-Chattanooga, Tennessee | Farley, 1994 |
| Boundary stone: "belongs to Rata" | Arkansas River, Warner, Oklahoma | Farley, 1994 |
| Stone Shelter land claim, about 900 C.E. | Oklahoma | Farley, Fell, 1978 |
| Coin from Athenian colony of Thurium, 200 B.C.E. | Red River, Terral, Okla. | Covey, 1975 |
| Coin from Athenian colony of Thurium, 200 B.C.E. | Illinois River, Black Gum, Okla. | Short, Totten; Farley, 1994 |
| Pegasus petroglyph, before 133 B.C.E. | Western Oklahoma | Farley, Fell, 1980 |
| Pegasus rebus petroglyph | Western Oklahoma | Farley, Fell, 1981 |
| Taurus-Hyades petroglyph | Picture Canyon, Colo. | Farley, 1973 |
| Possum Creek syllabary | Possum Creek, Oklahoma | Farley, 2002 |

# Chapter Notes

## Chapter 1

1. Robert Conley, *The Cherokee Nation: A History* (Albuquerque: University of New Mexico Press, 2005), esp. 1–13. Raymond D. Fogelson, "Cherokee in the East," in William C. Sturtevant, gen. ed., *Handbook of North American Indians*, vol. 14: *Southeast*, ed. Raymond D. Fogelson (Washington: Smithsonian Institution, 2004), 337–53.

2. Russell Thornton, *The Cherokees: A Population History* (Omaha: University of Nebraska Press, 1992), 5.

3. Narcissa Owens, *Memoirs of Narcissa Owen, 1831–1907* (Washington: Library of Congress, 1907); cf. *A Cherokee Woman's America*, ed. Karen L. Kilcup (Gainesville: University Press of Florida, 2005).

4. Howard L. Meredith and Virginia E. Milan, eds., *A Cherokee Vision of Eloh,'* trans. Wesley Proctor (Muskogee: Indian University Press, 1980), 11. Cf. "Red Man's Origin," *Indian Chieftain* (Vinita, Indian Territory), January 2, 1896, available at http://chroniclingamerica.loc.gov/lccn/sn83025010/1896–01–02/ed-1/seq-2/.

5. On Eubanks, see Daniel F. Littlefield, Jr., and James W. Parins, *Native American Writing in the Southeast: An Anthology, 1875–1935* (Jackson: University of Mississippi Press), 26–27.

6. On oral tradition, history and prophecy, see "Oral Traditions, Southeast," in *American Indian Religious Traditions: An Encyclopedia*, ed. Suzanne J. Crawford and Dennis F. Kelley (Santa Barbara: ABC-CLIO, 2005), 2: 698–99.

7. Personal communication, 11 November 2005. Wilkes is an active teacher of the Cherokee language in regional seminars and online and expert on Native American prophecies. He studied under Cherokee/Tuscarora medicine man John Pope (Rolling Thunder). Born in Georgia, he lives in Marion, Kentucky. On Pope, see Doug Boyd, *Rolling Thunder* (New York: Delta, 1976).

8. Meredith and Milan, 25–27.

9. Thomas E. Mails, *The Cherokee People: The Story of the Cherokees from Earliest Origins to Contemporary Times* (New York: Council Oaks, 1992), 162.

10. James Mooney, *Myths of the Cherokee and Sacred Formulas of the Cherokees* (Nashville: Elder, 1982), 8.

11. Stephen Oppenheimer, *Eden in the East* (London: Phoenix, 2001), 115, 356, 371.

12. Henry George Liddell and Robert Scott, comp., *A Greek-English Lexicon* (Oxford: Clarendon Press, 1996), s.v. κάθημι 2.: "esp. of courts, councils, assemblies, etc... of the βουλή."

13. Fogelson, "Cherokee in the East," 340–41. Cf. Mails 178, 90–94. Mails' source, in turn, is the John Howard Payne Papers, Ayer MS 689, in the Newberry Library, Chicago.

14. See Hornblower and Spawforth, ed., *The Oxford Classical Dictionary*, 1514, 118.

15. Mails, 162.

16. Liddell and Scott, s.v. ελαύνω, 529, and αλαινω, 60, for Mona, see s.v. μόνα, 1143.

17. On Russell, also known as Two White Feathers, see "Spiritual and Ceremonial Practitioners, Southeast (types)," in Crawford and Kelley 3: 1043.

18. On the suffix εθελο- "willing," Liddell and Scott, 479. On οικέω in the sense of "settle, colonize," s.v. A.2.

19. Fogelson, "Cherokee in the East," pp. 349–51, has a long discussion. Cf. personal communication from Brian Wilkes, 14 December 2006.

20. Brad Montgomery-Anderson, *A Reference Grammar of Oklahoma Cherokee*. Ph.D. dissertation, University of Kansas, 2008.

21. John McIntosh, *The Origin of the North American Indians* (New York: Nafis and Cornish, 1843), 93.

22. Montgomery-Anderson, 4.

23. As Montgomery-Anderson notes (25), an older scholar who first studied Cherokee in the 1960s, Lounsbury, using a list of 200 common words found only one-third inherited by Cherokee from the common ancestor. Cherokee has different words for the numbers '"four,"' '"six"' and '"seven."' Because of linguistic anomalies, Lounsbury thought Cherokee "widely separate" from the others. Its divergence "must be ascribed to a more complete, *though not earlier*, separation."

24. Personal communication of Brian Wilkes, 12 November 2005.

25. On Uktena, see Mooney, *Myths*, 541, 297–298. On κτεινω see Liddell and Scott, s.v.

26. Michael Gagarin and Elaine Fantham, eds., *The Oxford Encyclopedia of Ancient Greece and Rome* (Oxford: Oxford University Press, 2010), 6.396.

27. On *ustutli, dakwa, datsi*, see Mooney, *Myths*, 302–303, 543, 405, 514, 515. Liddell and Scott, s.v. Στυξ, δάκος and δασυς. Note that Cherokee phonetics renders *s, d, t, g*, and *k* sounds in various erratic ways. The Upper dialect uses *l* for the Lower dialect's *r*. Neither has a sound for *p* but changes it to *qu*.

28. See Hans Volkmann, "Kyrene," *Der Kleine Pauly* 3.410–413; *Oxford Classical Dictionary*, 421–22; and Barry Fell, "Sunset at Cyrene," in *Saga America* (New York: Times, 1980), 387–97.

29. Erich S. Gruen, "Hellenistic Judaism," in *Cultures of the Jews: A New History*, ed. David Biale (New York: Schocken, 2002), 76–132.

30. Shimon Appelbaum, *Jews and Greeks in Ancient Cyrene* (Leiden: Brill, 1979), esp. 170, 161, 164–67.

31. Josephus, *Complete Works*, trans. William Whiston (Grand Rapids: Kregel, 1976), 489.

## Chapter 2

1. Mark K. Stengel, "Diffusionists Have Landed: You've Probably Heard of Those Crackpot Theories about Ancient Phoenicians or Chinese in the New World. Maybe It's Time to Start Paying Attention," *The Atlantic Monthly* 285.1 (January 2000): 35–39, 42ff.

2. Fell broke the story of the settlement of the Pacific by ancient Greeks and related peoples in a series of articles contributed to *Epigraphic Society Occasional Publications* from 1974 onward and presented the accumulated evidence in his book, *Saga America* (New York: Times Books, 1980), esp. 238, 262.

3. Bryan Sykes et al., "The Origins of the Polynesians," *American Journal of Human Genetics* 57: 1463–75. Sadly for all who were thrilled with the story of the Kon Tiki and theories of Thor Heyerdahl, Sykes and his team proved once and for all that the Polynesians come from Southeast Asia, not the Americas. Thor Heyerdahl, *Kon Tiki: Across the Pacific by Raft* (Chicago: Rand McNally, 1960).

4. Gunnar Thompson, *American Discovery* (Seattle: Argonauts Misty Isles), 237–55.

5. On the inscriptions in New Guinea and Chile and Carter's decipherment, see Marjorie Mazel Hecht, "The Decipherment and Discovery of a Voyage to America in 232 B.C.," *21st Century Science and Technology* (1998/1999): 62–65.

6. *Der Kleine Pauly*, s.v. "Agatharchides."

7. Nicholas Nicastro, *Circumference: Eratosthenes and the Ancient Quest to Measure the Globe* (New York: St. Martin's, 2008), 135.

8. Manfred Kayser et al., "Reduced Y-Chromosome, but Not Mitochondrial DNA Diversity in Human Populations from West New Guinea," *American Journal of Human Genetics* 72.2 (2003): 281–302. See also M. Stoneking et al., "Geographic Variation in Human Mitochondrial DNA from Papua New Guinea," *Genetics* 124 (1990): 717–33. A recent report has called for the population history of Island Southeast Asia to be completely rethought: Catharine Hill et al., "A Mitochondrial Stratigraphy for Island Southeast Asia." *American Journal of Human Genetics* 80.1 (January 2007): 29–44.

9. Rick Sanders, "Ancient Navigators Could Have Measured Longitude," *21st Century Science and Technology* (Fall 2001): 58–60. Barry Fell, *America B.C.* (New York: Demeter, 1977), 118.

10. Jo Marchant, "In Search of Lost Time," News@nature.com, 29 November 2006. http://www.nature.com/news/2006/061127/full/444534a.html. Cf. *Nature* 444: 534–38, 551–52, 587–91. See now Jo Marchant, *Decoding the Heavens* (Cambridge: Da Capo, 2009).

11. Lionel Casson, *The Ancient Mariners* (Princeton: Princeton University Press, 1991), 6–22, 116–33, plate 24.

12. A different take is given by Gunnar Thompson, *Ancient Egyptian Maize* (Seattle: New World Discovery Institute, 2010).

13. Herodotus, *The Histories*, trans. Aubrey de Sélincourt (London: Folio Society, 2006), 229–30.

14. The figure of 30,000 colonists is made to be a medieval monk's error by most interpreters of this text. Casson writes that the 60 ships are probably nothing but "a good-sized fleet of merchantmen ... tagging along ... with far fewer than thirty thousand" (121).

15. Stephen C. Jett, "The Development and Distribution of the Blowgun," *Annals of the Association of American Geographers* 60 (1970): 662–88; *ibid.*, "Further Information on the Geography of the Blowgun and Its Implications for Early Transoceanic Contacts," *ibid.*, 81.1 (1992): 89–102.

16. Stephen Oppenheimer, *Eden in the East* (London: Phoenix, 1998), 23–48.

17. Oswald White Bear Fredericks and Frank Waters, *The Book of the Hopi* (New York: Viking, 1963), 16, 18–20.

18. On Pacific links, see Thompson, *American Discovery*, 236–55.

19. William Eubanks, *Cherokee Advocate*, January 12, 1901.

20. William Eubanks "Cherokee Legend of the Son of Man.... The Red Race, It is Claimed by this Writer, Were the Originators of the Ancient Apollo Worship, Now Known as the Christian Religion," in *A Collection of Works by William Eubanks*, eds. Doug Weatherly and Kristy Hales. American Native Press Archives and Sequoyah Research Center. Published online: http://www.anpa.ualr.edu/digital_library/WehEuba.html.

21. Personal communications of Brian Wilkes, 11 and 15 November 2005. "Vilcabamba, Valley of Longevity," at http://www.vilcabamba.org/. This Vilcabamba is in Ecuador and not to be confused with the Inca site of the same name in Peru.

22. On Seg, see "Austronesian Languages," *Encyclopaedia Britannica*, s.v. *Ethnologue, Languages of the World*, at http:www.ethnologue.com. *National Geographic Atlas of the World*, 6th ed. (Washington: National Geographic, 1990). Stephen Oppenheimer, *Out of Eden* (London: Robinson, 2004). P.V. Kirch, *The Lapita Peoples: Ancestors of the Oceanic World* (Oxford: Blackwell, 1997).

23. Oppenheimer, *Eden in the East*, 13, 184, 194, 465, 441–74, 456.

24. Personal communication of Paul Russell, 23 June 1996.

25. The best current overview of Madang society I have been able to find is Nancy Sullivan et al., *Tinpis Maror: A Social Impact Study of the Proposed RD Tuna Cannery at Vidar Wharf, Madan* (2003), available at http://www.nancysullivan.org/pdf/companyreport-rdtuna.pdf.

26. Johannes C. Andersen, *Myths and Legends of the Polynesians* (Tokyo: Tuttle, 1969), 362.

27. *Ibid.*, 216, 246, 377–80, 429.

28. *Ibid.*, 35.

29. *Ibid.*, 436. See under ΚΗΡΟΣ, Dor. Καρος in a Greek dictionary.

30. Notes on six Cherokee gentes [card files in the Smithsonian Institution], by Albert S. Gatschet, including notations by James Mooney and J.N.B. Hewitt recording information from Cherokee medicine man John Ax among others, together with manuscript materials by J.T. Garrett, interpreted by John D. Strange, Allogan Slagle and Mack Bettis, and kindly shared with the author by the last named. Also to be thanked is Herman Viola, director of the Smithsonian's Anthropological Archives, who facilitated access of these materials in 1974.

31. Mooney, *Myths of the Cherokee*, 239, 240, 252, 257.

32. *Eden in the East*, 319–54, 333.

33. Personal communication, 12 December 2006.

34. Since finishing the manuscript of this book, I read Terry Jones et al, eds., *Polynesians in America: Pre-Colulmbian Contacts with the New World* (Lanham: Altamira, 2011). This collection of essays devoted to the case for Polynesian contact with the New World amply documents "the material, linguistic, biological, mythological, nautical, chronological, and physical anthropological evidence" (263). In support of the Eshelokee's travels proposed in this chapter, "we identify three likely locations of contact: Southern Chile, the Gulf of Guayaquil in South America, and the Santa Barbara Channel in North America" (*ibid.*). Maps showing the sea routes and landfalls are on pp. 127–34.

## Chapter 3

1. Robert Wauchope, *Lost Tribes and Sunken Continents* (Chicago: University of Chicago Press, 1962), 2–3.

2. Luigi Luca Cavalli-Sforza et al., *History and Geography of Human Genes* (Princeton: Princeton University Press, 1994). On the controversy, see Mitchell Leslie, "The History of Everyone and Everything," *Stanford Magazine* (May-June 1999), online at http://www.stanfordalumni.org/news/magazine/1999/mayjun/articles/cavalli_sforza.html.

3. T.G. Schurr et al. (1990), "Amerindian Mitochondrial DNAs Have Rare Asian Mutations at High Frequencies, Suggesting They Derived from Four Primary Maternal Lineages," *American Journal of Human Genetics* 46 (1990): 613–23. See now his "Mitochondrial DNA and the Peopling of the New World," *American Scientist* 88.3 (2000): 246–53.

4. James L. Guthrie, "Human Lymphocyte Antigens: Apparent Afro-Asiatic, Southern Asian, and European HLAS in Indigenous American Populations" ," *Pre-Columbiana* 2/2–3 (2001): 90–163.

5. Peter N. Jones, *American Indian Demographic History and Cultural Affiliation: A Discussion of Certain Limitations on the use of mtDNA and Y Chromosome Testing* (Boulder: The Bäuu Institute, 2002), published in *AnthroGlobe Journal* online at http://www.bauuinstitute.com/Articles/JonesmtDNA.pdf.

6. Stephen C. Jett also reviewed American Indian genetics and categorized its numerous fallacies in the paper "Genetics Geography Implies a Minimum of Four Major Late Pleistocene Movements and Four Major Early to Middle Holocene Movements of Modern Humans into the Americas," International Science Conference, Los Angeles, May 2009.

7. Svante Pääbo et al., "Mitochondrial DNA Sequences from a 7000-year-old Brain," *Nucleic Acids Research* 16.20 (1988), 9775–9787. Pääbo went on to accomplish a partial sequencing of Neanderthal DNA and prove that early humans bred with Neanderthals in the Middle East of the Stone Age, the average European having 1–4 percent percent Neanderthal sequences in their DNA from that hybridization event.

8. A. Gonzalez-Oliver, "Founding Amerindian Mitochondrial DNA Lineages in Ancient Maya from Xcaret, Quintana Roo," *American Journal of Physical Anthropology* 116.3 (2001): 230–5.

9. F.M. Salzano, "Molecular Variability in Amerindians: Widespread but Uneven Information," *Annals of the Brazilian Academy of Sciences* 74.2 (2002), online at http://www.scielo.br/.

10. B.M. Sölder, "The Cayapa Indians of Ecuador: A Genetically Isolated Group with Unexpected Complement of C7 M/N Allele Frequencies," *International Journal of Immunogenetics* 23.3 (1996): 199–203.

11. D.C. Wallace et al., "Dramatic Founder Effects in Amerindian Mitochondrial DNAs," *American Journal of Physical Anthropology* 68 (1985): 149–55.

12. T.G. Schurr and S. Sherry, "Mitochondrial DNA and Y Chromosome Diversity and the Peopling of the Americas: Evolutionary and Demographic Evidence," *American Journal of Human Biology* 16.4 (2004): 420–39.

13. Michael H. Crawford, *Origins of the Native Americans: Evidence from Anthropological Genetics* (Cambridge: Cambridge University Press, 1998), 14. Cf. James Adovasio and Jake Page, *The First Americans* (New York: Modern Library).

14. Lance D. Green, "mtDNA Affinities of the Peoples of North-Central Mexico," *American Journal of Human Genetics* 66 (2000): 989–98.

15. Crawford, 182–193.

16. R.S. Malhi et al., "Distribution of Mitochondrial DNA Lineages among Native American Tribes of Northeastern North America." *Human Biology* 73 (2001): 17–55.

17. D.A. Bolnick and D.G. Smith, "Unexpected Patterns of Mitochondrial DNA Variation Among Native Americans from the Southeastern United States," *American Journal of Physical Anthropology* 122.4 (2003): 336–54.

18. J.T. Lell et al., "The Dual Origin and Siberian affinities of Native American Y Chromosomes," *American Journal of Human Genetics* 70.1 (2002): 192–206.

19. Raw data for the DNA studies of participants was published in *When Scotland Was Jewish* (Jefferson: McFarland, 2007), 215–17.

20. John Lawson, *A New Voyage to Carolina; Containing the Exact Description and Natural History of That Country: Together with the Present State Thereof. And a Journal of a Thousand Miles, Travel'd Thro' Several Nations of Indians. Giving a Particular Account of Their Customs, Manners, &c.* (1709), published online at http://rla.unc.edu/archives/accounts/Lawson/Lawson.html.

21. All genealogical information unless otherwise annotated comes from the author's "Cooper, Yates, Choctaw,

Cherokee and Sephardic in Ga.-Tenn.-Ala" database maintained by him in Family Tree Maker file format since 1992, published on Rootsweb beginning 1997 and available in updates at http://wc.rootsweb.ancestry.com/cgi-bin/igm.cgi?op=SHOW&db=dpanther&recno=2652.

22. Lars Menk, *A Dictionary of German-Jewish Surnames* (Bergenfield: Avotaynu, 2005), 552.

23. Kentucky State Historical Register, vol. 21, p. 97; Revolutionary War Pension #W3001 Filson Club, Louisville; Deed Books "C," "G," pp. 272, 374, and "M," p. 134, Clerk's Office, Wayne Co., Kentuckyfic.

24. *Record of the Tax, Paid for the paying of, the Militia employed in cutting the road and escorting families from the town and of Clinch Mountain to the Cumberland Settlements August 25th 1789*, Part I, by Linda Carpenter, compiled by E. James Keen (1997). On May 10, 1784, the legislature voted a grant to his heirs for the defense of Nashville.

25. See Doug Drake et al., *Founding of the Cumberland Settlements: The First Atlas, 1779–1804. Data Supplement 1* (Gallatin: Warioto, 2009), 277.

26. Samuel Kaye, Rufus Ward and Carolyn Neault, *By the Flow of the Inland River* (Littleton: Snapping Turtle Press, 1992), 22–24, 67; Monroe County Deed Book 1, page 118, Monroe County Chancery Clerk's Office, Aberdeen, Mississippi. See Jack D. Elliott, Jr., "The Plymouth Fort and the Creek War: A Mystery Solved," *Journal of Mississippi History* 62 (2000): 328–70. Thanks to D.J. Thornton for these references.

27. One can find several discussions of this point in Theresa M. Hicks, *South Carolina Indians, Indian Traders and Other Ethnic Connections Beginning in 1670* (Spartanburg: Reprint, 1998), esp. xiii.

28. Surnames of Sizemore marriage partners read like a Who's Who of Melungeon and crypto-Jewish genealogy: Adams, Asher, Bailey, Belcher, Blevins, Bondurant, Callicut, Canady, Chese, Colbert, Crownover, Dougherty, Emanuel, Ford, Gold, Harris, Minor, Moniac, Osborne, Pinte, Siler, Palmore, Shankles, Wade, Weir, West, Weston.

29. The most reliable Cherokee clan genealogies are in Emmet Starr, *History of the Cherokee Indians* (Oklahoma City: Warden, 1921), and George Morrison Bell, Sr., *Genealogy of "Old and New Cherokee Indian Families"* (Bartlesville: Watie Bell, 2006).

30. *Letters of Benjamin Hawkins, 1796–1806* (Savannah: Georgia Historical Society, 1974), 238.

31 Edward Andrew Rogers and Mary Evelyn Rogers, *A Brief History of the Cherokees 1540–1906*. E-book (1986 and 1988) available at http://www.innernet.org/tsalagi/index.html.

32. John Howard Payne (1832–38), papers on the Cherokee (mss. and typescripts available on DVD), Newberry Library, Chicago, Ayer MS 698.

33. R.S. Malhi, "Native American mtDNA Prehistory in the American Southwest," *American Journal of Physical Anthropology* 120 (2003): 108–24.

34. Ripan S. Malhi and Jason A. Eshleman, "The Uses and Limitations of DNA Ancestry Tests for Native Americans," online article retrieved in 2004: http://www.tracegenetics.com/newsevents.html. See also D.G. Smith et al., *Mitochondrial DNA Haplogroups of Paleoamericans in North America. Paleoamerican Origins: Beyond Clovis* (College Station: Texas A&M University Press, 2005).

35. Lowell Kirk, *Will Thomas, White Chief of the Cherokee*, e-publication (no date) at http://www.telliquah.com/Chief.htm.

36. M. Thomas et al., "Founding Mothers of Jewish Communities: Geographically Separated Jewish Groups Were Independently Founded by Very Few Female Ancestors," *American Journal of Human Genetics* 70 (2002): 1411–20.

37. On J, see J. Logan, "The Subclades of mtDNA Haplogroup J and Proposed Motifs for Assigning Control-Region Sequences into These Clades," *Journal of Genetic Genealogy* 4 (2008): 12–26.

38. Amid the tortuous bibliography, see Michael D. Brown et al., "mtDNA Haplogroup X: An Ancient Link between Europe/Western Asia and North America?" *American Journal of Human Genetics* 63.6 (1998): 1852–61, or R.S. Malhi and D.G. Smith, "Haplogroup X Confirmed in Prehistoric America," *American Journal of Physical Anthropology* 119 (2002): 84–86.

39. M. Thomas et al., "Origins of Old Testament Priests," *Nature* 9.394.6689 (July 1998): 138–40.

40. A. Torroni et al., "Classification of European mtDNAs from an Analysis of Three European Populations," *Genetics* 144 (1996): 1835–50. G. Passarino et al., "Different Genetic Components in the Ethiopian Population, Identified by mtDNA and Y-chromosome Polymorphisms," *American Journal of Human Genetics* 62.2 (1998): 420–34. V. Macaulay et al., "The Emerging Tree of West Eurasian mtDNAs: A Synthesis of Control-region Sequences and RFLPs," ibid., 64 (1999): 232–49.

41. S. Finnilä, S., et al., "Phylogenetic Network of the mtDNA haplogroup U in Northern Finland Based on Sequence Analysis of the Complete Coding Region by Conformation-sensitive Gen Electrophoresis," ibid., 68 (2000): 1475–84.

42. On the methods of identifying lineages with mitochondrial DNA mutation test results, see Martin Richards and Vincent Macaulay, "The Mitochondrial Gene Tree Comes of Age," *American Journal of Human Genetics* 68 (2001): 1315–20, available online at http://www.journals.uchicago.edu/AJHG/journal/issues/v68n6/012838/012838.web.pdf. Data and tables were published by Martin Richards et al., "Tracing European Founder Lineages in the Near Eastern mtDNA Pool," *American Journal of Human Genetics* 67 (2000): 1251–76. A standard nomenclature is in Mannis van Oven and Manfred Kayser, "Updated Comprehensive Phylogenetic Tree of Global Human Mitochondrial DNA Variation," *Human Mutation* 30.2 (2008): E386–E394.

43. Personal communication, 22 January 2010.

44. For genealogies of the Southern Yates family from colonial times to the present, see my *The Bear Went Over the Mountain* (Princeton: Cherokee, 1995).

45. See Richards et al., "Tracing European Founder Lineages."

46. D. Comas et al., "Geographic Variation in Human Mitochondrial DNA Control Region Sequence: The Population History of Turkey and Its Relationship to the European Populations," *Molecular Biology and Evolution* 13 (1996): 1067–1077.

47. L.I. Shlush et al., "The Druze: A Population Genetic Refugium of the Near East," *PLOS ONE* 3.5 (2009): e2105.

## Chapter 4

1. I follow the version (and spelling) given in David McCutchen, *The Red Record: The Wallam Olum* (Garden City Park: Avery, 1993).

2. De Villo Sloan, *The Crimsoned Hills of Onondaga: Romantic Antiquarians and the Euro-American Invention of Native American Prehistory* (Amherst: Cambria, 2008). For Rafinesque's life and bibliography, see T.J. Fitzpatrick, *Rafinesque: A Sketch of His Life with Bibliography*, revised by Charles Boewe (Weston: M&S, 1982).

3. He published a book titled *Genius and Spirit of the Hebrew Bible* (Philadelphia: Printed for the Eleutherium of Knowledge and Central University of Illinois, 1838).

4. Rafinesque's three works quoted here are available on the Web. Rafinesque, Constantine Samuel, *The American Nations, or, Outlines of Their General History, Ancient and Modern: Including the Whole History of the Earth and Mankind in the Western Hemisphere: the Philosophy of American History: the Annals, Traditions, Civilization, Languages, &c., of All the American Nations, Empires, and States ...* (Philadelphia: Printed for the Author, 1836), available at http://books.google.com/books?id=3mMFAAAAQAAJ. *A Life of Travels and Researches in North America and South Europe, or Outline of the Life, Travels and Researches of C. S. Rafinesque...* (Philadelphia: Printed for the Author, 1836), available courtesy of the Filson Historical Society and University of Chicago Press at http://memory.loc.gov/. *Ancient History, or Annals of Kentucky: With a Survey of the Ancient Monuments of North America, and a Tabular View of the Principal Languages and Primitive Nations of the Whole Earth* (Frankfort, Ky.: printed for the author, 1824), available courtesy of the Filson Historical Society and University of Chicago Press at http://memory.loc.gov/.

5. Richard Balthazar, *Remember Native America! The Earthworks of Ancient America* (Santa Fe: Five Flower, 1992), 17, 55.

6. According to the *Handbook of American Indians*, after the War of 1812 Tenskwatawa received a pension from the British government and resided in Canada until 1826, when he rejoined his tribe in Ohio and the following year moved to the west side of the Mississippi, near Cape Giradeau, Missouri (2.729–730). But according to Paul Russell, whose 3rd great-grandfather was one of the Potawatomi body guards accompanying Tecumseh on his visits to other chiefs, Tenskwatawa never left the main band. He would therefore have resided at its principal tribal seat in Illinois, Shawneetown, in 1818.

7. William W. Newcomb, Jr., "The *Walam Olum* of the Delaware Indians in Perspective," *Texas Journal of Science* 7.1 (March 1955): 57–63.

8. Retrieved online 4 April 2004 at http://www.geocities.com/wodwright/.

9. McCutcheon 37–38; cf. Eli Lilly, "Tentative Speculations on the Chronology of the Walam Olum and the Migration Route of the Lenape," *Proceedings of the Indiana Academy of Science* 54 (1944): 33.

10. Kristy Nease, "William Commanda, Algonquin Spritual Leader Dead at 97," *The Ottawa Citizen* (Aug. 4, 2011). See http://www.ottawacitizen.com/life/William+Commanda+Algonquin+spiritual+leader+dead/5199557/story.html.

11. See E.G. Squier and E.H. Davis, *Ancient Monuments of the Mississippi Valley* I (New York: Smithsonian Contributions to Knowledge, 1948).

12. Brinton once wrote that "all races were 'not equally endowed,' [some having] ...an inborn tendency, constitutionally recreant to the codes of civilization, and therefore technically criminal." He included American Indians in the criminal races. See Charles A. Lofgren, *The Plessey Case: A Legal-Historical Interpretation* (Oxford: Oxford University Press, 1988), 104–5. Brinton's shadow on American Indian studies is long. "A direct line has been traced in American linguistics from Humboldt through Brinton (who translated some of his publications), F. Boas, and E. Sapir to B.L. Whort, with particular reference to work on the languages of native America" (R.H. Robins, *A Short History of Linguistics*, Bloomington: Indiana University Press, 1974, 176).

13. Daniel G. Brinton, *The Lenape and their Legends* (New York: AMS), 14.

14. *Ibid.*, 148.

15. The search for Dr. Ward continues. The last word appeared in the *Indiana Magazine of History* in 1987 but was inconclusive. Since then, however, the federal census became available online for the pertinent Indiana counties and year in question. I was able to find a Thomas Ward in the 1820 schedule for Vanderburgh County, which borders on the township of Cynthiana. See also Harry B. Weiss, *Rafinesque's Kentucky Friends* (Highland Park: privately printed, 1936).

16. David M. Oestreicher, "The Tale of a Hoax: Translating the *Walam Olum*." In Brian Swann, ed., *Algonquian Spirit: Contemporary Translations of the Algonquian Literatures of North America* (Lincoln: University of Nebraska Press, 2005), 3–41.

17. Electa Fidelia Jones, *Stockbridge: Past and Present; or Records of Old Mission Station.* (Springfield: S. Bowles, 1854), 28–29.

18. Gen. 10:25: "In his days the earth was divided."

19. A good overview on the climatic rollercoaster is Brian M. Fagan, *The Complete Ice Age: How Climate Change Shaped the World* (London: Thames and Hudson, 2009).

20. Mary LeCron Foster, "The Transoceanic Trail: The Proto-Pelagian Language Phylum," *Pre-Columbiana* 1.1–2 (2002): 88–113.

21. Ironically, the best account of Atlantis may be the debunking survey by Sprague L. De Camp, *Lost Continents: The Atlantis Theme in History, Science, and Literature* (New York: Dover, 1970). Other accounts are Walter L. Friedrich, *Fire in the Sea: The Santorini Volcano: Natural History and the Legend of Atlantis* (Cambridge: Cambridge University Press, 2000) and Otto Muck, *The Secret of Atlantis*, trans. Fred Bradley (New York: Pocket, 1976).

22. Although the National Historic Landmarks Program describes Poverty Point as "the largest and most complex Late Archaic earthwork occupation and ceremonial site yet found in North America," excavation of the site has only been about 5 percent completed and publications regarding the findings have remained stillborn. Readers are still

probably best served by George R. Milner, *The Moundbuilders: Ancient Peoples of Eastern North America* (London: Thames and Hudson, 2004). An intriguing theory concerns its central position in the Minoan and Phoenician copper trade; see Jay Stuart Wakefield and Reinoud M. De Jonge, *Rocks and Rows: Sailing Routes Across the Atlantic and the Copper Trade* (Kirkland: MCS, 2010).

23. Brian M. Fagan, *Ancient North America: The Archaeology of a Continent,* 3rd ed. (London: Thames and Hudson, 2000), 399–400.

24. Gloria Farley, *In Plain Sight* (Columbus: ISAC, 1994), 11.

25. Donald Harden, *The Phoenicians* (New York: Praeger, 1963).

26. Clarence B. Moore, *The Tennessee, Green, and Lower Ohio Rivers Expeditions,* ed. Richard R. Polhemus (Tuscaloosa: University of Alabama Press, 2002), 19, 23, 301–2, Pl. V, VI. Cf. Thompson, *American Discovery,* 152.

27. See Adolph L. Dial and David K. Eliades, *The Only Land I Know: A History of the Lumbee Indians* (Syracuse: Syracuse University Press, 1996).

28. American Antiquarian Society, *Transactions and Collections of the American Antiquarian Society* I (Worcester: Manning, 1820), 273.

# Chapter 5

1. See C.J. Mulligan et al., "Population Genetics, History, and Health Patterns in Native Americans." *Annual Review of Genomics and Human Genetics* 5 (2004): 295–315.

2. Barry Fell, *Saga America* (New York: Times, 1980), 259–260.

3. David McCutcheon, *The Red Record: The Wallam Olum* (Garden City Park, Avery, 1993), 77. McCutcheon edits the text, dividing it into five books according to its redactors, then translates the pictograms verse by verse and supplies a running commentary with annotations. The version is endorsed by Linda Poolaw, grand chief, Delaware Nation Grand Council of North America, Anadarko, Oklahoma (ix–x).

4. The Wabash (White or Shining River in Algonquian) may have been called that because the newcomers found white people (i.e., Rafinesque's Atlans) living on it when they arrived, or it may already have carried that name, like many of the "white" place-names of the original settlers, as listed in Rafinesque.

5. Told to the author by Paul Russell about 1996.

6. McCutcheon, 125.

7. Timothy R. Pauketat and Diana DiPaolo Loren, eds., *North American Archaeology* (Oxford: Blackwell, 2005), 14–16.

8. Horatio Bardwell Cushman, *History of the Choctaw, Chickasaw and Natchez Indians* (Norman: University of Oklahoma Press, 1999), 22.

9. Nelson Lee, *Three Years Among the Comanches.* Albany: Baker Taylor, 1859), 194. See also Cyclone Covey, *Calalus: A Roman Jewish Colony in America from the Time of Charlemagne Through Alfred the Great* (New York: Vantage), 144–45.

10. Adair, 37.

11. Fell (1980), 88–116. See also Cyclone Covey, *A Critical Reprise of 'Aboriginal' American History,* 4th ed. (By the author, 2004).

12. Pauketat and Loren, eds., *North American Archaeology.*

13. Gates P. Thruston, *The Antiquities of Tennessee and the Adjacent States* (Cincinnati: Clarke, 1890), Plate II, pp. 87–97. This important witness to Tennessee's prehistory has been hidden away for years, and there are no good images available of it for examination by researchers or the public. A new study, which took private photos of the artifact, reaches very different conclusions from ours. See Vincas P. Steponaitis et al., "Iconography of the Thruston Tablet," in *Visualizing the Sacred,* eds. George E. Lankford et al. (Austin: University of Texas Press, 2011), 137–76. The smaller figure in a skirt clasping the larger chief's arm is explicated, for instance, as a male.

14. Thomas E. Mails, *The Cherokee People: The Story of the Cherokees from Earliest Origins to Contemporary Times* (Tulsa: Council Oak, 1992), 90.

15. R. Mack Bettis, personal communication, 2005.

16. John Ray Dillard, *Standing Stone, Tenn., Monterey, Early History* (Nashville: Harris, 1989), 106–118.

17. Speaking of metal, it is unusual that the Mound Builders of the Ohio Valley, who were but one step removed from Paleo-Indian hunter-gatherers, had Middle Eastern metallurgical traditions, such as the silver and copper sword scabbard and belt ornaments found at the Marietta, Ohio, mound June 1, 1819. These are described by Dr. Hildreth in Caleb Atwater's reports. Dr. Hildreth also claimed to find parts of a copper helmet and armor with one skeleton. Although we frequently hear that the Indians had no iron, a steel bow 5 to 6 feet long was found near Blacksburg, Virginia, and there are numerous accounts of oxidized iron traces in mound artifacts, including a large mica mirror on a plate of iron (Atwater, 83). A copper celt exactly like those found in Old Europe and the Middle East in the Copper and Bronze Age comes from an Ohio mound. The case for an American Copper and Bronze Age is made in C. Fred Rydholm, *Michigan Copper, The Untold Story: A History of Discovery* (Marquette: Winter Cabin, 2006). See also Roger L. Jewell, *Ancient Mines of Kitchi-Gummi: Cypriot/Minoan Traders in North America,* 3rd ed. (Fairfield: Jewell Histories, 2011).

18. Barry Fell, *America B.C.* (New York: New York Times Book, 1977).

19. *Archaeologia Americana* I 120. Cf. Robert Silverberg, *Mound Builders of Ancient America: The Archaeology of a Myth* (Greenwich: New York Graphic Society, 1968).

20. I was gratified that the reference librarian at the state archeological museum pointed me to one article on American ogam. A favorable review, it is D.H. Kelley, "Proto-Tifinagh and Proto-Ogham in the Americas," *The Review of Archaeology* 2.1 (1990): 1–9.

21. *Ibid.,* 122.

22. David Sansone, *Greek Athletics and the Genesis of Sport* (Los Angeles: University of California Press, 1992), 50–59.

23. Pauketat, 196.

24. Margaret Bender, "Framing the Anomalous: Stoneclad, Sequoyah and Cherokee Ethnoliteracy," in *New Perspectives on Native North America*, ed. Sergei Kan and Pauline Turner Strong (Lincoln: University of Nebraska, 2006), 46.

25. James Mooney, *Myths of the Cherokee and Sacred Formulas of the Cherokees* (Nashville: Cherokee Heritage, 1982), 319.

26. Suzanne Crawford and Dennis Francis Kelley, ed., *American Indian Religious Traditions: An Encyclopedia*, "Spiritual and Ceremonial Practitioners, Southeast," III (Santa Barbara: ABC-CLIO, 2005), 1040–44.

27. Bender, "Framing the Anomalous."

28. Ellen Kuskoff, ed., *Music Culture in the United States: An Introduction* (New York: Routledge, 2005).

29. Charlotte Heth, *Stomp Dance Music of the Oklahoma Cherokee: A Study of Contemporary Practice with Special Reference to the Illinois District Council Ground* (dissertation, University of California at Los Angeles, 1975).

30. Barry Fell, *Saga America* (311–314) found parallels between Greek music and poetry and "the Hohokam relics that we can now recognize in the Pima Chants collected by the Smithsonian ethnological expedition led by Frank Russell in 1901–02." See also George List, *Stability and Variation in Hopi Song* (Philadelphia: American Philosophical Society, 1993). David Nicholls, ed., *Cambridge History of American Music* (Cambridge, UK: Cambridge University Press, 1998), 5–14. William Nelson Fenton and John Gulick, *Symposium on Cherokee and Iroquois Culture* (Washington: U.S. Government Printing Office).

## *Chapter 6*

1. See R.H. Popkin, ed., *Christian Millenarianism and Jewish Messianism in English Literature and Thought* (Leiden: Brill, 1989).

2. Pt. 1, Ch. 3, pp. 6–7. Illustrations depict America's original inhabitants as sinful, warlike cannibals awaiting the Gospel, with Caucasian features.

3. Jefferson, *Writings*, 226. See Daniel Boorstin, *The Lost World of Thomas Jefferson* (Chicago: University of Chicago Press, 1993), 67.

4. John Filson, *The Discovery, Settlement and Present State of Kentucke* (Wilmington: 1789), 98–99.

5. Daniel T. Pasher, "The New Jerusalem: The Jewish-Indian Hypothesis and Christianity in America," online article retrieved November 23, 2000, at http://www.carleton.ca/~mwtyrrel/54–100/.

6. Elizabeth C. Hirschman and Donald N. Yates, *Jews and Muslims in British Colonial America: A Genealogical History* (Jefferson: McFarland, 2011) in the chapter, "Mapmakers, Privateers and Promoters."

7. Moses Wall, trans., *Menasseh ben Israel, The Hope of Israel: The English Translation by Moses Wall, 1652*, edited with an introduction and notes by Henry Méchoulan and Gérard Nahon (Oxford: Oxford University Press, 1987).

8. Cecil Roth, *The Life of Menasseh Ben-Israel: Rabbi, Printer and Diplomat* (New York: Arno, 1961), 164.

9. Hirschman and Yates (2011), Chapter 2, "Sephardim in the New World."

10. Cecil Roth, *The Spanish Inquisition* (New York: W.W. Norton, 1937).

11. Rick Aharon Chaimberlin, "Crypto-Judaism in America," *Petah Tikvah* (Door of Hope), 16.2 (n.d.), 165. Retrieved online Nov. 17, 2001, at http://www.nashuanh.com/bmy/Crypto.htm (since removed).

12. Samuel Kurinsky, "Gomez House," factsheet on Hebrew History Federation Web site available at http://www.hebrewhistory.org/factpapers/30gomez.html.

13. Perhaps Robert I the Bruce, ruled 1306–1329.

14. Hirschman, 2005.

15. See, for instance, Alan Taylor, *American Colonies: The Settling of North America* (New York: Penguin, 2000), 140–50.

16. See Archibald Henderson, "A Pre-Revolutionary Revolt in the Old Southwest" ," *The Mississippi Valley Historical Review* 17/2 (1930): 191–212.

17. A good resource for studying these families is George Morrison Bell, Sr., *Genealogy of Old and New Cherokee Indian Families* (Bartlesville: Watie Bell, 2006).

18. Charles Hudson, "James Adair as Anthropologist." *Ethnohistory* 24.4 (1977): 311–28.

19. Wauchope, 57.

20. "Take her as his wife and perform the levir's (husband's) duty" (Deut. 25:5).

21. The best account seems to be *Dictionary of American Biography* (1928–1936), published by the American Council of Learned Societies, I (New York: Scribner, 1928), s.v. "Adair, James."

22. See Lisa M. Bowes, "James Adair," Web page available at http://www.adair-holland.com/james.html. The source of the will is Elizabethtown, Bladen Co., North Carolina, Record of Wills No. 1, p. 476, reprinted in *Kinfolks* by William Harllee (1245–1247).

23. Box 2, bundle: S.C. Minutes of House of Burgesses (1730–35), 9, Parish Transcripts, N.Y. Historical Society, by Jordan, *White over Black*, 172. For a lengthy list of "Indians Recorded as Mulatto," see Steven Pony Hill's page "A Rose by Any Other Name is a Cactus—— Defining Mixed-blood Indians in Colonial Virginia and the Carolinas," available at http://sciway3.net/clark/freemoors/ARose.htm.

24. Hirschman, *Melungeons: The Last Lost Tribe* (2005).

25. On Chavis and other Sephardic surnames, consult Guilherme Faiguenboim, Paulo Valadares and Anna Rosa Campagnano, *Dicionário Sefaradi de Sobrenomes. Dictionary of Sephardic Surnames*, 2nd ed. (Rio de Janeiro: Fraiha, 2004).

26. See Lilian Friedberg, "Dare to Compare: Americanizing the Holocaust," " *American Indian Quarterly* 24/3 (2000): 353–380.

27. As, for instance, Paul Heinegg, "Free African Americans of North Carolina and Virginia," available at http://www.genealogy/genealogy/12_heing.html.

28. William Curry Harllee, *Kinfolks* II (1937), 337.

29. On crypto-Jews' antipathy towards Catholics, see David Gitlitz, *Secrecy and Deceit: The Religion of the Crypto-Jews* (Albuquerque: University of New Mexico Press, 2002), "Attitudes toward Christian Beliefs," 135–82.

30. Even though this word is usually spelled *julark* today and is apparently not derived from "Jew," John Adair evidently thought it was; compare Fenimore Cooper's spelling and use of the same word in the book *The Pioneers* (1823).

31. Maria Eugenia Aubet, *The Phoenicians and the West: Politics, Colonies, and Trade* (Cambridge: Cambridge University Press, 2001), 9–12. Cf. *Oxford Classical Dictionary*, s.v. "Phoenicians."

32. "...of complexion black, but by design, as the gypsies in England. They grease themselves with bear's fat clarified, and using no defense against sun or weather, their skins must needs be swarthy. Their eye is little and black, not unlike a straight-looked Jew. The thick lip and flat nose, so frequent with the East Indians and blacks, are not common to them; for I have seen as comely European-like faces among them, of both [sexes], as on your side [of] the sea; and truly an Italian complexion has not much more of the white, and the noses of several of them have as much of the Roman.... In the next place, I find them like countenance, and their children of so lively resemblance that a man would think himself in Duke's Place or Berry Street in London when he sees them." William Penn, *The Select Works of William Penn*, vol. IV (London: Philips, 1782), 312, 317.

33. Charles Mackay, *Extraordinary Popular Delusions and the Madness of Crowds*, with a foreword by Bernard M. Baruch (New York: Barnes and Noble, 1959), esp. 2–5. Adolphe Thiers, *The Mississippi Bubble: A Memoir of John Law* (New York: Townsend, 1959).

34. The name of the chief suggests he was a Keetoowah and of the Panther or Blue Paint Clan. Beverly Baker Northrup, *We Are Not Yet Conquered: The History of the Northern Cherokee Nation of the Old Louisiana Territory* (Paducah: Turner), 18–20, 38–39.

35. See Donald N. Yates and Elizabeth C. Hirschman, "Toward a Genetic Profile of Melungeons in Southern Appalachia," *Appalachian Journal* 38.1 (Fall 2010): 106.

36. Charles Reagan Wilson and William Ferris, co-editors, Ann J. Abadie and Mary L. Hart, associate editors, *Encyclopedia of Southern Culture* (Chapel Hill: University of North Carolina Press, 1989), 435.

37. Zadok Cramer, *The Navigator, Containing Directions for Navigating the Monongahela, Allegheny, Ohio, and Mississippi River*, 9th ed. (Pittsburgh: Cramer, Spear and Eichbaum, 1817) [102].

38. Benjamin Hawkins, *Letters of Benjamin Hawkins, 1796–1806* (Savannah: Georgia Historical Society, 1974), 231.

39. Starr, *History of the Cherokee Indians*, esp. 403. See also Bell, *Old and New Cherokee Indian Families*, under Bell, Adair and Watie.

## Chapter 7

1. Carolyn Thomas Foreman, *Indians Abroad 1493–1938* (Norman: University of Oklahoma Press, 1943).

2. The title comes from the only published catalog description of the painting (Acc. No. 56.567), Edgar P. Richardson, *American Paintings and Related Pictures in the Henry Francis du Pont Winterthur Museum* (Charlottesville: University Press of Virginia, 1986), 124–125.

3. For a reproduction, see Hirschman and Yates (2011), Chapter 9, "Georgia, the Last Colony."

4. Georgia Department of Archives and History, "A Representation of the Audience Given by the Trustees for Establishing the Colony of Georgia in America, to Tomo Chachi [sic] Mico of Yamacraw and his Indians on the 3rd day of July in the Year of Our Lord 1734," LRV #213.

5. Richardson, 124.

6. See Foreman, 34–39. The five Indians were (1) Sa Ga Yean Qua Prah Ton, chief of the Maquas (Mohawks), (2) Te Yee Neen Ho Ga Prow (Mohawk), (3) Etow Oh Koam, (4) Oh Nee Yeath Ton No Prow (river sachem), and (5) an unnamed Ganojahhore sachem. Their English names were Hendrick, or Henrick, John, Joseph Brant and Etawa Causne. Two of the portraits became part of the collection of the National Archives of Canada: Etow Oh Koam (c92421) and Saa Ga Yeath Qua Pieth Tow (c92419).

7. A key from the Winterthur Museum gives the following identities: 1. Earl of Egmont, president, 2. Anthony Ashley, Earl of Shaftesbury, 3. Lord Viscount Tyreconnel, 4. James, Lord Viscount Limeric, 5. George, Lord Carpenter, 6. Sir William Heathcote, baronet, 7. Robert Kendall, esquire, 8. Edward Digby, esquire, 9. James Oglethorpe, esquire, 10. George Heathcote, esquire, 11. Thomas Towers, esquire, 12. Robert More, esquire, 13. Robert Hucks, esquire, 14. Roger Holland, esquire, 15. William Sloper, esquire, 16. Francis Eyles, esquire, 17. John Laroche, esquire, 18. James Vernon, esquire, 19. Rev. Dr. Hale, 20. Rev. Dr. Bundy, 21. Richard Chandler, esquire, 22. Thomas Frederick, esquire, 23. Henry L. Aposter, esquire, 24. John White, esquire, 25. Probably clerks, 26. Indian boy.

8. Emma Lila Fundaburk, *Southeastern Indians: Life Portraits; A Catalogue of Pictures 1564–1860* (Fairhope: American Bicentennial Museum, 1958), pl. 112. Bureau of American Ethnology, neg. 1129-a. On Tomochichi's life, see C.C. Jones, *Historical Sketch of Tomochichi*, originally published 1868 (Savannah: Oglethorpe, 1998).

9. Patricia Seed, *Ceremonies of Possession in Europe's Conquest of the New World, 1492–1640* (New York: Cambridge University Press, 1995).

10. "An Essay on Plantations by Sir Francis Bacon Ld. Verulam.," in *The Most Delightful Country of the Universe: Promotional Literature of The Colony of Georgia 1717–1734*, introduction by Trevor R. Reese (Savannah: Beehive, 1972), 82.

11. *A New and Accurate Account of the Provinces of South-Carolina and Georgia (1732)*, attributed variously to James Edward Oglethorpe or Benjamin Martyn, the secretary of the Trustees of Georgia. It is reprinted in Reese, 115–156. The quotation is on p. 129.

12. On Iroquois visit, see Foreman 34–39, on the Cummings mission, 44–55, on the Yamacraw visit, 56–64, and on the Timberlake delegation, 65–81. The three chiefs in the Timberlake visit in 1762 are identified in admiralty records as (1) O Tacita Ostinaco Sky Augusta (Judds Friend, Outacity, Ostenaco), (2) Wooe Pidgeon (The Pidgeon), and (3) Conney Shota, or Shoatt (Standing Turkey). There is some question whether Oconostota was the same as Outacity ("Mankiller"), whether he was part of the 1730 delegation or whether he went to England at all. A descendant, Narcissa Owen, in *Memoirs of Narcissa Owen, 1831–1907* (Washington, D.C.: Library of Congress, 1907) claimed Oconostota was part of the 1730 delegation; he may have been "Oukah Ulah," called "the king to be." Oukah Ulah was quite tall, like the "giant" Great Warrior Oconostota. Most Cherokee newspaper reports identify Oconostota with the Ostenaco of the 1762 delegation (the one painted by Sir Joshua Reynolds). The Reynolds portrait of Ostenaco and painting of Standing Turkey by Francis Parsons are owned by the Thomas Gilcrease Institute of American History and Art, Tulsa, Oklahoma.

13. D'Abbeville quoted in Seed, 61–62.

14. Foreman, 58.

15. *Gentleman's Magazine* (August 1, 1734), quoted in Jones, 64–65.

16. Jones, 58.

17. Foreman, 58.

18. See Jones, 30.

19. *The Colonial Records of Georgia: Original Papers, Correspondence to the Trustees, James Oglethorpe, and others 1732–1735*, vol. 20, eds. Kenneth Coleman and Milton Ready (Athens: University of Georgia Press, 1982), 49–50.

20. Foreman, 44–55. See also William O. Steele, *The Cherokee Crown of Tannassy* (Winston-Salem: Blair, 1977); Samuel G. Drake, *Early History of Georgia, Embracing the Embassy of Sir Alexander Cuming to the Country of the Cherokees, in the Year 1730, with a Map of the Cherokee Country, from a Draft Made by the Indians* (New-England Historical and Genealogical Register, July 1872) (Boston: Clapp, 1872). The Coopers are also mentioned by James Adair, 238n.

21. See Hirschman and Yates (2007) on Scottish Jews.

22. J.H., "Sir Alexander Cumming," *Notes and Queries* 5 (March 20, 1852), 278–79.

23. Steele, 148.

24. Fundaburk, No. 109, reproduced from Neg. 1063-h-2 of the Smithsonian Institution, Bureau of American Ethnology, which reflects an original in the British Museum. Our study copy comes from the Hargrett Rare Book and Manuscript Library, University of Georgia Libraries. See Donald N. Panther-Yates, "A Portrait of Cherokee Chief Attakullakulla from the 1730s? A Discussion of William Verelst's 'Trustees of Georgia' Painting." *Journal of Cherokee Studies* 22: 5–20.

25. Steele, 136.

26. On the Sephardic surname Benamor (formed from Arabic *amor* "life"), see Faiguenboim et al. (2005), 177, 198. This surname is found in Oujda, Debdou, Fez, Sefrou, Tanger, Boujad, Tunis, Algiers, Mascara, Meknes, Gibraltar, Lisbon, Madrid, Jerusalem, London, Paris, Saïda, Buenos Aires and Panama. Our Beamers probably came from London or Paris.

27. Cox, 115.

28. Cox, 210.

29. R.S. Cotterill, *The Southern Indians: The Story of the Civilized Tribes before Removal* (Norman: University of Oklahoma, 1954), 213.

30. Charles Hudson, *The Southeastern Indians* (Knoxville: University of Tennessee Press, 1992), 202–34.

31. See Mails, *Cherokee People*, 94.

## Chapter 8

1. Louis Philippe, *Diary of My Travels in America*, trans. Stephen Becker (New York: Delacorte), 149.

2. Cox, 191.

3. *Ibid.*, 48 n. 9.

4. Nabil Matar, *Turks, Moors, and Englishmen in the Age of Discovery* (New York: Columbia University Press), 61–62.

5. The exciting cops-and-robbers story of the statue's theft and reappearance in a New England antiques collection is told, with updates, on "D. Ray Smith's Nancy Ward Page," available at http://smithdray.tripod.com/nancyward-index-5.html.

6. Hirschman (2005), 63–84.

7. According to the Washington County deed book, William Bean first entered his land shortly after the treaty of Sycamore Shoals on April 3, 1775, and recorded deeds for nearly 2000 acres on Boons Creek and elsewhere in Watauga, Nov. 18, 1775.

8. Also spelled Roberson, Robeson, Robinson, the same family as that for which Robeson County in North Carolina, center for the Lumbee Indians, was named.

9. Samuel Cole Williams, *Tennessee During the Revolutionary War* (Nashville: Tennessee Historical Commission, 1944), 19–23; cf. Cox, 44–78.

10. Williams, 189.

11. Quoted in Jedidiah Morse, *A Report to the Secretary of War of the United States on Indian Affairs* (New Haven: Converse), 168.

12. Morse, 152.

13. Shmuel Gorr, *Jewish Personal Names: Their Origin, Derivation and Diminutive Forms*, ed. Chaim Freedman (Bergenfield: Avotaynu, 1992), 266. The Sephardic form is Gracia.

14. In the Bible, Perez is the son of Judah and Tamara.

15. Mooney, 362.

16. This detail is reminiscent of the ancestral demigods in the Shalako Ceremony (from Eshelokee?) who emerge from their underwater lodge outside Zuni pueblo in every New Year's festival.

17. Lynn King Lossiah, *The Secrets and Mysteries of the Cherokee Little People* (Cherokee: Cherokee Publications, 1998), 39.

18. See Katharine Briggs, *The Vanishing People* (London: Routledge, 2000).

19. *Ibid.*, 263.

20. Gitlitz, 384.

21. Collected by the author from Paul Russell, Hartsville, Tennessee, May 14, 1997. Compare a shorter version titled "The Deluge" in Mooney, 261.

22. Adair, 152–53.

23. Riane Eisler, *The Chalice and the Blade* (San Francisco: Harper and Row, 1987), 105–6.

24. Marija Gimbutas, *The Language of the Goddess* (London: Thames and Hudson, 2006). Erich Neumann, *The Great Mother: An Analysis of the Archetype*, trans. Ralph Manheim (Princeton: Princeton University Press, 1974). Jane Ellen Harrison, *Prolegomena to the Study of Greek Religion* (1903; with an introduction by Robert Ackerman, Princeton: Princeton University Press, 1991).

25. Mooney, 342, 358–9.

26. *Ibid.*, 379.

27. *Ibid.*, 375–378.

28. Apuleius, *The Golden Asse of Lucius Apuleius*, trans. William Adlington (first pub. 1562) with introduction by E.B. Osborn (New York: Rarity, 1931), 262–65.

29. See, for instance, George E. Lankford, "The Swirl-Cross and the Center" in George E. Lankford et al., ed., *Visualizing the Sacred* (Austin: University of Texas Press, 2011), 251–75.

30. James R. Duncan and Carol Diaz-Granados," "Empowering the SECC: The 'Old Woman' and Oral Tradition," in *The Rock-Art of Eastern North America* (Tuscaloosa: University of Alabama Press, 2004), 195.

31. Thruston, 167.

32. Robert V. Sharp, Vernon James Knight, Jr., and George E. Lankford, "Woman in the Patterned Shawl: Female Effigy Vessels and Figurines from the Middle Cumberland River Basin," in ibid., 177–98.

33. See Neumann's chapter on "The Positive Elementary Character," 120–46, where two clay face urns from the fourth and fifth levels of ancient Troy are of particular interest.

34. Ruth Bradley Holmes and Betty Sharp Smith, *Beginning Cherokee*, 2nd ed. (Norman: University of Oklahoma Press, 1989), 19.

35. The name may be compared with that of a famous medicine woman, Ko-Kelus (Big Bottle). According to a Tihanama tradition, the chiefs of the Central Cumberland summoned her from Florida when their people began dying of plague in the early years of contact with Europeans. She came borne on a litter and brought her temple vessel, an enormous clay sarcophagus. She lived to be over a hundred years old and was buried with her healing vessel in the floor of the temple the chiefs raised for her at what is now the mound site of Hurricane Mills.

## *Chapter 9*

1. James Mooney, qtd. in Arlene Hirschfelder and Paulette Molin, eds., *Encyclopedia of Native American Religions*, rev. ed. (New York: Checkmark, 2001), 22.

2. Jim Hicks, "Descendants of John Vann," online genealogy page retrieved at http://familytreemaker.genealogy.com/users/h/i/c/James-R-Hicks-VA/GENE1-0005.html.

3. Qtd. in William G. McLoughlin, *Cherokee Renascence in the New Republic* (Princeton: Princeton University Press, 1992), 357.

4. *Ibid.*, 132.

5. *Ibid.*, 385–93.

6. H.B. Cushman, *History of the Choctaw, Chickasaw and Natchez Indians* (Norman: University of Oklahoma Press, 1999), 163.

7. Benjamin Hawkins, *Letters*, 202.

8. Of the Cherokee country, Lawson wrote: "Besides, it is worthy our Notice, that this Province has been settled, and continued the most-free from the Insults and Barbarities of the Indians, of any Colony that was ever yet seated in America." John Lawson, *A New Voyage to Carolina; Containing the Exact Description and Natural History of That Country: Together with the Present State Thereof. And a Journal of a Thousand Miles, Travel'd Thro' Several Nations of Indians. Giving a Particular Account of Their Customs, Manners, &c.*: (London 1709), available at http://rla.unc.edu/archives/accounts/Lawson/Lawson.html.

9. James W. Parins, *John Rollin Ridge: His Life and Works* (Lincoln: University of Nebraska Press, 2004), 189.

10. Mahir Abdal-Razzaaq El, "Message of a Cherokee Muslim," Web site retrieved 12 December 2008 at http://www.geocities.com/embracing_islam/mahir_abdal_razzaaq_el.html.

11. Parins, 116.

12. Papers on the Cherokee (mss. and typescripts available on DVD), Newberry Library, Chicago, Ayer MS 698.

13. Farley, 11.

14. "Mound Explorations," in *Twelfth Annual Report of the Bureau of Ethnology to the Secretary of the Smithsonian Institution, 1890–91* (Washington: Government Printing Office, 1894), 391–4.

15. Cyrus Gordon, *Before Columbus* (New York: Crown, 1971), 136–7, Appendix.

16. Robert C. Mainfort, Jr., and Mary L. Kwas, "The Bat Creek Stone Revisited: A Fraud Exposed," *American Antiquity* 69.4 (2004), 761–69.

17. J. Huston McCulloch, *The Bat Creek Stone*, article available online at http://www.econ.ohio-state.edu/jhm/arch/batcrk.html.

18. See *Pre-Columbiana* 3.4/4/1–2 (2005–2007), 257–58. "The authors endeavor to put the apparently Hebrew-language Bat Creek inscription (announced in 1889), into the context of the era's 'frauds,'" among which they include the Michigan Relics ... the Davenport Tables and pipes ... the Neward Holy Stones ... and even the Kensington Rune-stone ... regarding which their most recent reference dates to 1968." *The Encyclopedia of Dubious Archaeology*, citing only Mainfort and Kwas and no other literature, still calls their work "the definitive debunking" (Kenneth L. Feder, Santa Barbara: ABC-CLIO, 2010).

19. Covey (1993), 76.

20. Gordon, Appendix.

21. Beverly Baker Northrup, *We Are Not Yet Conquered: The History of the Northern Cherokee Nation of the Old Louisiana Territory* (Paducah: Turner, 2001), 10–11.

22. Kennedy, 37–42, 134, 172.

23. Yates and Hirschman, "Toward a Genetic Profile of Melungeons," 98–99.

24. Jacobs and Meyerling in *Jewish Encyclopaedia* (1906–1911), s.v. ""Marranno."

25. B. Netanyahu, *The Marranos of Spain from the Late 14th to the Early 16th Century, According to Contemporary Hebrew Sources*, 3rd ed. (Ithaca: Cornell University Press, 1999), 59.

26. Joesph M. Modrzejewski and Shayne J.D. Cohen, *The Jews of Egypt* (Princeton: Princeton University Press, 1997).

27. Immanuel Velikovsky, *Peoples of the Sea* (New York: Doubleday, 1977), 62–65.

28. Hirschman and Yates, *When Scotland Was Jewish*, 159–63.

29. Robert R. Stieglitz, *Maritime Activity in Ancient* Israel (Ph.D. dissertation, Brandeis University, 1973), 297. Cf. his "Long-distance Seafaring in the Ancient Near East," *Biblical Archaeologist* 47 (1984): 134–42.

30. Thompson, 28.

31. Biale, 162–65.

32. Fell, *Saga America*, esp. 164.

33. Mails, 180.

34. Mails, 173–79; cf. Adair, 101–103.

35. Mails, 145.

36. The Cherokee word is usually spelled *igagadi*.

37. I follow Eubanks' (and Sakiyah Sander's) original text in the *Indian Chieftain*.

38. Kule, Acorn, Dove or Bird Clan. See Gatschet (ca. 1900), Notes.

39. These are elsewhere called "the lowest grade clan of the wise men, the terrible Sa-ho-ni clan." I have suggested in Chapter 1 that the Panther or Blue Paint or Blue Holly Clan is the one that includes African peoples. If this interpretation is correct, the prophecy at the end of their national narrative predicts the Cherokee people will not escape the influence of the white man until the end of rule by the lowliest and, at present, most marginalized of the clans.

40. On Danaoi and Danauna, see *Der Kleiny Pauly* 1.1380.

41. Cornelis van Dam, *The Urim and Thummim: A Means of Revelation in Ancient Israel* (Winona Lake: Eisenbrauns, 1997).

42. Raymond D. Fogelson, "The Conjuror in Eastern Cherokee Society," *Journal of Cherokee Studies* 5.2 (1980): 64.

43. Biale, 161.

44. Gatschet, Notes.


# *Chapter 10*

1. Cecil R. Ison, "Farming, Gender, and Shifting Social Organization," in *The Rock-Art of Eastern North America*, eds. Carol Diaz-Granados and James R. Duncan (Tuscaloosa: University of Alabama Press, 2004), 181.

2. On Red Bird, see Kenneth Barnett Tankersley, "Red Bird (Dotsuwa) and the Cherokee History of Clay County, Kentucky," http://freepages.genealogy.rootsweb.ancestry.com/~brockfamily/ChiefRedBird-byKBTankersley-3.html (accessed on July 14, 2009).

3. Fred E. Coy, Jr., Thomas C. Fuller, Larry G. Meadow and James L. Swauger, *Rock Art of Kentucky* (Lexington: University Press of Kentucky, 1997), 7, 31–39.

4. Eric A. Powell, "ᏍᎥᎥᏩ [sic for ᏍᏉᎥᏩ, Sequoyah] Was Here, "*Archaeology* 62/4 (2009): 9. As a sub-note, Sequoyah signs his name with a double *s* at the beginning, not a single *s*. The reason, according to Cherokee language teacher and United Keetoowah Band chief George Wickliffe, is that the name is pronounced with an initial–*es* or–*is* sound (interview with Mack Bettis and Donald N. Yates, Tahlequah, Oklahoma, July 30, 2010). A more accurate transcription therefore would be Essiquoya. Such a spelling casts into doubt the often-cited etymology from *siqua*, "'pig." An analogous word is Issaqueena, the name of a chief's daughter who befriends the first English settlers near Lower Cherokee Keowee-Town in South Carolina. For the "Essiquoya-signed syllabary" in the collection of the Gilcrease Museum in Tulsa, see Willard Walker and James Sarbaugh, "The Early History of the Cherokee Syllabary," *Ethnohistory* 40.1 (Winter 1993): 70–94.

5. John Nobel Wilford, "Carvings from Cherokee Script's Dawn," *The New York Times* (June 23, 2009): D3.

6. M.F. Hammer et al., "Extended Y Chromosome Haplotypes Resolve Multiple and Unique Lineages of the Jewish Priesthood," *Human Genetics* 126 (2009): 707–17.

7. Hans Jenson, *Sign, Symbol and Script: An Account of Man's Efforts to Write* (New York: G.P. Putnam's Sons, 1969), 295 col. 5. Isaac Taylor, *The Alphabet: An Account of the Origin and Development of Letters*, Vol. I: *Semitic Alphabets* (London: Kegan Paul, Trench, 1883), 245.

8. On ogam and other types, also see David Diringer and Ellis Minns, *The Alphabet: A Key to the History of Mankind* (New York: Philosophical Library, 1948).

9. James H. Burchell, *The Stone of Witness*, unpaged booklet in newsprint from the author, P.O. Box 132, Manchester, KY 40962.

10. Personal written communication, 19 December 2007.

11. See Cyclone Covey, *The Yuki/Yuchi Nonplus* (Columbus: Institute for the Study of American Cultures, 1993), 76.

12. Gloria Farley, "In Plain Sight," vol. II (unpublished manuscript). Farley's essay on the Possum Creek stone forms a chapter in her book *In Plain Sight*, vol. II, being published by her executor, Bart Torbert. Farley died March 18, 2006. There are no Greek or Cherokee inscriptions in her first volume (Golden: Gloria Farley Publications, 2007).

13. Barry Fell attempted a decipherment of Linear A in *Epigraphic Society Occasional Publications* 4.77 (1977): 1–134.

14. See also Susan Kalter, "'America's Histories' Revisited: The Case of *Tell Them They Lie*," *American Indian Quarterly* 25.3 (Summer 2001): 329–351.

15. I make use of personal written communications of Gloria Farley of various dates, 2003–2006, and those of Brian Wilkes, 15 July 2009.

16. Letter from Gloria Farley to the author, 4 November 2003.

17. Personal communication, March 22, 2010.

18. For others, either in stone or on Greek vases, see Panos Valavanis, trans. Dr. David Hardy, foreword by Sir John Boardman, *Games and Sanctuaries in Ancient Greece: Olympia, Delphi, Isthmia, Nemea, Athens* (Los Angeles: J. Paul Getty Museum, 2004), 110, 126, 146, 374.

19. See report by R.B. Myers and photograph in "Tanith in North Carolina," *Epigraphic Society Occasional Publications* 18 (1989): 259.

20. Traveller Bird, *Tell Them They Lie: The Sequoyah Myth* (Los Angeles: Westernlore, 1971). See also Kalter, "'America's Histories' Revisited."

21. "The 'source' of what I have written comes from more than six hundred documents written by George Guess himself on thick ruled ledger books, small leather-bound notebooks, scraps of paper, edges of early eighteenth and nineteenth century newspapers, white buckskin, corn shuck paper, and mulberry and cedar bark. It comes from the mass of writings by his children, grandchildren, and great grandchildren...." (Traveller Bird 143). Traveller Bird remains unidentified. Gloria Farley attempted to contact Traveller Bird in the 1990s to no avail. Sources in the Keetoowah Society are reportedly skeptical about his trustworthiness as a language authority or historical expert.

22. E.g., Willard Walker and James Sarbaugh, "The Early History of the Cherokee Syllabary," *Ethnohistory* 40.1 (1993): 70–94.

23. Samuel Cole Williams, "Nathaniel Gist, Father of Sequoyah." *East Tennessee Historical Society Publications* 4 (1932): 39–54. George Lowery [Lowrey], "Notable Persons in Cherokee History: Sequoyah or George Gist/George Lowery and John Howard Payne," *Journal of Cherokee Studies* 2.4 (1977), 385–93.

24. Jean Muir Dorsey and Maxwell Jay, *Christopher Gist of Maryland and Some of His Descendants 1679–1957* (Chicago: Swift, 1969).

25. Charles Royster, *The Fabulous History of the Dismal Swamp Company* (New York: Knopf, 1999).

26. On the Gists, see Hirschman and Yates, *Jews and Muslims in British Colonial America*, 137–39.

27. Norman Golb and Omeljan Pritsak, *Khazarian Hebrew Documents of the Tenth Century* (Ithaca: Cornell University Press, 1982), 35–40.

28. Malcolm Stern, *First American Jewish Families, Third Edition* (Baltimore: Ottenheimer, 1991).

# *Chapter 11*

1. Robert Conley, *The Dark Way* (New York: Doubleday, 1993), 122. For "The Massacre of the Ani-Kutani," see Mooney, 392–3.

2. Mooney, 392.

3. Conley, *The Cherokee Nation*, 11.

4. "...although from the dimness of the tradition it is evident that it must have been much earlier" (Mooney 292–3).

5. Fogelson, "Cherokee in the East," 338.

6. William McLoughlin, *Cherokee Renascence in the New Republic* (Princeton: Princeton University Press, 1992), 284.

7. Emma Lila Fundaburk, *Southeastern Indians: Life Portraits; A Catalogue of Pictures 1564–1860* (Tallahassee: Rose, 1996), 116.

8. *Ibid.*, 189.

9. McLoughlin, *Cherokee Renascence*, 176.

10. Thompson, *American Discovery*, 289.

11. Ivan Van Sertima, *They Came Before Columbus* (New York: Random House, 2003), 252–53.

12. Harold Lawrence, "African Explorers in the New World" (Heritage Program Reprint, 1962), discussed by Van Sertima, 254–55.

13. Fell, *Saga America*, 173–89.

14. Albert Hourani, *A History of the Arab Peoples* (Cambridge: Belknap, 1991), 108.

15. *Ibid.*, 128.

16. *Ibid.*, 115.

17. See Rennard Strickland, *Fire and Spirits: Cherokee Law from Clan to Court* (Norman: University of Oklahoma Press, 1975). All Cherokee treaties are published in Charles C. Royce, *The Cherokee Nation of Indians*, intro. by Richard Mack Bettis (Chicago: Aldine, 1975).

18. Hourani, 114.

19. See Cynthia Cumfer, "Local Origins of National Indian Policy: Cherokee and Tennessean Ideas about Sovereignty and Nationhood, 1790–1811," *Journal of the Early Republic* 23 (2003), 21–46.

20. On the Dutch-Portuguese Marranos, see Miriam Bodian, *Hebrews of the Portuguese Nation: Conversos and Community in Early Modern Amsterdam* (Bloomington: Indiana University Press, 1997).

21. See Jacobs I: 231–33; *Journal of Cherokee Studies* 1.1 (1976): 17–22.

22. Cumfer, 30–35.

23. *Ibid.*

24. *Ibid.*, 46.

## Chapter 12

1. The earlier stages of it appeared in *The Bear Went Over the Mountain* (Princeton: Cherokee, 1995).

2. Lanny R. Slavey, "History: Salt Works of the Big South Fork," genealogy post in Cumberland-River-L Archives, retrieved Oct. 15, 1998, at http://news.rootsweb.com/th/read/CUMBERLAND-RIVER/1998–10/0908478847.

3. For sources and more names and dates and connections, consult my Rootsweb WorldConnect project, "Cooper, Yates, Choctaw, Cherokee, Sephardic in Ga.-Tenn.-Ala." at http://wc.rootsweb.ancestry.com/cgi-bin/igm.cgi?op=SHOW&db=dpanther&recno=2652. Also see my *Yates and Cooper Choctaw-Cherokee-Sephardic Genealogies*, Genealogy.com page available at http://familytreemaker.genealogy.com/users/p/a/n/Donald-N-Pantheryates/.

4. Hirschman and Yates, *Jews and Muslims* (2011), "Appendix A: Jewish Naming Practices and Most Common Surnames (Including the 'Good Name')."

5. George Powell, "A Description and History of Blount County," *Transactions of the Alabama Historical Society at the Annual Meeting in the City of Tuscaloosa* (July 9 and 10, 1855), 60–64.

6. Marcus, I.35, II.249.

7. I do not pretend to understand the math.

8. Henry's brother Thomas Cooper was the provincial grand master. See Hirschman and Yates, *Jews and Muslims* (2011), Chapter 10, "Beacon of Freemasonry: Elias Ashmole, John Skene and Early American Lodges."

9. Information of Pam Kahler of Vian, Oklahoma, from *Pioneers of Oklahoma*, Oklahoma Historical Society, and an article in *Ohoyohoma*, a publication by the Ohoyohoma Club at McAlester, Oklahoma, probably written by Juanita and Jewel Nichols.

10. All of the sons of Mahala Jane Blevins, called Linny, my 3rd-great-grandmother, including my great-great-grandfather Jackson Cooper, went blind, probably from a congenital disorder passed from mother to offspring. Mahala's mother was Lottie Muse, the wife of Jonathan Blevins, and Lottie's mother was Margaret Strother, the wife of Richard Muse. Since a full-blown case requires a "double hit," Jackson Cooper's father, Zack Cooper, whose mother was Nancy Blackfox, probably had the defective genes as well. Nancy's mother and the wife of Chief Black Fox was a Paint Clan woman (of the same clan as he was). Leber's Hereditary Optic Neuritis has been studied in Ashkenazi Jews but not American Indians. There is a 100 percent rate of LHON in males inheriting the gene T14484C, the primary mutation, and four secondary mutations (T4216C, G13708A, G15812A, G15257A). These marks of the genetic disorder belong to mitochondrial haplogroup J. Mahala Jane Blevins was evidently of the classic Jewish genetic type, although she could have received her rare disorder from a Cherokee ancestor. J is responsible for about one-quarter of Jewish female lines. See N. Povalko et al. (2005), "A New Sequence Variant in Mitochondrial DNA Associated with High Penetrance of Russian Leber Hereditary Optic Neuropathy," *Mitochondrion* 5.3 (2005): 194–99.

11. Hirschman and Yates, *When Scotland Was Jewish*, 81–85.

12. Bell, 163–65.

13. See Bell, 193–96.

14. See Hirschman and Yates, *Jews and Muslims*, cChapter 2, "Mapmakers, Privateers and Promoters."

15. *Ibid.*, "Pennsylvania: Quakers and Other Friends."

16. Faiguenboim et al., 314.

17. Information from Chief Rolling Thunder Justice (24 November 2006).

## Appendix A

1. Interestingly, the letters ZY (in Hebrew order, that is, from right to left) appear on a very old cattle brand that was maintained in my family when they came from Virginia to colonial Georgia. It was supposedly taken away when an ancestor in my branch married an Indian. At last report, it was in the possession of Ruth Yates Spence of the Osceola County Historical Society in Kissimmee, Florida.

2. A spreadsheet with data on individual haplotypes and mutations is available at DNA Consultants' Cherokee DNA Studies page at http://dnaconsultants.com/Cherokee/index.htm.

# Bibliography

Abdal-Razzaaq El, Mahir. "Message of a Cherokee Muslim." Website retrieved 12 December 2008, http://www.geocities.com/embracing_islam/mahir_abdal_razzaaq_el.html.

Adair, James. *Adair's History of the American Indians*, ed. by Samuel Cole Williams, originally published London, 1775. Johnson City, TN: Watauga Press, 1930.

Adovasio, James, and Jake Page. *The First Americans.* New York: Modern Library, 2003.

Alther, Lisa. *Kinfolks: Falling Off the Family Tree— The Search for My Melungeon Ancestors.* New York: Arcade, 2007.

American Antiquarian Society. "Archaeologica Americana." *Transactions and Collections of the American Antiquarian Society* I. Worcester: Manning, 1820.

Andersen, Johannes C. *Myths & Legends of the Polynesians.* Tokyo: Tuttle, 1969.

Anderson, S., et al. "Sequence and Organization of the Human Mitochondrial Genomes." *Nature* 290 (1981):457–465.

Andrews R.M., et al. "Reanalysis and Revision of the Cambridge Reference Sequence for Human Mitochondrial DNA." *Nature Genetics* 23 (1999): 147.

Appelbaum, Shimon. *Jews and Greeks in Ancient Cyrene.* Leiden: Brill, 1979.

Apuleius. *The Golden Asse of Lucius Apuleius.* Trans. by William Adlington with intro. by E. B. Osborn. New York: Rarity, 1931.

Atmon, Gil, et al. "Abraham's Children in the Genome Era: Major Jewish Diaspora Populations Comprise Distinct Genetic Clusters with Shared Middle Eastern Ancestry." *American Journal of Human Genetics* 86.6 (3 June 2010): 850–59.

Aubet, Maria Eugenia. *Phoenicians and the West.* Cambridge: Cambridge University Press, 2001.

Bacon, Josephine, ed. *The Illustrated Atlas of Jewish Civilization.* London: Quantum, 2005.

Balthazar, Richard. *Remember Native America! The Earthworks of Ancient America.* Santa Fe: Five Flower, 1992.

Barnavi, Eli, gen. ed. *A Historical Atlas of the Jewish People from the Time of the Patriarchs to the Present.* New York: Schocken, 1992.

Bartram, William. *Travels.* Ed. Francis Harper. New Haven: Yale University Press, 1958.

Becket, Jan, and Joseph Singer. *Pana O'ahu: Sacred Stones, Sacred Land.* Honolulu: University of Hawaii Press, 1999.

Behar, Doron M., et al. "The Genome-wide Structure of the Jewish People." *Nature* 466 (8 July 2010): 238–42.

Bell, George Morrison. *Genealogy of "Old & New Cherokee Indian Families."* Bartlesville, OK: Watie Bell, 2006.

Biale, David, ed. *Cultures of the Jews: A New History.* New York: Schocken, 2002.

Bird, Traveller. *Tell Them They Lie: The Sequoyah Myth.* Los Angeles: Westernlore, 1971.

Boaz, Franz, and J. W. Powell. *Introduction to Handbook of American Indian Languages* together with *Indian Linguistic Families of America North of Mexico.* Ed. Preston Holder. Lincoln: University of Nebraska Press, 1991.

Bodian, Miriam. *Hebrews of the Portuguese Nation: Conversos and Community in Early Modern Amsterdam.* Bloomington: Indiana University Press, 1997.

Boewe, Charles. *Profiles of Rafinesque.* Knoxville: University of Tennessee Press, 2003.

Bolnick, D. A., and D. G. Smith. "Unexpected Patterns of Mitochondrial DNA Variation Among Native Americans from the Southeastern United States." *American Journal of Physical Anthropology* 122.4 (2003): 336–54.

Boorstin, Daniel J. *The Lost World of Thomas Jefferson.* Chicago: University of Chicago Press, 1993.

Bowes, Lisa M. "James Adair." Website available at http://www.geocities.com/Heartland/Valley/9708/james.html.

Boyd, Doug. *Rolling Thunder*. New York: Delta, 1976.

Braund, Kathryn E. Holland. *Deerskins & Duffels: The Creek Indian Trade with Anglo-America 1685–1815*. Lincoln: University of Nebraska Press, 1993.

Briggs, Katharine. *The Vanishing People*. London: Routledge, 2000.

Brinton, Daniel G. *The Lenape and Their Legends*. New York: AMS Press, 1969 [1885].

Brook, Kevin Alan. *The Jews of Khazaria*. 2nd ed. Lanham: Rowman & Littlefield, 2006.

Brown, John P. *Old Frontiers*. Kingsport: Southern, 1938.

Brown, Michael D., et al. "mtDNA Haplogroup X: An Ancient Link between Europe/Western Asia and North America?" *American Journal of Human Genetics* 63.6 (1998): 1852–61.

Burchell, James H. *The Stone of Witness*. Unpaged booklet in newsprint from the author, Manchester, KY.

Bury, J. B., and Russell Meiggs. *A History of Greece to the Death of Alexander the Great*. 4th ed. with revisions. London: Macmillan, 1975.

Butler, John M. *Fundamentals of Forensic DNA Typing*. Amsterdam: Elsevier, 2010.

Byington, Cyrus. *A Dictionary of the Choctaw Language*. Ed. John R. Swanton and Henry S. Halbert. Asheville: Global Bible Society, 2001.

Casson, Lionel. *The Ancient Mariners*. Princeton: Princeton University Press, 1991.

_____. *Libraries in the Ancient World*. New Haven: Yale University Press, 2001.

_____. *Ships and Seamanship in the Ancient World*. Princeton: Princeton University Press, 1971.

Cavalli-Sforza, L., et al. *History and Geography of Human Genes*. Princeton: Princeton University Press, 1994.

Champagne, Duane. *Social Order and Political Change: Constitutional Governments Among the Cherokee, the Choctaw, the Chickasaw, and the Creek*. Stanford: Stanford University Press, 1992.

Chiltoskey, Mary Ulmer. *Cherokee Words with Pictures*. Cherokee: Cherokee Publications, 1972.

Coleman, Kenneth, and Milton Ready, ed. *The Colonial Records of Georgia. Original Papers, Correspondence to the Trustees, James Oglethorpe, and others 1732–1735*. Athens: University of Georgia Press, 1982.

Comas, D., et al. "Geographic Variation in Human Mitochondrial DNA Control Region Sequence: The Population History of Turkey and Its Relationship to the European Populations." *Molecular Biology and Evolution* 13 (1996): 1067–1077.

Comrie, Bernard, et al. *The Atlas of Language*. Rev. ed. New York: Facts on File, 2003.

"Concordance of Nucleotide Substitutions in the Human mtDNA Control Region." Online database made available by the Department of Biological Anthropology of the University of Cambridge. By K. W. P. Miller & J. L. Dawson, 1997 & 1998. Version 2.0. Available at http://www.bioanth.cam.ac.uk/mtDNA/toc.html.

Conley, Robert. *The Cherokee Nation: A History*. Albuquerque: University of New Mexico Press, 2005.

_____. *The Dark Way*. Norman: University of Oklahoma Press, 1993.

Cook, Warren, ed. *Ancient Vermont*. Rutland, VT: Academy Books of Castleton State College, 1978.

Cooper, William Ross. *History of the Cooper and Ross Families of England, Scotland, Ulster & America*. Privately printed, 1932.

Cotterill, R. S. *The Southern Indians: The Story of the Civilized Tribes Before Removal*. Norman: University of Oklahoma Press, 1954.

Covey, Cyclone. *Calalus: A Roman Jewish Colony in America from the Time of Charlemagne Through Alfred the Great*. New York: Vantage, 1975.

_____. *A Critical Reprise of 'Aboriginal' American History*. 4th ed. Printed by the Author, 2004.

_____. *The Yuchi/Yuki Nonplus*. Columbus: ISAC, 2001.

Cox, Brent Alan Yanusdi. *Heart of the Eagle: Dragging Canoe and the Emergence of the Chickamauga Confederacy*. Milan: Chenannee, 1999.

Coy, Fred E., Jr., Thomas C. Fuller, Larry G. Meadow and James L. Swauger. *Rock Art of Kentucky*. Lexington: University Press of Kentucky, 1997.

Cramer, Zadok. *The Navigator, Containing Directions for Navigating the Monongahela, Allegheny, Ohio, and Mississippi River*. 9th ed. Pittsburgh: Cramer, Spear & Eichbaum, 1817. Available online at http://onlinebooks.library.upenn.edu/webbin/book/lookupname?key=Cramer%2C%20Zadok.

Crawford, Michael H. *Origins of the Native Americans: Evidence from Anthropological Genetics*. Cambridge: Cambridge University Press, 1998.

Crawford, Suzanne J., and Dennis Francis Kelley, ed. *American Indian Religious Traditions: An Encyclopedia*. Santa Barbara: ABC-CLIO, 2005.

Cumfer, Cynthia. "Local Origins of National Indian Policy: Cherokee and Tennessean Ideas about Sovereignty and Nationhood, 1790–1811." *Journal of the Early Republic* 23 (2003): 21–46.

Cunliffe, Richard John. *A Lexicon of the Homeric Dialect.* Norman: University of Oklahoma Press, 1980.

Cushing, Frank H. *Zuñi: Selected Writings of Frank Hamilton Cushing,* ed. Jesse Green. Lincoln: University of Nebraska Press, 1979.

Cushman, H. B. *History of the Choctaw, Chickasaw and Natchez Indians,* ed. with a foreword by Angie Debo, intro. by Clara Sue Kidwell. Norman: University of Oklahoma Press, 1999.

Cyr, Donald L., ed. *The Diffusion Issue.* Santa Barbara: Stonehenge Viewpoint, 1991.

Deal, David Allen. *The Nexus: Spoken Language: The Link between the Mayan and Semitic, During Pre-Columbian Times.* Columbus: ISAC, 1993.

Debo, Angie. *A History of the Indians of the United States.* London: Folio, 2000.

De Camp, Sprague L. *Lost Continents: The Atlantis Theme in History, Science, and Literature.* New York: Dover, 1970.

Deloria, Vine, Jr. *God Is Red: A Native View of Religion: The Classic Work Updated.* Golden, CO: Fulcrum, 1992.

_____. *Red Earth, White Lies.* Golden, CO: Fulcrum, 1997.

Dial Adolph L., and David K. Eliades . *The Only Land I Know: A History of the Lumbee Indians.* Syracuse: Syracuse University Press, 1996.

Diaz-Granados, Carol, and James R. Duncan, ed. *The Rock-Art of Eastern North America: Capturing Images and Insight.* Tuscaloosa: University of Alabama Press, 2004.

Dillard, John Ray. *Standing Stone, Tenn., Monterey, Early History.* Nashville: Harris, 1986.

Diringer, David, and Ellis Minns. *The Alphabet: A Key to the History of Mankind.* New York: Philosophical Library, 1948.

Dixon, Max. *The Wataugans.* Johnson City, TN: Overmountain Press, 1976.

Dorsey, Jean Muir, and Maxwell Jay. *Christopher Gist of Maryland and Some of His Descendants 1679–1957.* Chicago: Swift, 1969.

Drake, Samuel G. *Early History of Georgia, Embracing the Embassy of Sir Alexander Cuming to the Country of the Cherokees, in the Year 1730, with a Map of the Cherokee Country, from a Draft Made by the Indians.* New-England Historical and Genealogical Register, July 1872. Boston: David Clapp & Son, 1972.

Eggan, Fred, ed. *Social Anthropology of Eastern American Indian Tribes.* Chicago: University of Chicago Press, 1937.

Einhorn, Lois J. *The Native American Oral Tradition: Voices of the Spirit and Soul.* Westport, CT: Praeger, 2000.

Eisler, Riane. *The Chalice and the Blade.* San Francisco: Harper & Row, 1987.

Elliott, Jack D., Jr. "The Plymouth Fort and the Creek War. A Mystery Solved." *Journal of Mississippi History* 62 (2000): 328–70.

*Encyclopedia of Southern Culture.* Charles Reagan Wilson and William Ferris, coeditors. Chapel Hill: University of North Carolina Press, 1989.

Endress, Gerhard. *Islam: An Historical Introduction.* Trans. Carole Hillenbrand. New York: Columbia University Press, 2002.

Epigraphic Society Occasional Publications (ESOP). 1974-present.

Eterovich, Adam S. *Croatia and Croatians and the Lost Colony 1585–1590.* San Carlos, CA: Ragusan, 2003.

Eubanks, William (Unenudi, Cornsilk). *A Collection of Works by William Eubanks.* Ed. Doug Weatherly and Kristy Hales. American Native Press Archives and Sequoyah Research Center. Published online: http://www.anpa.ualr.edu/digital_library/WehEuba.html.

_____. "Red Man's Origin. The Legendary Story of His Rise and Fall, His Victories and Defeats and the Prophecy of His Future, As Related by Saki-yah Sanders." *Indian Chieftain* (Jan. 2, 1896). Archived newspaper image provided by Oklahoma Historical Society at http://chroniclingamerica.loc.gov/lccn/sn83025010/1896–01–02/ed-1/seq-2/.

Fagan, Brian M. *Ancient North America: The Archaeology of a Continent.* 3d ed. London: Thames & Hudson, 2000.

_____. *The Complete Ice Age: How Climate Change Shaped the World.* London: Thames and Hudson, 2009.

Faiguenboim, Guiherme, Paulo Valadares and Anna Rosa Campagnano. *Dicionário Sefaradi de Sobrenomes [Dictionary of Sephardic Surnames].* 2nd ed. Rio de Janeiro: Fraiha, 2004.

Farley, Gloria. *In Plain Sight: Old World Records in Ancient America.* Columbus, GA: ISAC, 1994.

Feeling, Durbin. *Cherokee-English Dictionary.* Tahlequah: Cherokee Nation of Oklahoma, 1975.

Fell, Barry. *America B.C.* Rev. ed. New York: Pocket, 1989.

_____. *Saga America.* New York: Times, 1980.

Fenton, William Nelson, and John Gulick. *Symposium on Cherokee and Iroquois Culture.* Washington: USGPO, 1958.

Filson, John. *The Discovery, Settlement and Present State of Kentucke.* Lexington: Adams, 1784.

Finnilä, S., et al. "Phylogenetic Network of the mtDNA Haplogroup U in Northern Finland Based on Sequence Analysis of the Complete Coding Region by Conformation-sensitive Gen Electrophoresis." *American Journal of Human Genetics* 68 (2000): 1475–84.

_____. "Phylogenetic Analysis of mtDNA haplogroup TJ in a Finnish Population." *Human Genetics* 46 (2001): 64–69.

Fitzpatrick, T.J. *Rafinesque: A Sketch of His Life with Bibliography.* Rev. by Charles Boewe. Weston, MA: M & S, 1982.

Fogelson, Raymond D. "Cherokee in the East." in *Handbook of North American Indian.* Vol. 14: *Southeast,* 337–53. Washington: Smithsonian, 2003.

_____. "Cherokee Little People Reconsidered." *Journal of Cherokee Studies* 7.2 (1982): 92–98.

_____. "The Conjuror in Eastern Cherokee Society." *Journal of Cherokee Studies* 5.2 (1980): 60–87.

Force, M. F. *Some Early Notices of the Indians of Ohio.* Cincinnati: Clarke, 1979.

Foreman, Carolyn Thomas. *Indians Abroad 1493–1938.* Norman: University of Oklahoma Press, 1943.

Foster, J. W. *Pre-historic Races of the United States of America.* Orig. pub. Chicago: S.C. Griggs and Co., 1873; Colfax, WI: Ancient American Archaeology Foundation, 2005.

Foster, Mary LeCron. "The Transoceanic Trail: The Proto-Pelagian Language Phylum." *Pre-Columbiana* 1.1–2 (2001): 88–113.

Friedberg, Lilian. "Dare to Compare: Americanizing the Holocaust." *American Indian Quarterly* 24.3 (2000): 353–80.

Friedrich, Walter L. *Fire in the Sea: The Santorini Volcano: Natural History and the Legend of Atlantis.* Cambridge: Cambridge University Press, 2000.

Fundaburk, Emma Lila. *Southeastern Indians: Life Portraits, a Catalogue of Pictures 1564–1860.* Tallahassee, FL: Rose Printing Company, 1996.

Gagarin, Michael, and Elaine Fantham, ed. *The Oxford Encyclopedia of Ancient Greece and Rome.* Oxford: Oxford University Press, 2010.

Gallegos, Eloy J. *The Melungeons: The Pioneers of the Interior Southeastern United States 1526–1997.* Knoxville, TN: Villagra, 1997.

Galloway, Patricia, and Clara Sue Kidwell. "Choctaw in the East." in *Handbook of North American Indian.* Vol. 14: *Southeast,* 499–519. Washington: Smithsonian, 2003.

Gatschet, Albert S. Notes on Six Cherokee Gentes [card files in the Smithsonian Institution], including notations by James Mooney and J.N.B. Hewitt recording information from Cherokee medicine man John Ax among others, together with manuscript materials by J.T. Garrett, interpreted by John D. Strange, Allogan Slagle and Richard Mack Bettis.

Gerber, Jane S. *The Jews of Spain: A History of the Sephardic Experience.* New York: Free Press, 1994.

Gilmore, E. L. *Cherokee Dictionary.* Tahlequah, OK: Cherokee Studies Institute, 1986.

Gimbutas, Marija. *The Language of the Goddess.* London: Thames & Hudson, 2006.

Gitlitz, David. *Secrecy and Deceit: The Religion of the Crypto-Jews.* Albuquerque: University of New Mexico Press, 2002.

Golb, Norman, and Omeljan Pritsak. *Khazarian Hebrew Documents of the Tenth Century.* Ithaca, NY: Cornell University Press, 1982.

Golden, Mark. *Sport and Society in Ancient Greece.* Cambridge: Cambridge University Press, 1998.

Gonzalez-Oliver A., et al. "Founding Amerindian Mitochondrial DNA Lineages in Ancient Maya from Xcaret, Quintana Roo." *American Journal of Physical Anthropology* 116.3 (2001): 230–5.

Gordon, Cyrus H. *Before Columbus.* New York: Crown, 1971.

Graves, Robert. *The Greek Myths.* London: Folio, 1996.

_____. *The White Goddess.* New York: Farrar, Straus and Giroux, 2000.

Green, Lance D., et al. "mtDNA Affinities of the Peoples of North-Central Mexico." *American Journal of Human Genetics* 66 (2000): 989–98.

Greenberg, Joseph H. *Indo-European and Its Closest Relatives: The Eurasian Language Family.* Vol. 2: *Lexicon.* Stanford: Stanford University Press, 2002.

_____. *Language in the Americas.* Stanford: Stanford University Press, 1987.

Greenwood, Val D. *The Researcher's Guide to American Genealogy.* 2nd ed. Baltimore: Genealogical Publishing, 1990.

Guthrie, James L. "Human Lymphocyte Antigens: Apparent Afro-Asiatic, Southern Asian, and European HLAS in Indigenous American Populations." *Pre-Columbiana* 2.2–3 (2001): 90–163.

Hamer, Philip M. "The Wataugans and the Cherokee Indians in 1776." *East Tennessee Historical Society Publications* 3 (1931): 108–26.

Hammer, M. F., et al. "Extended Y Chromosome Haplotypes Resolve Multiple and Unique Lineages of the Jewish Priesthood." *Human Genetics* 126 (2009): 707–17.

_____. "Jewish and Middle Eastern Non-Jewish Populations Share a Common Pool of Y-chromosome Biallelic Haplotypes." *PNAS* 97.12 (2000): 6769–74.

Harden, Donald. *The Phoenicians*. New York: Praeger, 1963.

Harllee, William Currie. *Kinfolks*. 3 vols. New Orleans: Searcy & Pfaff., 1937.

Harrison, Jane Ellen. *Prolegomena to the Study of Greek Religion*. Intro. by Robert Ackerman. Princeton: Princeton University Press, 1991.

Harvey, L. P. *Muslims in Spain, 1500–1614*. Chicago: Chicago University Press, 2005.

Hawkins, Benjamin. *Letters of Benjamin Hawkins, 1796–1806*. Savannah: Georgia Historical Society, 1974.

Hecht, Marjorie Mazel. "The Decipherment and Discovery of a Voyage to America in 232 B.C." *21st Century Science & Technology* 1998/1999 (1998): 62–65.

Heinegg, Paul. "Free African Americans of North Carolina and Virginia." Article available at http://www.genealogy.com/genealogy/12_heing.html.

Herm, Gerhard. *The Phoenicians: The Purple Empire of the Ancient World*. Trans. Caroline Hillier. New York: Morrow, 1975.

Herodotus. *The Histories*. Trans. Aubrey de Sélincourt. London: Folio, 2006.

Heth, Charlotte. "Stomp Dance Music of the Oklahoma Cherokee: A Study of Contemporary Practice with Special Reference to the Illinois District Council Ground." Diss., University of California at Los Angeles, 1975.

Heyderdahl, Thor. *American Indians in the Pacific*. Chicago: Rand McNally, 1953.

_____. *Kon Tiki: Across the Pacific by Raft*. Chicago: Rand McNally, 1960.

Hicks, Jim. *Cherokee Lineages*. Book published online at http://familytreemaker.genealogy.com/users/h/i/c/James-R-Hicks-VA/.

Hicks, Theresa M. *South Carolina Indians, Indian Traders and Other Ethnic Connections Beginning in 1670*. Spartanburg, SC: Reprint Co., 1998.

Hill, Catherine, et al. "A Mitochondrial Stratigraphy for Island Southeast Asia." *American Journal of Human Genetics* 80.1 (2007): 29–44.

Hill, Steven Pony. "A Rose by Any Other Name Is a Cactus—Defining Mixed-blood Indians in Colonial Virginia and the Carolinas." Webpage available at http://sciway3.net/clark/freemoors/ARose.htm.

Hirschfelder, Arlene, and Paulette Molin. *Encyclopedia of Native American Religions*. New York: Checkmark, 2001.

Hirschman, Elizabeth C. *Melungeons: The Last Lost Tribe in America*. Macon, GA: Mercer University Press, 2005.

Hirschman, Elizabeth C., and Donald N. Yates. *Jews and Muslims in British Colonial America: A Genealogical History*. Jefferson, NC: McFarland, 2011.

_____. *When Scotland Was Jewish: DNA Evidence, Archeology, Analysis of Migrations, and Public and Family Records Show Twelfth Century Semitic Roots*. Jefferson, NC: McFarland, 2007.

Holmes, Ruth Bradley, and Betty Sharp Smith. *Beginning Cherokee*. 2nd ed. Norman: University of Oklahoma Press, 1989.

Homer. *The Odyssey of Homer*. Trans. By S. H. Butcher and A. Lang. Danbury, CT: Grolier, 1980.

Hopper, R. J. *The Early Greeks*. New York: Harper & Row, 1977.

Hornblower, Simon, and Anthony Spawforth, ed. *The Oxford Classical Dictionary*. 3d ed. Oxford: Oxford University Press, 2003.

Hourani, Albert. *A History of the Arab Peoples*. Cambridge: Belknap, 1991.

Hudson, Charles. "James Adair as Anthropologist." *Ethnohistory* 24.4 (1977): 311–28.

_____. *The Southeastern Indians*. Knoxville: University of Tennessee Press, 1992.

Hunley, K., and J. C. Long. "Gene Fow Across Linguistic Boundaries in Native North American Populations." *PNAS* 1.102.5 (2005): 1312–7.

Jefferson, Thomas. *Writings*. New York: Library of America, 1984.

Jenkins, Timothy R. *The Ten Tribes of Israel! or The True History of the North American Indians*. Orig. pub. Springfield, OH: Fireside Friend Pub. Co., 1883; Colfax, WI: Ancient American Archaeology Foundation, 2005.

Jensen, Hans. *Sign, Symbol and Script.* 3d ed. New York: Putnam, 1969.

Jett, Stephen C. "The Development and Distribution of the Blowgun." *Annals of the Association of American Geographers* 60 (1970): 662–88.

_____. "Further Information on the Geography of the Blowgun and Its Implications for Early Transoceanic Contacts." *Annals of the Association of American Geographers* 81.1 (1991): 89–102.

_____. "Pre-Columbian Transoceanic Contacts: The Context of Alleged Old World Inscriptions." *Epigraphic Society Occasional Papers* 25 (2007): 13–17.

Jewell, Roger L. *Ancient Mines of Kitchi-Gummi: Cypriot/Minoan Traders in North America.* 3d ed. Fairfield, PA: Jewell Histories, 2011.

Jewish Historical Society of New Jersey. "Biography of Luis Moses Gomez 1660–1740." article available online at http://www.jewishgen.org/jhscj/Feature.html.

Jobling, M. A., and C. Tyler-Smith. "The Human Y Chromosome: An Evolutionary Marker Comes of Age." *Nature Genetics* 4 (2003): 598–612.

Jobling, Mark A. "In the Name of the Father: Surnames and Genetics." *Trends in Genetics* 17.6 (June 2001): 353–57.

Jones, C.C., Sr. *Historical Sketch of Tomochichi.* Savannah, GA: Oglethorpe, 1998 [1868].

Jones, Electa Fidelia. *Stockbridge: Past and Present; or Records of Old Mission Station.* Springfield, MA: S. Bowles, 1854.

Jones, Peter N. *American Indian Demographic History and Cultural Affiliation: A Discussion of Certain Limitations on the Use of mtDNA and Y Chromosome Testing.* Boulder, CO: Bäuu Institute, 2002. Published in *AnthroGlobe Journal,* available online at http://www.bauuinstitute.com/Articles/Jonesmt DNA.pdf.

Jones, Terry L., et al. *Polynesians in America: Pre-Columbian Contacts with the New World.* Lanham, MD: Altamira, 2011.

Josephus. *Complete Works.* Trans. William Whiston, with foreword by William Sanford LaSor. Grand Rapids, MI: Kregel, 1976.

Josephy, Alvin M., Jr. *500 Nations: An Illustrated History of North American Indians.* New York: Gramercy, 2001.

Kalter, Susan. "'America's Histories' Revisited.'" *American Indian Quarterly* 25 (2001): 329–62.

Kan, Sergei, and Pauline Turner Strong. *New Perspectives on Native North America.* Lincoln: University of Nebraska Press, 2006.

Kayser, Manfred, et al. "Reduced Y-Chromosome, but Not Mitochondrial DNA, Diversity in Human Populations from West New Guinea." *American Journal of Human Genetics* 72.2 (2003): 281–302.

Kelley, D. H. "Proto-Tifinagh and Proto-Ogham in the Americas." *The Review of Archaeology* 2.1 (1990): 1–9.

Kelly, James C. "Notable Persons in Cherokee History: Attakullakulla." *Journal of Cherokee Studies* 1 (1978): 2–34.

_____. "Oconostota." *Journal of Cherokee Studies* 3.4 (1978): 221–38.

Kennedy, N. Brent. *The Melungeons: The Resurrection of a Proud People.* Macon, GA: Mercer University Press, 1998.

Kirch, P. V. *The Lapita Peoples: Ancestors of the Oceanic World.* Oxford: Blackwell, 1997.

Kirk, Lowell. *Will Thomas: White Chief of the Cherokee.* Book available online at http://www.telliquah.com/Chief.htm.

Klein, Harriet, E. Manelis and Louisa R. Stark, eds. *South American Indian Languages: Retrospect and Prospect.* Austin: University of Texas Press, 1985.

Kurinsky, Samuel. "Gomez House." Factsheet on Hebrew History Federation; website available at http://www.hebrewhistory.org/factpapers/30gomez.html.

Kuskoff, Ellen, ed. *Music Culture in the United States: An Introduction.* New York: Routledge, 2011.

Lankford, George E., et al. *Visualizing the Sacred: Cosmic Visions, Regionalism, and the Art of the Mississippian World.* Austin: University of Texas Press, 2011.

Lawson, John. *A New Voyage to Carolina; Containing the Exact Description and Natural History of That Country: Together with the Present State Thereof: And A Journal of a Thousand Miles, Travel'd Thro' Several Nations of Indians: Giving a Particular Account of Their Customs, Manners, &c.* London, 1709. Available online at http://docsouth.unc.edu/nc/lawson/menu.html.

Lee, Nelson. *Three Years Among the Camanches.* Albany: Baker Taylor, 1859.

Leeds, Georgia Rae. *The United Keetoowah Band of Cherokee Indians in Oklahoma.* New York: Peter Lang, 1999.

Lell J. T., et al. "The Dual Origin and Siberian Affinities of Native American Y Chromosomes." *American Journal of Human Genetics* 70.1 (2002): 192–206.

Leslie, Mitchell. "The History of Everyone and Everything." *Stanford Magazine* (May-June 1999), online at http://www.stanfordalumni.org/news/magazine/1999/mayjun/articles/cavalli_sforza.html

Levine, L. I. *Judaism and Hellenism in Antiquity*. Seattle: University of Washington Press, 1998.

Lewis, Thomas M. N., and Madeline Kneberg. *Tribes That Slumber: Indians of the Tennessee Region*. Knoxville: University of Tennessee Press, 1994.

Liddell, Henry George, and Robert Scott, comp. *A Greek-English Lexicon*. Oxford: Clarendon, 1996.

List, George. *Stability and Variation in Hopi Song*. Philadelphia: American Philosophical Society, 1993.

Littlefield, Daniel F., Jr., and James W. Parins. *Native American Writing in the Southeast: An Anthology, 1875–1935*. Jackson: University of Mississippi Press, 1995.

Lilly, Eli. "Tentative Speculations on the Chronology of the Walam Olum and the Migration Route of the Lenape." *Proceedings of the Indiana Academy of Science* 54 (1994).

Lossiah, Lynn King. *The Secrets and Mysteries of the Cherokee Little People, Yunwi Tsunsdi*. Cherokee, NC: Cherokee Publications, 1998.

Louis Philippe. *Diary of My Travels in America*. Trans. Stephen Becker. New York: Delacorte, 1977.

Lowery, George [Lowrey]. "Notable Persons in Cherokee History: Sequoyah or George Gist/ George Lowery and John Howard Payne." *Journal of Cherokee Studies* 2.4 (1977): 385–93.

Macaulay, V., et al. "The Emerging Tree of West Eurasian mtDNAs: A Synthesis of Control-region Sequences and RFLPs." *American Journal of Human Genetics* 64 (1999): 232–49.

Mackay, Charles. *Extraordinary Popular Delusions and the Madness of Crowds*. Foreword by Bernard M. Baruch. New York: Barnes & Noble, 1989.

Mahan, Joseph B. *North American Sun Kings: Keepers of the Flame*. Columbus, GA: ISAC, 1992.

Mails, Thomas E. *The Cherokee People: The Story of the Cherokees from Earliest Origins to Contemporary Times*. Tulsa, OK: Council Oak, 1992.

Mainfort, Robert C., and Mary L. Kwas." The Bat Creek Stone Revisited: A Fraud Exposed." *American Antiquity* 64 (Oct. 2004): 761–69.

Malhi, R. S., et al. "Demystifying Native American Genetic Opposition to Research." *Evolutionary Anthropology* 15 (2006): 88–92.

_____. "Distribution of Mitochondrial DNA Lineages Among Native American Tribes of Northeastern North America." *Human Biology* 73 (2001): 17–55.

_____. (2003). "Native American mtDNA Prehistory in the American Southwest. *American Journal of Physical Anthropology* 120:108–24.

_____. "The Structure of Diversity within New World Mitochondrial DNA Haplogroups: Implications for the Prehistory of North America." *American Journal of Human Genetics* 70 (2001): 905–919.

Malhi, R. S., and D. G. Smith. "Haplogroup X Confirmed in Prehistoric America." *American Journal of Physical Anthropology* 119 (2002): 84–86.

Mallery, Arlington, and Mary Roberts Harrison. *The Rediscovery of Lost America*. New York: Dutton, 1979.

Mange, E. J., and A. P. Mange. *Basic Human Genetics*. Sunderland, MA: Sinauer, 1994.

Mann, Charles C. *1491: New Revelations of the Americas Before Columbus*. New York: Knopf, 2006.

Marchant, Jo. "In Search of Lost Time." News@nature.com, 29 November 2006. http://www.nature.com/news/2006/061127/full/444534a.html.

_____. *Decoding the Heavens*. Cambridge: Da Capo, 2009.

Marcus, Jacob Rader. *Early American Jewry*. Vol. I: *The Jews of New York, New England and Canada 1649–1794*; Vol. II: *The Jews of Pennsylvania and the South 1655–1790*. New York: KTAV, 1973.

Markoe, Glenn E. *The Phoenicians*. London: Folio, 2005.

Matar, Nabil. *Turks, Moors & Englishmen in the Age of Discovery*. New York: Columbia University Press, 1999.

McAdams, William. *Records of Ancient Races in the Mississippi Valley*. Orig. pub. St. Louis, MO: C. R. Barns Pub. Co., 1887. Colfax, WI: Hayriver, 2010.

McClure, Tony Mack. *Cherokee Proud: A Guide for Tracing and Honoring Your Cherokee Ancestors*. Somerville, TN: Chunannee, 2006.

McCulloch, J. Huston. *The Bat Creek Stone*. 2004 publication available online at http://www.econ.ohio-state.edu/jhm/arch/batcrk.html.

McCutchen, David. *The Red Record, the Wallam Olum: The Oldest Native North American History*. Garden City Park, NY: Avery, 1993.

McIntosh, John. *The Origin of the North American Indians*. New York: Nafis & Cornish, 1843.

McLean, B. H. *An Introduction to Greek Epigraphy of the Hellenistic and Roman Periods from Alexander the Great Down to the Reign of Constantine (323 B.C.— A.D. 337)*. Ann Arbor: University of Michigan Press, 2002.

McLoughlin, William G. *The Cherokee Ghost Dance: Essays on the Southeastern Indians, 1789–1861.* Macon, GA: Mercer University Press, 1984.

Menk, Lars. *A Dictionary of German-Jewish Surnames.* Bergenfield, NJ: Avotaynu, 2005.

Meredith, Howard L., and Virginia E. Milan, ed. *Cherokee Vision of Eloh.'* Trans. Wesley Proctor. Muskogee, OK: Indian University Press, Bacone College, 1981.

Methvin, J. J. "Legend of the Tie-Snakes." *Chronicles of Oklahoma* 5.4 (1927): 391–6.

Metzger, Hans Dieter. "Heiden, Juden oder Teufel? Milleniarismus und Indianermission in Massachusetts 1630–1700." *Geschichte und Gesellschaft* 27.1 (2001): 118–48.

Milner, George R. *The Moundbuilders: Ancient Peoples of Eastern North America.* London: Thames & Hudson, 2004.

Mira, Manuel. *The Portuguese Making of America: Melungeons and Early Settlers of America.* N.p.: P.A.H.R. Foundation, 2001.

Modrzejewski, Joseph M., and Shayne J.D. Cohen. *The Jews of Egypt.* Trans. Robert Cornman. Princeton: Princeton University Press, 1997.

Montgomery-Anderson, Brad. "A Reference Grammar of Oklahoma Cherokee." Ph.D. Diss., University of Kansas, 2008.

Mooney, James. *Historical Sketch of the Cherokee.* Foreword by W.W. Keeler, intro. by Richard Mack Bettis. Chicago: Aldine, 1975.

_____. *Myths of the Cherokee and Sacred Formulas of the Cherokees.* Nashville, TN: Cherokee Heritage, 1982.

Moore, Clarence Bloomfield. *The Tennessee, Green, and Lower Ohio Rivers Expeditions.* Ed. Richard R. Polhemus. Tuscaloosa: University of Alabama Press, 2002.

Morse, Jedidiah. *A Report to the Secretary of War of the United States on Indian Affairs.* New Haven: Converse, 1822.

Mulligan, C. J., et al. "Population Genetics, History, and Health Patterns in Native Americans." *Annual Review of Genomics and Human Genetics* 5 (2004): 295–315.

Myers, R. B. "Tanith in N.C." *Epigraphic Society Occasional Publications* 18 (1989): 259.

*National Geographic Atlas of the World.* 6th ed. Washington: National Geographic, 1990.

Nease, Kristy. "William Commanda, Algonquin Spritual Leader, Dead at 97." *The Ottawa Citizen* (Aug. 4, 2011). Published online at http://www.ottawacitizen.com/life/William+Commanda+Algonquin+spiritual+leader+dead/5199557/story.html.

Netanyahu, B. *The Marranos of Spain from the Late 14th to the Early 16th Century, According to Contemporary Hebrew Sources.* 3d ed. Ithaca, NY: Cornell University Press, 1999.

Neumann, Erich. *The Great Mother: An Analysis of the Archetype.* Trans. Ralph Manheim Princeton: Princeton University Press, 1974.

Newcomb, William W., Jr. "The *Walam Olum* of the Delaware Indians in Perspective." *Texas Journal of Science* 7.1 (March 1955): 57–63.

Nicastro, Nicholas. *Circumference: Eratosthenes and the Ancient Quest to Measure the Globe.* New York: St. Martin's, 2008.

Nicholls, David, ed. *Cambridge History of American Music.* New York: Cambridge University Press, 1998.

Northrup, Beverly Baker. *We Are Not Yet Conquered: The History of the Northern Cherokee Nation of the Old Louisiana Territory.* Paducah, KY: Turner, 2001.

Oestreicher, David M. "The Tale of a Hoax: Translating the *Walam Olum.*" In *Algonquian Spirit: Contemporary Translations of the Algonquian Literatures of North America,* ed. Brian Swann, 3–41. Lincoln: University of Nebraska Press, 2005.

_____. "Unraveling the Walam Olum." *Natural History* 105/10 (1996): 14–21.

Oppenheimer, Stephen. *Eden in the East.* London: Phoenix, 2001.

_____. *Out of Eden.* London: Robinson, 2004.

_____. *The Real Eve: Modern Man's Journey Out of Africa.* New York: Carroll & Graf, 2003.

Owen, Narcissa. *Memoirs of Narcissa Owen, 1831–1907.* Washington: Library of Congress, 1907.

_____. *A Cherokee Woman's America.* Ed. Karen L. Kilcup. Gainsville: University Press of Florida, 2005.

Pääbo, Svante, et al. "Mitochondrial DNA Sequences from a 7,000 Year-old Brain." *Nucleic Acids Research* 16.20 (1988): 9775–87.

Panos, Valavanis. *Games and Sanctuaries in Ancient Greece: Olympia, Delphi, Isthmia, Nemea, Athens.* Trans. Dr. David Hardy, foreword by Sir John Boardman. Los Angeles: J. Paul Getty Museum, 2004.

Panther-Yates, Donald N. "A Portrait of Cherokee Chief Attakullakulla from the 1730s? A Discussion of William Verelst's *Trustees of Georgia* Painting." *Journal of Cherokee Studies* 22 (2001): 5–20.

_____. "Shalom and Hey, Y'all: Jewish-American Indian Chiefs in the Old South." *Appalachian Quarterly* 7.2 (2002): 80–89.

Parins, James W. *John Rollin Ridge: His Life and Works*. Lincoln: University of Nebraska Press, 2004.

Pasher, Daniel T.. "The New Jerusalem: The Jewish-Indian Hypothesis & Christianity in America." 2000, article available online at http://www.carleton.ca/~mwtyrrel/54–100/.

Passarino G., et al. "Different Genetic Components in the Ethiopian Population, Identified by mtDNA and Y-chromosome Polymorphisms. *American Journal of Human Genetics* 62.12 (1998): 420–34.

Patterson, Alex. *A Field Guide to Rock Art Symbols of the Greater Southwest*. Boulder, CO: Johnson, 1992.

Pauketat, Timothy R., and Diana DiPaolo Loren, ed. *North American Archaeology*. Oxford: Blackwell, 2005.

Payne, John Howard, and Daniel Sabin Butrick. *The Payne-Butrick Papers*. Ed. William L. Anderson, Jane L. Brown and Anne F. Rogers. Lincoln: University of Nebraska Press, 2010.

Peet, Stephen D. "Ancient Village Architecture in America: Indian and Mound Builders' Villages." *The American Antiquarian and Oriental Journal* 5.1 (1883): 4–30.

Penn, William. *The Select Works of William Penn*. Vol. IV. London: Philips, 1782.

Popkin, R. H., ed. *Christian Millenarianism and Jewish Messianism in English Literature and Thought*. Leiden: Brill, 1989.

Powell, Eric A. "4ᐯꞨ Ꮹ [sic for ᎤᏓᏅᏥ Ꮹ, Sequoyah] Was Here, " *Archaeology* 62/4 (2009): 9.

Priest, Josiah. *American Antiquities and Discoveries in the West*. Orig. pub. Albany, NY: Hoffman & White, 1834; Colfax, WI: Ancient American Archaeological Foundation.

Raban, Avner, and Robert Stieglitz. *Phoenicians on the Northern Coast of Israel in the Biblical Period*. Haifa: Reuben and Edith Hecht Museum, 1993.

Rafinesque, Constantine Samuel. *The American Nations, or, Outlines of Their General History, Ancient and Modern: Including the Whole History of the Earth and Mankind in the Western Hemisphere: The Philosophy of American History: The Annals, Traditions, Civilization, Languages, &c., of All the American Nations, Empires, and States...* Philadelphia: Printed for the Author, 1836. Available online at http://books.google.com/books?id=3mMFAAAAQAAJ.

_____. *Ancient History, or Annals of Kentucky: With a Survey of the Ancient Monuments of North America, and a Tabular View of the Principal Languages and Primitive Nations of the Whole Earth*. Frankfort, KY: Printed for the author, 1824. Available online courtesy of the Filson Historical Society and University of Chicago Press at http://memory.loc.gov/.

_____. *A Life of Travels and Researches in North America and South Europe, or Outline of the Life, Travels and Researches of C. S. Rafinesque...* Philadelphia: Printed for the Author, 1836. Available online courtesy of the Filson Historical Society and University of Chicago Press at http://memory.loc.gov/.

Randall, E. O. *The Masterpieces of the Ohio Mound Builders: The Hilltop Fortifications Including Fort Ancient*. Columbus: Ohio State Archaeological and Historical Society, 1916.

Read, M. C. *Archaeology of Ohio*. Orig. pub. Cleveland, OH: Western Reserve Historical Society, 1879; Colfax, WI: Hayriver Press.

Reese, Trevor R., ed. *The Most Delightful Country of the Universe: Promotional Literature of the Colony of Georgia, 1717–1734*. Savannah: Beehive, 1972.

Richards, M., et al. "Tracing European Founder Lineages in the Near Eastern mtDNA Pool." *American Journal of Human Genetics* 67 (2000): 1251–76.

Richards, Martin, and Vincent Macaulay. "The Mitochondrial Gene Tree Comes of Age." *American Journal of Human Genetics* 68 (2001): 1315–1320.

Richardson, Edgar P. *American Paintings and Related Pictures in the Henry Francis du Pont Winterthur Museum*. Charlottesville: University Press of Virginia, 1986.

Robins, R. H. *A Short History of Linguistics*. Bloomington: Indiana University Press, 1967.

Robinson, Prentice. *Easy to Use Cherokee Dictionary*. Tulsa: Cherokee Language and Culture, 1996.

Rogers, Edward Andrew, and Mary Evelyn Rogers. *A Brief History of the Cherokees, 1540–1906*. 1986; 1988. E-book available at http://www.innernet.org/tsalagi/index.html.

Rosenberg, Stephen B. "The Jewish Temple at Elephantine." *Near Eastern Archaeology* 67.1 (2004): 4–13.

Roth, Cecil. *The Life of Menasseh Ben-Israel: Rabbi, Printer and Diplomat*. New York: Arno, 1961.

_____. *The Spanish Inquisition*. New York: W. W. Norton, 1937.

Rottenberg, Dan. *Finding Our Fathers: A Guidebook to Jewish Genealogy*. Baltimore: Genealogical Publishing, 1995.

Royce, Charles. *The Cherokee Nation of Indians*. Intro. by Richard Mack Bettis. Chicago: Aldine, 1975.

Royster, Charles. *The Fabulous History of the Dismal Swamp Company*. New York: Knopf, 1999.

Ruhlin, Merritt. *On the Origin of Languages: Studies in Linguistic Taxonomy*. Stanford: Stanford University Press, 1994.

Rydholm, C. Fred. *Michigan Copper, the Untold Story: A History of Discovery*. Marquette, MI: Winter Cabin, 2006.

Salzano, F. M. "Molecular Variability in Amerindians: Widespread but Uneven Information." *Annals of the Brazilian Academy of Sciences* 74/2 (2002). Published online at http://www.scielo.br/.

Sanders, Rick. "Ancient Navigators Could Have Measured Longitude." *21st Century Science & Technology* (Fall 2001): 58–60.

Sansone, David. *Greek Athletics and the Genesis of Sport*. Los Angeles: University of California Press, 1992.

Sarton, George. *Hellenistic Science and Culture in the Last Three Centuries*. New York: Dover, 1987.

Schmidt, Hanns-Peter. "The Semurw. Of Birds and Dogs and Bats." *Persica* 9 (1980): 1–85.

Schroedl, Gerald F. "Cherokee Archaeology Since the 1970s." *Archaeology of the Appalachian Highlands*, ed. L. P. Sullivan and S.C. Prezzano, 278–97. Knoxville: University of Tennessee Press, 2001.

Schurr, T. G., et al. "Amerindian Mitochondrial DNAs Have Rare Asian Mutations at High Frequencies, Suggesting They Derived from Four Primary Material Lineages." *American Journal of Human Genetics* 46 (1990): 613–23.

_____. "Mitochondrial DNA and the Peopling of the New World." *American Scientist* 88.3 (2000): 246–53.

_____. "Mitochondrial DNA and Y Chromosome Diversity and the Peopling of the Americas: Evolutionary and Demographic Evidence." *American Journal of Human Biology* 16.4 (2004): 420–39.

Schwab, Gustav. *Gods & Heroes: Myths and Epics of Ancient Greece*. Intro. By Werner Jaeger. New York: Pantheon, 1974.

Seed, Patricia. *Ceremonies of Possession in Europe's Conquest of the New World, 1492–1640*. New York: Cambridge University Press, 1995.

Semino, O., et al. "Origin, Diffusion, and Differentiation of Y-chromosome Haplogroups E and J: Inferences on the Neolithization of Europe and Later Migratory Events in the Mediterranean Area." *American Journal of Human Genetics* 74.5 (2004): 1023–34.

Servadio, Gaia. *Motya: Unearthing a Lost Civilization*. London: Phoenix, 2000.

Shackel, Paul A. "Public Memory and the Search for Power in American Historical Archaeology." *American Anthropologist* 103.3 (2001): 655–670.

Shlush, L. I. et al. "The Druze: A Population Genetic Refugium of the Near East." *PLoS ONE* (2009): 3.5:e2105.

Sider, Gerald M. *Lumbee Indian Histories: Race, Ethnicity, and Indian Identity in the Southern United States*. Cambridge: Cambridge University Press, 1993.

Silverberg, Robert. *Mound Builders of Ancient America: The Archaeology of a Myth*. Greenwich: New York Graphic Society, 1968.

Singer Isidore, and Cyrus Adler, ed.. *The Jewish Encyclopedia: A Descriptive Record of the History, Religion, Literature, and Customs of the Jewish People from the Earliest Times to the Present Day*. Orig. published London: Funk & Wagnalls, 1901–1906. Reprint by KTAV Publishing House, 1980. Available online at http://www.JewishEnclopedia.com/.

"Sir Alexander Cumming." *Notes & Queries* 5 (March 20, 1852): 278–79.

Skorecki K., et al. "Y Chromosomes of Jewish Priests." *Nature* 2.385.6611 (1997): 32.

Smith, D. G., et al. *Mitochondrial DNA Haplogroups of Paleoamericans in North America. Paleoamerican Origins: Beyond Clovis*. College Station: Texas A&M University Press, 2005.

Smith, D. Ray. "Nancy Ward Page." Available at http://smithdray.tripod.com/nancyward-index-5.html.

Smith, Ethan. *View of the Hebrews; or The Tribes of Israel in America*. 2nd ed. Orig. pub. Poultney, VT: Smith & Shute, 1823; Colfax, WI: Ancient American Archaeology Foundation, 2002.

Sölder, B. M., et al. "The Cayapa Indians of Ecuador: A Genetically Isolated Group with Unexpected Complement of C7 M/N Allele Frequencies." *International Journal of Immunogenetics* 23.3 (1996): 199–203.

Sorenson, John L., and Carl L. Johannessen. *World Trade and Biological Exchanges Before 1492*. New York: iUniverse, 2009.

Sorenson, John L., and Martin H. Raish. *Pre-Columbian Contacts with the Americas Across the Oceans: An Annotated Bibliography*, 2nd ed. Provo, UT: Research, 1996.

Squier, E. G., and E. H. Davis. *Ancient Monuments of the Mississippi Valley I*. New York: Smithsonian Contributions to Knowledge, 1848.

Starr, Emmet. *History of the Cherokee Indians and Their Legends and Folk Lore*. Originally published Oklahoma City: The Warden Company, 1921; Millwood, NY: Kraus Reprint, 1977.

Steele, William O. *The Cherokee Crown of Tannassy*. Winston-Salem, NC: Blair, 1977.

Stengel, Mark K. "Diffusionists Have Landed: You've Probably Heard of Those Crackpot Theories...." *Atlantic Monthly* 285.1 (2000): 35–39, 42ff.

Stern, Malcolm H. *First American Jewish Families, Third Edition*. Baltimore: Ottenheimer, 1991.

Stieglitz, Robert R. "Long-distance Seafaring in the Ancient Near East." *Biblical Archaeologist* 47 (1984): 134–42.

_____. "Maritime Activity in Ancient Israel." Ph.D. Dissertation, Brandeis University, 1974.

Stoneking, M., et al. "Geographic Variation in Human Mitochondrial DNA from Papua New Guinea." *Genetics* 124 (1990): 717–33.

Strickland, Rennard. *Fire and Spirits: Cherokee Law from Clan to Court*. Foreword by Neill H. Alford, Jr. Norman: University of Oklahoma Press, 1975.

Sturtevant, William C., gen. ed. *Handbook of North American Indians*. Vol. 14: *Southeast*, ed. Raymond D. Fogelson. Washington: Smithsonian Institution, 2004.

Sullivan, Nancy et al. *IN PIS MAROR: A Social Impact Study of Proposed RD Tuna Cannery at Vidar Wharf, Madan* (2003). Retrieved online 11 Nov. 2005 at http://www.nancysullivan.org/pdf-/companyreport-rdtuna.pdf.

Swadish, M. *Indian Linguistic Groups of Mexico*. Mexico City: Escuela Nacional de Antropologia e Historia, 1956.

Swanton, John R. *The Indian Tribes of North America*. Orig. pub. Washington, DC: U.S. Govt. Print Office, 1952; Baltimore: Genealogical Publishing, 2003.

Sykes, Bryan, and Irven, Catherine. "Surnames and the Y Chromosome." *American Journal of Human Genetics* 66 (2000): 1417–19.

Sykes, B., et al. "The Origins of the Polynesians." *American Journal of Human Genetics* 57 (1995): 1463–75.

Tankerlsey, Kenneth Barnett. "Red Bird (Dotsuwa): And the Cherokee History of Clay County, Kentucky." Online article accessed on July 14, 2009 at http://freepages.genealogy.rootsweb.ancestry.com/~brockfamily/ChiefRedBird-byKBTankersley-3.html.

Taylor, Alan. *American Colonies: The Settling of North America*. New York: Penguin, 2000.

Taylor, Isaac. *The Alphabet: An Account of the Origin and Development of Letters*. Vol. I: *Semitic Alphabets*. London: Kegan Paul, Trench, 1883.

Ten Kate, Herman. *Travels and Researches in Native North America, 1882–1883*. Ed. Pieter Hovens et al. Albuquerque: University of New Mexico Press, 2004.

Terrell, John Edward. "Lost Continent." *Archaeology* 53.2 (2000): 70–74.

Thiers, Adolphe. *The Mississippi Bubble: A Memoir of John Law*. New York: Townsend, 1859.

Thomas, Cyrus. "Mound Explorations." *Twelfth Annual Report of the Bureau of Ethnology to the Secretary of the Smithsonian Insitution, 1890–91*. Washington: Government Printing Office, 1894.

_____. *The Problem of the Ohio Mounds*. Washington: Government Printing Office, 1889.

Thomas, M., et al. "Founding Mothers of Jewish Communities: Geographically Separated Jewish Groups Were Independently Founded by Very Few Female Ancestors." *American Journal of Human Genetics* 70 (2002): 1411–20.

_____. "Origins of Old Testament Priests." *Nature* 9.94.689 (1998): 138–40.

_____. "Y Chromosomes Traveling South: The Cohen Modal Haplotype and the Origins of the Lemba the "Black Jews of Southern Africa." *American Journal of Human Genetics* 66 (2000): 674–86.

Thompson, Gunnar. *American Discovery: Our Multicultural Heritage*. Seattle: Argonauts Misty Isles, 1994.

_____. *Ancient Egyptian Maize*. Seattle: New World Discovery Institute, 2010.

Thornton, Russell. *The Cherokees: A Population History*. Omaha: University of Nebraska Press, 1992.

Thorowgood, Thomas. *Jews in America; or Probabilities That Those Indians Are Judaical*. London: Henry Brome, 1660.

Thurston, Gates P. *The Antiquities of Tennessee and the Adjacent States*. Cincinnati: Clarke, 1890.

Torroni, A., et al. "Classification of European mtDNAs from an Analysis of Three European Populations." *Genetics* 144 (1996)1835–50.

Tyler, Hamilton A. *Pueblo Gods and Myths*. Norman: University of Oklahoma Press, 1884.

Van Dam, Cornelis. *The Urim and Thummim: A Means of Revelation in Ancient Israel*. Winona Lake: Eisenbrauns, 1997.

Van Oven, Mannis, and Manfred Kayser. "Updated Comprehensive Phylogenetic Tree of Global Human Mitochondrial DNA Variation." *Human Mutation* 30.2 (2008): E386-E394.

Van Sertima, Ivan. *They Came Before Columbus*. New York: Random House, 2003.

Velikovsky, Immanuel. *Peoples of the Sea.* New York: Doubleday, 1977.

Voegelin, C. F. *Walam Olum, or Red Score: The Migration Legend of the Lenni Lenape or Delaware Indians.* Indianapolis: Indiana Historical Society, 1954.

Wakefield, Jay Stuart, and Reinoud M. De Jonge. *Rocks and Rows: Sailing Routes Across the Atlantic and the Copper Trade.* Kirkland, WA: MCS, 2010.

Waldman, Karl. *Atlas of the North American Indian.* New York: Checkmark, 2000.

Walker, Willard, and James Sarbaugh. "The Early History of the Cherokee Syllabary." *Ethnohistory* 40.1 (1993): 70–94.

Wall, Moses, trans. *Menasseh ben Israel, the Hope of Israel: The English Translation by Moses Wall, 1652.* Edited with an intro. and notes by Henry Méchoulan and Gérard Nahon. Oxford: Oxford University Press, 1987.

Wallace, D. C., et al. "Dramatic Founder Effects in Amerindian Mitochondrial DNAs." *American Journal of Physical Anthropology* 68 (1985): 149–55.

Walker, Willard, and James Sarbaugh. "The Early History of the Cherokee Syllabary." *Ethnohistory* 40.1 (1983): 70–94.

Warrior, Robert Allen. *Tribal Secrets: Recovering American Indian Intellectual Traditions.* Minneapolis: University of Minnesota Press, 1994.

Waters, Frank. *Book of the Hopi.* Drawings and source material recorded by Oswald White Bear Fredericks. New York: Viking, 1963.

Wauchope, Robert. *Lost Tribes & Sunken Continents.* Chicago: University of Chicago Press, 1962.

Way of Plean, George, and Romilly Squire. *Scottish Clan & Family Encyclopedia.* New York: Barnes & Noble, 1999.

Wilfold, John Nobel. "Carvings from Cherokee Script's Dawn." *The New York Times* (June 23, 2009): D3.

Williams, Samuel Cole. "Nathaniel Gist, Father of Sequoyah." *East Tennessee Historical Society Publications* 4 (1932): 39–54.

_____. *Tennessee During the Revolutionary War.* Nashville: Tennessee Historical Commission, 1944.

Witthoft, John. "Notes on a Cherokee Migration Story." *Journal of the Washington Academy of Sciences* 37 (1947).

Yates, Donald N. *The Bear Went Over the Mountain. Genealogy and Social History of a Southern U.S. Family; the Story of the Native American-English Yates Family, from Colonial Virginia to Twentieth-century Florida.* Princeton: Cherokee Press, 1995.

_____. "Cooper, Yates, Choctaw, Cherokee and Sephardic in Ga.-Tenn.-Ala." Rootsweb WorldConnect project available at http://wc.rootsweb.ancestry.com/cgi-bin/igm.cgi?op=SHOW&db=dpanther&recno=2652

_____. "Yates and Cooper Choctaw-Cherokee-Sephardic Genealogies." Genealogy.com page available at http://familytreemaker.genealogy.com/users/p/a/n/Donald-N-Pantheryates/.

Yates, Donald N., and Elizabeth C. Hirschman. "Toward a Genetic Profile of Melungeons in Southern Appalachia." *Appalachian Journal* 38.1 (2010): 92–111.

Young, Bennett H. *The Prehistoric Men of Kentucky.* Louisville: Morton, 1910.

Ziegler, Konrat, and Walther Sontheimer, ed. *Der Kleine Pauly.* 5 vols. Munich: Deutscher Taschenbuch Verlag, 1979.

# Index

Numbers in *bold italics* indicate pages with photographs.

www.ingramcontent.com/pod-product-compliance
Lightning Source LLC
Chambersburg PA
CBHW080553270326
41929CB00019B/3294